The World History of Animation

"Art itself is really a form of exaggeration"

Oscar Wilde

The World History of Animation

Stephen Cavalier

UNIVERSITY OF CALIFORNIA PRESS

BERKELEY   LOS ANGELES

University of California Press, one of the most distinguished university
presses in the United States, enriches lives around the world by advancing
scholarship in the humanities, social sciences, and natural sciences. Its
activities are supported by the UC Press Foundation and by philanthropic
contributions from individuals and institutions. For more information,
visit www.ucpress.edu.

University of California Press
Berkeley and Los Angeles, California

Library of Congress Control Number: 2010931052
ISBN 978-0-520-26112-9 (cloth: alk. paper)

Published by arrangement with RotoVision SA
A RotoVision Book
www.rotovision.com

19 18 17 16 15 14 13 12 11
10 9 8 7 6 5 4 3 2 1

Art Director: Tony Seddon
Design: Morris and Winrow
Cover design: John Raimes
Cover illustration: Reproduced with the kind permission of King Features,
a division of Hearst Holdings, Inc.
Manufactured in China

Contents

Foreword
by Sylvain Chomet

This is the kind of book I would have dreamed of finding in my Christmas stocking as a boy. It represents a fascinating collection of arts, styles, and techniques, which one devours with passionate curiosity if your favorite pastime is to draw, to paint, or to sculpt.

In fact, when I was a boy, animation was the unreachable star—an art that only wizards from faraway countries could master. A magical power that could bring fossilized art forms to life. Born in the early 1960s, my wizards were Walt Disney's "nine old men" and their faraway country was called Burbank. Their films at that time included the likes of *The Jungle Book*, *One Hundred and One Dalmatians*, and *The Aristocats*. Not a bad upbringing, you would say. Quite frustrating, I would answer; I was born in France...

So I channeled my passion for drawing into comic books, but did so with an unnamed frustration hanging around in the air. My retrospective diagnosis is that I was longing for animation.

The defining moment finally happened for me in the mid-1980s, late one night in a London animation studio. Working all day on commercials, we were invited to work on our own projects in the evenings. That night I line tested 12 drawings of a loop sequence featuring an old bearded man playing a barbarie organ. It moved! It was alive! It was magic, but real magic, not the kind of magic you do when you know the trick. This one doesn't rely on sleight of hand—it tricks us without ever revealing itself. It is called "Animation."

L'illusionniste
(The Illusionist),
2010

This is the kind of book I would have dreamed of finding
in my Christmas stocking as a boy, and now I'm writing its
foreword... I'm not that old yet, and definitely not that wise.
I still live far away from Burbank. I am a very oblivious wizard,
or to rephrase, I am a fairly lucky sod whose life was
transformed by the magic of animation. Like many other kids
who never stopped drawing, modeling, painting—turning our
childhood dreams into films. Whatever the technique, whatever
the means, regardless of how successful, we all pretend to be
wizards, but in all honesty I believe we all share the same
wonder: How does it come to life?

I challenge the Lasseters, Parks, and Miyazakis of this
world to argue otherwise.

Sylvain Chomet *is one of Europe's foremost animation
directors. Born in France in 1963, he published his first
comic book,* Le Secret des libellules (The Secret of
Dragonflies) *in 1986. He began his animation career in
London, where he directed several animated commercials.
His first animated short film,* La Vielle Dame et les Pigeons
(The Old Lady and the Pigeons) *was released in 1996 and
was nominated for an Academy Award. Chomet has written
and directed two animated features,* Les triplettes de
Belleville (The Triplets of Belleville/Belleville rende-vous) *and*
L'illusionniste (The Illusionist), *both of which were nominated
for the Best Animated Feature Film at the Academy Awards.
He also wrote and directed a live-action short for the
anthology film,* Paris, Je T'Aime.

Introduction

Though there are various claims and theories as to the precise origins of animation, as there are for the origins of cinema itself, we can broadly speaking agree that animation has recently celebrated its first century.

During its first 100 years, animation has made a huge contribution to global popular culture. First, movie theater shorts captured the world's imagination, bringing us iconic characters such as Mickey Mouse, Popeye, Bugs Bunny, and Tom & Jerry. In the middle of the twentieth century, Walt Disney released stunning animated features, including *Snow White and the Seven Dwarfs*, *Pinocchio*, and *Dumbo*. After that came the animated television stars like *The Flintstones*, *The Simpsons*, and *Spongebob Squarepants*. Asian anime became a cultural phenomenon, with films such as *Akira* and *Sen to Chihiro no kamikakushi* (*Spirited Away*) achieving global appeal. Finally, who could imagine the multiplex theater experience of the early twenty-first century without the CGI marvels of Pixar—*Toy Story*, *The Incredibles*, and *Finding Nemo*—plus DreamWorks Animation's *Shrek*, Blue Sky's *Ice Age*, and a host of other CGI animated features.

Fantasmagorie vs Final Fantasy

When people describe animation, they often discuss whether it is "realistic" or "cartoony." This summarizes a fundamental split in animation between traditional cartoons aiming for a stylized realism and animation that attempts to imitate reality.

At the end of the nineteenth century, Emile Cohl was one of a small group of Parisian artists called the Incoherents, a group who were precursors to the surrealists, devoted to conceptual pranks and absurdist art. In 1908, beginning his work in film, Cohl created a revolutionary piece of animation into which he injected these anarchic ideas and opened up the wild possibilities of the form. *Fantasmagorie* has an antiplot in which anything goes and the impossible is certain. It might not look like much now, but in creating this universe of antirealism Cohl laid the blueprint for *Steamboat Willie*, Betty Boop, Daffy Duck, Road Runner, *South Park*, Wallace and Grommit, *Pokemon*, Super Mario, and all other works of this popular type of surrealism called animation, in which reality is twisted, stretched, chased, exploded, and run off a cliff.

Snow White and the Seven Dwarfs, Disney, 1937.
The first of Disney's animated features, Snow White set the standard for other movies to follow.

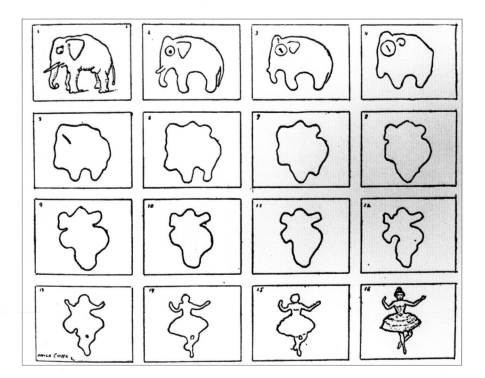

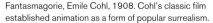

Fantasmagorie, Emile Cohl, 1908. Cohl's classic film established animation as a form of popular surrealism.

Minema Cinema, Tim Hope, 2004. Hope's work combines traditional 2D animation with digital 3D techniques for a purposely lo-fi look.

A few years later in Italy and Germany, in a further move away from figurative "reality," new modernist and abstract ideas were applied to film, and as a result an alternative path of animation began and experimental cinema was created.

In 1915 in New York, Max Fleischer invented the rotoscope in order to capture lifelike movements, and reality started to creep into animation. Later, Fleischer largely abandoned the rotoscope; as animators got better and faster at their work, he realized that the stylized work was funnier, cheaper, and more popular. In contrast, as the Disney Studio moved into feature films in the late 1930s, they applied meticulous levels of realism to the human figures and the environments, worried that cartoony designs would not have the emotional range to carry a long story and wanting to distinguish themselves from other studios' cartoons.

As modernist cartoon styles were being tried out in Europe, a breakaway group of Disney artists formed the UPA studio to take on Disney's realism with the sword of modern design. They largely won the battle and animation became more stylized again, now incorporating modernism and minimalism into the mix. This also highlighted the opposition between unreal and real and the divisions in animation; broadly speaking the animation genres were the realistic, the cartoony, the design based, the abstract, and the growing area of motion graphics, with little integration between these groups.

Apart from a blip in the style-free 1970s, it wasn't until the digital age that reality made another serious takeover bid with that aid to uniformity, the computer. The possibilities of 3D CGI meant that realism could be cut and pasted into cartoons and animation could be sampled into live action, precipitating a kind of digital goldrush for photorealism in movies and video games. In certain quarters, such is the prevalence of realism in animation that anything else is now seen as retro and nostalgic.

In live-action movies it is certainly a buzz to see convincing dinosaurs and monsters, and the possibilities are amazing, but maybe history has already proved that where cartoons are concerned, reality misses the point. After all, the best way to capture realism is to point a camera at it and make a live-action movie.

A groundswell of reaction against CG-style super-realism has formed into a genre of animation we can define as "lo-fi," in which the unreality of animation is underlined by the deliberate creation of imperfections, often with the use of "primitive" methods. Examples of this include Michel Gondry's music videos, the South Park series, the Parappa the Rapper video game, and the feature film Fantastic Mr Fox.

The Circle of Life

Although the differences between the animation of 100 years ago and the digital sophistication of today makes the two almost unrecognizable as the same art form, in some ways animation could now be said to have come full circle.

Much animation from the start of the twentieth century took the form of the primitive special effects featured in the earliest films. With similar appeal to the horrors depicted in lurid stage melodramas and the trash press of the time, these films were built around gimmicky set pieces designed to thrill. After separating itself out into its own genre for most of the rest of the century, animation in the digital age has reintegrated itself into mainstream cinema so as to be almost undetectable and inseparable from it. In the same way that early animation was just part of the whole fairground sideshow experience, CGI animation and special effects have become an integral part of the modern blockbuster, often a roller coaster/ghost-train type experience. Indeed, the *Pirates of the Caribbean* movies are a spin-off of a popular Disneyland attraction.

Much early animation took popular cartoons and comic strips of the time and turned them into animated characters. Similarly, a major trend in Hollywood today is for live-action comic-book adaptations, converted to the big screen with the aid of computer-generated animation and effects.

For a long time it was almost impossible to create animation without a team of people. Now, however, as at the beginning of animation when animators/inventors worked away in solitude on their obsessive ideas, the animation landscape is full of individuals sat at home computers creating their singular projects.

The origins of animation can be seen in the zoetrope (and similar inventions), based on the idea of a disc that spins sequential images. An amazing modern-day version of the zoetrope can be seen in the Ghibli Studio's museum in Japan, in which three-dimensional models of the studio's characters appear to be coming to life. Pixar created an equally spectacular version of this for their recent traveling exhibition.

Three Amigos

This book is divided into three broad eras of animation history: the age of film, the television age, and the digital age. Each new wave of technology is greeted by some with doomy predictions of the death of the old. In reality though, it generally means more choice for the artist, audience, or consumer. The invention of photography did not mean the end of painting, as some predicted. It meant the dwindling of some of the stale old styles of painting but generated new interest in images that weren't representational, and so abstract art was born. Similarly, the development of television did not signal the end of the movies, as predicted in the 1950s. Instead, audiences could choose between the big or the small screen.

The transition from the film age to the television age, and then on to the digital age, were painful times for some but created opportunities for those willing to adapt. The market fell away for traditional movie theater shorts in the 1950s, but opened up for television series and for television advertising. Likewise in the 1990s, traditional animation jobs like cell painting disappeared with the rise of digital technology and the consequent reduction in drawn animation, but parallel to that were new opportunities in the rapidly expanding video game, internet, and digital effects industries and a boom for 3D CG animation.

Techniques like drawn 2D animation and stop-frame animation have been popular for a century and will continue to be so, given a good script and decent characters. Audiences don't care about what technique or technology is involved, they just want to see a good story, well told.

Wallace & Gromit in The Wrong Trousers, Aardman Animations, 1993. Stop-frame animation is still popular with audiences if, like Aardman's work, it is based on great stories and appealing characters.

Short films have always been a big part of the development of animation, from the first short, wobbly experiments, like a baby's first steps, then the movie theater shorts of the "Golden Age" when Mickey Mouse and Bugs Bunny gleefully took on the world like hyperactive teenagers. Nowadays, shorts are generally used to explore mature ideas and experiments that, due to the pressure to find an audience, the feature film is often unable to do.

A lot of these films have up until now remained largely unseen, but one of the great things about the age of the internet is that an amazingly comprehensive collection of shorts, historic films from the dawn of animation, and trailers from the great animated features, can now be found and watched online.

About This Book

Films are arranged chronologically, with occasional detours to explore particular subjects in more detail. There are also short biographies of key people in the animation world, along with definitions of terms. My criteria for including any animation or technical innovation in this book was simple: anything that is important or interesting (historically, culturally, or otherwise) and that helps to tell the big story of animation's global history. Although it is impossible for any book to be an exhaustive survey of the entire industry, I have tried to include examples from as many different genres and styles as possible. In this book you will find the realistic and the stylized, the commercial blockbuster and the arthouse film, the traditional and the experimental, the children's classic and the adult cult favorite.

The book aims to take the reader on an exciting and inspirational journey through a broad sample of history and be a rough guide to the best of this animated universe, a place which is absolutely as limitless as the human imagination.

Big Hero, Short Sidekick

Aside from television and video games, animation is generally experienced as feature films and shorts. Features often represent the pinnacle of animated achievement and individuals have gambled fortunes and invested huge chunks of their working lives in making them. The effort of planning, funding, and producing the amount of animation required can be a mind-blowing task. It may require superhuman levels of dedication and often an obsession verging on insanity. Some animated features have had the most protracted schedules in the history of cinema. The investment of time and money required means that studios cannot afford to fail often, and a run of two or three unsuccessful features will close most studios down. This is why there are so few long-lasting feature animation studios.

Brief Histories of World Animation

Although this book is laying out a version of the *global* history
of animation, it is clear, at least until the explosion of Japanese anime
split off on its own trajectory, that the American animation industry has
been the driving force throughout most of that history; and that the history
of animation is largely the history of American animation. So we begin
this book with a brief overview of the development of the animation industry
in North America.

However, if American animation is the sun around which all other
animation has orbited, then it's also true that these other planets contain
weird and wonderful life-forms and mutations of their own that are worth
exploring. Western Europe led the way in the early days of cinema, and has
been a fertile area for experimental and avant-garde animation. For many
decades, Eastern European animation was funded by communist states,
which meant that animators had more financial security than their Western
counterparts, but also that they had less creative freedom. Although initially
taking inspiration from America and Europe, Japanese animators soon
developed their own distinctive traditions and styles, building a successful
industry that has attracted devoted fans around the world.

A brief history of North American animation

USA

Although many of the early pioneers of motion picture technology were European, it was in North America that the film industry, of which animation was an integral part, was really developed. The art of animation took a great leap forward with the refinements made by Winsor McCay around 1914, and at the same time, the industrialization of the animation industry was frantically establishing itself in New York. Canadian Raoul Barré and American Bill Nolan started the first commercial animation studio in The Bronx in 1914, and developed various animation techniques. John Randolph Bray was perhaps the most important figure in American animation in the years before World War I, establishing a studio and, somewhat unscrupulously at times, collecting, refining, and often patenting ideas such as celluloid overlays (cel animation) and color cartoons. Other studios developed the industrial "Taylorization" of the animation process further, following Frederick Winslow Taylor's theories of "scientific management" and industrial efficiency. Along with the newspaper publishers who often owned the cartoon characters, figures like the producer Pat Sullivan created early models for the mass-market exploitation of intellectual property via merchandise.

Toward the end of the 1920s, Walt Disney perfected the art of sound cartoons. Building on his huge success with this, his studio studied everything that had gone before in animation, as well as many other areas of art and design, and refined and developed the techniques, concentrating on quality rather than ease of production. Soon, with competition from the Fleischer Studios, Disney was the market leader. This precipitated what has become known as the Golden Age of American Animation, which lasted until the early 1960s.

By 1930, following Disney, who had relocated from Kansas City, most of the East Coast studios had moved west to Los Angeles for proximity with the rest of the movie industry in Hollywood. In the early 1930s, Leon Schlesinger Productions started making shorts for Warner Bros., in 1935 Tex Avery was hired as a director, and by the early 1940s, the popularity of the crazy and extreme Warner Bros. characters, along with MGM's cartoons, was rivaling Disney's.

Steamboat Willie,
Disney, 1928

Meanwhile Disney was keeping his lead on the pack by refining character animation to a fine art; his animators could now make their characters express emotion like real actors, and his company developed (although they did not invent) technical advances like the multiplane camera. To separate himself further from other cartoon companies, Disney imbued much of the new work with a detailed realism based on studies of live animals and landscapes. Armed with these new weapons, the Disney Studio moved into feature films in the late 1930s, a risky experiment that paid off handsomely with *Snow White and the Seven Dwarfs* (1937), and a string of other acclaimed features following closely behind.

World War II shattered the world economy, and Disney's main competitor, Fleischer Studios, was forced to close. Like other studios, Disney survived the war by making government information and propaganda films, but the failure of some big projects and a strike at the studio by the animators Walt Disney considered to be his "family" had come as big blows.

United Productions of America (UPA) was founded during the war by former Disney animators. The studio began work making information films and theater shorts, rejecting Disney's realistic style by featuring modernist designs and simplified characters and animation. This new approach won favor with the critics and made Disney's cartoons seem somewhat old-fashioned in comparison. UPA were widely influential in their modernist aesthetic, which was taken up by Warner Bros. directors like Chuck Jones, and even eventually in watered-down form by Disney artists. A less positive result, however, was the way that their approach to "limited animation" was taken up by television producers from the mid-1950s onward, for cost-cutting rather than artistic reasons, driving down the production values and quality of most animation for the next 30 years. During this age of cheap television cartoons, the prominent producers were ex-MGM directors William Hanna and Joseph Barbera, whose company, Hanna-Barbera, became the biggest name in TV animation.

Until the late 1950s, experimental animation was mainly a European phenomenon. Perhaps a by-product of the neurosis that seemed an undercurrent of America's economic success, "underground" filmmakers emerged, influenced by the New American Cinema of Maya Deren, the European avant-garde, and the freeform creativity encouraged by the "beat generation." Loose groups formed, such as the West Coast experimentalists who congregated around the Art in Cinema screenings that

Ryan, Chris Landreth,
2004

took place between 1945 and 1954 at the San Francisco Museum of Art. During the 1960s and 1970s avant-garde filmmakers used primitive computers to produce abstract animation, and it was these artists, hippies working with technology originally developed for military use, who pioneered computer animation. Their work led to some commercial experiments in the 1980s, such as Disney's *Tron* (1982).

In the world of commercial features, a breakaway group of Disney artists led by Don Bluth, disillusioned by the company's cost-cutting animation production and lack of artistic ambition, formed new companies and made animation features with ambitions toward the old levels of artistry, with some success.

The animation revival of the early 1990s was spurred by a few Disney smash-hit animated features, created by a new generation of artists determined to restore former glories. A new wave of innovative television series were also produced by the TV networks devoted to animation. These generally went back to retrospective attitudes of investing care, intelligence, and innovation, and often retro designs. New companies were formed to make animated features, such as Don Bluth Productions and DreamWorks Animation. Many quality feature films were made in this period but, as is often the case, many jumped on the bandwagon with diminishing care, intelligence, and innovation, and hence diminishing returns.

Many of the movies from the early 1990s featured CGI backgrounds, but it was not until the mid-1990s that John Lasseter's films proved, as Disney had done in the 1930s with drawn animation, that CGI characters could express emotion and humor. Lasseter and his animators achieved this success by applying the same innovative spirit, creativity, and artistry that Walt Disney had used in his heyday, and they reaped the rewards. The huge success of Pixar's Disney-financed movies precipitated another rush for CG cartoon features that lifted and propelled the box office viability of animated features into the new century, with Pixar, DreamWorks Animation, and Blue Sky as the leading players.

The success of animated features in the 1990s also enabled the big studios to green light more unusual works, and the films of Tim Burton and Henry Selick established pure stop frame as a valid option for commercial animation. Meanwhile the commercial viability of traditional drawn animation was questioned after the poor box office returns of several movies, and the Hollywood production of traditional animation was effectively closed down, even, incredibly, at Disney.

At the same time, the new sophistication of computer effects and animation meant that the vast majority of special effects were now created digitally and computer animation became an integral part of the multiplex blockbuster "event" film industry of the twenty-first century. The digital version of rotoscoping, motion or performance capture, was pushed as an alternative to the work of key frame animators, and a sequence of features were produced based on this technology, with mixed results.

In 2006, with their financing and distribution deal with Pixar coming to an end, The Walt Disney Company recognized that John Lasseter was the true modern day successor to Walt Disney's leadership, perhaps something they had been been missing since his death 40 years earlier. The corporation bought out Pixar and installed Lasseter as creative head of Disney. One of Lasseter's first acts in charge of the company was to reestablish the production of traditional drawn animation.

Canada

Canadian Raoul Barré was an important figure in the early animation industry, but aside from Barré's work in New York and the work of a few isolated individuals, such as Walter Swaffield, Harold Peberdy, and Bryant Fryer, Canadian animation did not really get going until the arrival of two men from Europe. John Grierson arrived from England in 1939 as the first director of the National Film Board of Canada (NFB) and in 1941 he appointed the Scot Norman McLaren to head the NFB's animation department. The original task of the NFB was to create wartime propaganda and, after some early collaboration with Disney in this area, the policy of animation production of the NFB moved away from mainstream cel animation. The NFB was inclined to explore more experimental forms in order to establish an identity for Canadian animation that differentiated it from the commercial mainstream of the USA. A huge success over the years, the NFB has won over 5,000 awards, including over 70 Academy Award® nominations, creating Canada's reputation as a world center of animation.

McLaren's pixillation classic *Neighbours* (1952) was a product of this NFB atmosphere of experimentation, winning an Oscar® (curiously, for best documentary). Another product of the policy was the innovative director George Dunning, who made a number of shorts for the NFB, including *Cadet Rouselle* (1946). Dunning worked briefly for UPA in New York

before moving to London, where he directed *Yellow Submarine* (1968). Another Canadian animation star was Richard Williams, who also worked at UPA and, like Dunning, moved to London where he established a world class studio and famously directed animation for *Who Framed Roger Rabbit* (1988). The first Canadian feature film, *Le village enchanté* (*The Enchanted Village*,1955) was made by NFB animators Marcel and Réal Racicot, and in 1966 the NFB split into two parts for French and English language work.

The television series *Rocket Robin Hood* (1966) was one of the first products of a slowly emerging Canadian animation industry proper; a forerunner of the TV animation boom of the 1970s, it was produced by TV impresario Al Guest and directed by American animator Ralph Bakshi. In 1971 animation giant Nelvana was formed in Toronto and successfully produces television animation to the present day, along with cult projects like *Rock & Rule* (1983), an ill-fated venture into feature films. In 1981 the French-speaking division of the Canadian Broadcasting Corporation won the Oscar for *Crac* in 1981 and again for the *The Man Who Planted Trees* in 1987, both directed by German-born animator Frédéric Back.

In recent years Canada has established itself as a world leader in digital animation, its technology companies working with animators to create much of today's widely used animation software such as Alias Wavefront's Maya and Softimage XSI. The production company Mainframe produced some of the best known early CG animation, including the first 3D CG television series, *Reboot* (1994). Today, Canada remains at the technological cutting edge of animation while retaining its tradition of artistry and experimentation. Both of these national strengths can be seen in Chris Landreth's Oscar-winning short film *Ryan*, about the great Canadian animator, Ryan Larkin.

A brief history of Western European animation

While many of the early developments in animation were made in Europe, animation never really took off as an industry there, as it did in the USA, until the 1950s. And even then, only London really developed and maintained a major industry comparable with Los Angeles, New York, and later, Tokyo.

While the USA strode ahead industrially, Europe was a fertile area for the experimental and the avant-garde. In the first few decades of the twentieth century many of the most revolutionary ideas in abstract and modern art were coming out of Europe, ideas and philosophies that spread out into film and animation. This cutting-edge work would then seep into the wider culture, influencing artists working in the rest of the world, crossing into the work of advertisers, and finding echoes in the movies of mainstream Hollywood filmmakers.

As with other art forms, at various stages throughout the history of animation there have been hotspots of invention and creativity, attracting more like-minded individuals and accelerating the process of change. This pattern can be seen in the major countries of Western Europe, as centers of animation bloom and die down again over a decade or two before blossoming elsewhere.

Experiments occurred in Italy as early as 1910 with painting directly onto film and a futurist manifesto mapped a blueprint for experimental film and animation to come. In the two decades after this, important developments in art and design in Germany based around the Bauhaus movement led to a group of artists who pushed the boundaries of abstract animation and cast an influence that would still be felt almost a century later.

World War II created economic chaos as capital was tied up in the war effort and postwar rebuilding. In this climate, most commercial animation went into decline. However in the larger economies, governments set aside funding for propaganda and public information and animation was understood to be an ideal medium for communicating these simple messages.

Key figures

Alexandre Alexeieff (France/Russia)

Dick Arnall (UK)

Berthold Bartosch (France/Hungary)

Bruno Bozzetto (Italy)

Sylvain Chomet (France)

John Coates (UK)

Emile Cohl (France)

Paul Driessen (Netherlands)

Michael Dudok de Wit (Netherlands)

George Dunning (UK/Canada)

Anson Dyer (UK)

Oskar Fischinger (Germany)

Ginger Gibbons (UK)

Terry Gilliam (UK/USA)

Bob Godfrey (UK)

Michel Gondry (France)

John Grierson (UK)

Oscar Grillo (UK/Argentina)

Paul Grimault (France)

John Halas (UK/Hungary) and Joy Batchelor (UK)

Jerry Hibbert (UK)

Jonathan Hodgson (UK)

Tim Hope (UK)

Clare Kitson (UK)

Réne Laloux (France)

Bill Larkins (UK)

Len Lye (UK/New Zealand)

Uli Meyer (Germany/UK)

Phil Mulloy (UK)

Michel Ocelot (France)

Nick Park (UK)

Richard Purdom (UK)

Joanna Quinn (UK)

Lotte Reiniger (Germany)

Martin Rosen (UK)

Georges Schwizgebel (Switzerland)

Shynola (UK)

Richard Taylor (UK)

Richard Williams (UK/Canada)

With the advent of war in Europe, many artists found their way not only to the USA and Hollywood, but also to the relative safe haven and freedom of expression that London offered. The UK, being culturally halfway between Europe and the USA, balanced the European experimental nature with a hard-headed American pragmatism, making serious attempts to industrialize animation in the years just before and after World War II, although the industry remained small until the explosion of TV advertising in London in the 1950s and 1960s. In a more experimental vein, The Greater Post Office Film Unit (GPO) was established in London in 1933 producing exploratory documentary and animation films.

In the 1940s a small UK cottage industry of animators developed to deliver simple messages with striking design through public information films and wartime propaganda. The result was a group of creative animators who were well versed in the art of fast, efficient communication of ideas. It was these traditions that from the advent of independent television in the late 1950s until the present day made for a large and successful advertising industry in London. Halas & Batchelor was formed in 1940 and became one of Europe's biggest, longest lasting, and most influential studios. In the 1960s

London became a world center of popular culture, with the energy of the pop music explosion feeding out into film and animation. In the 1980s and 1990s the UK's Channel 4 became one of the great supporters of animation, funding much work on the fringes as well as global mainstream hits, and supporting international as well as British animators. In the late 1990s the UK's instinct for invention put it at the forefront of the digital revolution as it become a world leader in video game, internet, and digital animation, producing CG animation for many Hollywood films. At the same time, Aardman Animations became one of the leading exponents of the traditional art of stop motion.

Since the pioneering days of Charles-Emile Reynaud, Georges Méliès, and Emile Cohl, France has maintained a passion for cinema, animation, and comic books. The world's foremost animation festival is held annually in Annecy and France is also home to many brilliant animators and directors, who are often the products of some of the best animation schools in the world. However, for many decades, this passion did not translate into a particularly successful animation industry, until the end of the twentieth century, when France seemed suddenly to come to life as a producer of animated

The Man with the Beautiful Eyes, Jonathan Hodgson, 2000

feature films. A string of independent movies were released by directors such as Michel Ocelot and Sylvain Chomet; wonderfully original and varied in tone and style, these films were all uniquely French in their sense of creativity.

In the late 1930s, around the end of the Spanish Civil War, a number of companies in Barcelona produced movie theater shorts in conjunction with popular published comics. The Baguna brothers' Hispano Grafic Films and Alejandro Fernandez de la Reguera's Dibonso Films were formed around the end of the 1940s, and a few years later merged into the larger studio Dibujos Animados Chamartín, which released three successful and long-lasting animated series. Estudios Moro was formed in 1955 in Madrid by the Moro brothers and became one of the biggest producers of animated commercials in Europe.

Like France, Italy has a tradition of popular adult comic books. A few isolated movies were made in the early years of animation and several Italian feature films were released postwar. In the 1950s the Italian Broadcasting Corporation started showing advertising, including a long-running advertising series called *Carosello*, almost single-handedly sustaining a small animation industry and allowing animators a surprising amount of freedom. In the 1960s one of the biggest animation studios in Europe was Gamma Film in Milan, specializing in advertising and occasional shorts. Bruno Bozzetto became a world-renowned animation director and auteur in the 1960s and 1970s with works such as *West and Soda* (1965) and *Allegro Non Troppo* (1976).

Until World War II, Germany had been home to several experimental animators, including Walther Ruttmann, Hans Richter, Lotte Reiniger, and Oskar Fischinger. When the Nazis came to power in the 1930s, they banned all "degenerate" art, which forced most of these animators to emigrate. The UFA studio became the Nazis' media corporation, often using animation in the propaganda they produced. The one outstanding animator producing work for UFA was Hans Fischerkösen, who managed to make charming children's animation, which seemed if anything to give out a message of freedom and tolerance rather than supposed racial superiority. Germany suffered an economic crash after the war, which set

back the development of the animation industry. In 1962, 26 filmmakers signed "The Oberhausen Manifesto," a statement intended to sweep away the past, to be a new start for German cinema, and to create a new wave of modernist films, which included animation.

The Belvision studio was founded in Belgium in 1955 and, with TVA Dupois, for the next 20 years would specialize in making movies based on popular comic strips, such as Tintin, the Smurfs, and Asterix.

Hungarian emigré George Pal established a tradition of puppet animation in the Netherlands in the 1930s before moving to the USA, and Dutch studios carried on with Pal's stop-frame style throughout the next couple of decades. Other notable Dutch masters include Marten Toonder and Paul Driessen.

What we now call the Global Economy took shape over the last decades of the twentieth century, homogenizing the world's markets and dissolving trade barriers. Most animation is now designed for an international audience, the biggest market being the USA. European productions, especially features, are often made with American viewers in mind, while many American producers have made their US-aimed movies in Europe. In the digital era the dramatic reduction of costs and increased ease of production has led to the fracturing of the animation industry worldwide. Once again, a large amount of smaller studios have appeared in competition with, or producing work for, the larger, more established studios.

The Western European countries have strong traditions of regularly producing internationally acclaimed live-action movies, and yet animation feature output has seemed in a sense inversely proportional to this. In contrast, Eastern European countries such as Croatia, Hungary, and the Czech Republic, with little history of international live-action success, have often punched above their weight in animation. Around the end of the twentieth century however, Spain, the UK, and France, taking advantage of the continuing international success of animated feature films, produced several features of their own.

Les triplettes de Belleville
(The Triplets of Belleville/
Belleville rende-vous),
Sylvain Chomet, 2003.

Key films

1902: Georges Méliès: Le voyage dans la lune

1908: Emile Cohl: Fantasmagorie

1924: Fernand Léger: Ballet Mécanique

1924: Viking Eggeling: Symphonie Diagonale

1926: Lotte Reiniger: Die Abenteuer des Prinzen Achmed

1933: Alexandre Alexeieff and Claire Parker: Une nuit sur le mont chauve

1935: Oskar Fischinger: Komposition in Blau

1945: Arturo Moreno: Garbancito de la Mancha

1949: Nino Pagot: I Fratelli Dinamite

1949: Anton Domenighini: La Rosa di Baghdad

1954: Halas & Batchelor: Animal Farm

1968: George Dunning: Yellow Submarine

1973: Réne Laloux: La planète sauvage

1976: Bruno Bozzetto: Allegro Non Troppo

1980: Paul Grimault: Le roi et l'oiseau

1982: Dianne Jackson: The Snowman

1995: Aardman Animations: Wallace and Gromit: A Close Shave

1998: Michel Ocelot: Kirikou et la Sorcière

2003: Sylvain Chomet: Les triplettes de Belleville

2007: Vincent Parronaud: Persepolis

2009: H5: Logorama

2010: Sylvain Chomet: L'illusionniste

A brief history of Russian and Eastern European animation

Key figures

Walerian Borowcyzk (Poland/France)

Piotr Dumala (Poland)

Zlatko Grgic (Croatia)

Ivan Ivanov-vano (Russia)

Piotr Kamler (Poland)

Fyodor Khitruk (Russia)

Andrei Khrjanovsky (Russia)

Jerzy Kucia (Poland)

Yuri Norstein (Russia)

George Pal (Hungary/USA)

Priit Pärn (Estonia)

Aleksandr Petrov (Russia)

Aleksandr Ptushko (Russia)

Aleksandr Shiryayev (Russia)

Nina Shorina (Russia)

Ladislaw Starewicz (Russia/France)

Jan Svankmajer (Czech Republic)

Genndy Tartakovsky (Russia/USA)

Jiri Trnka (Czech Republic)

Dusan Vukotic (Croatia)

Karel Zeman (Czech Republic)

Key films

1910: Ladislaw Starewicz: Prekrasnaya Lyukanida

1929: Mikhail Tsekhanovsky: Pochta

1935: Aleksandr Ptushko: Novvy Gulliver

1947: Ivan Ivanov-vano: Konyok-gorbunok

1948: Jiri Trnka: Cisaruv slavik

1958: Karel Zeman: Vynález zkázy

1958: Zagreb Film: Samac

1961: Zagreb Film: Surogat

1962: Russia: Fyodor Khitruk: Istoriya odnogo prestupleniya

1966: Russia: Andrei Khrjanovsky: Zhil-byl Kozyavin

1967: Zagreb Film: Professor Balthazar

1979: Russia: Yuri Norstein: Skazka skazok

1982: Jan Svankmajer: Moznosti dialogu

1987: Priit Pärn: Eine murul

1988: Jan Svankmajer: Neco z Alenky

2000: Piotr Dumala: Zbrodnia i kara

2000: Jerzy Kucia: Strojenie instrumentów

The large-scale development of animation in Russia, unlike in the USA, was driven by politics rather than economics. While American studios invested in animation for financial gain, soviet animation was primarily dictated by influences from within party ideology, as well as by a very differently-peopled landscape to the USA and Western Europe. Factors such as literacy levels, transport links, and the initial lack of electricity in many areas of the nation had as much impact on the art form in Russia as did the communist messages it was forced to contain.

Animation techniques were developed on a small scale in Russia before the turmoil of the revolution enveloped the nation. While Ladislaw Starewicz is usually hailed as Russia's first animator for his 1910 stop-motion work using dead insects, he was actually preceded by Aleksandr Shiryayev. A principal dancer and choreographer with the Imperial Russian Ballet, Shiryayev combined his love of movement with filmmaking. Between 1906 and 1909 he made animated ballet, first by drawing frame-by-frame dancers' positions, and then using puppets. Although he continued to work as a dancer, teacher, and choreographer in the Soviet Union until his death in 1941 (other than a short spell from 1909 to 1917 spent teaching in Europe), Shiryayev's animation was forgotten for almost a century until his films and drawings were rediscovered in 1995.

Starewicz's stop-motion films, although made a few years later than Shiryayev's, are still considered to mark the beginning of Russian animation proper. His work found favor with the Tsar, who loved the observations of middle-class life the films contained, but Starewicz did not care for the postrevolutionary regime and emigrated to France in 1919.

These achievements may seem insignificant compared with the work of the early animators in the USA and Western Europe, but they have to be put into technological context since the development of the animation industry in Russia was shaped as much by technological restrictions and political and social influences as by aesthetics and innovation. Before the revolution in 1917, Russia was still a largely underdeveloped and rural state, populated mainly by a peasant class and ruled over by Tsar Nicolas II. As in North America, railways had been established to link the vast country's disparate regions during

Professor Balthazar,
Zagreb Film

the nineteenth century. Following World War I and the revolution, however, most of the network was destroyed or rendered unusable. Electricity did not come to most rural areas until long after the revolution. To improve this situation, Lenin set up a commission to oversee the electrification of Russia. While this strategy was motivated with an eye to industry, Lenin said at the time that such a project would also, "make it possible to raise the level of culture in the countryside and to overcome, even in the most remote corners of the land, backwardness, ignorance, poverty, disease, and barbarism." Lenin's statements and the undoubted achievement of electrifying the country were notably celebrated in the Soyuzmultfilm short directed by Ivan Aksenchuk, *Plyus Elektrifikatsiya* (*Plus Electrification*).

With the railway network repaired and electricity powering the country, animated film could now be distributed to its potentially vast, yet still mainly illiterate, audience. Like the plays of the medieval church, animation would be sent out as one of the cultural vehicles to convey ideology and doctrine to the people. Key to this program was the employment of not only library trains, but also train carriages set up as movie theaters. In this way, prior to World War II, soviet culture, including animation, was distributed across the country to pervade every facet of life.

While this rather cold approach might have brought a rigid style to the output of Russia's animators, in fact, their way of working in groups that were more like artists collectives than production units meant a great deal of experimentation was possible. For this reason, the aesthetic of Russian animation initially drew heavily on, and was more akin to, art movements such as futurism, rather than a desire to achieve realism. Paid by the state irrespective of artistic success, animators experimented with not only different graphical styles, but also with different animation techniques.

Once into the Stalinist era, however, the nation underwent its own cultural revolution with artists, including animators, being compelled to work in the stultifying socialist realist tradition. This "realist" tradition was in fact more about communicating party propaganda than representing the reality of life in soviet Russia.

Russia's first feature-length animated film was Aleksandr Ptushko's *Novvy Gulliver* (*The New Gulliver*, 1936). Mixed with live action, the movie reworks Jonathan Swift's *Gulliver's Travels* with a communist slant. The success of this film at home and abroad placed Ptushko in a prime position to head up what was to become Russia's preeminent animation studio: Soyuzmultfilm.

Initially called Soyuzdetmultfilm and focused on children's animation, the studio was set up in 1936. The name was soon changed, removing the emphasis that animation was purely for children. During World War II, animators at Soyuzmultfilm, who until then had worked in smaller workshops, were evacuated en masse to Samarkand, Uzbekistan, so that they could continue to produce inspiring films for a battling nation. Following the war, the messages they put in their films became more focused on promoting the personality of one man, Stalin, and the vilification of the USA and NATO.

Not until 1953 and the slight thawing of the Cold War during the Kruschev era did Russian animation again take on the spirit and diversity that had been evident from its art-driven roots. This new dawn even survived the chill of the Brezhnev period despite the propagandist core of Russian animators still shaping the entertainment if not the aesthetics. In this way animators continued experimenting with techniques including puppet animation, painting on glass, cel, and cutouts. The results were such masterpieces as Fyodor Khitruk's *Istoriya odnogo prestupleniya* (*Story of One Crime*, 1962) and Yuri Norstein's *Yozhik v tumane* (*Hedgehog in the Fog*, 1975).

In the 1980s, as the Soviet Union opened up during Glasnost and then as it began to fall, animation turned to recording the new atmosphere just as, through most of the twentieth century, it had transmitted the desired ideologies of soviet leaders. For instance, *Seryy Volk end Krasnaya Shapochka* (*Grey Wolf and Little Red Riding Hood*, 1990) by Garri Bardin hinted at the collapse of communism to come.

What has been retained though in this new commercial age is the diversity, vision, creativity, and experimentation of noncommercial animation with international audiences now accessing and applauding Russian animation's eclectic styles and techniques.

In the rest of Eastern Europe, animation has also been shaped by politics. The animation industries of most of these regions have often been sustained by state funding at the expense of having to battle for their own heritage and identity during the various levels of an imposition of communism and its centralized cultural policies. Animators in these areas have endured the same battles to smuggle creativity, modernism, and any reflection on the hardships of life under the totalitarian regimes through the centrally imposed policies of socialist realism, often resulting in hidden, coded, and ambiguous meanings underlying the main narrative. When expression was allowed, the tendency was often for a general pessimism combined with a dark, sly, and often absurdist sense of humor.

Notable animators and studios in Eastern Europe include Croatia's Zagreb Film, which worked in the same kind of modernist style as America's UPA studio; Hungary's Pannonia Studio; the Czech surrealists Jan Svankmajer and Karel Zeman; and the "grotesque realism" of the Estonian Priit Pärn.

Mest Kinematograficheskogo
Operatora (The Cameraman's
Revenge), Ladislaw Starewicz, 1912

A brief history of Asian animation

For the first half of the twentieth century, Japanese animation developed along a similar path to that of the West, influenced by the European and American pioneers, and, more significantly, by the development of the flourishing trade in manga comic strips. Taking their inspiration from historical stories and social commentary with flourishes of humor or fantasy, the early animation works pictorially resembled much of the output of the American cartoon industry. However, they also included particular flavors and elements of the draughtsmanship and illustration styles found in ukiyo-e and other art and craft styles that emerged in Japan during the late Meiji and early Showa periods.

After the Pacific War, hand-in-hand with the massive growth of the manga industry, animation in Japan began to branch away from the trends observed in the West, developing its own broad range of distinctive styles—ultimately giving rise to the style known as anime—and expanding into the large-scale animation industry that exists today, with several world renowned studios, multiple blockbuster movie franchises, and a plethora of television series serving a global audience of devoted fans.

Anime can be a complex world to understand from the perspective of the curious observer. In keeping with the relatively rigid segregation of Japanese cultural creative expression, it can be categorized into a bewildering array of genres and subgenres, made for different niche audiences; including Mecha, Giant Robots, Real and Super Robots, Martial Arts Super Heroes, Transforming Heroes, Magical Girls, and the erotic Hentai. These genres intertwine with the stereotypical sci-fi and comic fantasies as enjoyed by their obsessive fans, often termed "otaku." A major part of the industry in Japan revolves around "O.V.A.s", or films made for direct to video or DVD release, often without theatrical or television screenings.

The other Asian countries with significant animation industries and traditions are Korea, India, the Philippines, Vietnam, and China. In the early years, their combined national output followed a similar, but more sporadic pattern to that of animation development in Japan, producing small numbers of animated shorts or features, often from studios financed by

Akira, Katsuhiro
Otomo, 1988

investment from their respective governments. Rather than becoming centers of creative originality, the overwhelming trend in recent years for many Asian nations has been to expand in the area of animation production services, as companies in Japan and the West outsource their animation products. However, in most cases these countries are rapidly evolving into dynamic and creative animation powerhouses in their own right.

The first generation of Japanese animation largely consisted of isolated experiments influenced by the early Western shorts screened to enthusiasts in urban picture houses. Most of the earliest animated films were lost following the earthquake that hit Tokyo in 1923, though recently a few long-lost prints have been discovered, remastered, and screened in retrospectives. The prestigious title of Japan's "first animated film" is debatable, though it is often attributed to Seitaro Kitayama's *Saru Kani Kassen* (*The Crab Gets His Revenge on the Monkey*, c.1917), though there were several other shorts released in theaters

over that summer. A later short animation, Kenzo Masaoka's *Chikara To Onna No Yononaka* (1932) was the first Japanese "talkie" animation with a prerecorded voice track.

Many of the second-generation Japanese animators developed their skills working at Kitayama's studio, although after the earthquake, the studio relocated to Kyoto and the former staff founded their own studios in the ruins of Tokyo. This emergent industry produced mainly cutout styles of animation, attempting approaches and methods similar to the use of cels, though overall these techniques proved costly to produce. These directors also faced increasing competition for their audience's interest from American movies. Through the 1930s and 1940s, the Japanese military government actively supported and endorsed the domestic animation industry by commissioning educational, information, and military films. The nature of these scripts turned their emphasis toward nationalistic themes, primarily made as propaganda, in the moral, ideological, and cultural battleground. The landmark film of this period was Mitsuyo Seo's *Momotaro no umiwashi* (*Momotaro's Sea Eagles*, 1943), which, at 37 minutes long, is regarded as the first Japanese feature-length animated film.

Though Japan possessed the logistical, social, and production infrastructures to rival movies made elsewhere, the first feature-length animated film by an Asian studio was *Tie shan gong zhu* (*Princess Iron Fan*, 1941). Directed by the pioneering Wan brothers in Shanghai, the script is based on the classical Chinese tale *Journey To The West*, and would have a far-reaching influence on its audiences, resulting in multiple animated interpretations in the ensuing decades.

The 1950s saw manga emerge as a huge cultural and social phenomenon in Japan, with an appeal across all age groups, and the development of the animation industry followed suit accordingly. By 1956, the remaining stalwarts of the animation industry—who remained active in the postwar era as the Nihon Doga Eiga-sha studio—were bought out by entrepreneur Hiroshi Okawa, leading to the formation of Toei Animation. With the intention of producing films akin to those of Walt Disney, Okawa and the Toei team embarked on producing a slate of annual features, commencing in 1958 with the release of Japan's first full-length animated color feature, *Hakuja den* (*Legend of the White Snake*) directed by Taiji Yabushita. Through their commitment to producing impressive animated features, and alongside the efficient development of an authentically Japanese creative process, style of artwork, and storytelling, Toei Animation originated the now distinctive anime look by using mainly limited animation on the majority of shots, saving the main resources for creating a series of spectacular sequences.

By the late 1950s, the legendary, highly-regarded manga creator Osamu Tezuka entered the world of animation, collaborating on the art direction for several early Toei feature films, before forming his own studio, Mushi Productions. Through the enormous popularity of his imaginative stories and characters, Tezuka became one of the most influential figures in Japanese animation history. His simplistically rendered, big-eyed characters provided the template for later anime character design. Mushi created animated features, as well as serialized

animations based on Tezuka's manga comics for the initial launch of the Japanese television industry, including *Tetsuwan Atomu* (1963). Bought by NBC for the US market, it was renamed *Astro Boy* and became the first Japanese animation to achieve significant success internationally.

In China, the Wan brothers were founding members of the government-funded Shanghai Animation Studio in 1950. Creating animation evolved from the traditional Chinese art of intricate paper silhouettes, they made the outstanding color feature, *Da nao tian gong* (*Havoc In Heaven*), a creative milestone in Asian animation. From 1967, Mao Zedong's cultural revolution appropriated the studio, and any animators seen as dissenters were sent away for "reeducation." China's progress in animation production in effect ceased for the next decade. By 1978 however, Shanghai Animation Studio had resumed production, releasing short films in its signature, traditional style.

With the rise of television through the 1960s, as elsewhere, the Japanese animation film industry downsized, while immensely popular genres such as Mecha were launched in television series from the late 1960s and on into the next decade. The popularity of material of this nature led to the rise of "otaku" culture—as observed and termed in the late 1980s—as well as a new wave of anime production. This period is seen as the Golden Age of Anime, with influences continuing to echo through the animation output produced in the present day.

Two influential Japanese studios rose to prominence during the 1980s: Studio Ghibli and Gainax. The huge demand for anime became such that films were made for growing tribes of fans, and released direct to video. Sharing futuristic themes and styling as imagined in the works of author William Gibson, as well as from director Ridley Scott's sci-fi movie *Blade Runner*, manga writers and anime directors like Katsuhiro Otomo began producing gritty sci-fi stories in the cyberpunk genre. Otomo's *Akira* (1988) and Mamoru Oshii's *Kokaku kidotai* (*Ghost in the Shell*, 1995) were also popular cult hits internationally.

Da nao tian gong
(Havoc in Heaven),
Wan Laiming, 1965

Aachi and Ssipak,
Jo Beom-jin, 2006

The Korean animation industry experienced a boom period through the 1990s, producing work for American television series such as *The Simpsons* and *Justice League Unlimited*, with the ensuing development of a new generation of skilled and talented animation artists across other parts of Asia.

Major 1990s television series in Japan included *Pokémon*, *Dragon Ball Z*, and *Sailor Moon*, each also popular with international audiences, and along with the Martial Arts Superhero and the Magical Girl anime genres, became increasingly dominant. Hayao Miyazaki's *Mononoke-hime* (*Princess Mononoke*, 1997) became simultaneously the most expensive anime and the highest grossing film ever at the Japanese box office. His next feature, *Sen to Chihiro no Kamikakushi* (*Spirited Away*, 2001) again broke box office records domestically, as well as scoring an international hit and winning an Academy Award® for best animated feature.

Other high profile Japanese animated features include Satoshi Kon's *Senen joyu* (*Millennium Actress*, 2001) and *Paprika* (2006), Michael Arias' *Tekkon kinkurito* (*Tekkon Kinkreet*, 2006), and, the most expensive of all, Otomo's *Steamboy* (2004). This set of movies were critically acclaimed by both domestic and international audiences, were beautifully realized in terms of their diversity of characters and storylines, and wonderfully represent the caliber of artistic visualization for which contemporary Japanese anime is renowned.

After some early experiments by film pioneer Dhundiraj Govind Phalke, the Indian animation industry truly began in 1956 with the establishment of the Cartoon Film Unit of the Ministry of Information. Disney animator Clair Weeks, who had grown up in India as the son of missionaries, along with Indian animation pioneer G.K. Gokhale, headed up the Unit. Ram Mohan began his career with this organization, where he was trained by Weeks. Mohan established his own company in 1972, producing films such as *Baap Re Baap* (1968). Over the course of a 50-year career, he made a significant contribution to Indian animation and trained and inspired a generation of animators.

In the 1990s, the Indian animation industry emerged as a center for outsourced Western television cartoons, and as a by-product of this, a few feature films were also produced. These movies included *Ramayana: The Legend of Prince Rama* (1992), a coproduction between Mohan and Japanese director Yugo Sako, and the American coproduction *Sinbad: Beyond the Veil of Mists* (2000), which used motion capture effects.

Freedom Song, Narayan Shi, 2000

Animation around the world

Outside of the main regions, animation has developed in a more sporadic, haphazard fashion. In the past, the financial resources required to create animation has been a drawback for areas without a developed industry, but the rise of digital technology has seen a change in the global animation map.

Nordic animation

1919: Denmark. Sven Brasch: *A Rather Good Intention*

1920: Denmark. Robert Storm-Petersen: *A Duck Story*

1924: Finland. Karl Salen & Yrjo Nyberg: *Aito Sunnuntaimetsastaja*

1925: Norway. Walter Fyrst: *Teddy*

1949: Norway. Ivo Caprino: *Tim og Toffe (Tin of Toffee)*

1966: Denmark. Kaj Pindal: *What on Earth!*

1967: Finland. Seppo Suo Anttila: *Impressario*

1969: Denmark. Jorgen Vestergaard: *Nattergalen (The Nightingale)*

1969: Sweden. Per Åhlin: *I huvet pa en gammal gubbe (Out of an Old Man's Head)*

1971: Denmark. Jannik Hastrup: *Benny's Badekar (Benny's Bathtub)*

1971: Norway. Trygve Rasmussen: *The Golden Coin*

1974: Sweden. Per Åhlin: *Dunderklumpen*

1974: Iceland. Jon Axel Egilsson: *The Pioneer*

1975: Norway. Ivo Caprino: *Flåklypa Grand Prix (Pinchcliffe Grand Prix)*

1976: Sweden. Stig Lasseby: *Agaton Sax och Byköpings gästabud (Agaton Sax and the Bykoebing Village Festival)*

1979: Finland. Riita Nelimarkka & Jaakko Seeck: *Seitseman Veljesta*

1980: Norway. Knut Eide: *The Tie*

1981: Sweden. Stig Lasseby: *Pelle Svanslös (Peter No Tail)*

1984: Denmark. Børge Ring: *Anna & Bella*

1984: Sweden. Per Ekholm & Gisela Friesen Ekholm: *It Was Year Zero*

1986: Denmark. Peter Madsen & Jeff Varab: *Valhalla*

1986: Finland/UK. Kari Leponiemi: *I'm Not a Feminist But…*

1988: Denmark. Lejf Marcussen: *Den offentlige røst (The Public Voice)*

1989: Iceland/UK. Inga Lisa Middleton: *Mummy, Daddy, Bobby and Debby*

1990: Denmark. Jannik Hastrup: *Fuglekrigen i Kanøfleskoven (War of the Birds)*

1995: Finland. Katarina Lillquist: *The Maiden and the Soldier*

1997: Denmark. Stefan Fjeldmark: *Når livet går sin vej (When Life Departs)*

1998: Norway. Pjotr Sapegin: *Salt Kvernen (The Salt Mill)*

1999: Norway. Torill Kove: *Min bestemor strøk kongens skjorter (My Grandmother Ironed the King's Shirts)*

2000: Denmark. Stefan Fjeldmark & Michael Hegner: *Hjælp, jeg er en fisk (Help! I'm a Fish)*

2002: Denmark/UK. Siri Melchior: *The Dog Who Was A Cat Inside*

2006: Sweden. Jonas Odell: *Aldrig som första gången! (Never like the First Time!)*

2006: Denmark. Anders Morgenthaler: *Princess*

2006: Norway. Christopher Nielsen: *Slipp Jimmy Fri (Free Jimmy)*

Australian and New Zealand animation

1914: Australia. Harry Julius: *Cartoons of the Moment*

1942: Australia. Eric Porter: Aeroplane Fruit Jellies commercials

1945: Australia. Will & Harry Owen: *First Victory Home Loan: Squander Bug*

1952: Australia. Eric Porter: *Bimbo's Auto*

1958: New Zealand. Fred O Neil: *Plastimania*

1962: Australia. Gus McLaren: *Freddo the Frog*

1962: New Zealand. Fred O Neil: *Hatupatu and the Bird Woman*

1970: Australia. Bruce Petty: *Australian History*

1972: Australia. Eric Porter: *Marco Polo Junior vs the Red Dragon*

1974: Australia. Bruce Petty: *Leisure*

1977: Australia. Yoram Gross: *Dot and the Kangaroo*

1978: Australia. Bruce Petty: *Karl Marx*

1978: New Zealand. Murray Freeth: *The Boy Who Bounced*

1984: New Zealand. Joe Wylie/Susan Wilson: *Te Rerenga Wairua*

1986: New Zealand. Murray Ball: *Footrot Flats, A Dog's Tale*

1986: New Zealand. Robert Stenhouse: *The Frog, the Dog and the Devil*

1992: Australia. Bill Kroyer: *Ferngully: The Last Rainforest*

1992: Australia. Yoram Gross: *Blinky Bill*

2001, 2002, 2003: New Zealand/USA. Peter Jackson: *The Lord of the Rings* trilogy

2003: Australia. Adam Elliott: *Harvie Krumpet*

2003: Australia. Peter Cornwell: *Ward 13*

2005: New Zealand/USA. Peter Jackson: *King Kong*

2006: Australia/USA. George Miller & Animal Logic: *Happy Feet*

2008: Australia. Tatia Rosenthal: *$9.99*

2010: Australia. Shaun Tan & Andrew Ruhemann: *The Lost Thing*

Latin American animation

1917: Brazil. Alvaro Marins:
O Kaiser

1917: Argentina. Quirino Cristiani:
El Apóstol (The Apostle)

1918: Brazil. Gilberto Rossi: *Aventuras de Bille e Bolle*

1918: Argentina. Quirino Cristiani: *Sin Dejar Rastros (Without a Trace)*

1929: Brazil. João Stamato & Luiz Seel:
Macaco Feio Macaco Bonito

1931: Argentina. Quirino Cristiani:
Peludópolis

1940: Argentina. Juan Oliva: *La Caza del Puma (Hunting the Puma)*

1942: Argentina. Dante Quinterno:
Upa en Apuros

1953: Brazil. Anélio Lattini Filho: *Sinfonia Amazônica (Amazon Symphony)*

1957: Brazil. Roberto Miller: *Rumba*

1958: Argentina. Carlos Gonzalez
Groppa: *Trio*

1959: Cuba. Jesus de Armas: *La Prensa Seria (The Serious Press)*

1961: Brazil. Lucchetti & Bassano
Vaccarini: *Fantasmagoricas*

1962: Cuba. Jesus de Armas:
El Cowboy

1965: Mexico. Fernando Ruiz:
El Musico

1967: Brazil. João de Oliveira: *Negrinho de Pastoreiro*

1972: Brazil. Ypê Nakashima: *Piconzé*

1976: Mexico. Fernando Ruiz:
Los Tres Reyes Magos (The Three Wise Men)

1976: Argentina. Simon Feldman:
Los Cuatro Secretes (The Four Secrets)

1978: Columbia. Fernando Laverde:
La Pobre Viejecita

1979: Cuba. Juan Padrón:
Elpidio Valdés

1981: Brazil. Marcos Magalhães: *Meow*

1982: Brazil. Maurício de Sousa:
Aventuras da Turma da Monica

1983: Cuba. Tulio Raggi: *El alma trémular y sola*

1983: Brazil. Maurício de Sousa:
A Princesa e o Robo

1984: Cuba. Mario Rivas: *El Bohío*

1985: Brazil. Marcos Magalhães, Céu
D'Ellia, Flávio Del Carlo: *Planeta Terra*

1985: Uruguay. Walter Tournier: *Nuestro Pequeño Paraíso*

1987: Argentina. Luis Palomares:
El escudo del cóndor

1994: Brazil. Otto Guerra & Adão
Iturrusgarai: *Rocky & Hudson*

1996: Brazil. Clovis Veira: *Cassiopeia*

2001: Brazil. Walbercy Camargo:
Grilo Feliz

2008: Brazil. Ale Abreu: *Garoto Cósmico*

2009: Brazil. Kiko Mistrorigo & Célia
Catunda: *Peixonauta*

2010: Brazil/Canada. Marcelo Fernandes
de Moura & Jean Cullen:
Doggie Day School

African animation

1936: Egypt. David & Shlomo Frenkel:
Mafish Fayda

1962: Egypt. Ali Mohib: *The White Line*

1963: Algeria. Mohamed Aram:
La fete de l'arbre (The Tree Party)

1963: Nigeria. Moustapha Alassane:
La mort du Gandji

1966: Nigeria. Moustapha Alassane:
Bon voyage Sim

1968: Egypt. Ihab Shaker:
The Flower and the Bottle

1969: Egypt. Noshi Iskander:
One and Five; Is It True; Abd Al; Question

1973: Ghana. John K. Ossei:
Annanse's Farm

1974: Egypt. Noshi Iskander: *Where?;
Room Number; Excellent*

1977: Nigeria. Moustapha Alassane:
Samba le grand

1988: Egypt/USA. Mona Abou
El Nasr: *Her Survival*

1989: Mali. Muambayi Coulibaly: *Segou
Janjo, la Geste de Segou*

1989: South Africa. William Kentridge:
*Johannesburg, 2nd Greatest City
After Paris*

1991: Egypt. Radha Djubran:
The Lazy Sparrow

1991: South Africa. William Kentridge:
Sobriety, Obesity and Growing Old

1993: Burkina Faso. Cilia Sawadogo:
Birth

1992: Republic of Congo. Jean Michel
Kibushi: *The Toad Visits His Family*

1994: South Africa. William Kentridge:
Felix in Exile

1996: Ivory Coast. Didier M. Aufort:
Grand Masque et les Junglos

1996: Benjamin Ntabundi, Michel
Castelain, Jacques Faton: *Carnet Noir*

1997: South Africa. William Kentridge:
Weighing and Wanting

1997: Egypt. Zeinab Zamzam:
A Terra-cotta Dream

1999: South Africa. William Kentridge:
Stereoscope

2000: Nigeria. Moustapha Alassane:
Kokoa 2

2000: Cameroon: Pierre Sauvalle:
The General Assembly of Diseases

2003: Zimbabwe. Phil Cunningham &
Roger Hawkins: *The Legend of the
Sky Kingdom*

2004: Republic of Congo. Jean Michel
Kibushi: *Prince Loseno*

2004: South Africa. Ancilla Berry:
Ummemo (The Echo)

2005: Burkina Faso. Cilia Sawadogo:
The Tree of Spirits

2005: Ethiopia. Shane Etzenhouser &
Bruktawit Tigabu: *The Great Animal Run*

2006: South Africa. Justine Puren:
Mbulu's Bride

2006: South Africa. The Blackheart Gang:
The Tale of How

2009: South Africa. Laszlo Bene: *Kalahari*

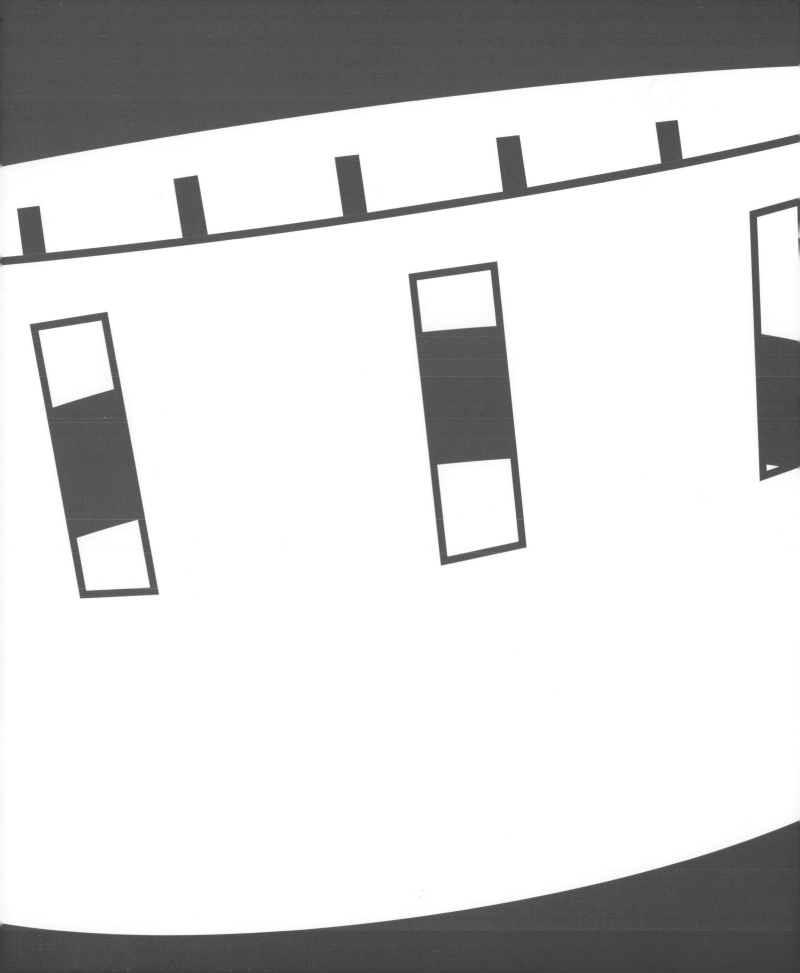

Pre-1900:
The Origins of Animation

Even though we think of cinema as a twentieth-century phenomenon, the art of animation can be traced back a lot further, depending on your definition of the word. Sequential drawings of human and animal figures have been found in ancient Egyptian artwork and many prehistoric cave paintings. Recent claims have been made for a 5,200-year-old bowl found in Iran's Burnt City, which apparently features a series of sequential images of a goat that could have possibly been designed to be spun, producing animation of a kind.

However, a generally agreed definition of animation would probably be along the lines of "single-frame images viewed in rapid succession by some form of mechanism, to create an illusion of movement." Using a definition of that kind, then possibly the earliest recorded animation was created for the devices of Chinese inventor Ting Huan around AD 180. Probably made purely for decorative purposes and as novelty items, these were primitive versions of what centuries later became known as the zoetrope. These early versions held series of drawings that rotated in the rising air when the device was suspended over a lamp, creating an illusion of movement when rotating at the right speed.

The beginnings of modern animation can perhaps be traced back to a paper published by Peter Roget in 1824 for The British Royal Society, titled "The Persistence of Vision with Regard to Moving Objects." This theory referred to the phenomenon whereby the eye's retina retains an image briefly after it has disappeared, which means that if images are flashed in rapid succession they appear to the human brain as one continuous image. If these images differ slightly, especially if they are sequential, then the images can appear to be one moving image. This discovery led ultimately to all cinema, television, and animation.

Spurred on by the persistence of vision discovery came the invention of many optical toys and devices. In 1825, English physician John Ayrton Paris produced his thaumatrope, featuring images on opposite sides of a disc that merged together when the disc was spun on strings. Later came the Belgian Joseph Plateau's phenakistiscope (1831) and Englishman William Horner's Daedalum (1834), essentially a spinning disc and a spinning cylinder in which a strip of sequential images are viewed. The crucial part of these inventions was that the image sequences were viewed through slits to ensure the drawings were seen one at a time to prevent them from appearing as a blur. Horner's name for the device, the Daedalum, means "the wheel of the devil," which perhaps explains why it did not become a popular optical toy until it was patented in the USA and UK in the 1860s and renamed more positively as the zoetrope ("the wheel of life") by the American developer, William F. Lincoln.

In 1877 Frenchman Charles-Emile Reynaud's praxinoscope improved clarity by viewing the sequence of drawings from mirrors mounted in the center of the cylinder. Reynaud later developed his praxinoscope into an early kind of film projector, which he called the Théâtre Optique. Reynaud's device proved a popular attraction in Paris until 1900 when audiences were drawn away from his primitive handpainted animated film strips by the Lumière brothers and their early cinema screenings. In a fit of rage, Reynaud smashed his beloved machines and died in poverty a few years later.

1872

USA/UK

Eadweard Muybridge: Sequential photographs

The collections of amazing photographs of animals and humans in motion produced by English photographer Eadweard Muybridge are still available in a series of reference books and are widely used by animators and artists to this day. The multitalented and inventive Muybridge had many strings to his bow, but his most famous work started as a small experiment. In 1872 the former Governor of California, Leland Stanford, engaged Muybridge to prove the hotly debated theory of "unsupported transit," which held that at some point in time during a horse's gallop, all its hooves were off the ground, contrary to the popular belief that at least one foot had to be on the ground at any one time.

By 1877 Muybridge had proved the unsupported transit theory by photographing Stanford's racehorse, Occident, in motion. Encouraged by Stanford to continue this work, he went on to produce a photographic sequence, using 12 stereoscopic cameras placed along a racetrack triggered by trip wires, which the horse passed through, an event which he invited the press to witness.

This project became Muybridge's life's work as he went on to produce series after series of his motion photographs. He galloped horses, flew birds, and walked any animals he could think of in front of his cameras, and after running out of animals, produced photostrips of humans performing a huge variety of different movements and actions.

His ingeniousness did not stop there as, in 1879, he created his own early cinema projector called the zoopraxiscope, a variant of the zoetrope designed to project his image sequences for public viewing. The device projected light through transparent spinning discs on which image sequences were handpainted or photographically transferred.

Muybridge's multicamera system has been adapted into a modern variation, the "bullet time" effect much used in movies such as *The Matrix*. This effect is also a feature of the work of quirky French genius, animator and director Michel Gondry. His early music videos involve a similar line of linked cameras, except they are generally arranged in a curve around the subject and are triggered simultaneously instead of split seconds apart. When viewed in rapid succession, the effect is almost the exact opposite of animation, giving the impression of a camera moving around a subject that is frozen in time.

Sequential photographs

1877
France

Charles-Emile Reynaud: The praxinoscope

Having developed a technical understanding of visual science as a photographer's apprentice and an aritistic sensibility from his mother, who had studied under the painter Pierre Joseph Redoute, Charles-Emile Reynaud had both the technical and artistic ability that has often produced good animators.

In 1877 he developed and patented an advancement of the zoetrope called the praxinoscope. The improvement basically consisted of adding a facility whereby mirrors, mounted in the center of the zoetrope's spinning cylinder, were fixed at such an angle that they would reflect the spinning strip of images one at a time in rapid succession as the cylinder whirled. This was a better experience for the viewer, compared with having to peep through the zoetrope's spinning slits. Reynaud achieved success in manufacturing his invention and selling it as a children's toy, but perhaps being wise enough to realize that this novelty would not last, he also looked to exploit his invention further.

Similar to Muybridge in his drive to move forward with his ideas and entertain larger audiences, he had the idea of developing his machine into a projecting device that would throw moving pictures onto a screen. In 1888 in front of a small invited audience, Reynaud demonstrated the device he called the Théâtre Optique, projecting a primitive film called *Un bon bock* (*A Good Beer*). The images for the machine were handpainted by Reynaud onto a perforated band or ribbon that unwound from one cylinder to another in much the same way as film projectors have done ever since. Meanwhile another projector created a still picture that was the backdrop for the projected animation.

The invention had to be operated by hand, and the complexity of this task dissuaded the potential buyers that Reynaud had hoped would create a kind of franchise network for his device and films. In 1892 Reynaud settled on a contract with the Grévin Wax Museum in Paris, which required him to perform daily screenings, produce regular new films, and give away the exclusive rights to his machine. By 1895 however, the writing was on the wall for his invention when the Lumière brothers began their early cinema screenings, also in Paris. In 1900 Reynaud closed his Théâtre Optique and soon afterward sunk into depression, smashing his machines and throwing his carefully painted films into the river Seine. He died in poverty in 1918. Despite his unhappy demise, the ingenious Reynaud, with his ribbons of handpainted moving figures, can be considered one of the true forerunners of modern animation, and indeed of cinema itself.

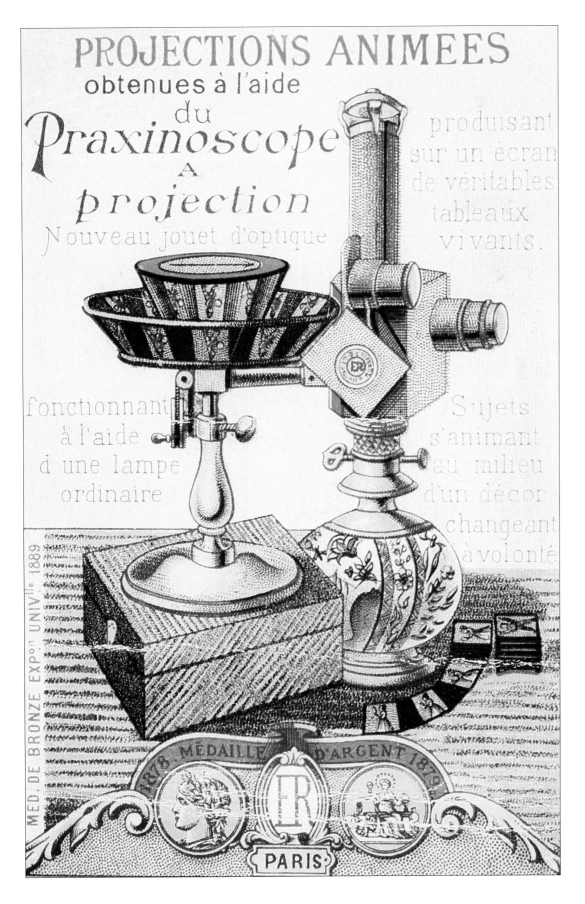

Reynaud's praxinoscope

1882
France

Etienne-Jules Marey: Motion photographs

A French scientist, Etienne-Jules Marey, later to also become a motion photographer, had proposed in his 1873 book *La Machine Animale* the unsupported transit theory concerning a horse's hooves all leaving the ground during a gallop, the theory that Muybridge would set out to prove a few years later.

After Eadweard Muybridge's first motion photographs appeared in the USA, Marey started producing his own photography of animals in motion, for which he had invented something called a chronophotographic gun in 1882. This device took 12 photos per second onto the same photographic plate. He used it for photographing birds in flight and then later a variety of animals falling and in various forms of motion.

Muybridge visited Marey in France and the two men seemed to inspire each other. While the more flamboyant Muybridge's work was part scientific, part artistic, and part showmanship, Marey, a leading scientist, continued his experiments in a more serious academic vein, nevertheless producing some equally remarkable and beautiful photographs, which still make a great resource for animators today.

Motion photographs

1889
USA

Thomas Edison and William Dickson: The kinetoscope

The kinetoscope was conceived in 1888 by Thomas Edison and developed between 1889 and 1892 by his talented employee, William Kennedy Dickson. Rather than being a projecting device, however, it was a box into which the viewer would peer through a viewfinder. Inside were strips of film spooling in front of a strong light that flashed behind a shutter, thus "freezing" each separate image as it passed. In 1894 Edison gave the first commercial motion picture screening with 10 of his kinetoscopes in New York. The first actual film show, however, seems to have been earlier the same year in that city, when Frenchman Jean Aimé "Acme" LeRoy showed his *Marvellous Cinematograph.*

Like most of cinema's pioneers, Edison seems to have been influenced by earlier inventions. He had met with Eadweard Muybridge and had possibly seen his zoopraxiscope in early 1888 when Muybridge gave a lecture close to Edison's headquarters in West Orange, New Jersey. The resourceful Muybridge had proposed a collaboration between himself and Edison to make a device that would produce both sound and vision, by adapting and combining Muybridge's zoopraxiscope and Edison's phonograph. Nothing came of that meeting, but later that year, Edison filed a preliminary patent for a device that would provide a filmed audio and visual experience. He later dropped the audio aspect of the device and concentrated instead on a silent version of the machine.

In 1899 Edison visited France for two months to attend a science and commerce fair called Exposition Universelle, where he would have seen Charles-Emile Reynaud's praxinoscope, with its strip of spooled perforated images. He would have also seen German inventor Otto Anschuetz's electrical tachyscope, which was a disc-based projector similar to Muybridge's, except that it used brief flashes of light to "freeze" the projected sequential images. While in France, Edison also visited Etienne-Jules Marey and saw his chronophotographic gun—the first real cine camera. A lot of the elements in these ideas found their way into his 1891 patents for the kinetoscope and his cine camera, the kinetograph.

What Edison can undeniably take credit for was for organizing, fully developing, and exploiting, all these various strands of ideas, including the use of George Eastman's photographic film, into one commercially viable package, and it would be from his invention that modern cinema would take its name and grow into an industry. As is often the case with history, it's not the individual with the original idea but the person who can see the "big picture" and then formalize, organize, develop, and profit from the idea, who takes the biggest prize. The only commercial mistake Edison seemingly made, perhaps mindful of similar inventions across the Atlantic, was to obtain only a US patent for the kinetoscope instead of a worldwide one.

1896

France

Georges Méliès: Early "trick" films

Georges Méliès, a succesful magician and owner of the Theatre Robert-Houdin in Paris, saw the Lumière brothers' Cinématographe near his own theater in 1895, and immediately set up his own moving picture show. The Lumières were unwilling to sell equipment to a rival, so Méliès had equipment custom-made and also improved on other people's designs.

After some early films which, like much of the Lumières' work, concerned simple landscapes and scenes of ordinary life, Méliès started to apply his magician's art and sense of showmanship to the filmmaking process and created some of the most imaginative and original work of his era. He discovered by accident, when his camera jammed and then restarted, the crucial magic trick of stop frame: stopping the film and moving or substituting objects before continuing the shot. He exploited this endlessly in his many fantasies and "trick films," and went on to pioneer the science fiction, fantasy, and horror genres. By 1899 he was creating films like the seven-minute *Cendrillon* (*Cinderella*), which used multiple scenes to tell the story, and in the process, was making the first true narrative films. He was also a pioneer in techniques like fade-in, fade-out, and dissolves, and he produced early crude animation, like making letters of the alphabet dance around.

His most famous and successful film was 1902's *Le voyage dans la lune* (*A Trip to the Moon*), which includes the iconic image of a rocket crashing into the eye of the "man in the moon." Although this film was a worldwide hit by the standards of the day, it appears to have been an early victim of piracy as Méliès received little financial benefits from its popularity. His best and most creative period of work was around 1899 to 1902; he made hundreds of other films after this, but his mighty burst of invention seemed to fade out and his later films are uninteresting in comparison.

He was left behind by the bigger film companies and when World War I began in 1914, he closed the doors of his theater. Like fellow French pioneer Reynaud before him, when he saw the success he had worked for unspooling in front of his eyes, he reportedly started to destroy his films one by one.

In the 1920s the French surrealist movement rediscovered and reevaluated Méliès' work and tracked him down to a kiosk in a Paris train station where he was selling candy and toys. In the last part of his life, at least, he achieved the recognition he deserved as one of the pioneers of cinema.

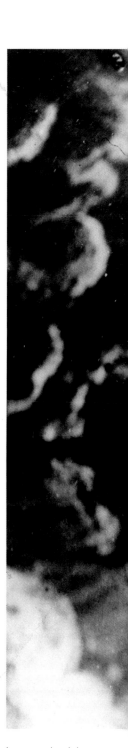

Le voyage dans la lune
(A Trip to the Moon), 1902

Stop-frame animation

Stop frame (also known as stop motion or claymation) is the process of using models, which are moved and filmed frame by frame. This is perhaps the oldest and simplest kind of animation, and was widely used in the past to animate realistic models of monsters, etc., which were then inserted into live-action scenes. It is still popular today thanks to the work of animators and directors such as Tim Burton and Nick Park.

1900-1927:
Film Animation: The Era of Experimentation

With the exploitation of cinema up for grabs worldwide, there were many developments and variations across Europe around the turn of the nineteenth century. All in the year 1895, the Lumière brothers in France opened their version of the Cinematograph; while in London, Robert W. Paul and his partner Birt Acres completed their 35mm cine camera, the Kinepticon; and in Berlin the Skladanowsky brothers showed films on their Bioskop projector.

With all the pockets of feverish development of film and animation in Europe and the USA, it is difficult to pinpoint the first real animator or the first real animation. It really depends on how you define these terms. In 1888 Charles-Emile Reynaud had projected his handpainted moving figures from image strips, but it seems to have been Thomas Edison's employee, the American Alfred Clarke, who in 1895 discovered the crucial magic trick of "stop-frame" cinematography and perhaps created the first special effect, while working on Edison's *The Execution of Mary, Queen of Scots*. At the crucial moment of the staged execution, Clarke stopped the camera, replaced the actress with a dummy, and cranked the machine again. French showman and early filmmaker Georges Méliès also accidentally discovered the stop-frame trick and was the first to crudely move objects around, but it was Englishman Arthur Melbourne-Cooper, an assistant of Birt Acres, who created perhaps the first animation proper in a film, with his stop-frame characters in *Matches: An Appeal* in 1899.

It was only at the turn of the nineteenth century that the history of animation really became distinguishable from the history of the cinema.

1899

UK

Arthur Melbourne-Cooper: Matches: An Appeal

In 1899 what many consider to be the first true filmed animation was made by Arthur Melbourne-Cooper of St. Albans, England, for the Bryant May match company. The son of a photographer, Cooper was working in the Barnet photographic company as an assistant to film pioneer Birt Acres when he created *Matches: An Appeal*, in which the public were asked to send money to British troops fighting the Boer War in South Africa. The film featured small characters made of matches, filmed frame by frame, as they wrote on a blackboard. For such a time of rapid progress when most innovations in the field seemed to be occurring simultaneously worldwide, it is impressive that Cooper's work was six or seven years ahead of the animation pioneers in France and America.

Cooper is also credited with inventing the close-up shot in film, when he edited close shots of faces into *Grandmother's Reading Glass* in 1900, although in the same year, fellow Englishman G. A. Smith is also credited with inventing the technique in his film *The Little Doctor*.

In 1904 Cooper set up the Alpha Trading Company and, with codirector Robert W. Paul, produced many films that experimented with animation ("stop and start" or "trick" films as Cooper referred to them), mixing these techniques with live action and fantasy to create charming work like *The Enchanted Toymaker* (1904) and *Dreams of Toyland* (1908).

Like an early model for a modern media corporation, at one stage his Alpha company produced, distributed, and exhibited his films, while next to the film studio in St. Albans, they ran an early multiplex-type development that incorporated a swimming pool, stores, and restaurants. After Paul retired in 1910, Cooper continued to make many animated films, such as *Cinderella* (1912), as well as commercials and newsreels, including *The Suffragette Derby* (1913) in which women's rights campaigner Emily Davison is seen being trampled to death by the King's race horse. Cooper retired in 1940 and died in 1961.

Dreams of Toyland, 1908

1905

Spain

El Hotel Eléctrico (The
Electric Hotel), 1905

Segundo de Chomón: El Hotel Eléctrico (The Electric Hotel)

Spain's Segundo de Chomón was a highly-skilled cameraman, special effects director, director of photography, and early pioneer of film techniques and methods. His movie *El Hotel Eléctrico* (*The Electric Hotel*), in which inanimate objects in a hotel come alive, was an early breakthrough in stop frame, using real objects in animation in a way years ahead of its time. Chomón was one of the early "nomadic" animators, traveling across Europe to work on projects in Barcelona, Paris, and Turin. He is credited with developing the "dolly," a camera on rails that is still used in live-action movies for tracking shots. Chomón did not really see himself as an animator; his skill with stop frame was just one of the many special effects in his armory.

1906
USA/UK

James Stuart Blackton: Humorous Phases of Funny Faces

What is said by some to be the first drawn animation recorded on film was *Humorous Phases of Funny Faces*, made by English-born James Stuart Blackton in New York. Blackton was working as a journalist at the time, and during an interview with Thomas Edison, he mentioned that he was interested in drawing. Edison asked Blackton to draw his portrait while being filmed. This changed the direction of Blackton's career and started him on the path to becoming a cameraman, director, producer, and one of the founders of animation.

Blackton had already had experience with a popular vaudeville act called "chalk takes" or "lightning sketches" in the UK, in which the performer drew a quick sketch, often a caricature of a member of the audience, modifying the drawing as he went along, to accompany a monologue. The earliest drawn animations were often simply films of these performances. Blackton made several films of this type including *The Enchanted Drawing* (1900) and, the most famous of these, *Humorous Phases of Funny Faces* (1906), which features various scenes, such as a man puffing smoke out of a cigar and a dog performing tricks.

Blackton's 1907 film *The Haunted Hotel* was his most successful. With a similar idea to Segundo de Chomón's *El Hotel Eléctrico* (*The Electric Hotel*), this was a live-action movie in which a hotel comes alive with ghostly stop-motion effects. This film achieved massive success and popularity worldwide, was much imitated, and inspired many others to become involved with the new magic of cinema.

Humorous Phases of
Funny Faces, 1906

1908
France

Emile Cohl: Fantasmagorie

Fantasmagorie was released on August 17, 1908, the title referring to the Fantasmograph, one of the nineteenth-century variants of the "magic lantern." The film contained over 700 drawings (each double exposed, or shot on "doubles" as animators call it), ran for nearly two minutes, and could be said to be the world's first fully-animated film. It used the same technique as James Stuart Blackton's of filming a black line drawn on white paper and then using the negative exposure to appear as a white line on a blackboard.

Considering its short length, *Fantasmagorie* contained an impressive number of transformations and wild scenarios, each joyously and spontaneously created by Cohl in his stream of consciousness, bohemian style as he traced over his own drawings, changing details frame by frame, and working out the timing as he went along.

Fantasmagorie, 1908

Biography

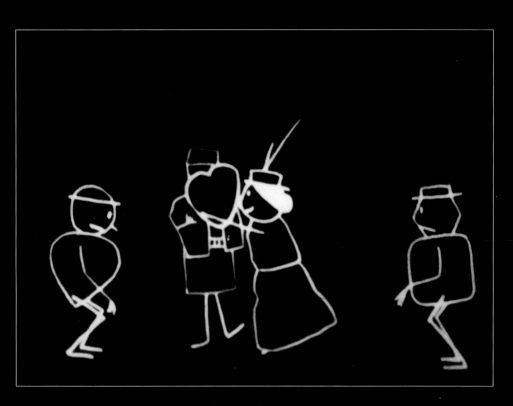

Une drame chez les fantoches (Drama Among the Puppets), 1908

Emile Cohl

Born Emile Courtet in Paris in 1857, this important animation pioneer first achieved fame, and some notoriety, as a political caricaturist. Cohl was also a member of certain subversive art movements, and a lot of his life's work was concerned with joyously satirizing and ridiculing convention, subverting and twisting reality, and caricaturing the lives of the establishment. It is therefore quite fitting and perhaps unsurprising that a lot of his own life has achieved the quality of legend and myth, to the extent that it is difficult to separate the stories about Cohl from the facts.

Cohl was a member of an art movement called The Incoherents, who believed in the power of the ridiculous and the ludicrous. They held art exhibitions of drawings by people who couldn't draw and of sculpture made of food. In this type of activity they challenged convention and closed thinking and were precursors of the dadaists, surrealists, and conceptual artists. Cohl took this attitude, creativity, and surrealism into the new medium of animation, and in doing so created a template for cartoons to come. His characters were distorted, stretched, came apart, transformed into objects and animals, and then afterward recovered as if nothing had happened. The impossible was not only possible, but certain to happen. Audiences were riotous with delight.

Cohl understood perfectly the whole point of cartoons—that anything can happen—and in demonstrating this he laid the path for Disney, Warner Bros., UPA, Pixar, and every other future creator of this new form of popular mass-market surrealism, before the idea of realism in animation spoiled the fun by making cartoons respectable.

Cohl first discovered his skill at drawing at boarding school, where he was sent by his father after his mother's death in 1863. In 1870 Paris was invaded during the Franco-Prussian War and, after his father lost his business, Cohl had to leave his boarding school. He began to spend a lot of time wandering the streets and observing

Emile Cohl

the political chaos around him. He discovered political caricature at this time as several caricaturists were based near his new school; these artists would post their work up around the city in protest at current events. He was also influenced by popular forms of puppet theater called Guignol and Fantoche.

Cohl's father, trying to provide him with some kind of stable occupation, got him jobs as a jeweler's apprentice, an insurance broker, and enlisted him in the army, where, despite his father's efforts, he persisted with his passion for cartoon drawing and produced sketches of his regiment. Cohl rejected all of these early occupations in favor of drawing, eventually ending up as an assistant to his hero, the caricaturist André Gill, who was his mentor for many years.

As he started to become successful, Cohl produced work for popular publications, including *Les Hommes d'aujourd'hui*, in which he caricatured famous figures of the day, such as the artist Toulouse-Lautrec and the poet Verlaine. He embraced the Parisian bohemian artist lifestyle and his work mocked authority, to the extent that he was jailed for one of his comic publications about the French president, making him a "cause célèbre."

Because of the instability and insecurity of many artists' lives, they often need to use their creativity in different ways in order to survive. As well as his early stints in various industries, the multitalented Cohl worked as a photographer, a comedy writer for the theater, and even used his interest in stamp collecting and dealing to survive. He also had a strong interest in magic tricks,

perhaps inherited from his father who was a part-time magician's assistant. Many of these experiences were called upon when, at 50 years of age, Cohl prepared to embark on something new. Cinema was the latest sensation in Paris and Cohl was curious about this new form of entertainment.

In 1907, at around the time that James Stuart Blackton's *The Haunted Hotel* was released in Paris, Cohl went to visit a film studio for the first time. The story of this visit has become one of the legends about his life about which there is some doubt. According to the story, after being enraged by a film poster he saw in the street that plagiarized one of his ideas, Cohl went straight to the office of producer Léon Gaumont to demand compensation. The producer, in honorable fashion, admitted his debt and in addition offered

Cohl a job as a creator of motion pictures. Blackton's film had caused much curiosity and debate and, again according to legend, Cohl was the only person able to figure out the methods behind the "magic" and set about using his talents and know-how to create his own films to better Blackton's achievements.

After a few months he released his first film, *Fantasmagorie* (1908); with its anarchic style of random transformations and absurd situations, the film can be seen as a tribute to Cohl's fondness for his Incoherent period of art. The success of this was followed by at least five more films that year and an estimated total of more than 500 shorts before 1923, an incredible output considering the amount of work involved and the lack of time-saving techniques available. His films between 1907 and 1910 were his best however, containing a joyous freedom and invention that liberated animation from the theatrical constraints that had held it rooted in the past and encouraged future animators to make the most of the possibilities of the medium. Although simple and naïve, mainly due to the simplification needed for quick drawing (the eternal problem for the animator), his drawings are sharp, clear, and inventive. As well as his drawn animation in this period—such as a series of adventures featuring the character Fantoche in films like *Un drame chez les fantoches* (*Drama Among the Puppets*, 1908)—his ever restless and curious nature led him to experiment with stop motion in *Les allumettes animées* (*The Animated Matches*, 1908) and painting directly onto film in *L'éventail animé* (*The Animated Fan*, 1909). Cohl would also later make the first film featuring the technique now known as pixillation.

The Animated Matches has had an extraordinary influence over the progress of animation worldwide, being named as an inspiration by artists in countries as widespread as Russia, India, and Argentina. This also demonstrates the widespread distribution and popularity that Cohl's films achieved. Like Georges Méliès and others before him, however, Cohl clearly did not always receive the royalties and financial rewards for this success, thus anticipating a problem that has plagued animators and filmmakers ever since, with particular echoes in the file-sharing download culture of the digital age.

In 1910 Cohl left Gaumont to work for Pathé and in 1912 he took a contract with the Éclair company. He was asked to work in Éclair's studio in Fort Lee, USA, where he animated a series called *Snookums*; taken from a popular comic strip by George McManus, it was one of the superior series of its time. Cohl enjoyed a happy time in the USA where he was impressed with the level of organization at the American studio and its highly-trained and well-paid artists. As he learned and was influenced by the American animators, they undoubtedly learned many animation tricks from him. In the next few years however, he came to regret sharing his secrets as he became disillusioned with the mechanization and economies of scale of the American studios that were producing such volumes of work that, when exported, made it impossible for individuals and smaller European companies to compete.

In 1914, just before the outbreak of World War I, Cohl returned to Paris and helped produce a series called *Flambeau*, which was similar to the series he had made in the USA, as well as some propoganda films for the war effort. His work after this never quite recaptured the magic of his early films, but with his last film, made when he was 64 years old, he went out on a high by reanimating his early character Fantoche for *Fantoche cherche un logement* (*The Puppet Looks for Lodging*, 1921). It was his early drawn animation films however which become a big influence on the next major figure to move animation forward, and perhaps the first truly great animator, Winsor McCay.

1910–1914
Italy/France

Experiments in abstract animation

Brothers and members of the Italian futurist movement, Arnaldo Ginna and Bruno Corra created four abstract films between 1910 and 1914 that are credited with not only being the first abstract animations, but also with starting the whole movement of avant-garde film.

The roots of abstract cinema came from their primitive experiments involving painting directly onto film. Ginna was a futurist painter who could also claim to have created the first abstract painting in *Neurasthenia* (1908) and would go on to direct the only official futurist film, *Vita Futurista* (*Futurist Life*, 1916). With his brother Bruno he sought to form a link between the harmony of colors and the harmony of music and develop a form of "visual music" created with "chromatic keys" linked to musical keys. After composing pieces of work on something they called their "light organ," they turned their attention to making films. Unable to find a movie camera that would take one frame at a time, the brothers improvised and painted directly onto film stock, creating the four films *A Chord of Colour*, *Study of the Effects of Four Colours*, *Song of Spring*, and *Flowers*. This radical new technique would be picked up again and further developed by Norman McLaren and Len Lye in London a quarter of a century later and also by fellow Italian Luigi Veronesi in 1938 in Milan.

Tragically all the films of Ginna and Corra, and almost all of Veronesi's, are believed to have been destroyed in the bombing of Milan in 1943.

Around 1912, Léopold Survage, a Paris-based artist of Russian/Danish/Finnish descent, produced a series of abstract paintings that he called "Colored Rhythm." He planned to animate these works, seeing their potential to flow together to form "symphonies in color" and intending to cross what he called "the glistening bridge" from still to moving images. He unsuccessfully applied for a patent for his idea and was unable to persuade the Gaumont Company in France to film his works with their new color film technique. He exhibited the paintings separately, however, in 1913 and 1914.

The avant-garde: an alternative history of animation

The roots of the avant-garde movement in animation can be traced back to Arnaldo Ginna and Bruno Corra's isolated experiments with painting on film in 1910 and the futurist manifesto they contributed to. The ideas they proposed would mushroom and grow in the rest of the twentieth century to become the basis of an underground universe encompassing a myriad of styles, techniques, and philosophies, often closer to the world of fine art than to the commercial realm. These influences have seeped into mainstream movies, advertising, design, and music videos; have provided the framework of ideas that early computer animation was built on; and became the inspiration for a million styles of abstract film in the digital age.

In the 1920s filmmakers, animators, and visual artists across Europe began to respond to the promptings of the futurists. Fernand Léger in France and Walther Ruttmann, Hans Richter, Oskar Fischinger, and the Swede Viking Eggeling in Germany created a connected body of inspirational abstract work. Most of this group of animators, along with many other artists, left Germany for the USA or UK during the rise of the Nazis.

In London in the 1930s, documentary maker John Gierson established the government-sponsored General Post Office Film Unit (GPO), which under his guidance invested in experimental film and animation. He funded the early films of Norman McLaren and Len Lye, who, although not as seriously theoretical and manifesto driven as their predecessors, were influenced by the German abstract animators. McLaren and Lye went on to produce some of the most influential abstract animation, playfully mixing techniques such as painting and dyeing film stock with filmed abstract work.

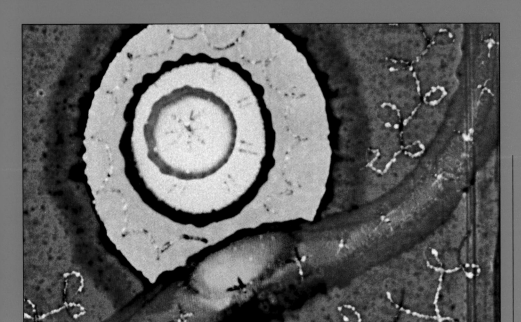

Begone Dull Care,
Norman McLaren, 1949

In 1938 the Government of Canada invited John Grierson to study Canadian film production. Grierson's report led to the establishment of the National Film Board of Canada (NFB) and he was appointed its first director. Grierson adopted the same philosophy of experimentation as at the GPO, appointing Norman McLaren as head of the animation unit and establishing the Board's reputation as one of the world's foremost centers for independent animation and film. Over the years, the NFB has won over 25 Oscars for animation and has funded films by experimental animators such as Caroline Leaf, Ryan Larkin, and Theodore Ushev.

Many influential live-action surrealist films were created in the 1920s and 1930s by French artists, who playfully attempted to uncover the subconscious mind through examining the inherent symbolism of dreams, inspiring work featuring surrealism and symbolism on the other side of the Atlantic.

Mary Ellen Bute was an animator working in New York at this time, experimenting with various machines associated with "the kinetic use of color" and collaborating with Norman McLaren. Maya Deren's live-action films are credited with kick-starting the New American Cinema

movement of the 1940s and 1950s and bringing a powerful spiritual dimension to avant-garde films. Marie Menken also created many experimental animated films in this period.

In the 1950s the "beat generation" started to emerge in the USA, with its philosophy of free-form, expressionist, "stream of consciousness" prose and art. The work of certain animators at the time seemed to relate to this style and they were loosely linked with the movement, although they later transcended the connection. Robert Breer started making his free-form animation in the mid-1950s, filming fast, sketchy, unrelated animation on filing cards. Harry Smith produced some of the twentieth century's most remarkable abstract animation and was a major influence on 1960s psychedelia. Smith associated with, and was influenced by, other California-based artists—including the great avant-garde pioneer Oskar Fischinger—and the scene based around the Art in Cinema screenings at the San Francisco Museum of Modern Art.

Another American abstract filmmaker with a long and varied career was Stan Brakhage, who made many films by scratching, painting, and pressing natural objects directly onto film stock. New York avant-gardist Stan Vanderbeek was

another 1950s filmmaker using wild, free-form types of animation incorporating performance art, whose "expanded cinema" shows differed for every performance and venue.

Despite working outside any movement, British filmmaker Jeff Keen's work has common ground with the free-flowing filmmakers and pop artists of the 1960s. His work often involves roughly-animated sequences, although the rapid pace of the editing in his pop-ephemera-laden collages makes it hard to know where the animation stops and the rest of the film begins.

Beginning in the early 1960s with his first student films, the Czech animator Jan Svankmajer combined his interest in surrealism with traditional Czech puppets and experimental theater, creating his own unique stop-frame universe in many award-winning and world-renowned shorts and features. His films were banned by Czechoslovakia's communist government, illustrating the power of surrealist and abstract art to represent freedom of thought and spirit, causing discomfort to those totalitarian governments who fundamentally dislike freedom.

Ryan Larkin made a series of influential and beautiful psychedelic short films for Canada's NFB between 1969 and 1972, after being taught animation by Norman McLaren. Larkin was later the subject of a semisurreal animated short by Chris Landreth in 2004, after his middle-aged descent into alcohol and drug abuse.

Outsider animator Bruce Bickford began working with rock musician Frank Zappa in California in the 1970s, sharing the same dark sense of the surreal and the absurd. Bickford's intense creations of constantly transforming and mutating stop-motion worlds feel anywhere between an amusing psychedelic trip and a Hieronymus Bosch–type nightmare vision.

In the 1960s and 1970s many computer animation pioneers took inspiration from the avant garde. John Stehura's *Cibernetik* (1963) used early computer algorithms, produced on a computer so primitive it didn't even have a screen, to manipulate and create images, and in so doing, created this psychedelic classic embraced by the hippie generation. Ed Emshwiller worked on early computer graphics systems in the 1970s after creating experimental films in the 1960s and produced some of the first 3D CGI.

After producing his abstract films in the 1940s and 1950s in a geometrical style influenced by the earlier German avant-garde, James Whitney used a primitive analogue computer built by his brother John to create work somewhere between computer animation and primitive spiritual art.

Hungarian Jules Engel, best known for his work on the great early Disney features and for being a founding member of the groundbreaking UPA studio, also made many abstract films, encouraged early on by Oskar Fischinger, who he met while working at Disney. Engel later founded the Experimental Animation Department at California Institute of the Arts in 1970.

Following his work as a programmer for John Whitney, Larry Cuba went on to produce his own groundbreaking computer-generated films, as well as commercial work, such as an animated Death Star for *Star Wars* (1977).

As is common in the world of art and culture, what is formerly considered avant-garde is soon absorbed into the mainstream and becomes just another flavor. Indeed, modern day corporations and their advertising teams are so sophisticated

and adept at this process of assimilation and commoditization that what seems underground and cutting-edge one month, is used to sell cars or phones the next. By the early 1970s, psychedelic images of hippies were being used to sell ice-cream.

Punk was in one sense the last gasp of a genuine revolutionary counterculture and created a powerful new direction that inspired a generation of musicians, artists, and animators with its "do-it-yourself" philosophy, but inadvertently in the act of making hippie culture seem antiquated overnight, it paved the way for the cynical consumer culture that would follow.

As abstract, symbolic, and psychedelic film lost the edge it once had, new ways of using moving images in the avant-garde were explored. In the 1970s and 1980s, installation,

Magnetic Movie,
Semiconductor,
2007

performance, and video art, and various combinations of these became widely explored methods of provoking engagement in galleries and public spaces. However, animation was unsuited to early video technology and was somewhat unfashionable in art at this time as it was generally associated with the worst of cheap, mindless television.

One gallery artist working with animation toward the end of the 1980s was William Kentridge. The South African artist achieved international acclaim with his figurative, animated charcoal sketches, in which drawings were photographed, erased, and overdrawn, producing a time trail of images. Kentridge often used these works to comment on South African politics and society.

In the mainstream politics of the 1980s and 1990s "the market" was everything. For the people controlling these markets, every product needed designers to create an image, packaging, and a "brand," leading to a worldwide growth in graphic design. With the explosion of computer graphics, the possibilities for creating animation, particularly abstract animation or "motion graphics," became open to anyone with a computer.

In this era of postmodernism every cultural and artistic movement of the past was used as a marketing gimmick, ruthlessly depoliticized and stripped of all meaning before being used as a wrapper for the next product variation. The kind of abstract moving imagery intended to be mind-expanding and revolutionary in the early years of the twentieth century was absorbed into the world of motion graphics to advertise brands, decorate nightclubs, and provide a coating of instant "cool." In some ways this was the futurist's dream—art that was produced by the masses, part of everyday industry and life—but the idea of

it comforting the mind into buying rather than stimulating it into thinking was a long way from the original intention.

At the cutting edge of the digital revolution, however, a new avant-garde emerged. Closer in spirit to the manifesto-led animators of the early twentieth century, these artists used computer technology to create new relationships between animation, music, and film; methods often impossible outside of the digital realm. Computer programmer, artist, and animator Yoichiro Kawaguchi was a pioneer in the creation of computer software that grows images in an organic way, developing brightly-colored psychedelic environments populated with metallic-shaded, organic life-forms. The process is one of the creation of environments with variable parameters in which various life-forms develop, flourish, or die away with infinite variety. Films produced in this way include *Ocean* (1986) and *Tendril* (1982). Later computer artists Karl Sims and William Latham also used software to grow their images, setting up digital ecosystems with complex mathematics to simulate natural evolution and produce images of "computer life-forms."

The UK's Animate! scheme, established in 1990, was a product of TV network Channel 4's animation initiatives and the British government's lottery funding for the arts. Along with organizations like the NFB, Animate! is one of the world's few government-sponsored initiatives with the explicit aim to fund projects that stretch the boundaries of animation in nontraditional directions. Managed by visionary producer Dick Arnall until his death in 2007, some of the many avant-garde artists to have benefited from its funding have been William Latham (*Biogenesis*, 1993), Run Wrake (*Jukebox*, 1994), Kayla Parker

(*Sunset Strip*, 1996), Semiconductor (*Magnetic Movie*, 2007), and Stephen Irwin (*The Black Dog's Progress,* 2008). onedotzero is a UK-based international organization formed in 1996 to promote digital film, by means of film festivals and events, often showcasing abstract and nontraditional short films.

Groups currently producing abstract digital animation include Tomato, an influential design collective based in London, and Insertsilence, an internet-based collective founded in 2001 to create abstract projects based on music, movement, and drawing. Satoshi Tomioka is a Japanese individualist CGI animator creating his own darkly absurdist and surrealist universes, often based on his observations of the corporate culture of downtown Tokyo. Theodore Ushev created the award-winning digital abstract films *Tower Bawher* (2005) and *Drux Flux* (2008) for the National Film Board of Canada; these works consist of a juxtaposition of images illustrating the inhuman effect of industrial progress on humans.

As perhaps a high watermark of contemporary gallery and installation art involving animation, the winner of Britain's prestigious 2008 Turner art prize featured a video of artist Mark Leckey giving a lecture about his love of animation. Also featured in Leckey's multimedia installation, entitled *Industrial Light and Magic*, were images of animated characters including Homer Simpson and Felix the Cat.

1910
Russia

Ladislaw Starewicz: Prekrasnaya Lyukanida (The Beautiful Leukanida)

The film that made Ladislaw Starewicz's name, like most of his early works, featured insects as its stars. He removed the legs from the embalmed bodies of beetles and then stuck them back to the insects' bodies using wax, so they could then be articulated and posed for the animation. *Prekrasnaya Lyukanida* (*The Beautiful Leukanida*), with insects dressed in clothes and walking upright like humans, features a fairy-tale-like plot about suitors fighting over a beautiful beetle bride. The film was a huge success and amazed audiences all over the world. When reviewed in the London papers, it was reported that the beetles were alive and had been trained by a Russian scientist!

Biography

Ladislaw Starewicz

Born in Moscow in 1882 of Polish parents, in the early decades of the twentieth century Ladislaw Starewicz broke new ground with stop motion, taking the technique to such levels that his films still have a huge influence on stop-frame animators today.

A keen entomologist, Starewicz made his first stop-motion film for purely scientific reasons as a means to an end. While making educational films for a museum, he found he was unable to film the nocturnal fighting of stag beetles as any light shone on them made them stop their activity, freeze, and fall asleep. After watching Emile Cohl's *Les allumettes animées* (*The Animated Matches*, 1908) he decided to try to recreate the fighting ritual using stop-frame techniques with dead and embalmed beetles. This resulted in the work that would change the course of his life and of animation history, *Lucanus Cervus* (*Battle of the Stag Beetles,* 1910). Considering Starewicz's total inexperience, this is a remarkably well-animated milestone in stop-frame animation.

For his next film made a few months later, *Prekrasnaya Lyukanida* (*The Beautiful Leukanida*, 1910), Starewicz abandoned reality and started to anthropomorphize his subjects. In the next few years Starewicz produced more films in Russia, both animated and live action, becoming an influential figure in early cinema by developing various techniques and effects. Among his best-known films at the time were *Mest Kinematograficheskogo Operatora* (*The Cameraman's Revenge*, 1912), a dark tale of infidelity among insects and *The Night Before Christmas* (1913).

Starewicz then moved on to working with puppets; although still lifelike representations of animals, they were often dressed in clothes and walked on their hind legs. These puppets gave his films the feel of the rather disturbing "comic" displays, popular in the Victorian age, of stuffed animals dressed and posed as humans.

During the Russian Revolution, Starewicz fled to Paris in 1919, where he continued his work, joining with other Russian émigrés working from George Méliès' old studio. At this time, he changed his first name from Wladislaw to Ladislaw, which was easier for French people to pronounce. He made one film *L'épouvantail* (*The Scarecrow*, 1921) for this company before it dissolved and he moved to Fontenay Sous-Bois in the Parisian suburbs, where he stayed for the rest of his long career. He made many more wonderful films, often with the aid of his wife, France, and daughter, Irene. The highlights included *Fétiche* (*The Mascot*, 1934) and *Le Roman de Renard* (*The Tale of the Fox*, 1930). (For more on *The Tale of the Fox*, see page 102.)

Starewicz carried on working right up until 1965, when he died during the making of his last film, *Like Dog and Cat*. Undoubtedly the father of stop-frame animation, his influence is so great that it can be clearly felt in modern-day classics like Tim Burton's *The Nightmare Before Christmas* (1993), made 80 years after Starewicz's own *The Night Before Christmas*.

Fétiche (The Mascot), 1934

1912
UK

Martin Thornton: In Golliwog Land (Gollywog's Motor Accident)

Credited as the first color animated film, *In Golliwog Land* combined stop frame with live action, and was made with the Kinemacolor process invented by George Albert Smith of Brighton, UK. (Smith is also credited, along with Arthur Melbourne-Cooper, with inventing the close-up in film). Produced by Charles Urban and directed and animated by Martin Thornton, the film depicted the misadventures of a group of toy dolls, culminating in the ringleader being involved in a car accident.

Although forms of color animation had been made before this time by painting or tinting individual frames by hand, Kinemacolor was the first widely-used color filmmaking process. It was a complex process involving a filter mechanism in the camera exposing alternate frames of the black-and-white film through different color filters and special projectors reversing this process by projecting alternate frames through filters. The special projectors were installed in movie theaters in the UK and the USA, but the expense of this equipment and limitations in quality made the system short lived. For this reason, *In Golliwog Land* was reissued in black and white in 1916.

1913–1914
USA

John Randolph Bray: Further breakthroughs in industrialization

Like many animators of the time, John Randolph Bray was a newspaper comic-strip artist who moved into animated cartoons. In 1913 he released a short called *The Artist's Dream* (aka *The Dachshund and the Sausage*), which won him a deal with distributor Charles Pathé. In *The Artist's Dream* he experimented with printing backgrounds rather than drawing them. His next film, *Colonel Heeza Liar in Africa*, is recognized as the first cartoon made to be part of a series.

Bray made several more developments in the animation process and patented various labor-saving techniques, including creating background elements on translucent paper and creating gray tones in the, at that time, black-and-white animated films. It was in this patent that the idea of celluloid sheets, later abbreviated to "cels," was first proposed. In 1915 he filed a further patent involving the backgrounds to be painted on cels to be overlaid on the characters. Bray later made what is often cited as the first color cartoon, *The Debut of Thomas Cat* in 1920, although the 1912 British stop-motion film *In Golliwog Land* can also be claimed as the first animation in color.

There is, however, controversy about the ownership of some of Bray's innovations and his ruthless business methods. Reportedly, Bray pretended to be a journalist writing about animation in order to visit Winsor McCay's studio to be given a demonstration of the animation pioneer's techniques. He then recreated these techniques in his own studio, patented many of them, and tried to sue McCay. Justice prevailed and McCay ended up receiving royalties from Bray. In a similar situation, Frank Nankivell claimed to have created a system of cel animation with his son Frank in his New York studio in 1914. Allegedly, animators from Bray's studio were allowed to visit in the usual spirit of cooperation among fellow animators, before again Bray reproduced the system and patented it as his own.

John Randolph Bray became an important figure in the industrialization and development of animation, building on the ideas of artists such as Winsor McCay and working out ways of saving labor and maximizing profits. For efficiency's sake he pioneered the breakdown of labor in animation into different roles, and to keep his studio productive, he made propaganda films for the US government during World War I—an early form of government information film—and corporate films for the auto industry under his subsidiary Jam Handy films run by Jamison "Jam" Handy in Detroit. Commercial activities like these would often underpin the animation industry worldwide and enable its survival in years to come. Bray's studio was the biggest in America in the years preceding World War I, and among the famous animators and producers who got their start working for Bray were the Fleischer brothers, Paul Terry, Earl Hurd, Walter Lantz, Pat Sullivan, Grim Natwick, and David Hand.

Bray's entertainment film business closed down after a takeover and reorganization by Samuel Goldwyn caused many of the animators to leave. The company was broken down and sold off, but the educational side of the business, Brayco, continued in production until 1963. The corporate filmmaking business, the Jam Handy Organization, stayed in operation until 1983, shortly outliving Bray himself. John Randolph Bray died in 1978, aged just short of 100 years.

Cel animation

Cel animation (also known as 2D or paper animation) is traditionally the most common form of animation, although since the 1990s, it has been superseded by CGI animation. The process of cel animation usually starts with an animator creating drawings at a light box, so he can look through the top drawing and see the other drawings in the sequence underneath it to use as a guide. In the past these drawings were then transferred onto cels, transparent plastic sheets, where they were painted by hand and then filmed, frame by frame, on top of the background painting. The use of cels was so that the background part of the drawing didn't need to be created over and over for every frame. Nowadays it is more common for the drawings to be scanned into a computer and then colored digitally, before being placed over the background image, also inside the computer.

1914
USA

1914
USA

Earl Hurd: The cel process and Bobby Bumps

It was yet another exnewspaper cartoonist, Earl Hurd, who hit upon the system that would become the standard method of animation production worldwide. In Hurd's patent, he describes the process of producing the background on paper while transferring the animated characters onto a cel, or different layers of cels overlaid on top, keeping any unmoving parts of the drawing on a separate level. Most early animation studios preferred John Randolph Bray's 1915 patented method of the background on an overlaid cel, giving the advantage of the drawing remaining on paper. It wasn't until at least a decade later that Hurd's development was widely taken up, went on to dominate the industry, and is still in common use by paper animators today.

Started in 1915 and distributed by Universal, Hurd's *Bobby Bumps* was an excellent series of shorts. Sophisticated for its time with its gray-toned backgrounds and characters (black-and-white lines were the contemporary norm) and well-structured and developed stories and characters.

Following the success of *Bobby Bumps*, Hurd was approached by Bray to make films for his organization and to set up the Bray-Hurd Patent Trust. With their combined patents, they demanded fees from any studio using the cel processes. During the 1920s most studios avoided these fees by continuing to work solely on paper, but with the general improvements in technical standards in the 1930s, most studios switched to cel and paid a fee to Bray and Hurd.

Winsor McCay: Gertie the Dinosaur

Winsor McCay first showed his masterpiece *Gertie the Dinosaur*—a breakthrough in precision, draughtsmanship, and "realistic" animation—at the Palace Theatre in Chicago on February 8, 1914, cleverly interacting with his projected creation onstage. During the performance McCay appeared to invite the huge cartoon brontosaurus-like creature onto the stage and, after shyly hiding behind some rocks, the loveable Gertie ate, drank, danced, and cried in response to her onstage "trainer." McCay's act was a sensation, no doubt aided by the advertising campaign that led the public to believe they would be seeing a live trained dinosaur onstage. When the posters proclaimed "She Eats, Drinks, and Breathes! She Dances the Tango!", how could anyone not buy a ticket?

Fellow animation pioneer Emile Cohl wrote the following description in a letter home to his native France: "The main actor, or perhaps the sole actor, was a prehistoric animal… McCay stood very elegantly in front of the screen armed with a whip. He would give a short speech and then, turning towards the screen like an animal trainer, he would call the animal." To the audience's amazement, the dinosaur would then come out of the rocks, and perform. The film is often regarded as the first instance of true character animation in the sense that, for the first time, an animated creation had a distinct personality of its own and gave an engaging performance. Master animator and cartoonist McCay had truly "breathed life" into his drawings, which is the essence of all great character animation.

McCay ended his theatrical productions of *Gertie the Dinosaur* soon after the newspaper he was working for claimed the rights to his performances. Instead, he added some extra footage to the film and sold it for distribution at movie theaters.

Biography

Gertie the Dinosaur, 1914

Winsor McCay

Although largely self-taught, Winsor McCay can be described as the first "classical" animator and also one of the world's leading cartoonists. The sophistication of his work, with its precise lines, realistic use of perspective, and intricate designs, set a standard that only a few would match in his lifetime in both the worlds of animation and newspaper comic strips. As if this wasn't enough achievement for one man, he was also a leading light in the world of vaudeville theater with his live-cartooning-based act, for which some of his greatest animation was designed.

Perhaps fittingly for someone with such a multiplicity of careers, McCay was born either in 1871 in Spring Lake, Michigan, as he claimed, or in 1867 in Canada, as his biographers

claim. He began his working life as a designer of advertising posters and vaudeville stage sets, and from 1903 he produced comic strips for the *Cincinnati Enquirer*. At first he illustrated other writers' work, and then later began to write his own strips, such as *Dreams of the Rarebit Fiend* and *Little Nemo in Slumberland*. It was *Little Nemo* that cemented his reputation after he was invited to New York by James Gordon Bennett, the publisher of the *New York Herald* and the *Evening Telegram*.

Apart from a small amount of tutoring during his spell at Business College in Michigan, McCay had no formal training, and yet his comic strip achievements were impressive enough on their own to ensure his reputation without even taking

into consideration his work as an animator. *Little Nemo in Slumberland*, precisely drawn and immaculately crafted in McCay's signature floral decorative style, is still regarded as one of the great comic strips. This distinct rococo masterpiece, although drifting in and out of fashion, has remained an influence on comic art ever since, including many psychedelic artists of the 1960s and contemporary greats such as Moebius and Chris Ware.

In addition to his comic strip work, the prolific McCay returned to work at vaudeville theaters, this time however as a performer on stage with an act based on creating chalk drawings of volunteers from the audience. McCay would then age the drawings to predict the future appearance of the subjects. He toured this act for 11 years while still maintaining his steady output of newspaper strips.

McCay's move into animation came about through this vaudeville act and as a result of a bet with other cartoonists who challenged him to film some of the many drawings he created. He would later also claim that he was inspired by a flick book that his son brought home.

Probably following technical advice from James Stuart Blackton, he decided to adapt *Little Nemo* into an animated film. Four thousand drawings and four years later, he incorporated the animated version of his newspaper creation into his stage act. The film had a similar dreamlike quality to his newspaper work, with every 35mm frame handcolored by McCay. Consisting of little more than the comic characters being brought to life, the impact of this film on audiences at its premiere in 1911 is hard to imagine. The excitement of the characters' motion is such that they spend much of the film discussing, in comic-strip speech bubbles, the very fact that they are moving.

As well as showing the film on stage, McCay also sold *Little Nemo* to movie theaters through Blackton's distribution company Vitagraph, where it was preceded by a short introduction featuring Blackton describing the bet and showing McCay at work.

No doubt aware of the limitations of his first film, McCay's next animated work, *The Story of a Mosquito* (aka *How a Mosquito Operates*, 1912), showed strong progression. Whereas the experimental *Little Nemo* was little more than a demonstration of his drawings in motion, *The Story of a Mosquito* was a clever comedy in which a mosquito drinks the blood of a drunkard. Every frame of the film is richly drawn in McCay's art-nouveau style, and carefully and precisely crafted. McCay was one of the first animators to meticulously preview and refine the animation, testing the flow of the drawings before filming them. This time McCay ensured that the film would not conflict with his stage act by stipulating that it would not run in movie theaters while he was using it in his vaudeville act. It was his next film, however, *Gertie the Dinosaur*, which cemented McCay's reputation as one of the great masters of animation.

Despite McCay's towering importance in animation history, he made relatively few films in his lifetime. His perfectionist approach and the fact that he did most of the work single-handed made for long production schedules. It must be remembered that in all his most famous films each frame is a complete drawing; the backgrounds were drawn on every frame, or traced back by an assistant, a process that seems insanely time-consuming and labor intensive today. This,

combined with his late start in the field and his parallel careers as a newspaper cartoonist and a stage performer, ensured that his film production was limited.

The Sinking of the Lusitania was McCay's last significant film. (For more on this film, see page 73.) For many of his later works he used the newly developed cel animation technique instead of working purely on paper, a method with which he never matched his earlier levels of quality. Among the later films produced were three adaptations of his early newspaper cartoon *Dreams of a Rarebit Fiend* (1921), produced with the aid of his son Robert.

Despite his achievements in many areas, McCay always considered himself as an animator first and foremost, and that was where his real passion lay, even in the last decade of his life after he had retired from the demands that animation brings to concentrate on illustrating. "Animation should be an art, that is how I conceived it," he famously berated an audience of animation industry figures, "but as I see it, what you fellows have done with it is make it into a trade."

1914–1915
USA/Canada

Raoul Barré and Bill Nolan: The peg bar and other innovations

In 1914 French-Canadian Raoul Barré, a newspaper cartoonist and fine art painter, and his colleague Bill Nolan set up what is credited as the world's first commercial animation studio in New York's The Bronx. This, along with several developments at the studio, were important steps in the industrialization of animation that was gathering pace in the USA.

Prior to opening their studio, Barré and Nolan had been producing primitive animated advertising work. Keeping the many drawings in registration had been an issue since the start of animation and various methods had been used; Winsor McCay had apparently used a paper cutter to give his drawings uniform right-angle corners, while Barré used the common printer's method of registering crosses in the corners of the drawing, a technique still used by paper animators for the "shift-and-trace" method of in-betweening breakdown drawings.

In 1914, however, Barré hit upon the method of registration that would come to be used by practically every animator in the world—the peg bar. With this method, the paper was uniformly perforated along either the bottom or the top and then held in place by a bar fixed to the drawing board and also to the camera, ensuring perfect registration. The drawings could then be flicked and rolled back and forth like a flick book as the animator worked through the sequence and perfected the movement.

Barré also developed the "slash" system, a method for separating the still background and the animated foreground, involving cutting or "slashing" the paper between the two areas. The character drawings would then exist on each sequential sheet of paper while the background remained on one static cut piece, which was overlaid on the others for filming.

Nolan also developed another important technique still in use today, the process of what is generally called "panning backgrounds." These are long background drawings that are moved along frame-by-frame under the camera to give the illusion of the camera tracking along a path with the character.

In 1915 Barré's studio created *The Animated Grouch Chasers*, a series of animated shorts whose crazy surrealism, based on childlike logic and zany humor, would prove influential on commercial animation for decades to come.

1915
Sweden

Victor Bergdahl: Trolldrycken (The Demon Drink)

Swedish cartoonist Victor Bergdahl was inspired to make his own animations after a Stockholm-based movie-theater proprietor asked him, in around 1912, how Winsor McCay made his cartoons. Three years later Bergdahl found a producer and the result was his first cartoon, *Trolldrycken* (*The* *Demon Drink*); a series of 13 shorts followed, featuring the character Kapten Grogg (Grogg being a Swedish nickname for alcohol). The hero (or, more appropriately, antihero) of these films had a liking for alcohol and was married to an unpleasant, nagging woman (both attributes, according to legend, of Bergdahl himself). To escape from the irritations of his family life, Kapten Grogg traveled the world in a balloon, drinking, womanizing, and getting involved in various adventures.

1916

USA

The Fleischer brothers: The rotoscope and Out of the Inkwell

In 1915 Max Fleischer, a young cartoonist working as art editor on *Popular Science Monthly* magazine, used his interest in science to develop an idea for a machine for capturing movement and making animated films. He patented his idea as the "rotoscope," and the name and variations of the technique are still in use today. The device projected film frame-by-frame onto a light table where an artist could trace the movements of figures. His mechanically-minded brother Joe helped make the machine, and another brother Dave posed in a clown suit for the film *Koko the Clown*.

Fleischer was soon hired by John Randolph Bray to make the *Out of the Inkwell* series as part of Paramount's monthly *Screen Magazine*, a short news and entertainment program shown before feature films. As the hand of Fleischer is seen drawing the animation, Koko the Clown grows out of the ink and interacts with the animator and the "real" world around him. *Out of the Inkwell* won much praise and success for its fluid and realistic rotoscoped movement and for its combination of live action and animation.

Rotoscoping

Rotoscoping is a process where characters in a live-action film are traced or drawn over in order to give a lifelike, smooth movement. Motion capture or performance capture, a 3D digital form of rotoscoping, is when actors' movements are recorded by a computer, using sensors on their body, and these movements are applied to CGI characters. This again produces a very lifelike and smooth movement, and means that the subtleties of an acting performance can be easily and quickly transferred into the CGI character.

Koko the Clown

Biography

Max & Dave Fleischer

In the first half of the twentieth century the Fleischer Studios, formed by brothers Max and Dave Fleischer, achieved levels of success second only to The Walt Disney Company. Although their achievements now seem insignificant relative to Disney's, the Fleischer brothers were responsible for characters that are still world famous today. In addition, Max Fleischer held 15 patents for inventions relating to animation and was responsible for many other developments in the animation industry.

After working at John Randolph Bray's studio, producing the successful *Out of the Inkwell* series among other projects, the Fleischer brothers formed their own studio, Out of the Inkwell Films, in 1921. They had an early success with the *Song Car-Tunes* series of musical shorts, which were some of the ealiest instances of films incorporating sound. (For more on *Song Car-Tunes*, see page 81.)

The studio was also reportedly the first to use the technique of "in-betweening," whereby trainees drew the in-between poses while the best animators concentrated on the main drawings. This efficient process became standard practice throughout the industry and continues to be used today.

Max soon stopped animating in order to concentrate on research, leaving the creative side to Dave and a small team of animators. It is probably fair to say that, while Max was a man of a great vision and invention and a talented artist to boot, like many creative people he was not a great businessman. Apart from his early appearances in *Out of the Inkwell*, he was never interested in self-promotion, and despite patenting many of his inventions, he never

secured proper ownership of his characters or had much time for financially exploiting their popularity. As well as a greater sophistication in production and drawing techniques, it is in the commercial area that Disney really pulled ahead of the Fleischers, using merchandising and licensing revenue to fund films and expand his company. "I'm in the business of making cartoons, I'm not in the merchandising business," Max is reported to have grumbled; a noble attitude perhaps, but this failure to financially capitalize on his works ultimately cost him control of his studio.

Dave was credited as a director, and to an extent he fulfilled this role, but the actual work he did seems more vague; he was a kind of producer and studio manager, but his main focus seems to have been on providing a nonstop supply of gags that were shoehorned into each show.

In 1928 the company was renamed as the Fleischer Studios, and in the early 1930s the studio really got into its stride, its supply of shorts often featuring a confident blend of quirky, surreal, and dark humor. They introduced two new characters, Betty Boop and Popeye, who became hugely successful in their time and continued to appear in cartoons and films for decades to come. (For more on Betty Boop and Popeye, see pages 100 and 108.)

During these early years, the Fleischer Studios maintained an endearingly human, loose, and somewhat wild approach to the production of animation. They allowed the kind of freedom of expression that can produce moments of genius, but also many mistakes. The artists swapped roles and worked in individual styles, which was in contrast to the increasingly regimented and industrialized division of labor becoming

predominant in other studios. The studio did not have a "story" department until the mid-1930s; instead the animators created their own stories as they went along and the characters they drew were not fixed by model sheets, meaning the design of the characters could fluctuate wildly. The advent of sound, which was pioneered by the studio, was also approached in a more casual manner than elsewhere. Characters' voices were dubbed on after animation and were largely improvised, unlike the conventional approach of recording all sound in advance and then creating the animation to match. This loose approach made for an unrestrained rawness and freshness, which contributed to the characters' popularity, although at times the indiscipline and juxtaposition of styles and techniques could also prove detrimental to the overall quality.

Another hindrance the Fleischers faced was the instability of their financiers and distributors, Paramount. The three-color Technicolor process was launched in the early 1930s, but Paramount considered it too expensive, which enabled the Disney Studios to secure a four-year exclusive deal and achieve great success with their color films. A couple of years later, Paramount funded the Fleischers' move into color, but only with the inferior processes available. The studio then produced the *Color Classics* series of shorts, as well as longer films, including three Popeye specials. These color films were notable for their use of another of the Fleischers' inventions, the stereotypical process. This was a technique of using three-dimensional model backgrounds to give the films a sense of depth, and was a precurser to Disney's development of the multiplane camera.

Max Fleischer

Unfortunately in other areas of the business, things weren't going so well. A feud had developed between Max and Dave, and by the time of *Mr. Bug Goes to Town*, the two were no longer speaking. Soon after the movie's release and shortly before the Fleischers' contract with Paramount was due for renewal, Dave left to take over as head of Columbia's Screen Gems animation studio in Los Angeles. This was a technical breach of the contract with Paramount, who had already started a takeover process in 1941. The brothers were removed from their own studio and new management was installed, the company was renamed Famous Studios and moved back to New York, surviving another few years making further Superman and Popeye films.

In later years, Max and Dave Fleischer worked for several other companies and developed other projects and innovations, none having the same impact as their previous work. Max worked for The Jam Handy Organization in Detroit, and later for his old boss John Randolph Bray. Dave worked for Columbia and then for Universal as a general problem solver on their live-action movies. The anonymity of the Fleischer brothers' later years should not detract, however, from their earlier achievements. Their ingenuity has rarely been matched and the determination and hard work it takes to put those ideas into practice and make a success of them should never be underestimated. Ultimately, the Fleischers' best films still impress and entertain, and many of their greatest inventions are still in use today.

In 1937 the studio achieved an undesirable milestone as its employees staged one of the first animators' strikes. The strike lasted for nine months and caused radical changes in the company. In contrast to the general trend at the time of studios moving to California to join the flourishing movie industry, Max decided to move from New York to Florida where the unions hadn't taken hold and the rent was cheaper. The cost of the strike and the move caused financial difficulties for the Fleischers, who were being pressured by Paramount to respond to the huge success of Disney's feature *Snow White and the Seven Dwarfs*. Paramount supplied the Fleischers with a loan to help them finance two feature films, which effectively put the studio in Paramount's hands until the debt was repaid.

The studio's first feature, *Gulliver's Travels*, was released in 1939. It fared relatively well at the domestic box office, but the outbreak of World War II meant a lack of foreign sales. (For more on *Gulliver's Travels*, see page 126.) Their second feature, *Mr. Bug Goes to Town* (aka *Mr. Hoppity Goes to Town*, 1941), was unfortunately released two days before the bombing of Pearl Harbor. The movie failed at the box office and contributed to the studio's insolvency.

A successful project for Fleischer Studios at this time was the *Superman* series, the first of which was released in 1941. They had a larger than usual budget to work with, and this, combined with the pressure of being faithful to the comic, encouraged the Fleischers to meticulously plan and execute the films. Consequently, the *Superman* cartoons were the most sophisticated films the Fleischers ever produced. (For more on *Superman*, see page 136.)

1916
USA/Canada

Raoul Barré: Mutt and Jeff

In 1916 Raoul Barré teamed up with cartoonist Charles Bowers who had bought the rights to turn the popular newspaper comic strip "Mutt and Jeff" into a series of animated movie theater shorts.

The cartoon strip had been a huge success for its creator, artist Bud Fisher, who kept a close grip on his public image as creator of the property. Fisher was featured in all publicity for the series with little acknowledgment that the animated cartoons were created by anyone other than himself. In actual fact, Fisher had practically nothing to do with the animated series. This denial of public credit for the animators' hard work was a common feature of the early years of industrialization, and is an often-heard complaint from animators throughout history.

The fact that *Mutt and Jeff* were entertaining and well-made shorts was down to the talents of Barré, Bowers, and the team of young animators they hired. Fisher's lack of involvement meant that, within the confines of producing a short film every week, they were free to experiment and come up with fresh ideas. However, the heavy workload took its toll on Barré, one of the early masters of animation, who in 1918 left the studio and took a break from the animation industry, apparently as a result of disagreements with Bowers. After a number of years producing advertising posters and paintings, he eventually returned to animation in 1925 to work on another popular character, Krazy Kat.

1916
Italy/Spain

Giovanni Pastrone and Segundo de Chomón: La Guerra et il sogno di de Momi (The War and Momi's Dream)

Spanish cinematography and special-effects pioneer Segundo de Chomón collaborated with Italian director Giovanni Pastrone on the semianimated, antiwar feature film, *La Guerra e il sogno di de Momi* (*The War and Momi's Dream*). The movie included a well-animated stop-frame sequence, very sophisticated for its time, in which a child called Momi falls asleep listening to his grandfather's war stories and dreams of a battle fought out by puppets.

1917
India

Dhundiraj Govind Phalke

Dhundiraj Govind Phalke: Agkadyanchi Mouj (Matchsticks Fun)

Dhundiraj Govind "Dadasaheb" Phalke is known as the founder of Indian cinema. Having previously worked as a photographer, printer, and magician, in 1912 Phalke traveled to England to learn the techniques of filmmaking and to purchase equipment. Later that year, he produced India's first feature-length film, *Raja Harishchandra*. Phalke created the first of his stop-frame animated shorts in 1917, *Agkadyanchi Mouj* (*Matchsticks Fun*). Featuring animated matchsticks and coins, the film was inspired by Emile Cohl's *Les allumettes animées* (*The Animated Matches*, 1908).

Throughout his career as a filmmaker, Phalke constantly experimented with camera and editing techniques, and although he died in obscurity in 1944, the prestigious Dadasaheb Phalke Award for lifetime contribution to Indian cinema was founded in his honor in 1969.

1917
Japan

Early Japanese animation

The earliest Japanese animated film screened publically is believed to be Hekoten Shimokawa's *Imokawa Muzako genkan-ban no maki* (*Imokawa Muzako the Doorman*), shown in 1917. (Although recently a short, 50-frame section of 35mm film was found in Kyoto, probably the work of a home enthusiast, which could be as much as 10 years older.)

Around 1913 Seitaro Kitayama began experimenting with ink drawings on paper, resulting in a number of animated films that were released a few years later, including *Saru Kani Kassen* (*The Crab Gets His Revenge on the Monkey*, c.1917). The inspiration for this film probably came from American and European cartoons that Kitayama had seen in Tokyo. He later established a small studio in 1921, although his work was somewhat curtailed by the devastating earthquake that hit the city in 1923.

Other early pioneers of what would one day become the huge Japanese animation industry include Junichi Kouchi, who produced cartoons with traditional cultural themes, such as the two-minute samurai comedy *Namakura-gatana* (*The Blunt Samuari Sword*, 1917). Like much of Japan's early film and animation, this was thought lost until a copy of this and another early film, Seitaro Kitayama's animated folk tale *Urashima Taro* (1918), were discovered by chance by a film historian at an antique fair in Osaka in 2007. The prints of both films have now been digitally restored by the National Film Center in Tokyo.

1917

Argentina/Italy

Quirino Cristiani: El Apóstol (The Apostle)

Argentina is not normally considered a leading animation country, and yet reportedly it is the home of the world's first animated feature in *El Apóstol* (*The Apostle*), animated and directed by the 20-year-old Italian-born cartoonist Quirino Cristiani. Although no copies survive to prove it was actually a feature-length film, it seems its length was somewhat over one hour, which may qualify it as feature length (the standard qualification is 70 minutes). If this is true, the release of *The Apostle* predates Lotte Reiniger's *Die Abenteuer des Prinzen Achmed* (*The Adventures of Prince Achmed*) by nine years and Walt Disney's *Snow White and the Seven Dwarfs* by 20 years. Regardless of the exact length of the film, it is without doubt a remarkable achievement, considering nothing like this would be attempted in the USA or Europe for years to come.

The Apostle was produced by another Italian, Federico Valle, who had previously hired the young political cartoonist Cristiani to produce a satirical one-minute long cartoon *La intervención a la provincia de Buenos Aires* for his newsreel *Actualidades Valle*. Cristiani learned the basics of animation by studying the work of Emile Cohl (probably *Les allumettes animées* [*The Animated Matches*]) from Valle's collection of films. The first work they produced followed a similar pattern to the cartoon segments in American newsreels at the time, which were derived from popular newspaper cartoons. The success of this venture prompted Valle to make the bold progression to commissioning a work of extraordinary length for that time from the young animator.

For *The Apostle* Cristiani was in charge of animation while Alfonso de Laferrére provided the script and leading caricaturist Diógenes "El Mono" Taborda designed the characters. The movie's central character was Hipólito Yrigoyen, the real-life president of Argentina since 1916, who, in the movie, dreams of realizing his ambitions of halting Argentina's decay by befriending the gods of Mount Olympus and becoming an apostle. Cristiani used a patented cutout animation technique that he would revisit for his next few productions.

Despite its limited distribution, *The Apostle* was a success with the public and critics and enabled Cristiani to create several more films, including several educational and advertising films and the World War I satirical feature *Sin Dejar Rastros* (*Without a Trace*, 1918). He achieved another landmark by making what is attributed as the world's first animated feature using sound, *Peludópolis* (1931), about the reelection of Hipolito Yrigoyen in 1928. Based on fact, the movie had to be reedited to keep pace with the rapidly changing political situation and the resulting film failed to achieve Cristiani's earlier success.

After the economic failure of *Peludópolis* Cristiani limited himself to advertising projects until 1938, when he departed from his cutout technique and made the short film *El Mono Relojero* (*The Monkey Watchmaker*) using the more conventional cel method.

1918
USA

Winsor McCay: The Sinking of the Lusitania

Perhaps the first significant animated film containing purely serious political content, this was an early example of animated propaganda. The film recreated the 1915 disaster when British ship the *Lusitania* was sunk by a German submarine, killing many passengers and crew, including 124 Americans. McCay created the film on the back of personal and public outrage as the incident became a major factor in American participation in World War I.

Like McCay's other films, *The Sinking of the Lusitania* is an example of the strong connection between newspaper cartoons and animation that was particularly prevalent in the early years of American animation. Many of the early animators, like McCay, started out as newspaper cartoonists, and much of their animation was created as adaptations of popular newspaper strips. In the case of *The Sinking of the Lusitania*, the film was an animated version of the illustrated recreations of disasters and big news stories that were common in the press of the day.

The use of animation for public information and propaganda was destined to become popular at times of war and austerity, due to the graphic clarity that the form can bring in delivering a message and transmitting information. The government spend on this type of work would save many animators and studios at times of economic hardship.

The Sinking of the Lusitania was however, like McCay's other work, self-funded and then sold to movie-theater distributors. Despite the gulf in subject matter between this and McCay's other films, and indeed popular animation in general, it retains McCay's detailed and realistic style and his precise perspective and draughtsmanship in its dramatic representation of the terrifying events of the loss of the ship and the subsequent plight of the passengers at the mercy of the sea.

The Sinking of the
Lusitania, 1918

1919
USA

Otto Messmer and Joe Oriolo: Felix the Cat

After the success of early American animators such as Winsor McCay, a lot of animation was made to cash in on the craze, most of it low-quality product, churned out cheaply. An exception to this, and perhaps the biggest cartoon star of the 1920s, was Felix the Cat.

Felix was created and animated by Otto Messmer and produced by Pat Sullivan. At the height of Felix's popularity, Sullivan took all the credit and toured Europe to meet crowds of cheering Felix fans, while the shy Otto Messmer was back in the studio drawing the cartoons. Indeed, so thorough was this camouflaging of the facts of Felix's true creator that for around the next 50 years Felix was solely attributed to Sullivan.

Sullivan had spotted Messmer's potential and hired him in 1915 to work at his newly-formed studio. In 1919 Messmer created Felix the Cat for Paramount's newsreel, *Screen Magazine*. Paramount trademarked the name and hired Pat Sullivan's studio to continue making the series.

In 1922 Sullivan acquired the rights to Felix from Paramount. With Messmer and his team, including his protégé Joe Oriolo, creating a steady supply of the cartoons—one every 15 days for a long period—Sullivan proceeded to practically invent merchandising by selling a vast array of Felix objects while traveling the world publicizing his property.

Messmer's previous experience of studying Charlie Chaplin's performances and animating Chaplin cartoons undoubtedly influenced the animation of Felix. Ingenious and entertaining, with a bold and simple style, Felix was a great example of the power of a design based on graphical shapes and a strong silhouette. A variety of devices negated the need for sound, such as his tail transforming into question and exclamation marks. Other characteristics included perspective tricks, such as distant objects being plucked from the background by Felix, and his trademark pacing round in circles when faced with a problem. Although not breaking any new ground technically, Felix the Cat was a step forward in terms of acting, performance, and connecting with the audience, qualities which led to his worldwide cult status.

With the advent of sound, Felix faded from public view; Sullivan's alcoholism and depression after the death of his wife sapped his energy and rendered him incapable of driving his company into the sound era. After Sullivan's premature death at the age of 48 in 1933, Joe Oriolo began working closely with Messmer on Felix. Oriolo brought with him almost two decades of animation and cartooning experience, having previously worked at the Fleischer Studios on the *Popeye* and *Superman* series and the *Gulliver's Travels* movie. Oriolo began to work solely on Felix and received "carte blanche" from Messmer to redesign Felix, with a new image and personality, and new supporting characters such as The Magic Bag of Tricks, Poindexter, The Professor, Rock Bottom, and Vavoom.

The only two cartoonists ever to draw the Felix comic strips in the early days were Otto Messmer and Joe Oriolo. Oriolo's son Don spent many hours looking over the shoulders of both his father and Messmer as they drew these newspaper strips and comic books. Near the end of his career in the late 1970s, Joe Oriolo, recognizing his son's imagination and passion for Felix asked him to bring Felix into the twenty-first century. With great admiration of all that is Felix, Don Oriolo continued the legacy of his father's work. He had learned well from his father, inheriting his gag development and storytelling talents. In 1988 he wrote and produced the feature-length *Felix the Cat: the Movie*, as well as keeping the character alive by producing new comic books and a television series entitled *Baby Felix and Friends*, coproduced with NHK-NEC in Japan. In 1996 Don Oriolo coproduced with Film Roman a TV series entitled *Twisted Tales of Felix the Cat*, which was broadcast worldwide, and in 2004 he produced a motion picture entitled *Felix Saves Christmas*. From licensing and merchandising to movies and promotional campaigns, Felix's popularity continues to grow and win over new audiences with his winning personality, humor, and visual appeal.

Felix the Cat

1920

USA

John Randolph Bray: The Debut of Thomas Cat

The Debut of Thomas Cat, a film about a kitten learning to hunt mice and coming up against a large rat, was made in color using a process called Brewster Color invented by Percy Brewster of New Jersey. Although the film was a success for producer John Randolph Bray, like other early color systems the process proved too expensive and the resulting film stock too fragile to be practical. Although earlier claims have been made for animation filmed in color, *The Debut of Thomas Cat* is the earliest recorded instance of a traditional drawn-animation film in color.

1920–1923
USA

Walt Disney: Laugh-O-grams and other early films

In 1920 a young Kansas City cartoonist called Walt Disney met another cartoonist named Ub Iwerks and set up a small company called Iwerks Disney Commercial Artists with the intention of creating newspaper ads. The 19-year-old Disney could never have imagined at the time what his company would one day achieve.

Unable to make much money from their first venture, Disney and Iwerks worked at the Kansas City Film Ad Company where they learned the rudiments of animation. Disney made several partly-animated shorts in his spare time, which he sold to Kansas City theater owner Frank Newman who screened them under the title of *Newman's Laugh-O-grams*. In 1922 Disney resigned from his job and formed Laugh-O-gram Films, and, after hiring Iwerks, he produced several more of the *Laugh-O-grams* cartoon newsreels.

When these films became successful locally, Disney then hired more young artists to make a series of short fairy-tale parodies such as *Cinderella* and *Puss in Boots*. At this stage Disney was far from a master of animation, having not yet benefited from absorbing all there was to learn from such works as *Felix the Cat* and the Fleischer brothers' work, but these early films nevertheless demonstrated a great sense of storytelling and comic timing. These shorts were moderately successful, but when their distributor went bankrupt, the fledgling company was plunged into financial difficulties.

Disney completed a pilot film for a new series, *Alice in Cartoonland*, before filing for bankruptcy himself. Disney and Iwerks went back to working for other people, and Disney even made plans to quit animation. But, as we know, this was far from the end of Disney's company; *Alice in Cartoonland* was picked up by a distributor, and Disney's determined belief in his own ideas, his preparedness to take financial risks, and his ability to inspire others, enabled him to persevere in the animation business and eventually become the world leader.

Laugh-O-grams

Such is the level of Walt Disney's success that he is not only a "household name," almost as universally well known as his characters, but his name and the imaginary universes his studio created have been so closely linked with the medium of animation that, for a lot of people, Walt Disney *is* animation. In fact, many people are surprised to hear that he didn't invent animation.

Born in Chicago in 1901, Walt spent the first years of his life moving from place to place until, from 1906 to 1910, his family settled in the rural town of Marceline, Missouri. This was a place Disney would talk fondly of in later years and hold up as a kind of ideal pastoral setting that formed the backdrop of much of his work. Following his childhood interest in drawing, Disney studied at the Kansas City Art Institute and the Chicago Art Institute, where he drew patriotic cartoons for the school newspaper. In 1918, he served with the Red Cross in France, where he entertained his colleagues with cartoons. After returning from duty, Disney moved back to Kansas City where he met a kindred spirit in another cartoonist, Ub Iwerks, with whom he struck up a great friendship. The two of them set up an artwork company called Iwerks Disney Commercial Artists.

Iwerks and Disney initially struggled to find enough work, so to make ends meet they found employment at The Kansas City Film Ad Company, where they learned the rudiments of animation by making movie theater commercials using primitive cutout techniques. It was here that Disney and Iwerks decided to become animators. After mastering the basics, they created several shorts, which they called *Laugh-O-grams*. A local theatrical promoter agreed to show them, and when they proved popular, Disney resigned from the Kansas City Film Ad Company and set up Laugh-O-gram Films. He hired Iwerks and several other local artists and started making a series of short fairy-tale parodies, including *Cinderella* and *Puss in Boots*, which were sold to a distributor. They followed this with a pilot for a series called *Alice in Cartoonland*, which Disney circulated in hope of a further deal. Unfortunately the distributor went bust and Disney had to declare himself bankrupt.

In 1923 a disheartened Disney set off for Los Angeles with the idea of trying his luck in live-action movies. A distributor in New York, Margaret J. Winkler, contacted him to order more *Alice in Cartoonland*. Walt and his brother Roy set up a new studio in their uncle's garage. They set to work on a series of combined animation/live-action shorts called the *Alice Comedies*. With Roy as business manager (a position he would retain for the rest of Walt's life and beyond), Walt set to work on the films alone. When the first shorts were successful, he hired Iwerks, and in 1927 they began production on another series, *Oswald the Lucky Rabbit*. This was also a success and Disney expanded the studio, bringing in more artists from Kansas City.

But there was bad news when Disney went to the distributor—now Margaret Winkler's husband Charles Mintz, funded by Universal Pictures—to negotiate another deal for *Oswald the Lucky Rabbit*. Mintz told him that the fee would actually be dropped, and furthermore, if Disney did not accept this, Universal had agreements with most of his animators to make *Oswald* directly for them. Disney was understandably hurt by this lack of loyalty from his artists, and, with most of his animators and his main character gone, Disney once more had to pick himself up off the floor. He created a new character with his only remaining animator, Ub Iwerks, who reworked Disney's sketches to create a design that incorporated some elements of Oswald. Walt provided the personality and the voice and his wife Lillian came up with the name: Mickey Mouse.

Mickey Mouse went on to become the most famous and successful cartoon character of all time and, as the foundation on which Disney's empire was built, is still the iconic emblem of the company today. Following his debut in *Steamboat Willie* (1928), Mickey Mouse became a huge worldwide phenomenon, the hysteria bigger than for any cartoon character before or since. Although appealing to look at, Mickey Mouse wasn't a particularly funny or interesting personality himself, the humor came from the situations Mickey found himself in—he reacted to events rather than driving the stories. In many of his outstanding films, such as *Barnyard Broadcast* (1931) and *The Band Concert* (1935), he is the straight man trying to control the chaotic characters and situations around him, a likeable character who children could relate to and parents could be comfortable with. His companions, the dogs Goofy and Pluto, constantly needed his help in a bright, magical, but familiar world. The whole scenario was cleverly designed to appeal to a child's mind and to "the child in all of us."

Disney's excellent commercial sense meant that he made the most of Mickey's popularity by producing a variety of merchandise, including clothes, figurines, and watches. In 2006, 78 years after losing the rights to Oswald and 40 years after Walt Disney's death, the company that Mickey Mouse built negotiated back the rights to Oswald the Lucky Rabbit from Universal Pictures.

Throughout his career, Disney pioneered the advancement of animation techniques; always willing to take financial risks, he wanted to raise the standard of animation as an art form. After the studio's breakthrough work with sound on *Steamboat Willie*, they produced the *Silly Symphonies*, a series of shorts in which the animation was used to enhance the music and not, as in *Steamboat Willie*, the other way round. As well as such early developments as the use of storyboards and pencil tests (the testing of the animation before producing the finished scene) Disney used the *Silly Symphonies* to experiment with further ways to refine animation. *Flowers and Trees* (1932) was Disney's first cartoon in color and *The Flying Mouse* (1934) experimented with color design to enhance the change in moods of the story. *Three Little Pigs* (1933) was the most successful of these shorts, and broke new barriers in character animation, with each of the pigs having a distinct personality. In *The Old Mill* (1937) Disney tested the multiplane camera to give a feeling of depth in its realistic portrayal of nature, a foretaste of the pursuit of realism in the feature films to come.

Although the growing confidence and ambition of the studio could be measured by the shorts they made in the mid-1930s, the cost of producing them was often far higher than for the average short and this expense was eating into the profits, but it was all part of Disney's "big picture," and in a sense the shorts were rehearsals for bigger events. Walt Disney was constantly looking for ways of pushing the medium of animation forward into becoming something bigger than just cartoons, he wanted to transform animation into a powerful storytelling medium that could draw a spectrum of emotions from an audience.

There had been various plans for feature films since 1933, such as versions of *Alice in Wonderland* and *Rip Van Winkle* featuring live-action stars in animated worlds, but these projects failed to get off the ground. Disney expanded his staff, training up his young artists with night classes in drawing and acting, creating a buzz of excitement and exploration with everyone from Disney downwards learning and moving forward together.

In December 1937 Walt Disney paced outside a gala premiere wondering if the audience was laughing with him or at him. He needn't have worried; this was another monumental film that would change movie history. After years of development and against all sensible advice, Disney had again stretched his finances to the point of bankruptcy to complete his first feature (and the first American animated feature), *Snow White and the Seven Dwarfs*. The movie ended up massively over budget, but Disney's risk-taking again paid dividends—from its release *Snow White* captivated audiences and critics alike and within a few months had made back its budget many times over. In addition, there was the profit from merchandising; after his success with Mickey Mouse, Disney had every manner of *Snow White* souvenir lined up to buy as people left the theater.

With the success of Mickey Mouse and *Snow White*, Disney had money rolling in to his company for the first time in his life. However, rather than simply repeating the same successful formulas, Disney was determined to keep moving forward. The number of employees grew from six in 1928 to 187 in 1934, and in excess of 1,600 in 1940 when the company moved to a large building in Burbank. *Snow White and the Seven Dwarfs* was the first of Disney's many classic

features; movies made during Walt's lifetime include *Fantasia, Pinocchio, Dumbo, Bambi, Cinderella, Alice in Wonderland, Lady and the Tramp, One Hundred and One Dalmatians, Mary Poppins*, and *The Jungle Book*. With such phenomenal success, The Walt Disney Company became for many decades the undisputed world leader in animated features.

Everything had looked rosy in the garden after *Snow White*, but as Disney should have learned from his own movies: beware the poison apples. He had needed all his powers of persuasion to keep the large team of talented artists working hard to realize his vision for the studio's extraordinary feature films. The way a number of the crew saw it, he had made promises he was unable to keep; the new deals offered failed to match the expectations of many of the staff, and that, coupled with a dissatisfaction with the amount of credit given to the artists, prompted the workforce to form a union. When Disney blocked this, perhaps seeing it as another act of betrayal, a strike was inevitable.

Although the likeable Mickey Mouse was in some ways Disney's alter ego, one can suspect elements of the explosive Donald Duck were also present as he often had a turbulent relationship with his staff. His musical collaborator Carl Stalling left after a year, Ub Iwerks left to start his own company in 1930 (although he later returned), and many other senior animators and artists left as a result of the strike of 1941. This difficult reputation must be balanced against the many positive aspects to Disney's personality; the charm, likeability, and persuasiveness needed to achieve his kind of success and popularity cannot be underestimated.

When Disney is mentioned it often seems that what the man *didn't* do is discussed far more

Walt Disney

After Walt Disney's death from lung cancer in 1966, the true value of his input to the movies was felt. The heart of the company was gone and for many years the films struggled to recapture the magic. The talent was still present, but without Disney's vision, inconceivably, several times the company nearly gave up on making the traditionally animated features that made them such a special organization. The studio slowly learned to live without Disney; a decade after his death *The Rescuers* (1977) was a return to form, and 10 years after that the successes of *Who Framed Roger Rabbit* (1988) and *The Little Mermaid* (1989) initiated a global animation revival and a new Golden Age.

Moving into the digital era, Disney's partnership with, and subsequent buyout of, Pixar meant that they maintained a strong lead in the field of animated features. With the Pixar merger, Walt Disney's company also at last found a new visionary figure in the form of John Lasseter to guide the movie-making side of the business. Lasseter, although mainly working with computers, is a keen disciple of Disney's approach, obsession with detail, and perfectionist working methods. One of Lasseter's first acts in creative charge of Disney was to recommence the production of traditionally-drawn animated features with *The Princess and the Frog*. This is a bold statement of intent that Walt Disney would have approved of, and one which confirms Lasseter as a kindred spirit and trustworthy figure qualified to keep the Disney magic alive.

than the incredible things that he *did* do, and the brilliant work that the man, the company, and its artists have produced has in some ways been taken for granted, devalued, and dismissed. For the truth is that many of Disney's movies are undeniably among the greatest achievements in animation, and the best of them are among the greatest movies ever made.

Disney's precise part in the making of his movies can seem mysterious; he stopped drawing early on in his career, so his role clearly wasn't that of an animator. He was not credited as a director or writer, and yet he received much more acclaim than the average producer. The truth is that Disney was all of these things, or at

least he was guiding all of these activities, and more. It was said of him that he was a director of men, not a director of movies; in other words, he directed the directors, writers, and animators, and was the driving force behind every other area of his movies. He started off as an artist, drawing and animating his own films single-handedly at times, but soon recognized that although he was talented, others were *more* talented. Disney was the visionary, the one who saw and controlled "the big picture," and in this role his abilities were proved close to genius. His talent, for instance, for reading a movie's storyboard and instantly knowing where the story slowed or needed improvements was legendary.

1921

Germany

Walther Ruttmann: Lichtspiel Opus 1

After early training in architecture and fine arts, Walther Ruttmann focused his efforts on abstract painting and engraving and through this formulated a theory of abstract cinema that he described as "painting with time." On April 27, 1921 in Berlin he presented *Lichtspiel Opus 1*, the first public screening of an abstract film. The music was specially composed by Max Butting and the film, somewhat of a modernist painting that moves and changes through time, received rapturous reviews from around the world. Ruttmann went on to make three follow-ups: *Opus 2, 3,* and *4.*

Ruttman also created animated dream sequences for Paul Wegener's *Lebende Buddhas* (*Living Buddhas*, 1923) and Fritz Lang's *Die Nieberlungen* (1924), and worked on Lotte Reiniger's feature film *Die Abenteuer des Prinzen Achmed* (*The Adventures of Prince Achmed*) in 1925. In 1927 he produced his final abstract animation, the opening sequence of *Berlin, Die Sinfonie der Großstadt* (*Berlin, Symphony of a Great City*). After this, he moved into an experimental documentary style of filmmaking.

Strangely for an intellectual, an abstract artist, and a supporter of the left, in later life he wholeheartedly backed the rise of Hitler. In 1941 he died of wounds suffered while working as a war photographer. *The Times* of London had written in 1925 that Ruttmann's films would be long remembered, and sure enough, it can be said that his small number of films cast a big influence over future abstract filmmakers.

Berlin, Die Sinfonie der Großstadt (Berlin, Symphony of a Great City), 1927

1924
USA

Max and Dave Fleischer: Song Car-Tunes

One of the Fleischer brothers' many developments in the sphere of film and animation was the visual idea of the "bouncing ball" moving along song lyrics on the screen, as a guide for the audience to sing along to (as still used in karaoke bars today). This device was used in a series of films called *Song Car-Tunes*. (The films were originally known by the rather tongue-twisting name *Koko Song Car-Tunes*, after the character Koko the Clown who "introduced" the cartoons.)

The first of these sound films were *Oh, Mabel, Come Take A Trip in my Airship*, *Mother Pin A Rose On Me*, and *Goodbye My Lady Love*, which were made in May and June, 1924. The bouncing ball itself was not in fact animated but was produced by filming someone holding a luminescent white ball on a stick and bouncing it over lyrics that were rolled past on a cylinder. The films contained animated sequences featuring Koko the Clown introducing the songs, and also featured various animated figures (appropriate to the song), which replaced the bouncing ball for the later choruses.

The accompanying sound was initially provided by a pianist or small orchestra, but these early experiments combining film and sound were further developed in 1924 using the Lee De Forest Phonofilm Sound-on-film System. This invention by American Lee De Forest improved on earlier experiments by Finnish inventor Eric Tigerstedt and German team Tri-Ergon. It was an early method of recording sound directly onto the film, in this case as lines of variable shades of gray, which, as with all sound-with-film technology, was then converted back into sound by special equipment when the film was projected. Like many true originals, it seems that De Forest was too far ahead of his time and the major Hollywood studios showed no interest in his work, or at least, they professed none. Films made using this system therefore had to play in smaller independent theaters outside the big chains owned by the studios, restricting their commercial viability. Three years later a different

system, Vitaphone, using similar ideas, was used in the musical *The Jazz Singer*, which proved to be a huge hit and established sound in film as the way forward.

The Fleischer brothers made 19 of the 36 *Song Car-Tunes* with the De Forest system, the first of which was *My Old Kentucky Home* in 1926, which includes a dog speaking a line of synchronized dialogue to the audience. However, in the same year, the US Division of De Forest Phonofilm closed due to bankruptcy, and a year later the Fleischers released their last *Song Car-Tune* entitled *By The Light of the Silvery Moon*. This proved to be somewhat unfortunate timing as "talking pictures" were just about to explode in popularity.

In response to the success of sound films, in 1929 Paramount rereleased some of the *Song Car-Tunes* with new soundtracks and new animation but with the Fleischers' names removed, and in the same year the Fleischers themselves revived the song/film/bouncing ball idea in a new series called *Screen Songs*.

1924

France

Fernand Léger: Ballet Mécanique (The Mechanical Ballet)

In 1924 the dadaist painter Fernand Léger completed his film *Ballet Mécanique* (*The Mechanical Ballet*), which, as well as being a classic of abstract animation, became one of the most famous and widely-distributed works of avant-garde cinema of its time and a hugely influential work. The American abstract filmmaker Dudley Murphy collaborated with Léger on the film, although to what degree is uncertain; some sources claim he was the codirector, others that he was the creative driving force, and others state that he merely collaborated on certain sequences. The surrealist artist Man Ray and the modernist writer and poet Ezra Pound are also believed to have had creative input on the film. Léger is, however, most commonly named as the sole director.

A masterful score by composer George Antheil, controversial for his use of mechanical devices, was composed for *The Mechanical Ballet*, designed to be performed on piano, percussion, airplane propellers, and electric buzzers. The music brings the film fully to life, although the unfathomably loose and eccentric nature of the collaboration between composer and filmmakers meant that the music and film were apparently not seen together until the 1990s.

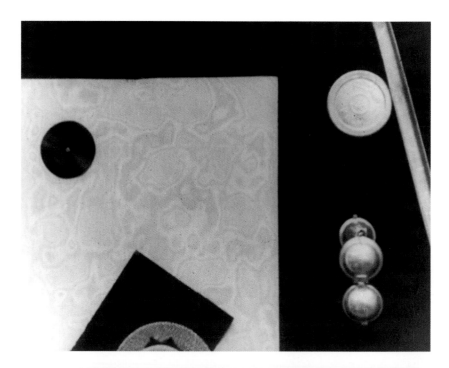

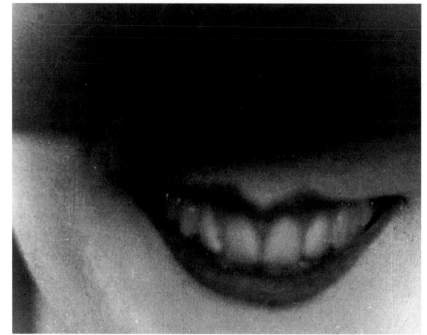

Ballet Mécanique (The
Mechanical Ballet), 1924

The Mechanical Ballet features a mixture of animation styles and techniques, such as painting on film and stop frame, plus live-action sequences. The film strongly shows its futurist and dadaist influences; geometric shapes moving mechanically are intercut with footage of machinery and close-ups of human faces and bodies; these body parts are isolated, reduced to the abstract, and engulfed by machines. In some ways these ideas anticipate the techno-fetish movements of the late twentieth century.

The film seems to pursue the idea that every object, whether natural or man-made, handcrafted or mass-produced, can be transformed into part of an artistic situation, an idea that echos down through the history of animation through artists such as Norman McLaren and Jan Svankmajer.

1924

Germany/Sweden

Viking Eggeling: Symphonie Diagonale (Diagonal Symphony)

Forced by economic conditions to leave his native Sweden, as a young man Viking Eggeling spent several years traveling around Europe. He spent time in Milan, Italy, where he attended the Brera Academy of Fine Arts, and Zurich, Switzerland, where he befriended artists and filmmakers loosely attached to the Dada movement. He later moved to Germany with his friend and fellow animator, Hans Richter, and settled in Berlin. His early experiments were funded by the German film studio UFA, which, in the 1920s liked to be seen as a progressive company, supporting the avant-garde. (In the 1930s and 1940s however, UFA produced propaganda for the Nazis.)

In 1923 Eggeling began work on the self-funded *Symphonie Diagonale* (*Diagonal Symphony*); battling against financial hardship, he completed the film a year later and it was shown to the public in 1925. The screening, organized by UFA, included Walther Ruttman's various *Opus* films, Fernand Léger's *Ballet Mécanique* (*The Mechanical Ballet*), and René Clair's *Entr'acte*. Tragically, Eggeling was unable to attend the show through illness, and he died of septic angina at the age of 45 just six days later.

Eggeling's *Diagonal Symphony* remains a minor classic of abstract film, a precise, graphical work that depicts a number of stark, futurist-style designs which grow, fade, and become more complex during the film's seven-minute length. Like much abstract animation of the era, the film attempts to express a complex philosophy; Eggeling believed that art should encompass political, ethical, and scientific ideologies, and that abstract work was the purest and freest way to try to demonstrate these beliefs. Dying too young to fully realize his vision, he spent much of his life in a monk-like existence, dedicating himself to developing his ideas in solitude and expressing them through his few animated films.

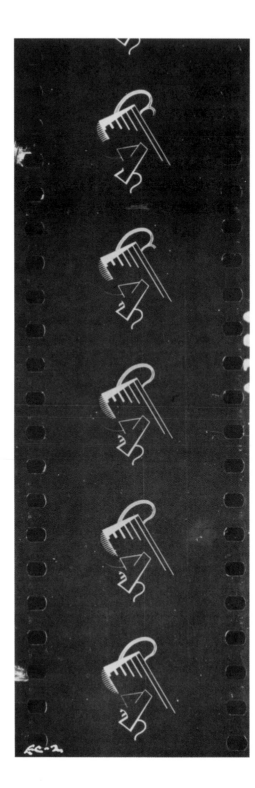

Symphonie Diagonale (Diagonal Symphony), 1924

UK

George Studdy: Bonzo the Dog

Like fellow Englishman Arthur Melbourne-Cooper before him, George Studdy was a pioneer in the commercialization of animation and a forerunner for the establishment of a British animation industry. Like many of his American contemporaries, Studdy began his career as a newspaper and magazine cartoonist before using his creations in animated movie-theater shorts. Studdy's best-known character Bonzo the Dog became a kind of European answer to the success of Felix the Cat, supported by extensive merchandising exploitation of the now familiar avenues, such as songs, books, posters, toys, etc. Bonzo was also the subject of one of the first neon signs in London's Piccadilly Circus when it was redesigned as a modern attraction in answer to New York's Times Square.

Born in Devon, England in 1878, Studdy tried a number of careers before he started to produce illustrations for adventure stories in publications such as *Boy's Own* at the turn of the century. A few years later he was creating his own humorous strips in publications such as *Pick-Me-Up* and *The Big Budget*, including a popular character called Professor Helpeman. By 1915 he was an established contributor to popular magazines such as *The Tatler* and *The Sketch*; his first experiments in animation began at this time as many propaganda cartoons were being produced in Britain during World War I. *The Studdy's War Studies* series featured a version of the "lightning sketches" popular at the time, in which Studdy was seen—with the use of stop-motion techniques—drawing cartoon sketches "magically" fast.

When Studdy's regular bull terrier puppy character Bonzo from *The Sketch* became popular enough to sell an array of merchandising, film producer Gordon Craig commissioned a series of animated shorts for his company, New Era Films. The Bonzo shorts stood up well to contemporary American animated films and 24 were made, directed by fellow cartoonist William A. "Billy" Ward, and drawn by Studdy, Ward, and around 10 other artists. Bonzo continued to be popular for another couple of decades. Despite Bonzo's success and the financial comfort this brought to Studdy and his family for the most part of his life, he died in relative poverty in 1948. After Studdy's death the Bonzo comic strips continued to be produced and drawn by other artists in publications such as *Bonzo's Laughter Annual*.

1925
USA

Harry O. Hoyt and Willis O'Brien: The Lost World

The Lost World tells the story of an expedition to a South American plateau mountain where dinosaurs are believed to still exist. Finding this to be true, the explorers bring a brontosaurus back to London where it runs amok before swimming out to sea. Based on a short story by Arthur Conan Doyle, the movie was directed by Harry O. Hoyt, but is remembered mostly for the pioneering animated dinosaurs created by Willis O'Brien.

    The Lost World was the first feature film to include stop-frame animation, and it left audiences and critics astounded by its combination of "lifelike" dinosaurs and human actors. This aspect, along with O'Brien's stop-frame animation and the plot device of captured prehistoric monsters escaping into the modern world, would later form the basis for the 1933 smash hit *King Kong* as well as many other "monster on the loose" movies.

The Lost World, 1925

Biography

Willis O'Brien

Willis O'Brien, commonly known as O'bie, perfected the work of early stop-frame pioneers such as Georges Méliès. Born in Oakland, California in 1886, O'Brien pursued early careers as a cartoonist and sculptor. He also worked as a guide for paleontologists in Crater Lake, Oregon, a job that surely influenced his later film work. His early experiments with stop-frame animation resulted in a showreel of a fight between a caveman and a dinosaur. Despite the crude animation in this homemade effort, the short film impressed Thomas Edison and he hired O'Brien. At Edison's studio, O'Brien produced a series of stop-frame shorts featuring clay models, many of which had prehistoric themes. In 1919 he worked on *Ghost of Slumber Mountain* for producer Herbert Dawley. In what sadly became a pattern for O'Brien, his experience with Dawley was not a good one: the film's running time was slashed from 45 to 15 minutes, O'Brien was poorly paid, and Dawley claimed the credit for the animation. This did however lead to a commission for his first feature film, *The Lost World*, for which, along with 1933's *King Kong*, O'Brien is best known. (For more on *King Kong*, see page 108.)

O'Brien's lost masterpiece is the movie *Creation*. He spent a year working on the film, which told the story of a secret island inhabited by dinosaurs. He developed and finessed the techniques used in *The Lost World*, and it doubtless would have been an impressive piece, but the film was dropped by RKO Pictures who were nervous about investing so much in a movie following the Wall Street Crash of 1929.

Following *King Kong*, O'Brien masterminded the animation in *Mighty Joe Young* (1949), where he trained future stop-frame legend Ray Harryhausen. O'Brien wrote concepts for several films, including a stop-frame adaptation of *Frankenstein*, but he failed to get financial backing and completed few projects. After his death in 1962, Harryhausen produced *The Valley of Gwangi* (1969), a western with dinosaurs, a project O'Brien had been developing for many years. Despite his achievements on *The Lost World* and *King Kong*, he received liitle acclaim or financial reward during his lifetime, but was awarded the Winsor McCay award for lifetime contribution to animation in 1997.

1925-1926

Germany

Lotte Reiniger: Die Abenteuer des Prinzen Achmed (The Adventures of Prince Achmed)

Die Abenteuer des Prinzen Achmed (*The Adventures of Prince Achmed*) is regarded as the earliest surviving animated feature film. The plot is an adaptation of "The Story of Prince Ahmed and the Fairy Paribanou" from Andrew Lang's *The Blue Fairy Book* (1889), which translated Middle Eastern and Asian fairy tales and folklore into English for the first time. The subject matter suited Lotte Reiniger's distinctive and delicate cutout silhouette style, which has the feel of traditional Asian shadow puppets.

 Prince Achmed is also known as the first film to use a form of multiplane camera (the traditional way of giving two-dimensional animation a feeling of depth), 10 years ahead of Walt Disney and Ub Iwerks in the USA. Created in 1925, the film failed to find a distributor for a year until, with the support of Reiniger's artist friend, Jean Renoir, it was shown at the Cannes Film Festival whereupon it became a hit with critics and public alike.

 This ambitious project was funded by a wealthy banker, Louis Hagen, to whose children Reiniger was teaching art. Hagen, no doubt wanting to keep an eye on his investment, had a studio built for the production above his garage in Potsdam. Reiniger enlisted the help of several other important animators from her circle in Berlin, including Walther Ruttman and Berthold Bartosch. The fact that these rather serious-minded artists agreed to work on such basically populist material demonstrates the close friendship that existed between the group of German animators at the time (and also perhaps a scarcity of paid work). Ruttman produced the abstract backgrounds while Bartosch worked on special effects along with Reiniger's husband, the director and producer Carl Koch.

The survival of the film is a story in itself. All original copies were destroyed during the bombing of Berlin in World War II, but a print was later found in the British Film Institute's archive in 1954. Further prints made from this were unable to reproduce the original colors as these had been handtinted, a process for which the instructions were not discovered till a later date, when, finally, in 1970, the restored film was screened in its original glory. Further restoration was undertaken in 1998 to produce the remastered copy now available on DVD.

Die Abenteuer des
Prinzen Achmed (The
Adventures of Prince
Achmed), 1926

Cutout animation

Cutout can be the simplest and quickest technique of all and the results are somewhere between cel animation and stop frame. The drawing is cut out and then cut into sections, which are put on a background and then moved frame by frame. It can be done using physical cutouts or cutout images inside a computer animation package.

Multiplane camera

The multiplane camera was used to give an illusion of depth to traditional 2D animation. To achieve this, pieces of artwork were moved past the camera at various speeds and at various distances. Some areas of artwork were left transparent so that layers below could be seen behind them.

Lotte Reiniger

Lotte Reiniger's unique style means that her work, unlike that of some of the other great animators, is instantly recognizable as her own. Her delicate cutout silhouette technique carried her through a long and productive career that spanned 60 years and many different countries, and enabled her to work simultaneously within the mainstream and avant-garde sectors of animation. Her passion for producing animated versions of fairy tales has perhaps influenced the course of mainstream animation and its association with stories of this type. Beginning her career as part of the group of ambitious and influential animators working in pre-World War II Germany, Reiniger was a central figure in the avant-garde movement, despite being distinct from the others in the group due to her generally more accessible figurative style and more traditionally narrative-led subject matter.

Born in Berlin in 1899, as a child she developed the seemingly self-taught technique of cutting out freehand paper silhouettes, often producing portraits of people and animals that she used in her homemade shadow theater productions. Later she developed a keen interest in cinema, firstly in the stage-magic-style special effects films of Georges Méliès and then in the work of Paul Wegener, the German expressionist director of The Student of Prague (1913) and Der Golem (1915, also remade in 1920). After attending a lecture by Wegener about "trick" films (or special effects, as we now call them), she knew that was what she wanted to be involved in.

Reiniger persuaded her parents to let her enroll in Max Reinhardt's theater school in Berlin as she knew Wegener was a member of the acting troupe there. In an attempt to get to know him, she made cutout silhouette portraits of the school's actors in their most famous roles. Due to her skill at creating these silhouettes, this plan worked splendidly and she was soon creating captions and title cards for Wegener, animating wooden rats in his Der Rattenfänger von Hameln (The Pied Piper of Hamelin, 1918), and even taking small roles in his films.

Wegener introduced her to a group who were setting up an experimental animation studio called the Institut für Kulturforschung (The Institute for Cultural Discovery), including animator Berthold Bartosch and the writer and director Carl Koch. Wegener suggested that Reiniger's silhouettes might have potential for interesting animation, and, after learning the techniques from Bartosch, she started to produce her own films, the first of which was Das Ornament des Verliebten Herzen (The Ornament of the Lovestruck Heart, 1919), concerning two lovers and an ornament that changed according to their moods. Her attraction to fairy tales soon became apparent as she produced Aschenputtel (Cinderella, 1922) and Dornröschen (Sleeping Beauty, 1922). She was also known for creating, along with avant-garde animator Walther Ruttman, a dream sequence featuring a silhouetted falcon in Fritz Lang's movie, Die Nibelungen (1924).

With financial backing from Louis Hagen, Reiniger was presented with an opportunity to make a feature film; the result was Die Abenteuer des Prinzen Achmed (The Adventures of Prince Achmed, 1926). The movie director and actor Jean Renoir helped to promote Prince Achmed in France where, as in other countries, it eventually achieved commercial and critical success. Renoir described Reiniger's work as "a visual interpretation of Mozart," an apt description as music and operas, along with fairy tales, were favorite themes of hers. In the 1930s she produced an adaptation of Carmen (1933), as well as Papageno (1935), based on Mozart's opera The Magic Flute, and then Helen La Belle (1957) from Offenbach's music, and A Night in a Harem (1958), again from Mozart. She also contributed a sillouette animation to Renoir's La Marseillaise (1938).

Further films made in Germany were the animated Doktor Dolittle und seine Tiere (Doctor Dolittle and His Animals, 1928) and the live-action Die Jagd nach dem Glück (Running After Luck, 1929). The latter, codirected with Rochus Gliese and starring Renoir and Bartosch, featured a 20-minute silhouette sequence. This film was unfortunately completed just before the advent of sound and was then hastily and unsuccessfully dubbed before its release.

Like fellow animator Oskar Fischinger and many other artists, Reiniger and her now husband Koch fled their native country when the Nazis came to power in the 1930s. As no country would take them as refugees or asylum seekers, they were forced to keep traveling around the world for six years, returning to Germany several times. Nevertheless they carried on working in Italy, France, and Great Britain during the prewar and war years, until they settled in London in 1948.

During their many years in England, Reiniger and Koch produced a huge volume of work including films for the BBC and the GPO Film Unit, such as The King's Breakfast (1936).

Sleeping Beauty, 1954

They also established a company called Primrose Productions. Among the many acclaimed animated films they made during their time in London were a series of fairy tales for producer Louis Hagen Jr. (son of the financier of *Prince Achmed*), including *The Gallant Little Tailor* (1954) and *Jack and the Beanstalk* (1955).

After Carl Koch's death in 1963, Reiniger took a break from making films and spent a number of years as a near recluse. In the late 1960s there was a revival of interest in her work and she was invited to visit Germany for the first time since her move to London. She was presented with several awards honoring her career. Later she was also invited to lecture in the USA, during which time she described herself as "a primitive caveman artist." Despite this rather deprecating view of her own art, the enthusiastic reception she received persuaded her to start work once again.

In 1976 Reiniger went to Canada where she made *Aucassin et Nicolette* and later *The Rose and the Ring* (1979) for the National Film Board. In her last decade she spent time lecturing and teaching around the world. Her final film was *Die vier Jahreszeiten* (*The Four Seasons*, 1980), made for the Filmmuseum Düsseldorf the year before she died.

1926

Germany

Hans Richter: Filmstudie (Film Study)

After early involvement as an artist in the cubist and Dada movements, Hans Richter befriended Swedish animator Viking Eggeling and the two began experimenting with animation in 1918. Richter made three early abstract animated films in the 1920s: *Rhythmus 21* (1921), *Rythmus 23* (1923), and *Rythmus 25* (1925). These consisted of minimalist animation of geometric shapes moving and growing, the forms increasing in complexity through the series. Although interesting and ambitious attempts to give modernist imagery the dimension of time, the rather primitive animation technique meant that they fell short of the ideal level of precision required for this kind of cold, mathematical style.

For the rest of his career, Richter incorrectly claimed that *Rhythmus 21* was the first ever abstract animated film, when in reality the Italian futurists Bruno Corra and Arnaldo Ginna had created experimental work in 1911 and Walther Ruttmann produced the more sophisticated *Lichtspiel Opus 1* in 1920.

In 1926 Richter produced *Filmstudie (Film Study)*, a richer and more dreamlike work in which, as in Léger's *Ballet Mécanique* (*The Mechanical Ballet*), he combined live action with animation, mixing surrealist imagery—disembodied eyeballs and multiple exposed faces—with geometric animation. This time Richter used more advanced camera tricks, such as superimposition to overlay patterns, and utilized the focal properties of the lens to blur and smear the imagery.

In 1940, like many of his fellow artists at this time, Richter emigrated from Germany and moved to New York, where he went on to make the live-action, surrealist classic feature films *Dreams That Money Can Buy* (1947), *8 x 8: A Chess Sonata in 8 Movements* (1957), and *Dadascope* (1961).

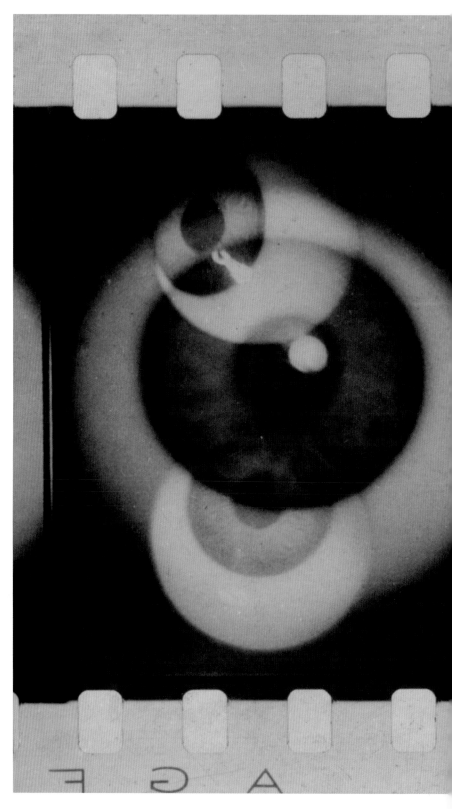

Filmstudie (Film Study),
1926

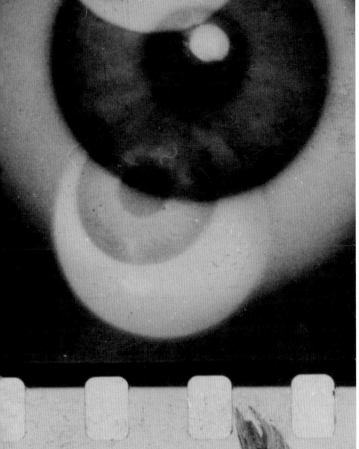

Japan

Noburo Ofuji: Kujira (Whale)

As a young man Noburo Ofuji was apprenticed to one of the pioneers of Japanese animation, Junichi Kouchi, who adapted traditional Japanese stories into simple cartoons such as *Hanawa Hekonai meitô no maki* (*The Sword of Hanawa Hekonai*) and *Namakura-gatana* (*The Blunt Samuari Sword*) both produced in 1917.

After working with Kouchi for a few years, Ofuji began making his own films, believing in animation as a serious art form and trying to create grown-up films for adult audiences. For his *Kujira* (*Whale*) he used a cutout sillouette technique, creating figures out of a semitransparent Japanese paper called chigoyami. These paper figures were then manipulated and filmed on different levels of glass plates, techniques similar to those used by Lotte Reiniger. *Whale* was one of the first Japanese animated films to be distributed worldwide and win international acclaim. Ofuji remade the film in 1952 in color.

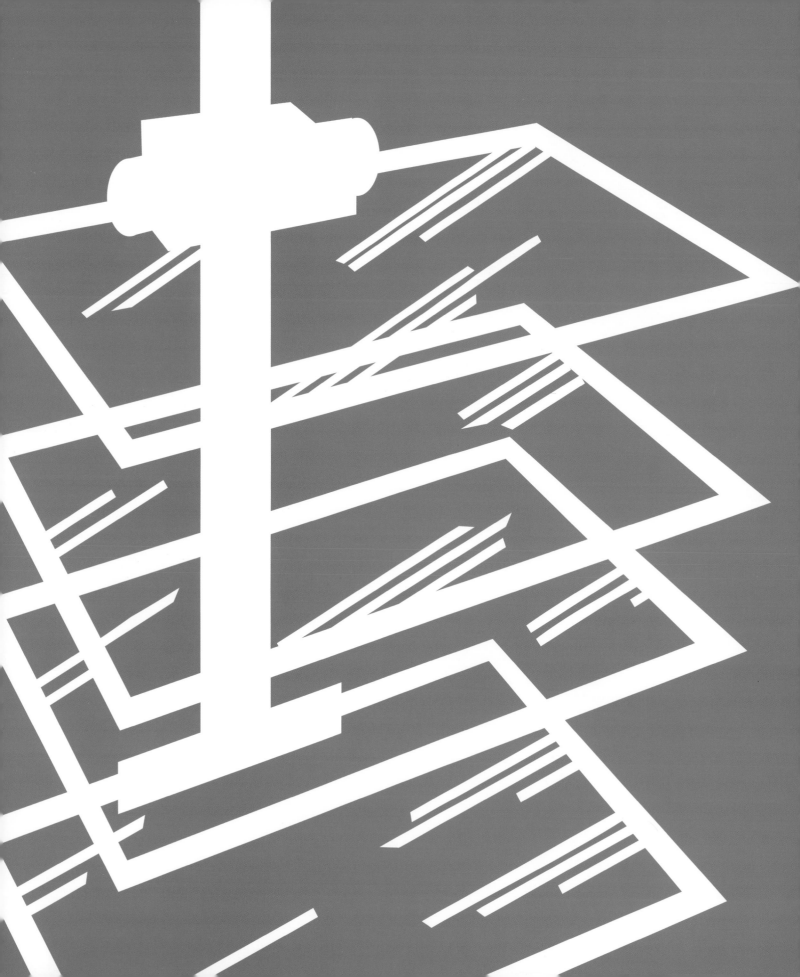

1928–1957:
Film Animation:
The Golden Age
of Cartoons

By 1928 animation had enough blueprints to work from for both commercial, technical, and artistic success. European abstract animators such as Oskar Fischinger, Walther Ruttman, Viking Eggeling, Fernand Léger, and Hans Richter had pioneered animation as high art, but the American Winsor McCay had shown that mainstream cartoons could also be beautifully crafted and of fine quality. American producers of animation like James Stuart Blackton, Otto Messmer, Pat Sullivan, Raoul Barré, Earl Hurd, the Fleischer brothers, Paul Terry, and John Randolph Bray, and to a lesser extent on the other side of the Atlantic, Charles-Emile Reynaud, Emile Cohl, Ladislaw Starewicz, Arthur Melbourne-Cooper, George Studdy, and Lotte Reiniger had created cartoons that could be funny, entertaining, and commercially successful, while developing and applying technical systems that moved the process of animation toward something practical and sustainable. It just needed someone to pull the best of these artistic and commercial ideas together: step forward, Walt Disney.

1928
USA

Paul Terry: Dinner Time

In 1928 Paul Terry and John Foster made a short with sync sound called *Dinner Time* at the Fables Studios in New York. The short was part of the *Aesop's Fables* series and starred Terry's character Farmer Al Falfa, in this case working as a butcher and battling with a bunch of hungry dogs. It was premiered in September and released in October, but failed to capture the public's imagination.

The reason for the film's failure in comparison to Disney's early sound work can be seen as symptomatic of Terry's whole approach to animation—he viewed it simply as a money-making exercise, churning out cheap cartoons with the minimum of effort and attention to detail. Terry was one of the pioneers of the cel-based system of animating on different layers so that parts of the drawing could be held rather than redrawn, later to become standard practice.

Terry cheerfully admitted that in animation terms he was the "Woolworths" while Disney was the "Tiffanys", an attitude that is somewhat ironic considering Terry, another exnewspaper cartoonist, was inspired to take up animation by master craftsman Winsor McCay, the era's fiercest opponent of the industrial approach to animation. The quote does however seem to typify Terry's reputation as one of the great characters of early animation, the many stories about him often funnier than his actual cartoons.

In Terry's defence, his approach seemed to have been shaped by some bruising early experiences in the industry. One of his best-known stories was how when he told one of his distributors that the price he was offering barely covered the price of the film stock, the distributor told Terry that he would have been offered a higher price if he hadn't put those cartoons all over it! He later said he was told by another distributor that he bought Terry's films to clear the theater between features so that the queue at the box office could move more quickly. Terry's work was also unexpectedly influential; Walt Disney once stated that "as late as 1930 my ambition was to make cartoons as good as the *Aesop's Fables* series."

The idea to make the move into sound had come from his business partner, Amadee Van Beuren, and was only reluctantly carried out by Terry. Later, when Van Beuren saw Disney's success and wanted more properly syncopated sound films, Terry disagreed, preferring to add cheap soundtracks to silent films, leading to a fall out with Van Beuren. Terry left to form his own studio, Terrytoons, where he continued to make *Aesop's Fables*. In the meantime, the newly christened Van Beuren Studio had its main characters Tom and Jerry, a pair of tramps bearing no relation to the famous cat-and-mouse cartoons of the same name.

Terry was not alone in his pragmatic attitude toward his work; this approach was common in the New York animation business of his day, and was also reflected in many studios worldwide. A great many of the cartoons were made with a similar factory-like approach and lack of artistry, care, and attention. Consequently the novelty of moving drawings wore off, the public was predictably tired of such weak, uninspired product, and needed something wonderful to make animation exciting again. As we shall see on the next page, that something was just around the corner.

USA

Disney: Steamboat Willie

In 1927 the sound feature film *The Jazz Singer* was a huge success at the box office. The next year saw the release of Walt Disney's *Steamboat Willie*. The large financial investment in sound of this quality was considered a huge risk after the failure of other cartoons with "sound on film" systems, but Disney was determined to persevere. *Steamboat Willie* caused a sensation, winning huge acclaim and igniting the box office. While some wrote its success off to the novelty of sound, it clearly wasn't that simple as both the Fleischer Studios and Paul Terry had previously released sound films with nowhere near the same level of success. Indeed, Terry's *Dinner Time* was released just a month before *Steamboat Willie*.

Disney used the Powers Cinephone sound system for his first sound film, a system that producer Pat Powers had copied from Lee De Forest's Phonofilm, knowing that, following the bankruptcy of his company, De Forest would be unable to afford a legal challenge to this copyright infringement. Powers and Disney later fell out over money arguments and the poaching of Disney's animator and colleague Ub Iwerks in 1930. Subsequently Disney switched to another sound system.

The plot of *Steamboat Willie* is slight; Mickey Mouse pilots a boat while having difficulties with a character called Pegleg Pete, involving his girlfriend Minnie. What makes this special is the sound synchronization, created with skill and creativity; everything and everyone seems to move in time with the music and anything from cow's teeth to the whistle of the boat can seemingly become a musical instrument.

The movie was already half-finished as a silent short before Disney had the idea to make it a synchronized sound film. A test screening was set up where what there was of the cartoon was projected in one room, while in another room some members of Disney's team played a mouth organ and created impromptu sound effects with tin cans and whistles. Bearing in mind that fully-fledged cartoon shorts had never convincingly "produced" any noise before, the invited audience was mesmerized, and

Steamboat Willie, 1928

Disney knew he had found a winner. A soundtrack was recorded, the timings of which were precisely noted, and the cartoon was carefully remade in time with the music. Disney was on his way to his first smash hit.

The success of the cartoon ushered in what has become known as the Golden Age of American Animation, which lasted until the early 1960s. The film is also noted for the introduction of Mickey Mouse, the most famous cartoon character in history. Disney had actually made a couple of other silent Mickey Mouse shorts before *Steamboat Willie*, but as he hadn't sold them to distributors at this point, they were unknown to the public. They were quickly converted to sound and released as follow-ups.

After the success of *Steamboat Willie*, the Disney Studio released all its animation with soundtracks, and Mickey Mouse took over from Felix the Cat as the number one cartoon star.

1929
USA

1929
Russia

The Skeleton
Dance, 1929

Disney: The Skeleton Dance

Following the successful release of *Steamboat Willie*, Disney began a series of musical shorts called *Silly Symphonies* in 1929. A popular series, these cartoons starred cheerful and optimistic characters that gave audiences a lift during the Great Depression of the 1930s.

The Skeleton Dance is the first of the *Silly Symphonies* and is one example from this musical series that never seems to date. A perennial classic that could, and should, be shown every Halloween, it could pass for a contemporary production by Tim Burton. Wonderfully animated by Disney's main man at the time, Ub Iwerks, it features four skeletons in a graveyard performing a variety of inventive and compelling dances. Composer Carl Stalling, who suggested the concept of the series, based the music on a foxtrot in a minor key. The film was a milestone not just in terms of timeless entertainment value, but also for the fact that it was constructed to fit around Stalling's music—an unusual way to work at this time—and because it had no main character or star.

Mikhail Tsekhanovsky: Pochta (Post Office)

Mikhail Tsekhanovsky, a Leningrad-based illustrator and painter, created *Pochta* (*Post Office*, also known as *Post*). The film is based on a children's book by Samuel Marshak about postmen and the global movement of letters. *Post Office* became known as an early masterpiece of soviet animation and received praise worldwide from many quarters, with the architect Frank Lloyd Wright apparently showing it to Walt Disney.

After receiving such acclaim for his strongly personal style, Tsekhanovsky was sadly then forced, along with other soviet animators, to change to a more bland, commercial form. This kind of restriction of artistic freedom lasted for the quarter century after the formation of the Soyuzmultfilm Studio, which happened soon after the unveiling of Disney's Mickey Mouse shorts at the Moscow Film Festival of 1934. Soon after that seminal screening, a group of writers and government officials decreed a new direction of "Soviet Realism" which meant pro-soviet children's films based on traditional stories and fairy tales, made with the approved technique of cel animation using Éclair, the Russian equivalent of rotoscoping.

In 1964, when government cultural controls were relaxing and Russian animators were once more able to express themselves individually, Tsekhanovsky remade *Post Office*, his most acclaimed and personal film, shortly before his death.

1930
USA

Ub Iwerks: Fiddlesticks with Flip the Frog

After working loyally side by side with Walt Disney almost nonstop since their Kansas City beginnings, producer Pat Powers eventually tempted star animator Ub Iwerks away from the Disney Studio in 1930. This must have seemed like a major coup for Powers and caused some raised eyebrows around the animation world as, at that time, it was widely believed that Iwerks was the talent behind Disney's success. The reasons for Iwerks' departure are not clear, but Disney's total domination of the relationship was probably instrumental.

The first cartoon Iwerks produced for Powers' Celebrity Productions studio starred a character called Flip the Frog—probably derived from the frog he created for the *Silly Symphonies* short *Night* earlier that year—a personality he hoped would rival Mickey Mouse. The first Flip the Frog film was called *Fiddlesticks* and featured Flip dancing on stage and playing the piano along with a character very similar in appearance to Mickey Mouse (another Iwerks cocreation, although of course owned by The Walt Disney Company). Despite not being radically different from Disney's shorts, the film was notable for being made in two-color Technicolor. Another technical milestone in Iwerks' films was the development of a multiplane camera (several years before Disney, but several years after the version used by Lotte Reiniger).

Iwerks built up a talented staff including Carl Stalling (the musician from the Disney Studio), and Grim Natwick and Shamus Culhane, the star animators from Fleischer Studios. Despite his ambitious approach, none of Iwerks' new characters really took off; he had the technical talent, but lacked Disney's vision and spark. In 1936 Powers withdrew his support and the Iwerks studio closed down.

In 1938 Iwerks made what must have been a difficult return to the Disney Studio. As with their parting, neither Disney nor Iwerks ever really discussed this reunion, or revealed whether they remained friends, but it was a professional success for both men. Iwerks spent the rest of his career there, although not as an animator; Disney's animation had made advances since *Steamboat Willie* and *The Skeleton Dance*, but Iwerks had not. Instead he became a technical supervisor, a role in which he excelled, and went on to mastermind some of the technical accomplishments in Disney's movies, winning two Academy Awards for technical achievement. He was also the brains behind the impressive animation/live-action sequences in *Song of the South* and *Mary Poppins*, and helped to develop Disney's theme park.

1930

USA

Max Fleischer: Dizzy Dishes

Dizzy Dishes was the sixth installment in the Fleischer brothers' series of shorts called *Talkartoons*. The character that would later be named Betty Boop was introduced here, created by Max Fleischer and worked on by one of the Fleischers' best animators, Grim Natwick. Although clearly recognizable in this cartoon, she had some canine characteristics along with a sexy female body, as a kind of companion for Bimbo the half-human dog.

By 1931 Betty had become a regular character and had lost her canine characteristics; by 1932 each of her cartoons was billed as "A Betty Boop Cartoon" (the first being *Stopping the Show*). She was the first sexy cartoon star and some of her cartoons dealt with the subject in a none too subtle way, while others were quite nightmarish in the kind of surreal scares Betty and Bimbo were subjected to. Then, as now, most cartoon characters were based on cute, humanized animals or objects, so Betty Boop stood out by being an adult character primarily aimed at an adult audience, based on a type of very modern young lady, a kind of party girl known as a "flapper." Her appeal was based on an innocent sexuality and some of her cartoons, perhaps for the first time in animation, dealt directly with the subject of sex, as she is pursued by lecherous men intent on taking away her innocence, or her "boop-oop-a-doop" as she seems to refer to it. While Disney's short films were concerned with childlike situations and problems, Fleischer cartoons like those of Betty Boop and Popeye were grounded in a much more adult kind of world. It was issues such as these that drew attention from concerned parents and, among many other perceived lapses in morality in the movies of the time, led to the introduction of the Production Code (known as the Hays Code) in 1934 to control the content of movies, which forced many changes in the tone of the Betty Boop cartoons.

The toned-down version of Betty survived for another few years, her last cartoon being *Rhythm on the Reservation* in 1939. Despite this short career she has remained one of the most famous and well-loved cartoon characters. Her cartoons enjoyed a television revival, with two TV specials made in the 1980s, along with a cameo appearance in *Who Framed Roger Rabbit* (1988).

Betty Boop

1930

France/Russia

Ladislaw Starewicz: Le Roman de Renard (The Tale of the Fox)

After leaving Russia during the Russian Revolution, Ladislaw Starewicz's first feature film was *Le Roman de Renard* (*The Tale of the Fox*), completed in France in 1930. Also known as *Reynard the Fox*, the film features Starewicz's signature model animation style of humanized, realistic-looking animals, often wearing clothes and walking on two legs.

After problems in adding a soundtrack for the new sound age, funding for a German soundtrack came from the Nazi regime, and the film had its world premiere in Berlin in 1937. It was later released with a French soundtrack in 1941, and this is the version that is more commonly viewed today.

The story comes from traditional Dutch and French folk tales, medieval fables of an amoral and crafty fox character who could charm his way out of any trouble he found himself in. The traditional version was translated into English and printed by William Caxton in the fifteenth century and also adapted in a book, *Renert the Fox*, in 1872, in a Luxembourg setting.

An anti-Semitic version of the story was published in Holland in 1937, which may have attracted the interest in the film project from Nazi Germany, although there is no suggestion that Starewicz's version has any such racist connotations. Another inferior animated version, a Dutch adaptation of the 1937 anti-Semitic text, was also funded by the Nazis and released in Holland in 1943, but was never given a full release. This poisonous version was rediscovered and restored for historical reasons in the later decades of the twentieth century.

Starewicz's *Tale of the Fox*, 10 years in the making, features stunningly sophisticated stop-frame animation for its time—more fluid than the more celebrated *King Kong* released three years later—and with beautiful black-and-white cinematography. It has the wicked sense of humor of the original stories and stands up today as a fascinating film and a true classic.

Le Roman de Renard
(The Tale of the Fox),
1930

Starewitch-Film
der Ufa

1930
France/Czech Republic

Berthold Bartosch: L'idée (The Idea)

Berthold Bartosch was born in 1893 in Bohemia (now the Czech Republic). He attended art school in Vienna, Austria, and, after graduation, created educational animated films "for the masses." In 1919 he moved to Berlin, where he met and collaborated with a group of animators and artists including Lotte Reiniger, Viking Eggeling, Hans Richter, and Walther Ruttmann, and also befriended the director Jean Renoir and writer Berthold Brecht.

In 1929 Bartosch was commissioned by publisher Kurt Wolff to create an animated film from an illustrated book of woodcuts by Frans Masereel and, after moving to Paris in 1930, started work on *L'idée* (*The Idea*). Using stylized cutout drawings, superimposed images, and multiplane techniques (similar to the techniques of Reiniger, with whom he had worked in Berlin), Bartosch strived in isolation for months, filming the cutout figures on multiple levels of glass and achieving soft lighting effects by backlighting and smearing the glass with soap. The resulting film, with a soundtrack by Arthur Honegger, bore little relation to the original woodcuttings.

The story concerns a young dreamer who conceives an idea, which appears in the visual form of a small, naked female figure. The strength and freedom of the Idea disturbs the conservative bourgeoisie, but no matter how hard they try, they can't own, destroy, hide, or corrupt the purity and beauty of the Idea, which lives only to help and empower the repressed poor. The workers rise up and are defeated and the Idea's creator is executed, but the Idea lives on. Unlike the Idea in Bartosch's film, *The Idea* did not inspire the masses; failing to obtain any kind of distribution, it was only seen by a small number of people.

Undaunted by this, and clearly the kind of artist who doesn't much care if anyone sees his work, Bartosch continued to plan more films. He was rescued from poverty by the English critic Thorold Dickinson, who admired his work and became his benefactor, helping to fund his next film. Bartosch used another elaborate and time-consuming technique on this project, an antiwar statement. This animation was in color, which was achieved by filming it separately three times on different kinds

L'idée (The Idea),
1930

of film stock sensitive to different parts of the color spectrum. After all this effort, and just as he was editing the film and preparing the soundtrack with Arthur Honegger, the film was, somewhat ironically considering its subject matter, destroyed in the outbreak of World War II. It was reported that only three people ever saw the film (referred to as *Cauchemar* [*Nightmare*] and also known as *Saint Francois*): Bartosch, his wife, and Thorold Dickinson.

Still undeterred, Bartosch started work on another film after the war ended. Never one to shy away from the big topics, this time Bartosch planned a film about the universe, the planets, and, one of his obsessions, the qualities of light. His failing health, however, meant that the long hours necessary standing at his multiplane camera system proved impossible. His passion and drive for making animated films never diminished, and right up to his death in 1968, Bartosch talked to his friend Alexandre Alexeieff about his plans for the next film.

1932
USA

Fleischer Studios: Minnie the Moocher

"Minnie the Moocher" was a jazz song recorded by bandleader Cab Calloway in 1931, which went on to sell over a million copies worldwide. The lyrics are often nonsensical and indecipherable, a characteristic of Calloway's ad-lib style of "scat" singing. The origins of "Minnie the Moocher" are in the 1927 song "Willie the Weeper" by Frankie "Half Pint" Jackson, featuring street-slang lyrics and drug references.

In 1932 the Fleischer Studios used Calloway's song as the basis for what is now regarded as one of their finest shorts and a classic of American animation. Cab Calloway appears in a live-action segment at the start of the cartoon, the earliest known film of him and his band. After this, any sense of reality is left behind as Betty Boop, along with her dog Bimbo, is involved in a wild fantasy journey in which she confronts her psychological fears and meets a singing ghost, whose movements are rotoscoped from Calloway's dancing.

Like *Minnie the Moocher*, a number of Betty Boop's other early films, such as *Bimbo's Initiation* (1931) and *Boop-oop-a-doop* (1932) were quite dark in subject and tone. The success of *Minnie the Moocher* gave birth to a follow-up the next year, the even more surreal *Snow-White*, again loosely constructed around a Cab Calloway song, "St James Infirmary Blues", and definitely not to be confused with Disney's version of *Snow White*, released four years later.

1933
USA

Disney: Three Little Pigs

Disney's *Three Little Pigs* was the most successful of the *Silly Symphonies*, became one of the most successful short films of all time, and won the Oscar for best short film. Its theme song, "Who's Afraid of the Big Bad Wolf?", became a huge hit in the Depression years, as the song, and therefore the film, came to express and symbolize the hope and resilience of the American people during harsh economic times. During the early years of World War II it was also used to refer to Hitler's expansion in Europe. This made it, whether by accident or intention, almost unique among Disney cartoons in that it could be considered a political allegory (another candidate would be the 1943 Donald Duck short, *Der Fuehrer's Face*).

In terms of the history of animation, *Three Little Pigs* represents a big step forward in the sophistication of character animation, pushing Disney another few light years ahead of the competition. The three pigs, although sharing almost identical character design, have very distinct personalities, which are defined by brilliantly expressive character animation.

Disney followed *Three Little Pigs* with three sequels, failing, however, to achieve the success of the original. This is believed to have convinced Walt Disney of the value of moving forwards with new ideas and taking risks, rather than adopting the cautious and short-sighted policy of sequels, an approach which reaped rewards for his company. After this, he was often heard to say "You can't top pigs with pigs!"

1933
USA

Fleischer Studios: Popeye the Sailor

Popeye the Sailor was actually a cartoon in the Betty Boop series, and was used, like several other Betty Boop films of this time, to try out a new character for whom the Fleischers had acquired the rights. Popeye had been the star of the King Features Syndicate *Thimble Theatre* newspaper comic strip, drawn by Elzie Crisler Segar, since his introduction in 1929. He soon took over from Betty Boop as the Fleischers' biggest cartoon star, and by 1935 was beating even Mickey Mouse in popularity polls.

Directed by Dave Fleischer, *Popeye the Sailor* starts with Popeye coming to life from a newspaper strip and then introducing his famous theme song, "I'm Popeye the Sailor Man," sung by his original voice artist William "Billy" Costello. (When Costello's behavior later became a problem, the actor was replaced with Jack Mercer, a Fleischer Studios "in-betweener" who could do a good Popeye impression.)

Later in the cartoon, Popeye is on shore with his rival Bluto, competing as usual for the affections of the squeaky-voiced Olive Oyl. When they come across Betty Boop performing at a carnival, Popeye dances with Betty, giving the brutish Bluto the opportunity to kidnap Olive and tie her to a railway track, prompting Popeye to swallow a can of spinach to gain his super strength and rescue his damsel in distress. This pretty much laid the blueprint for most Popeye cartoons from then on.

At around this time, Lillian Friedman was promoted to the position of animator at the Fleischers' studio, the first American woman to do this job professionally. (Edith Vernick had also worked in the animation department at the Fleischer studio for some time before this, but although she had produced some animation, she was never promoted to the position of animator.) Friedman worked on her one and only Popeye cartoon, *Can You Take It*, in 1934.

Popeye the Sailor

1933
USA

Merian C. Cooper, Ernest B. Shoedsack, and Willis O'Brien: King Kong

In the early decades of the twentieth century, few zoos had "monkey houses," and consequently knowledge about primates was low, whereas curiosity and fanciful stories were high. A few successful movies about apes had been made, almost enough in fact for the subject to qualify as a separate genre. *King Kong* producer/director Ernest B. Shoedsack had already made a couple himself: *Chang* (1927, also with Merian C. Cooper) and *Rango* (1931), both featuring live-action monkeys in jungle settings. The most successful of these ape movies was the hoax documentary exploitation flick, *Ingagi* (1930), which claimed to feature genuine footage of a woman being sacrificed to giant gorillas.

In this climate, Cooper was working on an ape movie in 1931 when he saw Willis O'Brien's stop-motion project, *Creation*, in development; he knew that he had found the way to tell his giant ape story. The film that resulted, *King Kong*, is a classic of cinema and one of the most famous movies of all time; it is a milestone, not just in animation history, but for movies in general.

King Kong amazed audiences on its release and was a huge commercial success. The movie contains many often-joked-about flaws, such as the animators' visible finger dents on the model's fur and the slight jerkiness of the stop-frame animation, but in actual fact these make little difference to the "believability" of the experience. We all know that giant apes don't exist and that it is an exercise in imagination, but the storytelling and animation not only help us believe in, but also sympathise enormously with, the giant ape who is kidnapped from the jungle where he is king and taken to New York to be the centerpiece of a freakshow. The pathos and empathy that are built for the monster and his doomed love for the heroine, played by Fay Wray, means there are very few better monster films in the history of cinema.

For the character of King Kong, O'Brien used a series of 18-inch high models, made from foam, rubber, and animal skins over metal skeletons. These were placed within miniature sets that provided the backdrops, although a few scenes involving close-ups between King Kong and the human actors were made using giant, "lifesize" models of the gorilla's head, hand, and foot. The prehistoric inhabitants of Skull Island were animated using similar models, and to prepare for the movie, O'Brien spent time at zoos studying the movements and behaviors of gorillas and other large animals.

The story has been remade several times, each time more "realistically," but the fact that this emotional connection with the audience has never been as strong in the later versions proves that the holy grail of some kind of technical reproduction of perfect reality is actually not the important thing in film or animation. In no movie since the original *King Kong* have we felt such sympathy for a monster in the process of smashing a city and killing innocent people.

1933
France/Russia/USA

Alexandre Alexeieff and Claire Parker: Une nuit sur le mont chauve (Night on Bald Mountain)

Alexandre Alexeieff was a Russian artist living in Paris, having left his native country after the October Revolution of 1917. He worked as a set designer and book illustrator before turning to filmmaking, and after considering his strengths as an artist and his lack of resources, he came up with an original idea for making animation. Alexeieff and his first wife Alexandra Alexandrovna Grinevskya (a self-taught engraver) built a pinscreen device composed of hundreds of pins that slid in and out of a grid, creating an infinitely pliable surface shape, which could produce relief shadow images especially when lit from the side (a similar idea to today's "executive toy" pinboards).

Alexeieff and Grinevskya were aided by Claire Parker, a young American living in Paris who had admired Alexeieff's book illustrations, asked him for lessons, and then offered to help. The two embarked on a long professional and personal relationship by starting work on *Une nuit sur le mont chauve* (*Night on Bald Mountain*) together in 1932. They worked intensively for 18 months on the film, shooting and reshooting the footage until Alexeieff was satisfied, the plans for the film mapped out in his head.

Night on Bald Mountain was based on Modest Mussorgsky's short symphony concerning the witches sabbath, which, according to folklore, occurs at summer solstice on Mount Triglav, Slovenia. The film avoids cute, Halloween archetypes, and instead opts for obscure and unsettling images of figures, animals, and footprints materializing out of the mist before marching or spinning off again, giving the film a feeling of the subconscious mind at work and a spontaneity that Alexeieff said he had "learned from surrealism." The film is often compared with the "Night on Bald Mountain" sequence from Disney's *Fantasia*, which, although very different and unambiguous in style, is equally powerful in its own way. Although probably influenced by the earlier film, the Disney version is so different in approach and execution, that comparisons are pretty futile.

Intended to be a new kind of serious animation similar to engraving, Alexeieff and Parker's film has a look that is certainly unique. Always heavily shadowed, it has a dreamlike, smeared quality. Often the figures are simple and stylized, but on other occasions they are astonishingly precise and lifelike, possibly these variations in style reflecting the different hands at work. Alexeieff and Parker described their relationship as the artist and the animator, implying that while Alexeieff had the vision and design sense, Parker had the greater eye for movement. While Grinevskya had an often-overlooked role in many of her husband's films—building sets and models, for instance, and contributing to the creative process—for the pinscreen films it seems Alexeieff worked just with Parker.

Some scenes in *Night on Bald Mountain*, such as the opening shot of a scarecrow in the wind, have an uncanny rotoscope-like reality, and at other times the subjects spin almost perfectly in three dimensions, the light and shadow eloquently picking out the volume. In other sequences, the animation is more basic, the stylized forms moving in a cutout, slidey manner. There is an overall haze present which makes it seem like it is filmed in thick fog or at the bottom of the sea, adding to the nightmarish atmosphere.

After receiving much praise but little financial reward from the project, Alexeieff and Parker moved into advertising, often using simpler and more conventional methods of animation than the pinboard. Later, after moving to the USA, Alexeieff returned to the pinboard to produce films for the National Film Board of Canada. Returning to Paris after World War II, he continued his experiments with different technical processes involving animation and light, and in 1962 he was invited by Orson Welles to make the title sequence to *The Trial*. Other famous works from Alexeieff and Parker include *The Nose* (1963), *Tableaux d'une exposition* (*Pictures at an Exhibition*, 1972), and *Trois Themes* (*Three Themes*, 1977). They died less than a year apart, Parker in 1981 and Alexeieff in 1982.

1934
USA

Mary Ellen Bute: Rhythm in Light

Experimental American filmmaker Mary Ellen Bute produced her first complete film, *Rhythm in Light*, in 1934, working with her future producer and husband, cameraman Ted Nemeth. *Rhythm in Light* is a musical film, based on the piece "Anitra's Dance" from Edvard Grieg's opera, *Peer Gynt*. Like many of Bute's films, it is concerned with experiments with the properties of light when refracted through glass and other materials, producing kaleidoscopic and psychedelic patterns. Bute believed that abstract animation like this could, and would, become very popular, and that it would achieve a recognition that, interestingly, this genre has somehow never really received, even in the art world. To this end she persuaded the programmers of New York's prestigious Radio City Music Hall to screen her films before the main features; the effect of these fresh and shimmering works on a huge screen can only be imagined. Presumably because of its intended presentation to the general public, *Rhythm in Light* is preceded by rather unintentionally funny title cards using the formal language of the day to instruct the audience in how to experience the film. Best ignored, these cards can detract from what is often quite beautiful imagery.

Bute went on to produce many more experimental films, discovering many talented people to collaborate with. Thelma Schoonmaker, who would later become Martin Scorsese's favored editor, worked on Bute's 1965 live-action feature-length adaptation of James Joyce's *Finnegan's Wake*; and *The Boy Who Saw Through* (1954), another of Bute's narrative live-action films, stars an 11-year-old Christopher Walken.

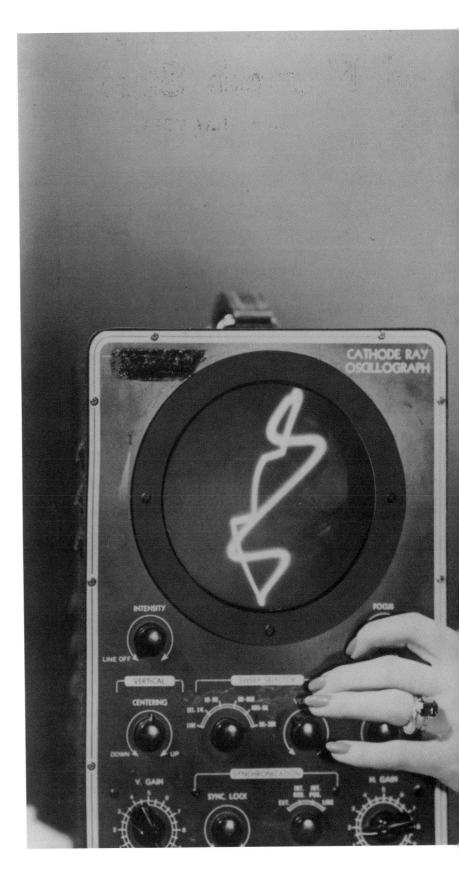

Mary Ellen Bute

USA

Disney: The Wise Little Hen

The 1934 short *The Wise Little Hen*, part of the *Silly Symphonies* series and based on the fairy tale *The Little Red Hen*, is notable for including the first appearance of a sailor-suit-wearing, rather bad-tempered duck, who would end up taking Mickey Mouse's position as Disney's most popular character at the box office.

In the cartoon, Donald Duck—here looking much more duck-like, with a smaller, rounder head and a longer neck than his later, more humanized design—and Peter Pig, a lazy friend of Donald's, avoid helping the busy hen, until at last they realize the value of hard work. Being a *Silly Symphony*, this is all set in musical time to a song about the hen and her corn-growing antics, and, while Peter and Donald are too lazy to help her out, they have lots of energy for dancing around. When we first see Donald he is on a boat, perhaps explaining the origins of his sailor suit.

Clarence Nash, who voiced Donald so memorably and helped define his strong character for the next four decades, was recruited after passing by the Disney Studios by chance as he toured the area with a team of miniature horses giving out candy in a publicity drive for a milk company. Walt Disney recognized Nash's voice from a radio show on which he had performed a routine where he recited "Mary Had a Little Lamb" in the character of an irritated duck. When Disney heard Nash do his routine again in an impromptu audition, he cast him as Donald Duck in *The Wise Little Hen*. A perfect example of the right person being in the right place, at the right time.

1934
France/UK/USA

Anthony Gross and Hector Hoppin: La Joie de Vivre

British-born animator Anthony Gross teamed up with American producer/animator/director Hector Hoppin in Paris to form the production company Animat, later renamed Societe Hoppin et Gross. Their short film, *La joie de vivre*, established them as talents to be reckoned with.

This gracefully designed and animated piece follows a couple of carefree young women dancing through a twentieth-century urban landscape, their happiness seeming to enable them to escape gravity and soar high into the sky. The two friends are followed by an eager young man on a bicycle who tries to return a lost shoe. As the happy trio move from city to country to coast, they unite and fly away together on the bicycle.

La joie de vivre is a kind of delightful animated precursor to the life-affirming, freewheeling nature of French movies of the 1960s' "nouvelle vague" (New Wave) movement, such as *Jules et Jim* and *À bout de souffle*. Despite its lack of "gags," its feeling of being an animated ballet also makes *La joie de vivre* seem like a French version of one of Disney's *Silly Symphonies*. The film captures the happy-go-lucky feeling of its title perfectly; perhaps it was this particularly French idea of the "joy of living" that drew Gross and Hoppin to France to begin with. The art-deco-inspired stylization of the animation, reminiscent of fashion magazine design, locates the film perfectly in its era.

The film's happy feel was perhaps a form of escapism from the reality of Europe at the time: fascism was on the rise and war was just around the corner. Shortly after completing *La joie de vivre*, Gross and Hoppin moved to London to work for producer Alexander Korda on another brilliant short, *The Fox Hunt* (1936), before embarking on the ill-fated feature-length *Le Tour du Monde en 80 Jours* (*Around the World in 80 Days*). The production of this film was curtailed by World War II, and the work was subsequently lost.

Gross became an official war artist for Britain, and later, when some old film stock of *Around the World in 80 Days* was rediscovered in an archive, he worked with the British Film Institute to restore it as a short, retitled *Indian Fantasy* (1955). This was Gross's last animated project before concentrating on his work as a painter.

Japan

Momotaro Vs Mickey Mouse
(Toy Box: Picture Book 1936)

After the Japanese invasion of Manchuria, China, in 1931, Japan withdrew from the League of Nations in response to international condemnation of the incident. Japanese propaganda attempted to motivate the public of Japan and its occupied regions toward building up military resources against supposed American plans to invade in 1936.

Momotaro was a popular character based on a traditional folktale, who appeared in a number of propoganda cartoons. In this rather crudely animated example from the *Toy Box* series, he jumps out of a picture book to fight off fanged Mickey Mouse look-alikes attempting to invade a peaceful island. The island is inhabited by dolls, rather strange-looking cat-like creatures, and other characters relating to Japanese folklore. The American invaders are represented by snakes, alligators, and bats who spit missiles. In one scene, an island cat (who bears a strong resemblance to Felix the Cat) tears up a treaty that presumably represents the Washington Naval Treaty of 1922, which restricted the Japanese Navy to a percentage of the American and British fleets. The invasion is successfully repelled and the cartoon ends with cherry trees blossoming and the characters singing the folk song, "Tokyo Ondo."

A young Yoshitsugu Tanaka worked on this and other *Toy Box* shorts before becoming one of the better-known postwar Japanese animators.

Joie de vivre,
1934

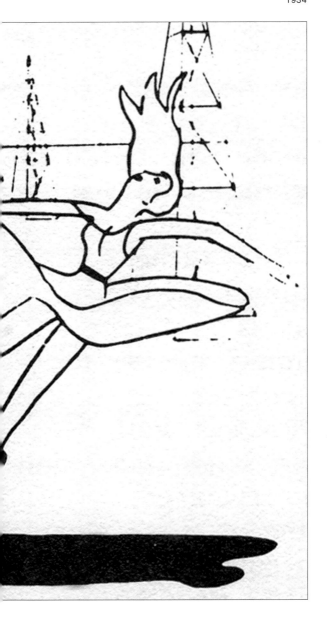

1935

Germany

1935

Russia

Oskar Fischinger: Komposition in blau (Composition in Blue)

In 1933 the Nazi party took control in Germany and put in place policies against "degenerate art," or, in other words, modernist or abstract art. Oskar Fischinger was a member of the German abstract animation movement, creators of what some were calling "Visual Music." After creating special effects for films like Fritz Lang's *Die Frau im Mond* (*The Woman in the Moon*, 1929), he made many of his own abstract films, including the series *Studies 1-12*. These were widely distributed and a few of the films were used to advertise new record releases by Electrola.

While most of the other abstract animators stopped work or moved abroad under the new fascist regime, Fischinger continued to work by defining his films as "decorative" rather than "abstract". He produced advertising, creating a popular series of commercials for Muratti tobacco, where stop-motion cigarettes danced around the screen. Fischinger also somehow managed to make, and even have approved by the authorities, the abstract piece *Komposition in Blau* (*Composition in Blue*, 1935). The film was made as an accompaniment to the overture from Otto Nicolai's opera *The Merry Wives of Windsor* and was described by Fischinger as an attempt to express joy. It is notable for its three-dimensional qualities, which bestow the abstract images with a huge amount of depth.

Composition in Blue, along with his cigarette commercials, was screened in Los Angeles. It was praised by critics, and led to Fischinger being offered a contract to work for Paramount in California, an offer which he quickly accepted. Fischinger worked for short periods at Paramount in 1936, MGM in 1937, and Disney from 1938 to 1939. However, he found working in a studio difficult and, with the patronage of Hilla Rebay, curator of the Solomon Guggenheim Foundation, he worked on oil paintings and independent films. In 1947 he fell out with Rebay over his film *Motion Painting No.1*, and never received enough finanicial backing to complete another film. He died in 1967.

Aleksandr Ptushko: Novyy Gulliver (The New Gulliver)

Aleksander Ptushko built his reputation as a great filmmaker on his adaptations of fairy tales, something that has led some to christen him the "Soviet Disney."

Ptushko began his career in the field of mechanical engineering (he invented a type of adding machine that was used in the USSR for 50 years), but in 1927 he joined Moscow's Mosfilm studio as a puppet maker. He was soon making his own short films, starting with *Sluchay na stadione* (*It Happened at the Stadium*, 1928), followed by other works featuring a character called Bratsihkin.

He assembled a team of animators and puppet makers, and in 1935 embarked on his first feature, and what would be the first Russian animated feature film, *Novyy Gulliver* (*The New Gulliver*). Willis O' Brien (perhaps a more accurate comparison for Ptushko than Disney) had earlier combined human actors with stop-frame models in *The Lost World* (1925) and *King Kong* (1933), but for *The New Gulliver* Ptushko and his team topped these achievements with a cast of 3,000 puppets.

The film was an adaptation of *Gulliver's Travels* with Gulliver becoming passionately involved in a proworker, antielitist struggle. This was in line with the USSR's policy at the time of creativity geared toward "soviet realism." Artists and filmmakers were encouraged by the state to steer away from avant-gardism and intellectualism in favor of more populist, moralistic works, as well as traditional children's stories that often incorporated none too subtle pro-soviet propaganda.

Leaving the politics aside, the film is an amazing achievement, both in the intricacy of animating all the puppets while combining them with live action, but also for the high quality of the animation and lip-synch. This was a highly intricate process, as the puppets of the main characters had many different heads, each with various expressions and mouth shapes, which had to be constantly swapped over.

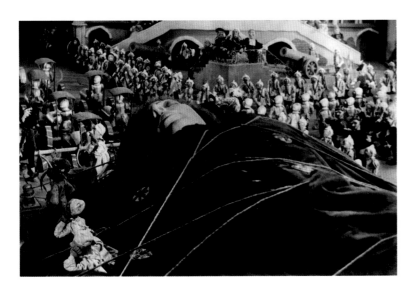

1936
USA

The New Gulliver was shown in many festivals worldwide and achieved great acclaim. Ptushko was made head of a new animation studio, Soyuzdetmultfilm (later renamed Soyuzmultfilm), which was set up in 1936 to create a new breed of populist and patriotic soviet animation. At this studio, Ptushko supervised the production of many more animated shorts, but did not usually take on the director's role.

In 1936 Ptushko and his team started work on *Zolotoy klyuchik* (*The Golden Key*), another feature film incorporating live action and stop-frame animation, based on Alexsei Tolstoy's version of *The Adventures of Pinocchio*. The film was released in 1939 in the Soviet Union only, predating Disney's adaptation by two years. It is another beautiful and extraordinary-looking film; scenes such as the living dolls and puppets in the clockmaker's workshop are quite magical and eerie.

The Golden Key was to be Ptushko's last extensively-animated film, as after this he produced his epic, fairy-tale-type of cinema mainly in live action. His later work included such award-winning and milestone films as *Kamennyy tsvetok* (*Stone Flower*, 1946), which was the first Russian film in color; *Sadko* (*The Magic Voyage of Sinbad*, 1953); and *Ilya Moromets* (*The Sword and the Dragon*,1956), which, like several of his later films, featured some stop-motion effects, and claims the award for the most people (106,000) and horses (11,000) used in a film.

Novyy Gulliver
(The New
Gulliver), 1935

Fleischer Studios: Popeye the Sailor Meets Sinbad the Sailor

Popeye the Sailor Meets Sinbad the Sailor was the first of three 16-minute-long color specials, three times as long as the normal Popeye cartoons, made by the Fleischer Studios at the height of Popeye's popularity. The draw these specials had at the box office was such that they were often billed higher than the main feature.

The entertaining story features Sinbad declaring that he is the world's greatest sailor, before Popeye shows up, leading to the hard-bitten New Yorker having to undertake a series of challenges and battles to prove his worth, ending with a battle with Sinbad himself. Lots of scenes include the Fleischers' tabletop three-dimensional technique, their version of the rotoscope, which produced an interesting and original look. The film hinted at the Fleischers building up for a feature film, and perhaps shows how colorful and popular that film could have been, had they not been sidetracked by the success of Disney and as a result decided, or were pressured by their financiers Paramount, into going down a more traditional fairy-tale route.

This film is a little gem right from the very first scene, as the brutish, Bluto-like Sinbad stomps through the lovely tabletop 3D background of his island, bellowing out a swaggering song to his menagerie of monsters: "Who's the most remarkable extraordinary kind of fellow..?" The animation is smooth, flowing, and funny, and the film remains a treat through to the climactic battles.

1936
UK/New Zealand

Len Lye: A Colour Box

After moving to London from New Zealand in 1927, eccentric genius Len Lye became involved with modernist art associations where he showed his paintings and sculptures, shared and absorbed ideas, and met like-minded people. Through this he started to make films; his first effort *Tusalava* (1929), made with cel animation and inspired by the native aboriginal art of his homeland, was funded by the London Film Society and apparently took him 10 hours a day for two years to complete.

With the reaction to *Tusalava* somewhat underwhelming, Lye found himself without any funding. Unable to afford a camera, he started making a film by drawing, scratching, and painting directly onto some discarded film stock he had found at Ealing Studios. He edited it together and persuaded John Grierson, head of the Greater Post Office Film Unit, to buy the resulting film. Grierson paid for a soundtrack to be added, as well as some totally out-of-context graphics advertising the Post Office.

Displaying easily as much "joie de vivre" as Anthony Gross' film released two years before, *A Colour Box* was the first film painted or scratched onto filmstock, or "direct" film, to be shown to general audiences. It established the style with which Len Lye would be associated and would return to many times over his long and varied career.

A Colour Box, 1936

Drawn-on film animation

Also known as direct animation, with this technique, images are scratched or painted directly onto the film strip.

Biography

Len Lye

An experimental artist and animation pioneer, Len Lye spent his long career attempting to "compose motion," a theme he explored through many different media, including film, painting, drawing and sculpture. Born in New Zealand in 1901, Lye had a tremendously varied life. Before moving to London in 1926, he spent much time with Aboriginal and Samoan peoples studying their art, which had a great influence on his later work.

In London he joined the Seven and Five Society, an art group that also contained abstract painters and sculptors like Henry Moore, Ben Nicholson, and Barbara Hepworth, and exhibited in the 1936 International Surrealist Exhibition. He began making experimental films and, unable to afford a camera, he scratched, painted, and stenciled directly onto the film. His first films *Tusalava* (1929), *Kaleidescope* (1935), and *A Colour Box* (1936) were animation landmarks of huge influence. *Tusalava* was self-financed by using these camera-free methods, and as a result the next two were commissioned. *A Colour Box* was made for John Grierson's General Post Office Film Unit (GPO) to publicize a new, faster parcel service. The first "direct film" (a term for film created with images rendered in any way directly onto the film stock) to be shown to a general cinema audience and therefore a milestone in the popularity of abstract film,

A Colour Box has been voted one of the top 10 most significant animation films of all time by a panel of experts at the 2005 Annecy Film Festival. The film inspired Lye's contemporary Norman McLaren, who was experimenting with similar techniques at the time, to take up animation as his main work.

In 1944 Lye left London for New York where he met, and found great similarities with, many of the famous abstract expressionist artists of the day, who would show his films at their parties. Lye also created kinetic sculptures (a lifelong passion that began in 1918 when he was 17 years old) believing them to be closely linked with his animation in creating a new art of motion. Years after his death, the Len Lye Foundation in New Zealand is still building the many huge kinetic sculptures that he left detailed designs for before his death in 1980.

Eleven years after his death, Lye was included as one of the 100 great innovators of the twentieth century in a major exhibition in Germany along with artists like Duchamp and Picasso. Len Lye urged all animators to be "free radicals," considered that no film was ever great unless it was made in the spirit of the experimental filmmaker, and was described as the "least boring person who ever lived" by the Scottish poet and film director Alistair Reid.

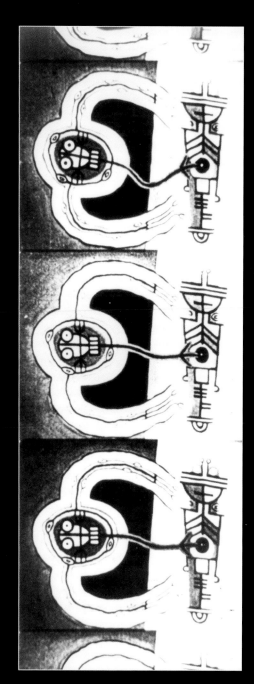

Tusalava, 1929

1936
USA

1937
USA

Disney: The Old Mill

Like the other shorts he produced around this time, Walt Disney used *The Old Mill* as a way to test out his new techniques in establishing realism in animation, in preparation for making his first feature film. He was motivated by a desire to reestablish his company as the leaders in animation by differentiating them from the mere cartoons that the others made, and his belief that in order to sustain an audience's interest for over an hour, he would need to create a realistic, believable world and characters.

The short, a story of animals in an old windmill sheltering from a storm, features extensive use of the multiplane camera to give depth to the images, a concentration on rotating objects drawn in three dimensions, and realistic-looking animals and the natural world, including effects of rain, water, and a storm. *The Old Mill* marks the defining moment when animation moved into realism, and is possibly one of Disney's most technically-advanced shorts.

Disney: Snow White and the Seven Dwarfs

Snow White and the Seven Dwarfs was Walt Disney's first feature film and was a huge financial gamble. When Walt announced his intentions to the *New York Times* in 1934, many were sceptical that the studio would be able to reproduce the success of its shorts with a full-length movie. The press called it "Disney's Folly" and even his wife Lillian and brother Roy tried to persuade him to abandon the idea, with Lillian saying "No one's gonna pay a dime to see a dwarf picture."

Like the personal risk he took with the expensive sound on *Steamboat Willie* in 1928, *Snow White* went six times over its initial budget as Disney employed somewhere between 750 and 1,000 artists. This led to an estimated budget of $1.7 million, eventually causing Disney to remortgage his house to keep the production going. Had it not succeeded, Disney could have faced ruin and it would have been a very different history of animation. Instead *Snow White* was a monumental success around the world and set a sky-high standard for all future animated features to aspire to. It became the highest grossing film that year and Disney was awarded an honorary Oscar for innovation, one full-size statuette and seven small ones.

The progress the studio had made in less than a decade since *Steamboat Willie* is incredible—from monochrome rhythmic rubberyness to an animated feature so brilliantly realized it has rarely been matched in the decades since its launch. All of Disney's experiments in those years came together and fell into place to create one intensely visually lush and exotic experience; *Snow White*'s world is the definitive fairy-tale landscape of idyllic green meadows, dense forests thick with life, atmosphere, light, and shadow, with huge turreted castles towering over all. Although a children's fairy tale, the movie certainly had its dark moments, the sequences involving the evil Queen and her machinations and the forest at night are, like any proper fairy tale, genuinely frightening. Like the many colors and shades of the forest itself, the movie contains the full emotional spectrum from light to dark, good to evil, merry to terrifying, Happy to Grumpy.

Despite his belief in the idea of animated features, Disney paid great attention to the concerns that long cartoons would not work because audiences would not be able to empathise with cartoon characters or care about their fate. For example, the chilling scene where the Queen's hunter takes Snow White to the forest to kill her took months to complete until Disney was satisfied that the necessary emotional impact was there. Other frightening moments in the forest were influenced by horror movies such as F. W. Murnau's *Nosferatu* (1922) and James Whale's Frankenstein films. British censors considered some moments to be so frightening that they banned certain scenes for young audiences.

The film's color palette was muted due to concerns that audiences would not be able to sit through the usual bright colors of a cartoon for an extended length of time. According to later interviews with Disney, the efforts to make Snow White a real character even extended to the women in the trace and paint department applying their own makeup to her painted face to put color in her cheeks.

This last story perhaps illustrates that the central characters, although beautifully crafted, suffer a bit from the dullness that essentially rotoscoped characters usually have—a limited appeal that any animation that is captured directly from reality will invariably suffer from. However, *Snow White*'s

Snow White and the
Seven Dwarfs, 1937

central characters were also elaborated and worked up to become something between hand-animated and enhanced rotoscope work.

Perhaps the most memorable feature of the movie is the animation of the seven dwarves. Using all of the sophisticated techniques developed on *Three Little Pigs* and many other shorts, the seven superficially similar characters were given completely differing personalities and emotions through the superb character animation.

By modern standards the film does slow in the middle section, being mostly concerned with the Dwarfs and the broad comedy interplay between their different personalities. Perhaps Disney and director David Hand may have been falling slightly into the animator's trap of wanting to show off great animation at the expense of story momentum, but audiences at the time were no doubt charmed and enthralled at these new heights of character animation. Indeed the animation of the Dwarfs and animals is so good that it has the effect of highlighting the deficiencies of the more realistic human characters who are largely rotoscoped. Although also beautifully crafted, the movement of the features on these human characters sometimes seems to waver in comparison with the beautiful flow of the hand animation.

In many ways, Disney's first few features were aimed as much at adults as children, or probably more accurately, they were aimed squarely at a universal audience, perhaps even more so than the "hip and sophisticated" animated features of the 1990s boom, which while aiming for universal audiences, did so by going primarily through the kids and then adding irony, referential humour, and sly jokes for the grown-ups.

Snow White and the Seven Dwarfs, 1937

1937
USA

1938
USA

Warner Bros. and Tex Avery: Porky's Duck Hunt

Daffy Duck was created by Tex Avery for the Warner Bros.' short *Porky's Duck Hunt*. In his typically frenetic way, Daffy turns the tables on duck-hunter Porky Pig. He torments the slow-witted pig mercilessly until Porky protests "That wasn't in the script," at which point Daffy bounces and whoops into the distance shouting "Don't let it worry you skipper—I'm just a crazy darn fool duck." This would set the tone for his anarchic, abrasive character from then on.

The public responded enthusiastically to this new crazed, screwball character and for his next cartoon, *Daffy Duck and Egghead* (1938) he was given a name and a starring role. Avery seemed to prefer the character of Egghead (later to become Elmer Fudd) and dropped Daffy, who was then seized upon by animator Bob Clampett, who, with voice artist Mel Blanc, developed him into the well-loved Warner Bros. star, rivaling Bugs Bunny for popularity.

Over the years Daffy's design was often modified and was passed on from animator to animator, including Robert McKimson, Friz Freleng, Art Davis, and Chuck Jones. Indeed the development of Daffy's design and personality shows the whole spectrum, and also the common development pattern, of an animal-based cartoon character. Beginning as basically a cartoon animal with some human characteristics, Daffy evolved into an anthropomorphic character who is primarily human, but with some animal characteristics.

Warner Bros. and Bob Clampett: Porky in Wackyland; Warner Bros. and Ben Hardaway: Porky's Hare Hunt

In the fantastically imaginative *Porky in Wackyland*, director Bob Clampett showed that in a Warner Bros. cartoon anything really could happen, and probably would. In fact when Porky the perennial big-game hunter arrives in Wackyland, in deepest darkest Africa, a sign proclaims "It Can Happen Here," which could have been the sign outside the Warner Bros. studio. What follows packs more surrealism into five minutes than Salvador Dalí could have dreamed up in five years. There are dementedly strange animals, complete bending of the laws of time and space, and an appearance from the last Dodo who, like most of Porky's prey, runs rings round him in an ever-increasingly mind-bending manner.

In *Porky's Hare Hunt*, Bugs Bunny (almost unrecognizable from his later design) makes his debut. He behaves rather a lot like Daffy Duck, sounds rather a lot like Woody Woodpecker (Bug's voice artist Mel Blanc also provided the voice for Woody two years later), and looks rather unlike Bugs Bunny, particularly as he is all white. He has the same wisecracking personality, though, that audiences would became familiar with in years to come. The character's name comes from animator Ben Hardaway's nickname, Bugs; when he drew the first design for the rabbit, it was known as Bug's Bunny.

Warner Bros.

The Warner Bros. movie studio was founded by Albert, Harry, Sam, and Jack Warner in 1923, and in 1927 producer Leon Schlesinger was invited to open an animation studio on their site. Hugh Harman and Rudolf Ising originated the *Looney Tunes* series of animated shorts in 1930 and *Merrie Melodies* in 1931. Both cartoon series were produced by Schlesinger at the Harman-Ising Studio for Warner Bros. The first *Looney Tunes* character was Bosko, The Talk-ink Kid. Bosko was reasonably popular, but never matched the popularity of the Disney or the Fleischer studios' characters. In 1933 Harman and Ising fell out with Schlesinger and left for MGM, taking Bosko with them.

In 1935, the same year that Porky Pig made his debut, Warner Bros. hired a young animation director called Fred "Tex" Avery, who had risen through the ranks at Walter Lantz's studio. Schlesinger teamed him up with animators Chuck Jones, Bob Clampett, and Robert "Bobe" Cannon, moved them away from the main team, and installed them in a cabin that they nicknamed Termite Terrace. Something special started to happen with the work produced by these animators, and within a few years Warner Bros. became the world's leading studio for animated shorts and made some of the funniest cartoons of all time. Tex Avery and his team reinvented animation by taking the developments that had been made in character animation and pushing them to the limits with a zany, exaggerated, and extreme style. Together they created some of the world's greatest and most enduring cartoon characters, including Porky Pig, Daffy Duck, Bugs Bunny, Speedy Gonzales, Wile E. Coyote, and Road Runner.

Other important parts of the Warners identity were the voice artist Mel Blanc and the composer Carl Stalling. Blanc was a former radio performer whose first job at Warners was to find a voice for Porky Pig. The stammering child-like voice he created pushed the character into stardom and from then on Blanc became the voice of Warner Bros. Carl Stalling had started out at the Disney Studio, having known Walt in Kansas City in the early days. After a fallout with Disney he went to work with Ub Iwerks and then moved to Warners in 1936 when Iwerks' studio closed. Stalling had learned his ability to complement film with music during his time as an accompanist for silent films.

The *Merrie Melodies* series went to full Technicolor in 1936, while *Looney Tunes* stayed in black and white for seven years longer. In 1938 Chuck Jones was promoted to director and was given his own unit. At first he dealt with cartoons featuring "cute" characters, like *Tom Thumb in Trouble* (1940) and *Joe Glow, the Firefly* (1941), which were made in a Disney-esque style. He soon began to specialize in cartoons of the new gag-heavy, crazier type that Warner Bros. were making their own, such as *A Wild Hare* and *Elmer's Candid Camera* (both 1940).

Warner Bros. had a serious side too at this time. They were the first American studio to take a stand against Hitler and the Nazis in their work, declaring war long before the American government. This was understandable as they had closed their German office after one of their representatives was beaten to death by Nazi thugs. In 1940 when Bugs Bunny first appeared, Bob Clampett described him as "a symbol of America's resistance to Hitler and the fascist powers."

Tex Avery left the studio to join MGM in 1941 following disagreements with Schlesinger. Chuck Jones, along with Avery's replacement Frank Tashlin and the other star animators Friz Freleng and Bob Clampett, carried on in the new Warners fashion with countless crazy classics such as *Porky in Wackyland* (1938), *Hare-um Scare-um* (1939), *You Ought to be in Pictures* (1940, one of the few Warners cartoons to include live-action sequences), *Wabbit Twouble* (1941), *Tortoise Wins by a Hare* (1943), the now perhaps politically-incorrect *Coal Black and de Sebben Dwarfs* (1943), and *What's Cookin' Doc?* (1944).

In 1944, Schlesinger sold his company to Warner Bros. and it was run as Warner Bros. Cartoons, Inc. until 1963. The man appointed by Warner Bros. to replace Schlesinger was Edward Selzer, who, according to several of the animators who worked for him, had no sense of humor or fondness for animation. By 1946, Tashlin and Clampett had left, but there was enough talent remaining to maintain the high standards, and later succesful Warner Bros. creations include Yosemite Sam, Sylvester the Cat, Foghorn Leghorn, Speedy Gonzales, and Road Runner.

In 1953, during the first 3D craze, Warner Bros., in what now seems like a moment of insane panic, shut its cartoon studio down, worried that 3D cartoon production would be too expensive. One 3D cartoon was produced, Bugs Bunny in *Lumber Jack-Rabbit* (1954). Chuck Jones moved to Disney to work on the feature-length *Sleeping Beauty*, and the other animators were snapped up by rival companies. Warner Bros. Cartoons reopened five months later after the 3D fad had, somewhat predictably, ended. By the mid-1950s, after it was ruled by the courts that Warner Bros. could no longer force the "block booking" of their features and cartoons together, the price for animated shorts fell and Selzer forced a stringent five-week production schedule on each cartoon, meaning a fall in quality was inevitable.

Selzer retired in 1956 and John Burton took over the studio. Warner Bros. Cartoons branched out into television. *The Bugs Bunny Show*, featuring Warner Bros. theatrical shorts, remained on the air on US television until 2000. *Looney Tunes* and *Merrie Melodies* were briefly subcontracted to Freleng's DePatie-Freleng Enterprises studio from 1964 until 1967, and the Warner Bros. Cartoons studio briefly reopened in 1967 before shutting its doors for good in 1969.

In 1961, as David H. DePatie became the last boss of the Warner Bros. Cartoon studio, Chuck Jones moonlighted to write the script for *Gay Purr-ee* at UPA. When Warner Bros. found out, Jones was fired. Freleng left four months later. In 1962 DePatie was forced to shut the studio due to decline in demand for movie theater shorts. The final short was Bugs Bunny in *False Hare* (1964), directed by Robert McKimson, followed later the same year by a final project to produce the animated sequences for the Warner Bros. feature *The Incredible Mr. Limpet*, also directed by McKimson.

A new studio, Warner Bros. Animation was set up in 1980, with Friz Freleng returning as its executive producer. For the next decade, the studio created movie theater shorts, television specials, and features starring *Looney Tunes* characters. A separate television animation studio

Hanna-Barbera staff members. The new division produced several successful series, including *Tiny Toon Adventures* (based on *Looney Tunes* characters) and *Animaniacs*, which continued the Warner Bros. tradition of crazy, humorous cartoons. The studio also made animated versions of DC Comics characters, such as *Batman: The Animated Series*, *Superman: The Animated Series*, and *Justice League*. (For more on *Batman: The Animated Series*, see page 288.) In 1996 Warner Bros. acquired Hanna-Barbera and took over the production of its classic television series.

In the mid-1990s Warner Bros. began to invest more heavily in animated movies, establishing Warner Bros. Feature Animation as a separate division. Its first release was *Space Jam* (1996), which combined live action with animation and starred basketball legend Michael Jordan alongside Bugs Bunny and other *Looney Tunes* characters. *Space Jam* was a huge hit at the box office, but further films, such as *Cats Don't Dance* (1997), *The Iron Giant* (1999), and *Osmosis Jones* (2001) were less successful commercially. *The Iron Giant*, directed by Brad Bird, won critical acclaim and has now become a much-admired classic. (For more on this film, see page 318). Investment in the feature animation division was scaled back due to this lack of success at the box office.

In the twenty-first century however, Warner Bros. has been behind many successful features that have blended animated special effects with live action, such as *The Matrix* series, the *Harry Potter* franchise, and *The Lord of the Rings* trilogy

1938

Germany

Hans Fischinger: Tanz der Farben (Dance of the Colors)

Hans Fischinger was the younger brother of the more celebrated Oskar. The pair collaborated on Oskar's *Studies No. 9* and *10*, and Hans completed *No 12* on his own, before the two fell out over the never-to-be-completed *Study No 14*.

Hans moved to Alzenau near Frankfurt where he continued with his abstract work. Although possessing similarities, his style differed from his brother's, as Hans prefered to work with charcoal rather than paint. However, Hans clearly shared Oskar's skill in getting abstract work passed by the Nazi regime, as his *Tanz der Farben* (*Dance of the Colors*) was freely distributed in Germany. Admired by critics and audiences, it was the last great film of the German abstract animation movement of the 1920s and 1930s.

1938

UK

Norman McLaren: Love on the Wing

This was Norman McLaren's last film for John Grierson's Greater Post Office Film Unit (GPO) in the UK before he moved to New York in 1939. It was McLaren's first real foray into "direct animation," meaning drawing straight onto the film, in the way that his colleague at GPO Len Lye had helped to pioneer three years earlier.

Love on the Wing features a Dali-esque surrealist background that scrolls in multiplane, on which is painted a frantically-animated love story of a man and a woman who communicate by letter (the GPO films existed to publicize the Post Office). The figures are painted in broad white strokes but are gracefully animated in their frenzied scurrying, embracing, fighting, and making up as they continually morph into symbolic images, invoking the surrealist movement's love for images of the subconscious. Some of these images, however, clearly proved a bit too symbolic for the Post Office, who banned the film for its "Freudian" imagery.

Biography

Norman McLaren

Norman McLaren was born in Stirling, Scotland in 1914. He studied interior design at the Glasgow School of Art, but, distracted by his interest in amateur filmmaking, he did not complete his diploma. Inspired by the films of Oskar Fischinger and Emile Cohl he experimented with stripping film stock of its images and then applying dyes to it to create abstract color pieces, which he accompanied with jazz music soundtracks. His film *Colour Cocktail* (1935) won him prizes and the attention of John Grierson at the GPO film unit, who hired McLaren to make government information films. After an assignment in Spain filming the civil war, he made two films for the GPO, *Many a Pickle* (1938), which explored pixillation, a technique he had seen in some of Cohl's films, and *Love on the Wing* (1938), which used the drawing on film technique.

In 1939 John Grierson was asked by the Canadian Government to set up the National Film Board (NFB). He immediately set up an animation unit, which was to become one of the greatest supporters of animation worldwide. Grierson invited Norman McLaren, who was now in New York, to come to Canada and make films for the NFB. McLaren recruited a team of animators and set to work on a series of groundbreaking films.

After a series of wartime propoganda films, this team went on to produce one of McLaren's greatest shorts, *Begone Dull Care* (1949). He later continued his experiments with pixillation in films like *Neighbours* (1952), as well as continuing his work with animated sound. (For more on *Neighbours*, see page 159.)

In 1973 he made *Pinscreen*, a documentary about the animation techniques used by Alexandre Alexeieff and Claire Parker. McLaren retired from the NFB in 1983 and died in 1987.

Love on the Wing, 1938

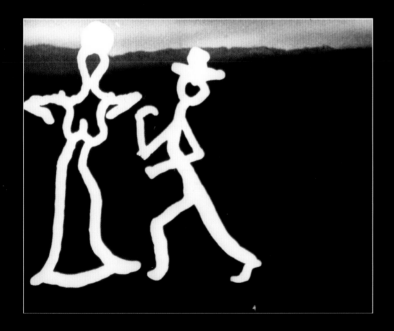

1939
USA

Fleischer Studios: Gulliver's Travels

Gulliver's Travels was the first of the Fleischer Studios two feature films, a loose adaptation of Jonathan Swift's allegorical tale of a shipwrecked man washed ashore on an island populated by a society of tiny people, the Lilliputians. The rotoscope technique (a Fleischer brothers' invention) used to create the central character of Gulliver still stands up as impressive work, and the movie features some memorable and spectacular sequences, such as the opening shipwreck, and some entertaining comedy from the tiny Lilliputians. *Gulliver's Travels* was a moderate box office success, but suffered financially from the outbreak of World War II in Europe, which curtailed its foreign sales.

The movie was well received by the public although critically it suffered (and still suffers) from comparison with the Disney features of the time, which unfortunately can only highlight the weaknesses of *Gulliver's Travels*. The comparison is hardly surprising as the movie was conceived and released by Paramount (who effectively financially controlled Fleischer Studios at the time) as the Fleischers' answer to the massive success of Disney's *Snow White and the Seven Dwarfs*.

Gulliver's Travels is often criticised for its mixing of realistic, rotoscoped human characters with others of a stylized, cartoon look (both styles widely used in the Fleischer brothers' earlier work). However, it should be remembered that *Snow White and the Seven Dwarfs* used similar techniques, although in Disney's film the more realistic characters were stylized enough to feel like cartoons and the cartoonish characters were crafted with enough realism to make the blend a success. In *Gulliver's Travels*, although the Lilliputians are literally a race apart from Gulliver, the realism of the central character does at times sit fairly uncomfortably alongside the cartoon style of the little people.

The main problem with *Gulliver's Travels* though, as is so often the case with animated features, is the script. Where Disney progressed slowly over a number of years toward making a feature film, creating ever more elaborate shorts with more and more depth and emotion to the characters, the Fleischers struggled with the big step up to a feature-length story from their crazy gag-strewn Popeye and Betty Boop cartoons. The characters in *Gulliver's Travels* have no real depth and so consequently the story lacks any emotional power. Where Disney instinctively understood how to craft a perfect story arc that would hold the viewer's interest for over an hour, *Gulliver's Travels* simply doesn't have the same flow and momentum. The Fleischers also made the mistake of shying away from featuring any evil characters, or scenes that might frighten children, in response to some parent's complaints about the scariness of some parts of Disney's *Snow White*. This may have pleased a minority of sensitive souls, but for the majority of children and adults alike, that kind of approach generally makes for a duller movie.

The title sequence of *Gulliver's Travels* of the ship at sea is a highlight and uses the Fleischers' "tabletop" 3D filming technique, used so memorably in earlier work such the Popeye specials. Mysteriously though, the technique isn't seen again in the rest of *Gulliver's Travels*, perhaps a missed opportunity to create something to stand up alongside Disney's impressive use of their multiplane system in *Snow White*, *Pinocchio*, and *Bambi*.

1940
USA

Walter Lantz: Knock Knock

Walter Lantz began working in the camera room at the William Hearst International Studio at the age of 15, from which point he learned to be an animator. He ran his own studio from 1929 until his retirement in 1972, aged 72. In 1940 animator Ben Hardaway joined Lantz's studio as a storyboarder after helping to create the "screwball" characters Bugs Bunny and Daffy Duck at Warner Bros. Later that year, the cartoon *Knock Knock*, which starred Lantz's character Andy Panda, introduced a zany woodpecker character who would go on to be Lantz's most popular creation.

Lantz later told the story of how, on his honeymoon, a woodpecker annoyed him by pecking away at his roof, and while he wanted to kill the bird, his wife suggested making a cartoon out of it instead. He also claimed that Woody's trademark manic laugh came from the woodpecker's cry. The trouble with this story is that the honeymoon was a year after the first Woody cartoon and that voice artist Mel Blanc had used a similar laugh even before that.

Blanc initially provided Woody's voice before he was contracted full time to Warner Bros., at which point Ben Hardaway took over, doing an excellent impersonation of Blanc's vocal creation. After the studio closed briefly from 1948–50, Lantz needed a new voice for Woody. His wife, the actress Grace Stafford, secretly slipped her audition into a pile of tapes and Lantz picked her without knowing her identity (although this story could be another of Lantz's embellishments). Stafford then provided Woody's voice for the next two decades.

Lantz continued to make Woody Woodpecker cartoons until 1972 (albeit with a few short breaks), long after most studios had ceased production of their shorts, arguably making Woody Woodpecker the cartoon character with one of the longest shelf lives.

1940
USA

William Hanna and Joseph Barbera: Puss gets the Boot

Working at the MGM animation studios in the late 1930s were director William Hanna and Joseph Barbera, a storyboard artist and character designer. When the two were paired, one of the first cartoons they made was *Puss Gets the Boot*. This concerned a cat called Jasper trying to catch a mouse. Evidently no one thought it was anything special until it later emerged that it had become a big favorite with theater audiences and that it had then been nominated for an Academy Award.

In *Puss Gets the Boot* Jasper's design is quite different from what would later become the look for Tom. Jasper's body is more kittenlike, with a rounder face, fluffier fur, and bigger feet, although, somewhat contradictorilly, Jasper's face is also more aggressive and adult. The design of the unnamed mouse in the cartoon is virtually unchanged from the later look of Jerry, however. One difference is that we hear the mouse saying a prayer in a squeaky little voice, whereas a familiar characteristic of the pair in future years was their speechlessness. The story follows the now-familiar path of the mouse managing to turn the tables on the bullying cat, this time by breaking, or threatening to break, the glass and crockery in the house after the cat is told by the maid, Mammy Two-Shoes, that he will be evicted if there are any more breakages.

After the success of *Puss Gets the Boot*, Hanna and Barbera were set to work making more shorts about the cat and mouse. A competition was held among MGM staff to choose a new name for the duo, and Tom and Jerry was selected. They became MGM's most popular characters and are among the most famous of all cartoon personalities. The theater shorts were made right up until 1967 and after that were created for television, with the TV production ongoing, practically to the present day.

1940
USA

Disney: Pinocchio

Pinocchio is considered by many to be Disney's masterpiece, the culmination of the previous two decades of phenomenal progress. Certainly the six years after *Snow White and the Seven Dwarfs* produced the most astonishing boldness, quantity, and quality of work from any animation studio before or since, and it seems incredible that five of the greatest animated features of all time were produced in this short burst of activity.

The large use of rotoscoping of the human characters in *Snow White* was hardly apparent in *Pinocchio*, leaving more room for the brilliant character animation that the Disney Studios was now effortlessly achieving. Here, the animation of the Blue Fairy alone was rotoscoped and is therefore somewhat dull in comparison with the lively animation elsewhere. The sparkly effect of the fairy's wand was animated by an unlikely new recruit to the studio, German abstract animation legend Oskar Fischinger.

The animation of the evil characters (and this is one cartoon where they really are evil) is particularly memorable. The scene where Stromboli, the greedy and bullying puppet showman, rages in his cluttered and bouncing gypsy caravan, is a brilliant sequence, as are the spectacular undersea moments featuring the unforgettable and terrifying Monstro the Whale. The utterly amoral Honest John and his idiot sidekick Gideon are perhaps the seediest and most reprehensible duo in the whole history of animation.

Other treasures to be found in the movie are the scenes where characters take long walks through the richly-painted environments, the camera seeming to follow them into the frame and back through the multiple layers of background and foreground detail.

The fact that a masterwork like *Pinocchio* was a financial failure, on initial release at least (like other Disney classics it has since multiplied its earnings through theatrical rerelease over the decades) has been put down to many reasons, mainly to do with the outbreak of World War II and the subsequent loss of foreign markets. Even the previous year's release of the Fleisher Studios' disappointing *Gulliver's Travels* was blamed by some at Disney for spoiling the public's appetite for animation. But with the innocent Pinocchio being sucked into one nightmarish experience after another by a succession of sleazy bad guys, perhaps the film was darker than the public expected and so did not provide the escapism that the USA needed in a time of depression and looming world war.

As with many early Disney films, *Pinocchio* went way over its original budget, as Walt Disney called a halt to production halfway through and demanded a whole new approach to the designs and personalities of Pinocchio and Jiminy Cricket. The initial, more "realistic" designs, although closer to the concept of Carlo Collodi's original book, were deemed not appealing enough to audiences. Pinocchio's character was also thought too harsh and needed to be rewritten as more innocent and childlike. Another change made was that, while originally Gideon was voiced by Mel Blanc, the legendary voice artist behind Warner Bros. characters such as Bugs Bunny, Daffy Duck, and Porky the Pig, it was later decided to make the character mute and all that survives of Blanc's performance is a hiccup.

Pinocchio, 1940

1941

USA

Disney: Fantasia

Fantasia began life as a special-edition *Silly Symphonies* short, designed as a vehicle to launch a redesigned Mickey Mouse and boost his flagging popularity. It soon became clear to Walt and Roy Disney that the huge expense of the ambitious cartoon they were planning meant that it could never turn a profit as a short. As the idea developed into a feature film, with the involvement of composer and music critic Deems Taylor and leading conductor Leopold Stokowski, it became in some ways Disney's attempt to be taken seriously as an artist and provide a showcase for his best animators. By attempting to visualize and even enhance the work of the great composers, Disney ambitiously wanted to create the ultimate experience with the idea of using animation as a form of visual music. It was a typically bold venture, which can be considered a success as a spectacle, for raising the idea of animation as an art form, and for introducing classical music to children and mainstream audiences. However, on initial release at least, it was a financial failure.

    Fantasia includes eight different segments set to eight different pieces of music. While all of them are superbly animated, some sequences of the movie have been criticized for straying too far into kitsch. The sequences consist of:

    • "Toccata and Fugue in D Minor": Johann Sebastian Bach. Features footage of the orchestra and then segues into Disney's first abstract animation, inspired by the work of Oskar Fischinger, who briefly worked on the movie.

    • "The Nutcracker Suite": Pyotr Ilyich Tchaikovsky. Features dancing mushrooms, fairies, and flowers as the seasons change into one another.

    • "The Sorcerer's Apprentice": Paul Dukas. Features Mickey Mouse as the trainee wizard who tries to use his master's powers to save him from chores, with disastrous consequences. This is one of Mickey's most famous roles, brilliantly animated and probably the only Mickey film in which the comedy is overtaken by truly frightening events.

Fantasia, 1941

• "The Rite of Spring": Igor Stravinsky. An illustration of prehistory, from the birth of the planet flowing with volcanic lava to the dawning and then extinction of the dinosaurs.

• "Intermission/Meet the Soundtrack": In the original movie theater screenings of *Fantasia*, the orchestra were shown leaving the "stage" in live-action footage, and an intermission followed. Afterward there was a short jazz "jam session" during which elaborate animated waveforms of music were shown as an illustration of how a soundtrack is recorded.

• "The Pastoral Symphony": Ludwig van Beethoven. Features a festival taking place with Greek gods, centaurs, fauns, and other mythological creatures, which is interrupted by the god Zeus hurling lightning bolts. This sequence first attracted controversy for the female centuars' nudity and then in later years for the African appearance of the servant figures.

• "Dance of the Hours": Amilcare Ponchielli. This comedic sequence is notable for the genuinely funny and beautifully animated ballet sequences of ostriches, then elephants, hippopotamuses, and alligators, and the ensuing chaos when they all attempt to dance together.

• "The Night on Bald Mountain": Modest Mussorgsky, and "Ave Maria": Franz Schubert. In which the demon Chernabog summons various monstrous creatures of the night. This section is a pièce de résistance for animator Bill Tytla and again shows Disney's willingness to tackle dark and powerful subject matter. The sequence ends with the tolling of a bell and a procession of monks walking through a forest near the mountain to the accompaniment of "Ave Maria."

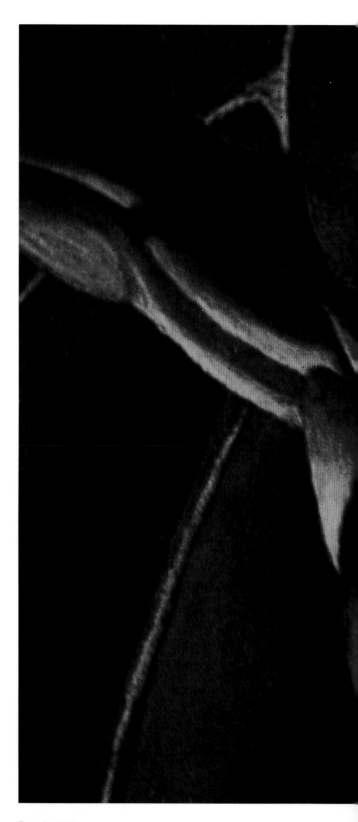

Fantasia, 1941

1941

USA

Disney: Dumbo

Dumbo was in many ways a back-to-basics exercise for Disney after the ambition and elaborations of *Pinocchio* and *Fantasia*, with the aim of making some money back from the losses of these two features. Despite this relative lack of artistic ambition, the movie is a perennial favorite and is recognized as one of the Studios' greatest achievements, mainly because it does what the Disney Studios does best: tells a good story using superb, emotive animation.

The story was adapted from an obscure children's book by Helen Aberson and Harold Pearl, which Walt Disney came across and gave to his team. The plot was fleshed out, storyboarded, and was proceeding toward production when Disney cancelled the project. Two staff writers, Dick Huemer and Joe Grant, were convinced the project had potential;

they picked it up and started working on it again before showing sections of the new version to Walt Disney, who put it back in production.

Dumbo is the shortest of Disney's features, but even taking that into account, the production was apparently one of the cheapest, fastest, and easiest of all, with everyone responding to the simplicity and charm of the project. The story concerns a female elephant, Jumbo, who longs for a child. When the stork brings her a precious bundle she is filled with happiness, only to be shocked by the cruel taunts of the other elephants, who mock her baby's unusually large ears and name him Dumbo. Eventually driven into a rage by the jibes, Jumbo lashes out and is imprisoned as a mad elephant, leaving her heartbroken child to fend for himself. Rejected by the other elephants, Dumbo befriends a mouse called Timothy, who, needless to say, the other elephants are scared of. Timothy has the idea for Dumbo

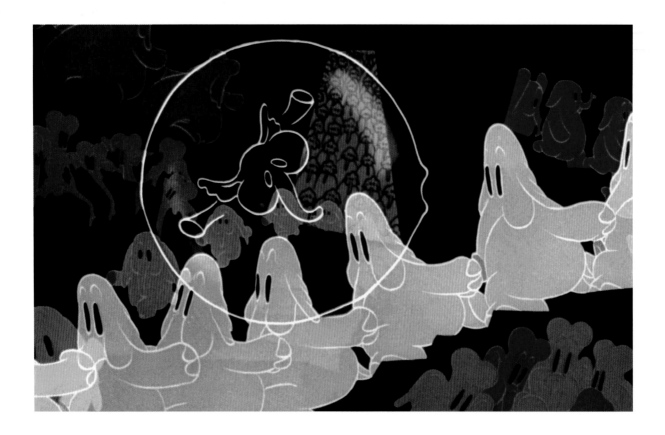

to become the star of the circus by using his big ears to fly, thus turning a problem into an advantage.

The emotionally punchy nature of the story was translated into many powerful character scenes; the mother's joy and then shock turning to pain and anger at the cruelty of the other elephants is gut-wrenching stuff, and the elation of the shy, sad, and confidence-drained Dumbo eventually managing to fly is heart-warming indeed. Perhaps the most famous sequence is the surreal fantasy that accompanies the "Pink Elephants on Parade" song, in which an accidentally inebriated Dumbo hallucinates marching and dancing elephants. A beautiful, purely surreal sequence, it is impossible to do justice to it by describing it in words—it simply has to be seen.

Some discontent had been brewing for a while at the Disney studio, and during the production of *Dumbo* a strike broke out. Disney was hurt by what he saw as disloyalty after everything he had done for his workforce and for animation in general. The strikers are thought to be caricatured in the movie when a group of drunken clowns march off to "hit the big boss for a raise."

Dumbo succeeded in its basic aim of making money back for Disney after his recent losses and, despite the bombing of Pearl Harbor just after its release, became Disney's biggest grossing film of the 1940s.

Dumbo, 1941

1941
USA

Fleischer Studios: Superman

After the feature film *Gulliver's Travels* had disappointed financially and the *Betty Boop* shorts had finished production, the Fleischer brothers were struggling to find new material and new sources of income. When their financiers Paramount suggested an animated version of the popular *Superman* comics, Dave Fleischer was reluctant, saying it would be too expensive. Paramount were willing to pay, however, and the resulting series was one of the Fleischers' finest hours.

With larger budgets the animators were able to spend time designing, animating, and creating rich special effects for the series. Unlike in previous Fleischer productions, they were able to pencil test the animation, and after they were animated, the figures were often handrendered with a three-dimensional look. The stylization of the camera angles and the design also gave the series a film-noir feel.

In the series, plucky journalist Lois Lane pursues her story into dangerous situations and uncovers evil plots with photographer Clark Kent trailing behind. But when trouble looms, Superman appears to save the day. The Fleischers appear to have learned the lesson from *Gulliver's Travels* and here they did not avoid the scary stuff—giant robots, mad scientists, escaped gorillas, and mummies on the loose are all seen off by the caped crusader in splendid fashion.

The Fleischer brothers made eight *Superman* cartoons before they lost control over their studio following Paramount's takeover in 1941. Paramount renamed the company Famous Studios and made nine more *Superman* episodes. The Famous Studios episodes differed from the first eight in that they were more concerned with gung-ho patriotic stories, no doubt relating to America's war effort, rather than the classic, giant-robot-type science fiction of the Fleischers' episodes.

Superman, 1941

As is often the case with work from this era, *Superman* now seems rather slow-paced and the stories may seem slightly banal to modern audiences who have been bombarded with sophisticated twists on the superhero idea. Despite this, the Fleischers' *Superman* series is still regarded as one of the best animated superhero adaptations. Its strong 1940s style was a big influence on such creations as the acclaimed 1990s TV superhero revivals *Batman: The Animated Series* and *Superman: The Animated Series* (both produced by DC Comics and Warner Bros.), as well as the award-winning graphic novel *Batman: The Dark Knight Returns* by Frank Miller.

China

Wan brothers: Tie Shan gong zhu (Princess Iron Fan)

The Wan brothers, Wan Laiming, Wan Guchan, Wan Chaochen, and Wan Dihuan, were China's animation pioneers. While working as live-action movie set designers for the Great Wall Film Company in Shanghai, Laiming and Guchan made China's first animated film, the short *Uproar in the Studio* in 1924, an experiment inspired by the Fleischers' *Out of the Inkwell*. They continued to produce shorts throughout the 1920s and 1930s; at first these were based on traditional stories but then became more patriotic in nature around the time of the Japanese attack on Shanghai in 1932. When the Japanese army invaded Shanghai in 1937, the Wan brothers fled to unoccupied Wuhan, from where they made several politically-motivated films in protest at the invasion. When Wuhan also fell to the Japanese, the Wan brothers returned to Shanghai and, now working for the Shinhwa company, they opened a studio in the area known as the French Concession, which had a degree of independence respected by the Japanese. In 1939 they saw Disney's *Snow White and the Seven Dwarfs,* which inspired them to make China's first animated feature film, *Tie shan gong zhu* (*Princess Iron Fan*), based on part of the sixteenth-century Buddhist tale, *Journey to the West.*

The movie's characters, animated using rotoscoping in their movements, have a half-animal, half-man type of design. This look, typical of much Asian animation, differs from the Western style of anthropomorphized, cute, animal-based characters, in that while having animal's heads or faces, the bodies are generally very human (and thus more easily rotoscoped). The story concerns a monk, a priest, a pig, and a monkey king who travel up a mountain of flames to find sacred Buddhist texts. The monkey king obtains a magic fan from the queen of the buffaloes in order to help them on their adventures.

Princess Iron Fan is a remarkable achievement considering the very difficult circumstances under which it was made. It was produced during the turmoil of war by 70 artists working for 16 months solid in a small and basic space that left them at the mercy of the cold of winter and the heat of summer. It went on to achieve success in China and the South Pacific area during the war years, possibly due to its underlying theme of people joining forces to defeat an oppressor.

1942
USA

Disney: Bambi

Disney's *Bambi* was based on Felix Salten's bestselling book, *Bambi, a Life in the Woods*, the story of a deer and the animals around him in the forest as he grows to become a mighty stag. The movie was developed to be less hard-hitting than the book, but despite this it contains some powerful emotional scenes; the sequence where Bambi's mother is killed by hunters, although done with subtlety, is one of the most moving scenes in animation history and is often described as one of the saddest moments in cinema.

The development process of *Bambi* was fairly extended. This was partly due to the need to adapt the book into something with a different tone, requiring a difficult combination of naturalistic animals living serious lives in a realistic forest (as in the book) with Disney-style humanized animals and character gags. That the combination works and that the stylization never pushed far enough from the natural forms that the different tones ended up clashing, is a tribute to the years of planning that went into the movie. The rich forest environment is also one of Disney's best examples of multiplane camera use, the techniques learned in previous movies were here used to perfection and pushed to give the forest three-dimensionality and a real, living atmosphere.

Other reasons for the five-year development time before production began include the research and training that Disney asked his main animators and artists to undertake in order to achieve the naturalistic look of the film. Artists and background designers were sent to forests in Vermont and Maine to sketch and photograph the wildlife; a pair of fawns were borrowed by the studio for a period, and a mini zoo was set up on site to study other animals. Unused to drawing animals realistically, the animators worked much slower, only managing to produce a fraction of the amount of their usual output.

Although a critical success, *Bambi* lost money on its initial release, but went into profit after its 1947 rerelease. The reasons for its initial failure were the USA's entry into World War II, and possibly the slightly difficult appeal for some of a story where humans are essentially the bad guys. There were also some voices of protest from the American gun lobby that the film was "antihunting," but these probably had little impact on most potential audiences. Despite these initial hiccups, it has now been recognized as one of the greatest animated movies of all time, and regularly comes near the top of critics' and public polls. The techniques of animating and designing realistic nature perfected here were invaluable in future Disney movies.

Bambi, 1942

1942
USA

1942
USA/Hungar

Paul Terry: The Mouse of Tomorrow

The character of Mighty Mouse came about, like a lot of cartoons, as a spin-off or parody of something else, in this case, Superman. Indeed, the character was originally called Super Mouse, a name that makes sense in his first adventure, *The Mouse of Tomorrow*, which explains his transformation from repressed mouse into Super Mouse as a result of the dubious gag of eating "super" foods from the "super" market. (The reason the character's name was changed to Mighty Mouse is often attributed to legal threats from Superman's creators, but reportedly it had more to do with an exemployee of Paul Terry's who published an unrelated comic strip entitled "Super Mouse" just as *The Mouse of Tomorrow* was released.)

The cartoon's plot involves all of the many mice in a town being chased by an equal number of cats, before their climactic rescue by the superhero. This provided the basic formula for most of the Mighty Mouse episodes—mice are in trouble, Mighty Mouse shows up and rescues them. The film was one of Terry's most successful and demanded a return from its hero, and the second in the series was released a month later.

Mighty Mouse went on to be a popular character in theater shorts, but it was not until Terry sold his company to CBS in 1955 that Mighty Mouse became a beloved fixture of children's television worldwide. For the television transmissions, the title graphics of the Super Mouse cartoons were changed to Mighty Mouse, and the new name was also dubbed over the old soundtracks.

In 1987 Ralph Bakshi, who had worked on *Mighty Mouse* cartoons while employed at Terrytoons at the beginnng of his career, produced *The New Adventures of Mighty Mouse*. This ran for two series, but caused some controversy due to its somewhat adult humor and alleged references to drug use.

George Pal: Tulips Shall Grow

After his early life in Hungary, George Pal worked as a set designer in Germany for the giant state-run UFA film company from 1930, where he founded Trickfilm-Studio and patented his Pal-doll system, or Puppetoons as it was known in the USA. This was a system of animation involving puppets with replaceable parts, such as heads and hands, enabling controlled expression and lip-synch.

In 1933 Pal was investigated by the Getsapo for no other reason than being Hungarian; he left Germany for Czechoslovakia, then Paris, and ended up working in Holland from 1934 until 1940, when, with the help of his friend Walter Lantz, he was invited to work for Paramount in the USA. He stayed in the USA for the rest of his life, becoming one of Hollywood's most famous producers of live-action science fiction movies.

One of his first American short cartoons, *Tulips Shall Grow*, was made in Pal's distinctive Puppetoon style, and was motivated by revenge toward the Nazis who had victimized him in Germany and forced him to flee Holland. A thinly-disguised attack on the Nazi invasion, the film shows two young Dutch lovers happily romancing until the idyllic cartoon version of Holland is torn apart by the arrival of a "screwball army" of metal robotic creatures with their tanks and bat-like planes.

1942
USA

Warner Bros. and Chuck Jones: The Dover Boys at Pimento University

The Dover Boys, as this Warners Bros. short is commonly known, is often cited as the first example of the simplified, stylized animation that became the hallmark of the UPA studio in the next few years, although there had been experimental movements in this direction previously from other studios, including Disney in the USA and Larkins Studio in the UK.

The characteristics of this new form of "limited animation" included heavily stylized, simplified character designs, using lots of angular shapes in contrast to the soft, rounder designs that were typical of the Disney style. The poses were most often held quite still in profile, before invariably whipping from pose to pose in one or two frames, sometimes using a smear technique that blends and trails the image across to the next extreme position, a technique that would come to typify Chuck Jones' style in future Bugs Bunny and Road Runner cartoons.

The title and characters are a parody of *The Rover Boys*, a popular series of young people's adventure books that were published in the early twentieth century. The cartoon has some genuinely funny moments, particularly the character who crops up from time to time, interrupting the proceedings like someone who has mistakenly wandered across stage.

As the director, Chuck Jones had been encouraged to simplify his more elaborate design tendencies, and this was the result. Producer Leon Schlesinger and the Warner executives apparently found its experimental style too extreme however, and nearly fired Jones, who only kept his job as he was deemed too hard to replace.

John Hubley, one of the founders of the UPA studio, cited *The Dover Boys* as an influence on the UPA style. Bob Canon, an animator on the film, went on to be a key member of the UPA team and Chuck Jones would later direct the milestone UPA political campaigning film, *Hell Bent for Election* in 1944.

Biography

Chuck Jones

Chuck Jones is recognized as one of the greatest ever animators, and was the man behind some of the world's most famous and best-loved cartoon characters. Born in 1912, Jones grew up in Hollywood, and his childhood included early experiences with the entertainment business as he worked as an extra on comedy films. He studied at the Choinard Art Institute (now known as the California Institute of the Arts), and in 1932 he got a job working for Ub Iwerks. In 1936, he was hired as an animator at the Leon Schlesinger Studio, which was later sold to Warner Bros.

His time at Warner Bros. is now seen as a golden age for the studio, as Jones worked alongside fellow animation greats Friz Freleng, Tex Avery, and Bob Clampett. Jones directed *The Dover Boys* in 1942, a project which taught him to simplify his design style, and after this he created his best-known characters, including Road Runner, Wile E. Coyote, and Pepe le Pew. While at Warner Bros., Jones also worked on other iconic characters, such as Bugs Bunny, Daffy Duck, and Porky Pig. He pushed animation to its imaginative limits, creating self-aware characters who interacted with their animator, as in the classic *Duck Amuck* (1953). (For more on *Duck Amuck*, see page 160.)

After the Warner Bros. animation studio closed in 1962, Jones joined MGM, where he worked on several *Tom & Jerry* cartoons, produced the perennial Christmas classic *How the Grinch Stole Christmas!* (1966) and directed the feature-length *The Phantom Tollbooth* (1970). (For more on these films, see pages 195 and 216.)

In 1962 he established Chuck Jones Enterprises, making television specials, and he also collaborated with the UPA studio on *Gay Purr-ee* (1962). (For more on *Gay Purr-ee*, see page 186.) His later work included animated segments in the 1992 movie *Stay Tuned*.

Jones received three Oscars, as well as an Academy Award for lifetime achievement, along with numerous awards from other organizations around the world. His 1957 Wagner-inspired comedy short *What's Opera, Doc?*, which featured Elmer Fudd as Siegfried and Bugs in disguise as Brunhilde, was added to the American National Film Registry in 1992. Chuck Jones died in 2002.

1943

USA

Biography

Tex Avery

Tex Avery: Red Hot Riding Hood

Red Hot Riding Hood is the first of Tex Avery's *Red Riding Hood* films, which were made soon after his arrival at MGM from Warner Bros., and proved to be MGM's most successful cartoons to date. Avery's style of wildly pushing the gags to their limits, into areas of the surreal, had a big effect at MGM and on the cartoon world in general.

Red Hot Riding Hood starts off as the traditional fairy tale, but Avery's typically self-aware characters rebel and demand the cartoon does something different for a change. The story restarts with the wolf, a regular Avery character, as a city slicker in a nightclub being driven to distraction in extreme, snappy eye-popping style by Red Riding Hood as a sexy showgirl, later pursuing her to Granny's penthouse apartment. The wolf's lust-crazed antics were frowned upon by the censor for being too suggestive, and cuts were demanded.

The cartoon is often cited as one of the all-time greats and was immensely popular at the time. The "red hot" showgirl, physically based on Betty Grable and later an influence on the Jessica Rabbit character in *Who Framed Roger Rabbit*, was animated by Preston Blair, author of *How to Draw Animated Cartoons*, one of the best "how to" animation series of books, still in use by students and animators today.

Born Frederick Bean Avery in Texas in 1908, Tex Avery is one of America's greatest animators, whose distinctive style and sense of humor set the tone for much of the best work produced by Warner Bros. and MGM. He began his career in the early 1930s working as a painter and storyboard artist at Walter Lantz's studio, where he worked on Oswald the Rabbit cartoons. During his time there, he lost his sight in one eye in an accident, which affected his depth perception.

Avery worked at the Warner Bros. animation studio between 1935 and 1941, where he created Porky Pig and Daffy Duck. He also invented Bugs Bunny's catchphrase, "What's up, doc?" A perfectionist and a master of comic timing, Avery devoted huge amounts of time and effort into perfecting the gags with which he filled each cartoon he worked on.

In 1941 he joined MGM, where he further developed his distinctive animation style. He preferred to focus more on slapstick and gags, rather than creating enduring characters who could star in series of cartoons. Like his Warner Bros. colleague Chuck Jones, Avery rejected realism in favor of pushing the limits of animation, creating surreal cartoons whose sophisticated humor appealed to adults as much as children. At MGM, he made cartoons that subverted traditional fairy tales, as characters such as Cinderella and Little Red Riding Hood became sexy, modern women.

Avery briefly returned to Lantz's studio in 1954, where he worked on the penguin character, Chilly Willy. In later years, he worked on television commercials, including successful campaigns for Raid and Frito-Lay.

An inspiration to many future animators, Tex Avery received the Winsor McCay award in 1974. He died in 1980.

1943
USA

Disney: Der Fuehrer's Face and World War II propaganda

During World War II, like many other animators and animation companies worldwide, the Walt Disney Studios produced a number of propaganda films for the US government in order to help the war effort and to help the company survive this time of economic hardship. Another motive was to try and recoup the losses suffered from *Pinocchio* and *Fantasia*, although the profit margins that Disney charged on many of the government films were small or nonexistent as part of his contribution to the war effort. Disney was contracted to make 32 propaganda, training, and educational shorts from 1941–1945; this kind of volume multiplied the studios' output many times over and was achieved by producing the films in a much simpler animation style than usual.

The best-known of these propaganda films was the Donald Duck short *Der Fuehrer's Face*, winner of the 1943 Oscar for best animated short. In this satirical cartoon directed by Jack Kinney, Donald is a rather unwilling citizen of Hitler's Germany, which is plastered with images of Hitler's face, each of which Donald is expected to salute, even when working an intensive 48-hour shift on a production line. The film is a typically wonderfully-animated Donald short, and a lot of the humor rests in the volatile duck's growing rage at the ridiculous and increasingly surreal demands put on him by the Nazi state. The title of the film was changed from *Donald Duck in Nutzi Land* in order to relate to a hit novelty tune "Der Fuerher's Face" by Spike Jones and his City Slickers, which voiced contempt toward the Nazi leader and his delusional master race egotism.

Other Disney wartime propaganda films included *Education for Death; the Raising of a* Nazi (1943), the story of how a German child called Hans is brainwashed from birth to be a good Nazi and a cold killer. The film is as strange as it sounds; its Disney stylings and gags are at odds with the rather disturbing subject matter and depictions of a sinister fascist state. *Reason and Emotion* (1943) is an interesting short with an adult psychological theme, again not something usually associated with Disney, concerning the struggle between our sense of reason and our emotions, and how Hitler used the rabble-rousing potential of the latter. This film is a good example of how these projects allowed the animators to experiment with different styles from the usual Disney house style; the characters here are often more caricatured, simplified, and stylized, at times going toward the kind of designs that UPA would become known for in the 1950s.

Victory Through Air Power (1943) was a feature-length PR push for Major Alexander de Seversky's proposal for more resources to be concentrated on building war planes. Disney felt strongly enough about this issue to devote his own resources to making the film. The realistic designs and the lovely 1940s-style special effects details recall the Fleischers' popular *Superman* series. Reportedly, it was not until Franklin D. Roosevelt had watched *Victory Through Air Power* that he decided that the long-range bombing strategy would be part of the USA's battle plan.

1943

Japan

Kenzo Masaoka: Kumo to Chûrippu (The Spider and the Tulip)

Kenzo Masaoka was one of Japan's animation pioneers, beginning work in 1930 when he used his redundancy deal from a film studio to make his first animated film *Nansensu monogatari dai ippen: Sarugashima* (*The Monkey Island*, 1931). He then worked at a number of companies as animator, actor, and also as a special effects artist, a talent for which he became known as the "Japanese Méliès." He created the first Japanese animation with sound, *Chikara to onna no yo no naka* (1933), and the first made entirely using cel animation, *Chagama Ondo* (*The Dance of the Chagamas*, 1934).

He later established his own studio, but at the outbreak of World War II small animation companies were consolidated into larger units and pressed into producing propaganda. Masaoka took a job as head of the Shouchiku Animation Production Department, where he made a series of shorts. The most famous of these films is *Kumo to Chûrippu* (*The Spider and the Tulip*), based on a prize-winning short story about a lothario spider who tries to trap a cute ladybug, only to be thwarted by a kind tulip. The cute character animation is silky smooth and the multiplane effects are excellent as the camera moves around the beautiful, Japanese-style garden backgrounds. At a running time of 15 minutes, the slight musical story is perhaps overstretched, but overall this short compares very well technically with most American shorts released at the time, even without color. The Japanese authorities took a different view and reprimanded the filmmakers for producing a film with no propaganda angle. This was a disappointing reaction, as films like this stand as testaments to Japan's status as a cultural superpower.

1944–1945

USA

UPA's early films

In 1943 the ex-Disney artists Zack Schwartz, David Hilberman, and Stephen Bosustow formed what would later be called United Productions of America (UPA), with the idea of pursuing the modernist "ideal future" of animation. In 1942, Hilberman, one of the leaders of the 1941 strike at the Walt Disney Studios, was working at Warner Bros. where he participated with other artists in making a film for the Office of War Information. The film, made in the evening with the artists giving their time free of charge, was entitled *Point Rationing of Foods*, with Hilberman designing and Chuck Jones directing. With its simplified design and limited animation, the film does not look much like the other Warner Bros. cartoons made at the time.

In 1943 another ex-Disney artist, John Hubley, received a commission from the United Auto Workers union to make a film supporting Franklin D. Roosevelt's reelection. He designed and storyboarded the film and took it to Hilberman, Schwartz, and Bosustow's new company, then operating as Industrial Film and Poster Service.

Without a premises or a staff, the fledgling company made the film in Zack Schwartz's apartment with animators moonlighting from other studios. Chuck Jones, sneaking away from his post at Warner Bros., directed the film, called *Hell Bent for Election* (1944). It depicts a fast modern train, representing Roosevelt, racing with a broken-down old steam train, representing the Republican candidate, Thomas E. Dewey. A working man operating the switches must choose between the trains while being bugged by a cranky old Dewey-supporting goblin. The animation of the characters is not very different from general cartoon designs, but the stylings of the backgrounds, trains, colors, and camera angles feels modernist and fresh, giving the overall feel of something halfway between Chuck Jones' films for Warner Bros and the future UPA style of "limited" animation.

Flat Hatting (1945), an instructional film for the Navy, shows a new modernist graphic style beginning to emerge in the context of a clever, satirical script. *The Brotherhood of Man,* directed by Robert Cannon in 1945, is less well known than *Hell Bent for Election*, but it is a better film and more definitively UPA in style. It was beautifully designed and animated by Hubley and tells a progressive lesson about racial integration. Also sponsored by the United Auto Workers, this time to address tensions at the Union's branches, the film depicts a man living in a mixed ethnic neighborhood. While he is excited by the diversity around him, his mean-spirited alter ego whispers dark thoughts to him about the differences between men. The narrator corrects these fears with scientific material from the 1943 anthropological leaflet "Races of Mankind" about how we are all the same under the skin and behind superficial cultural differences. *The Brotherhood of Man* was nominated for an Oscar in 1943.

Hell Bent for Election, 1944

The Brotherhood of Man, 1945

1945
Spain

1945
UK/Hungary

Arturo Moreno: Garbancito de La Mancha (The Enchanted Sword)

While looking for a distributor for his animated short, *El capitan Tormentoso* (*The Boisterous Captain,* 1942), Arturo Moreno, a screenwriter and director, met producers and distributors Ramón Balet and José María Blay. Impressed with his short, Balet and Blay asked Moreno to make Spain's first animated feature film.

Garbancito de La Mancha (*The Enchanted Sword*), adapted from a poem by Julian Pemartin, concerns the boy Garbancito (meaning little chickpea) and his efforts to free the Spanish region of La Mancha from a man-eating ogre with the aid of a magic sword, a goat, and a fairy who gives him the ability to change into a chickpea.

The movie was successful with audiences in Spain and abroad, leading to a sequel *Alegres vacaciones* (*Happy Holidays*, 1948), in which the characters travel to surrounding lands. Another follow-up film was made by the studio Balet y Blay, *Los sueños de Tay-Pi* (*The Visions of Tay-Pi*, 1951). However, Moreno had moved to Venezuela by this time, so the Austrian Franz Winterstein took over the directing duties. The movie, a jungle story, was a commercial failure and led to the studio's closure.

Halas & Batchelor: Handling Ships

During World War II, the newly-established British studio Halas & Batchelor, like many other animation studios worldwide, made a variety of government-sponsored propaganda and information films. The studio, based around the talents of Jewish Hungarian émigré John Halas and his wife Joy Batchelor, made military training films, as well as a series of anti-Nazi films for the Middle East featuring an Arab boy character called Abu, a Nazi snake, and an Italian bullfrog.

These were all shorts with the exception of *Handling Ships*, a 70-minute feature-length instructional film explaining how to pilot ships, made for the Navy and never shown in public theaters. Director John Halas used stop-frame animated models of Naval craft to produce what was Britain's first feature-length animated film. In 1948 *Water for Fire Fighting*, a second feature-length instructional film, was commissioned by the Home Office.

Halas & Batchelor

Founded in 1940 by married couple John Halas and Joy Batchelor, Halas & Batchelor became the most influential animation studio in Britain and one of the largest in Europe.

John Halas was born in Hungary in 1912; influenced by the Bauhaus movement, he initially trained as a painter, before learning the art of animation from George Pal. After various artistic endeavors in Budapest and Paris, Halas formed his own studio in 1932. He was then offered a contract in London and while there, he met English animator Joy Batchelor, who answered a job advert Halas had placed. One of the few female animators working at the time, Batchelor wrote, directed, and designed many of the company's films.

After setting up their studio in London, they produced commercials and then, with encouragement from influential producer John Grierson, made animated information and propaganda films as part of Britain's war effort. After the war, Halas and Batchelor created the character Charley to introduce the government's new social security system. They followed this with many more examples of sophisticated adult-aimed work, such as their masterpiece, *Animal Farm*. (For more on *Animal Farm*, see page 162.) Halas & Batchelor has been called the British UPA, although they had been experimenting with modernist design before the establishment of the American company, who they were friendly with due to Halas' international links.

Both Halas and Batchelor believed that animation was an art form that could be used to do good, and these humanitarian concerns inspired much of their work. Halas, a founder member of ASIFA (Association Internationale du Film d'Animation), believed in building bridges between animators of different nations as a way to work toward world peace.

During its 50-year existence, the studio constantly experimented with different techniques, from low-tech paper cutouts through to pioneering work with computer animation. Halas' background in Bauhaus philosophies of modernism and technology in art meant he saw computer technology as an aid rather than a threat to animators. (For more on Halas & Batchelor's computer animation, see *Autobahn* on page 239 and *Dilemma* on page 244.) Due to their invention and creativity and their resistance to turning their animation production into an industrial conveyor belt, the studio became one of the world's most influential, long lasting, and prolific, producing over 2,000 films, in genres ranging from propaganda and information films, to television series and feature films.

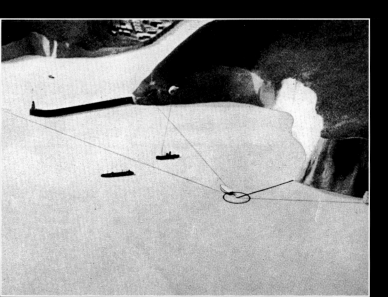

Handling Ships, 1945

1946
USA

Disney: Saludos Amigos, The Three Caballeros, and Song of the South

During the war years, as well as producing government propaganda films, the Walt Disney Studios consolidated by making a few cheaper B-movie-type features that were "package" movies, or collections of shorter subjects packaged together (also known as "anthology" or "portmanteau" films). *Saludos Amigos* (1943), made up of several South American-based shorts on the general theme of "love thy neighbor," was inspired by Disney's 1941 trip to the area along with his top artists. It was popular enough to lead to a follow-up, *The Three Caballeros* (1945). This film was based around the idea of Donald Duck opening seven presents from his South American friends, which link up short stories of his travels around the continent.

The Three Caballeros was nothing special in the story department, but was interesting and fresh visually due to some experimental special effects supervised by Ub Iwerks, who had returned to the studio a couple of years earlier after an unsuccessful attempt to start a rival studio. The film was Disney's first since the *Alice* comedies in the 1920s to mix live action and animation, and was the most sophisticated use of this technique to date.

When *Song of the South* was released in 1946 however, it became clear that the live action/animation sequences in *The Three Caballeros* were just a rehearsal for the spectacular use of the technique in the new film. *Song of the South* presents several of the Uncle Remus stories from the books of Joel Chandler Harris. The animated stories are linked by scenes featuring live-action actors portraying Uncle Remus and two children. As Uncle Remus tells his stories, the film dissolves in and out of animation to see the stories played out. In the final magical sequence, the animated characters arrive in the live-action scene and the live-action world turns to animation as the characters walk into the sunset singing the theme song. Animation and live action would not be mixed together as successfully as this until Disney's *Mary Poppins* in 1964. The song from this final sequence, "Zip-A-Dee-Doo-Dah," was a

Song of the South, 1946

popular hit and won the 1947 Oscar for best song. *Song of the South* has never been released on video or DVD in the USA because of racial sensitivity to the portrayed image of the happy slave, although it has been rereleased theatrically and released in all formats in other areas of the world. According to writer Neal Gabler however, in his book *Walt Disney: The Triumph of the American Imagination* (2006), Walt Disney was sensitive to the potential for racial stereotyping or "Uncle Tom" accusations in this movie, and did what he could to prevent this by assigning Jewish left-wing writer Maurice Rapf to work on the script alongside southern writer Dalton Raymond.

UK

Larkins Studio: T for Teacher

After a short partnership with veteran producer Anson Dyer, animator Bill Larkins opened his own studio in London in the early 1940s. Producing training films for the army during World War II, his design skills were later put to good use getting the message across in information films like *Without Fear* and *The Spivs*.

Peter Sachs, a German émigré with an elegant design style based on German expressionist ideas, became a director at the studio. Larkins also worked with directors, animators, and trainees who would later become mainstays of the British animation scene, such as Denis Gilpin, Bob Godfrey, Philip Stapp, Ginger Gibbons, and Richard Taylor. Together they created films that were modernist and nonrepresentational in style. Along with the UK's Halas & Batchelor, America's UPA, and Croatia's Zagreb Film, Larkins Studio spearheaded the advance toward a stylized, simplified form of animation based on cutting-edge contemporary illustration and design, something that would become a tradition of the London animation scene in years to come. The reason Larkins Studio is not remembered as well as these other studios is probably that they produced only information films and no entertainment work of the kind that would be shown in later years on television or in movie theaters.

T for Teacher was a short film made for the tea bureau, giving instructions on how to make a cup of tea properly using the permitted rations. The animation and design are pushed to angular, jagged, and graphic extremes, that were very progressive for the time.

1947
Russia

Ivan Ivanov-Vano: Konyok-gorbunok (The Humpbacked Little Horse)

Ivan Ivanov-Vano was probably the most influential personality in Russia's conservative animation industry in the 1950s. The style of animation produced at this time is known as Soviet Realism, and was centered around the state-run Soyuzmultfilm studio. The general policy was of animation as a public service, providing traditional folk stories and educational films for children. Animators were told to use the system known as Éclair, which involved rotoscoping from live actors' movements. Influenced by Disney's popularism and often beautifully-crafted, the early creativity of soviet animation was however abandoned in favor of a rigid system of cel animation and a factory-like division of labor. The animators from the early years either adapted to the new methods or left animation entirely.

Ivanov-Vano's *Konyok-gorbunok* (*The Humpbacked Little Horse*) was a popular feature-length film based on a poem by Pyotr Pavlovich Yershov with a rather complicated plot about three brothers and a magic flying horse, with all the dialogue in rhyme. It was later remade by Ivanov-Vano and Soyuzmultfilm in 1975 due to deterioration of the original print; the original was also restored in 2004 for a DVD release.

Ivanov-Vano went on to make other successful films in this traditional style, including *The Story of a Dead Princess and a Brave Family* (1951); *Snegurochka* (*The Snow Maiden*, 1952); *Moidodyr* (1939, also remade 1954); *12 Mesyatsev* (*The Twelve Months*, 1956); and *Priklyucheniya Buratino* (*The Adventures of a Puppet*, 1959), based on the *Pinocchio* story.

Other notable Soyuzmultfilm works from this era were Zinaida and Valentina Brumberg's *Noch pered Rozhdestvom* (*The Night Before Christmas*, 1951), Lev Atamanov's *Zolotaya antilopa* (*The Golden Antelope*, 1954) and *Snezhnaya koroleva* (*The Snow Queen*, 1957). These films were popular in the USSR and were often successfully distributed and screened abroad.

1948
UK

Gaumont-British Animation: Animaland and Musical Paintbox

In 1945, David Hand, the director of Disney's *Snow White* and *Bambi*, was hired by the British film producer J. Arthur Rank to set up a Disney-style animation studio in the UK. In its short existence, the Gaumont-British Animation studio was a hive of creativity, and many animators learned their trade in its training school from the Disney masters hired to come over as supervisors. Gaumont-British made a series of commercials and instructional films, as well as two series of shorts for movie theaters: *Animaland*, consisting of nine films, and *Musical Paintbox*, for which 10 shorts were made. The main character in many of these films was a squirrel called Ginger Nutt. The first of these was *The Cuckoo* from the *Animaland* series.

The films were beautifully made, with the overall feel being somewhere between the lush, homely nature of Disney shorts and the madcap nature of Warner Bros. cartoons. Before the studio could really get underway however, Rank pulled the plug in 1949 because the films were unable to find a US distributor.

Konyok-gorbunok
(The Humpbacked Little Horse), 1975

1948

Czech Republic

Cisaruv slavík
(The Emperor's
Nightingale), 1948

Jirí Trnka and Milos Makovec: Cisaruv slavík (The Emperor's Nightingale)

Jirí Trnka learned his trade at an early age by making puppets with his grandmother; he then studied at the prestigious Prague School of Applied Arts. In 1936 he started a puppet theater that was dissolved at the outbreak of World War II. He soon translated his skill with puppets into animation and started to gain a reputation as one of the world's foremost masters of the art of stop-frame animation. From 1948, the Czech communist regime funded his films, although he was allowed to retain his artistic freedom.

In 1948 his first feature film, the first Czech animated feature, *Cisaruv slavík* (*The Emperor's Nightingale*) won worldwide acclaim and was picked up by Rembrandt Films in 1951 for distribution in the USA, for which a narration by Boris Karloff was added. The beautiful film is based on a Hans Christian Andersen tale and has been amazing audiences in the decades since its release.

Others of his highly-rated films include a western parody *Arie prerie* (*Song of the Prairie*, 1949); an adaptation of a short story by Anton Chekhov, *Román s basou* (*The Story of the Bass Cello*, 1949); a version of Jarosev Hasek's classic comic novel *Dobry voják Svejk* (*The Good Soldier Svejk*, 1955); an adaptation of Shakespeare's *A Midsummer Night's Dream*, *Sen noci svatojánské* (1959); and *Ruka* (*The Hand*, 1965).

1949
USA

Chuck Jones: Fast and Furry-ous

The Road Runner cartoons were created by Chuck Jones and writer Mike Maltese; their aim was to parody the chase scenes in other cartoons, such as MGM's *Tom and Jerry* series. They did this by creating the craziest chase of all, in which, instead of the pursued character winning by turning the tables on the pursuer, the chaser defeated himself through his own ineptitude. The series they created became perhaps the purest expression of the Warner Bros. style.

When it was made, *Fast and Furry-ous* was never considered the start of a series, yet despite this, the two characters are formally introduced to the audience. At the start of the cartoon the characters are "frozen" in a held frame with parodic scientific names presented in captions onscreen; the Coyote is "carnivorous vulgaris" and the Road Runner is "accelleratti incredibus." This became a tradition in the series.

Another tradition is Acme, the mail order company that supplies a variety of (usually malfunctioning) traps and gadgets. There have been various theories about the origin of this name, such as the acronym "A Company that Makes Everything," but the most likely theory is that Acme appeared as a brand in the Sears mail order catalogs in the early twentieth century.

Neither of the characters speak, although Wile E. Coyote (voiced by Mel Blanc) speaks in some cartoons he appeared in with Bugs Bunny. The Road Runner makes a "beep beep" noise, which was taken from the noise a Warners background artist called Paul Julian made when he was carrying large backgrounds about. Jones recorded Julian's "beep beep," speeded it up, and used it in the cartoons.

1949
USA

UPA: Ragtime Bear

In 1947 the FBI started searching for people with "communist leanings," and the free-thinking artists of UPA came under suspicion. With government films drying up, Columbia pictures stepped in and offered UPA a contract. The first films they produced were vehicles for characters called Fox and Crow entitled *Robin Hoodlum* (1948) and *The Magic Fluke* (1949). When these proved a critical and commercial success, UPA were allowed to create their own characters and they came up with Mister Magoo.

Magoo's character is that of a grumpy old man who refuses to admit his chronic near-sightedness. He was created by John Hubley and writer Millard Kaufman. Hubley apparently partly based him on his uncle Harry Woodruff, with W. C. Fields being another inspiration. Magoo was originally supposed to be a right-wing type, full of crazed ranting about everything and nothing, as a sort of revenge by Kaufman who had been blacklisted by Senator Joseph McCarthy's committee. The political-based rantings were toned down though, to leave just a few random, nonsensical outbursts.

In the first Magoo short, *Ragtime Bear*, the short-sighted Magoo mistakes a bear for his banjo-playing nephew, Waldo. Columbia suggested a series starring the bear, but Hubley and UPA thought the human character woud be better, after all the cartoon market was already flooded with animal stars. After this first short, Hubley took a back seat in the project and Pete Burness directed the shows.

The main character design is not particularly stylized, but the backgrounds are very graphic, stripped down, and modernist, featuring oblique angles and forced symmetry, in the UPA style.

Mister Magoo was a critical and commercial success. *When Magoo Flew* won the Academy Award in 1954 for animated short subject, and *Magoo's Puddle Jumper* won again in 1956. This ensured that Columbia continued to fund UPA, enabling directors like John Hubley and Robert Cannon to make their more experimental and groundbreaking one-off films.

Italy

Nino Pagot: I Fratelli Dinamite (The Dynamite Brothers); Anton Domenighini: La Rosa di Bagdad (The Rose of Baghdad)

I fratelli Dinamite (*The Dynamite Brothers*) and *La rosa di Bagdad* (*The Rose of Baghdad*) were two animated features produced independently of each other during the troubled war and postwar years in Italy, and therefore the fact that they were completed at all is somewhat of an achievement. The first Italian features in color (of the two *The Dynamite Brothers* was apparently completed first), both movies were launched at the Venice Film Festival in 1949 and were released simultaneously in the USA, so inevitably they have always been linked and compared to one another. The timing of their releases was a shame as, in any contest like this, there has to be a winner and a loser, whereas a few years' gap between their releases may have allowed them both success.

Nino Pagot's *The Dynamite Brothers* is notable for the involvement of several future big names of the Italian cartoon scene. Pagot later achieved success in the 1960s with his character Calimero the chicken, Osvaldo Cavandoli worked as an animator on the film years before he became famous for *La Linea* (*The Line*, 1972), and Attilo Giovaninni later worked with Bruno Bozzetto on *West and Soda* (1965). *The Dynamite Brothers* relates a series of misadventures that befall three young brothers, linking the tales together through the device of their aunt telling the stories to her friends. The stories are of variable interest, and the film is well crafted for its time although the animation is unspectacular. It fared poorly at the box office and the production company moved away from animated features to advertising.

La rosa di Bagdad (The Rose of Baghdad), 1949

The Rose of Baghdad was seven troubled years in the making. The film was director Anton Domenighini's way of keeping his team, who had previously worked on advertising films, together through the war years. They moved their studio away from their base in Milan to the less war-torn town of Bornato in Brescia. The *Arabian Nights*-type story tells of a boy rescuing a princess from an evil sultan with the inevitable involvement of a genie in a lamp. While not plotted as well as it could be, the film's animation and the rich visual style compares very well with the work of the big American companies and other productions worldwide. While *The Rose of Baghdad* was a success with the public, Domenighini and his team, perhaps finding the whole experience a bit too stressful, went back to advertising work. A measure of the film's quality and ability to stand the test of time is that it was rereleased in the USA in 1967 as *The Singing Princess* and dubbed into English with the voice of Julie Andrews.

An animated feature version of *Pinocchio* was produced in Italy in 1936, but was never completed and is considered a lost film and so is here discounted as the first Italian animated feature.

1950-1953
USA

Disney: Cinderella, Alice in Wonderland, and Peter Pan

After *Song of the South* (1946), a financial success which saw advances in mixing animation with live action, the 1950s and 1960s at Disney were short on innovation and progress compared with the previous decades. Although they continued to make high-quality animated feature films, most of the changes at Disney were to do with increasing industrialization and profit rather than any aesthetic or technical improvements.

After getting his fingers burnt in the war years and now forced to be more cautious in his approach by postwar economic austerity, Walt Disney did not make another top-grade animated feature for eight years after *Bambi* (1942). In 1950 the studio released *Cinderella* followed in quick succession by *Alice in Wonderland* (1951) and *Peter Pan* (1953), after Disney stated his intention of releasing one major movie a year. These were all brilliantly crafted films but lacked the innovation, inspiration, and pioneering spirit of his earlier work. Part of the reason for this is that Walt Disney's passion for animation had faded, probably due to the pains of the 1941 animators strike, and to reservations from some critics about his beloved projects *Fantasia* and, to a lesser extent, *Pinocchio*. His interest had now spread to a different area where his empire might expand—theme parks. His creativity was focused on his ideas for Disneyland and he left the animation department largely in the hands of his trusted "nine old men," his famous senior team of super-skilled animators.

Cinderella was in many ways a back-to-basics exercise for Disney, returning to the fairy-tale world of princesses, princes, castles, and wicked stepmothers. The traditional fairy tale was again fleshed out with comedy characters, catchy songs, and great animation. The film is said to have cost nearly $3 million and, not for the first time, Disney staked everything on its success, as failure would apparently have meant the closure of the studio. *Cinderella* fulfilled its purpose, thankfully, and became one of Disney's biggest hits with audiences.

Alice in Wonderland may seem like a more adventurous choice of material, but it is not so surprising when it's remembered that Disney's first success was with the *Alice* comedies of the 1920s, and Disney had intended to tackle an Alice feature for some years. For the first time a daring and rather modernist approach was taken to the design, with background artist Mary Blair simplifying and streamlining shapes. Like some of Disney's "package" features of the 1940s, the audience's interest was intended to be maintained with songs and visual appeal rather than overall storyline. Unfortunately *Alice in Wonderland* was not a big success, with fans of Lewis Carroll's classic disapproving of the Disneyfication, and Disney fans a bit uncomfortable with the story's surrealist episodes and the spiky and somewhat grotesque nature of the supporting characters.

Alice in Wonderland,
1951

Alex Anderson and Jay Ward:
Crusader Rabbit

The first cartoon made specifically for television, *Crusader Rabbit* was created by animator Alex Anderson and producer Jay Ward. The first episode was broadcast on August 1, 1950, on the KNBH network in Los Angeles, and was then syndicated across other channels. Anderson was working for Terrytoons when he had the idea, but Terrytoons wanted to stay with theatrical shorts so Anderson approached Ward.

To say the *Crusader Rabbit* episodes feature limited animation is something of an understatement–it is in fact barely animated at all. The experience is like watching an "animatic," a device used at the development stage of an animated film, in which the storyboard is filmed and edited in holds to coincide with the soundtrack, with some limited pose-to-pose movement thrown in here and there for clarity. The strengths of *Crusader Rabbit* are clearly not in the animation but in the zany writing and the comic-strip-style stills of the characters.

One hundred and ninety five, five-minute episodes of *Crusader Rabbit* were created, which were rerun for many years as a break between programs or inserted into children's Saturday morning shows. Later the series was picked up again and, after a legal battle, 250 more color episodes were made by a company set up by Shull Bonsall, one of the animators on the original show. *Crusader Rabbit* inspired many other TV series, and Jay Ward would go on to produce the similarly zany, but slightly more visually advanced, Rocky and Bullwinkle cartoons. This series from the early 1960s was another huge success, and combined the talents of ex-UPA animators and directors Ted Parmelee, Bill Scott, Bill Hurtz, Pete Burness, and Lew Keller.

The next feature, *Peter Pan*, was another version of a classic children's story, and one that Disney had been preparing for a few years. He started trying to buy the licence to J.M. Barrie's tale in 1935, and four years later reached an agreement with the Great Ormand Street Hospital, to whom Barrie had bequeathed the rights. Designs for the movie can be seen in the 1941 "behind the scenes" documentary, *The Reluctant Dragon*. Like *Cinderella*, there were no surprises in the look of the film, just great drawing and animation–the Walt Disney Studios were making it look easy by now. Captain Hook is an enjoyable over-the-top baddie, and the Crocodile makes a great nemesis, but perhaps due to complaints from oversensitive parents about scaring children, there is a distinct lack of chills or evil bad guys in any of these three movies, which makes them feel blander than the Disney classics of the early 1940s.

1951-1953
USA

UPA: Gerald McBoing-Boing and other UPA shorts

UPA gained both critical acclaim and public affection with a number of stylish one-off shorts. *Gerald McBoing-Boing* was a charming children's film that won the animated short film Oscar for 1951. The success of this heart-warming short spawned a number of sequels and a television series, and with its deliberate antirealism, established UPA as the front-runners in progressive animation. What the studio's films lacked of the laughs of Warner Bros. and MGM, or the storytelling of Disney, they made up for with pure style and charm.

Gerald McBoing-Boing, adapted from a story by Dr Seuss, concerns a young boy who can only produce sound effects instead of words, and how he turns the embarrassment of this into an advantage. Looking for simplicity, the designer Bill Hurtz reduced the design to a few elemental lines, getting rid of all walls, floors, horizon lines, and skies, and complementing this with a graceful spread of muted flat colors, which subtly change with the mood of the story. The minimalist *Gerald McBoing-Boing* compensated for its lack of rich animation and detailed backgrounds with personality, charm, and bags of style.

Prolific director Robert Cannon followed *Gerald McBoing-Boing* with films such as *The Oompahs* (1952), about a family of musical instruments, and a series of charming shorts about small children: *Georgie and the Dragon* (1951), *Madeline* (1952), and *Christopher Crumpet* (1953).

John Hubley's *Rooty Toot Toot* (1951) was a more grown-up and sophisticated affair. A brilliant piece of "beat" animation inspired by a jazz version of the traditional song "Frankie and Johnny," it tells a murder story from different perspectives. The flat, angular design by Paul Julian has a refreshingly loose connection between the colors and the lines, with paint spilling out over its borders at will. The cool, Jazz Age characters prowl languidly around each other like panthers, and every movement, line, and color fits the music like a glove in what has been described as one of the greatest animated short films.

The Tell Tale Heart, 1953

The Unicorn in the Garden, 1953

Gerald McBoing-Boing,
1951

Hubley followed this with another grown-up subject, in the animated segments for the live-action feature film *The Fourposter* (1952). An adaptation of Jan de Hartog's stage play showing the different stages of a marriage over 35 years, this was one of UPA's finest pieces of work and later, when distributed to Yugoslavia (now Croatia), inspired a group of animators to form what would become the award-winning Zagreb School of Animation with its own modernist style. This was to be Hubley's last work for UPA before they fired him, under pressure from the House Un-American Activities Committee, for being a former member of the Communist party.

New Yorker magazine illustrator and humorist James Thurber was much admired by the UPA directors, and in 1953 Bill Hurtz adapted his typically black-humored story *A Unicorn in the Garden* for UPA, featuring Thurber's own drawings, creating what is one of the studio's best-loved shorts.

The Tell Tale Heart (1953) was a straight-ahead horror cartoon, something almost unheard of at the time (and still pretty rare today), adapted from Edgar Allen Poe's grisly short story. Originally made in 3D, the typically striking design by Paul Julian creates a cold atmosphere for James Mason's chilling narration. Today *The Tell Tale Heart* is a cult favorite, and, along with *Gerald McBoing Boing* and other UPA shorts, is a greatly admired example of animation design.

1951
USA

1951
UK

Massachusetts Institute of Technology: The Whirlwind computer

Development of the Whirlwind computer began at the Massachusetts Institute of Technology (MIT) in 1944, and the system was first demonstrated on April 20, 1951. This was a milestone in computer graphics as it was the first digital computer capable of displaying real-time text and graphics on a video terminal, which at this time was a large oscilloscope screen. Later at MIT, computers were output onto cathode ray tubes, familiar as television screens until digital screens became the norm. This is the point at which computer graphics proper became a possibility and led to the development of the software called Sketchpad by Ivan Sutherland, recognized as the beginning of modern day computer graphics.

Norman McLaren: Stereoscopic films for the Festival of Britain

The development of dual camera printing and projection enabled Scottish animator Norman McLaren to make the three-dimensional films *Around Is Around* and *Now Is the Time* for the Festival of Britain. Both films are 10-minutes long with stereo soundtracks and use McLaren's favored technique of drawing directly onto the film strip. For *Around Is Around*, McLaren filmed oscilloscope patterns, pioneered by the American artist Mary Ellen Bute, and gave them stereoscopic form through differing the left and right eye image positions.

These three-dimensional films were shown at the Telekinema Cinema at the South Bank in London, a state-of-the-art movie theater that showed television and cine film presentations. The Telekinema was a central part of the spectacular Festival of Britain celebrations, which marked an end to wartime austerity and gave an optimistic view of the future. Despite being the only part of the Festival that charged admission, the Telekinema was sold out for every performance. The Telekinema later became the National Film Theatre.

This was not the first time that three-dimensional films had been shown to the public; in 1924 a program of films had been shown in London, and the USSR had already perfected stereoscopic projection without the need for the audience to wear special glasses.

The Whirlwind computer

1951
Yugoslavia

1952
Canada

Duga Film: Veliki Miting (The Big Meeting)

In 1950 a group of cartoonists from the satirical magazine *Kerempuh*, including Fadil Hadzic, Borivoj "Bordo" Dovnikovic, and Walter and Norbert Neugebauer set out to learn about animation and make an animated short that would celebrate the Yugoslavian identity. They created the first Yugoslavian cartoon *Veliki miting* (*The Big Meeting*), and with government support, founded the studio, Duga Film. This expanded to include over 100 artists and later formed the basis of the Zagreb Film studio, which would develop its own style of design-based "limited" animation inspired by the work of American studio, UPA.

Norman McLaren: Neighbours

Norman McLaren made his pixillation classic *Neighbours* on return from China, where he had been working with local artists in a war-torn region of Szechuan. The film is constructed with many types of effect, only some of which can be classified as animation. McLaren's colleagues at the National Film Board of Canada, Grant Munro and Jean Paul Ladouceur, played the two main parts in the film about neighbors who go to war over a flower that grows on the boundary between their gardens. The two neighbors end up killing the flower, their families, and each other. For submission to the Oscars, the scene in which they kill each other's wives and children was edited out, but was reinstated in later years. Strangely the film was entered into, and won, the documentary category of the Oscars.

Neighbours, 1952

1953
USA

1953
USA

Chuck Jones: Duck Amuck

In this, one of Chuck Jones' greatest moments of animated genius, his relationship with the character Daffy Duck has a real tangible quality as the boundaries of the cartoon are broken apart with the furious Daffy railing against his animator. Characters in many of the more manic Warners' cartoons often seem to be trying to break out of the frame, as they address the audience, remark on the fact that they are in a cartoon, and sometimes run off the filmstrip itself.

In this short, Jones perfectly demonstrates that the greatest thing about animation is that the animator can do absolutely anything, absolutely easily. Like all art, it's not about reproducing reality it's about altering reality and looking at it from a different perspective. In this case, the joke is that the animator is altering reality too fast and too much for the character's liking. Daffy is trying to hang on to some semblance of logic as the animator changes the background, the sound, the frame, and, eventually, even Daffy himself.

Jones later explained that in *Duck Amuck* he was proving that the character of Daffy was now something that existed outside his appearance, voice, or cartoon setting, as here he is transformed into many different forms and yet still remains Daffy. Perhaps Jones is trying to show us that Daffy is now so real that he has a soul.

Analysis aside, this is one of the cleverest, funniest, and best-known cartoons produced by Warner Bros. It polled second in the 1994 book *The 50 Greatest Cartoons: As Selected by 1,000 Animation Professionals* by Jerry Beck, in which Chuck Jones' films accounted for four of the top five.

Ray Harryhausen: The Beast From 20,000 Fathoms

Directed by Eugèné Lourie, *The Beast From 20,000 Fathoms* was conceived by producers Jack Dietz and Hal E. Chester after being inspired by the successful 1952 rerelease of *King Kong*. Hoping to tap into growing fears about the effects of testing nuclear weapons, the film's success inspired the giant monster movie genre of the 1950s, in which various prehistoric creatures were awoken or mutated by nuclear weapons, before going on the rampage in the nearest metropolis.

The producers became aware of a short story by Ray Bradbury, which had a similar theme to what they were planning; they bought the rights to the story and changed the name of their project to *The Beast From 20,000 Fathoms*, although their film was only superficially similar and was advertised as being merely "suggested" by Bradbury's tale.

The Beast From 20,000
Fathoms, 1953

For the film's central monster Dietz and Chester hired Ray Harryhausen, a talented young stop-frame animator who had worked on gorilla movie *Mighty Joe Young* (1949) with Willis O'Brien, the creator of *King Kong*. O'Brien had also made the similarly-themed *The Lost World* (1925) in which a brontosaurus ran amok in London. The monster in Bradbury's short story was also a brontosaurus-type dinosaur, while the The Beast in the movie was a "Rhedosaurus," a four-legged lizard predator with a spiny back, a forked tongue, and dragging tail. However scientifically unlikely the monster was, Harryhausen brought it to life in splendid fashion; despite having very big claws, spikes, and sharp teeth, the monster has a cute, almost puppy-like quality that, like King Kong before it, creates some kind of empathy between audience and monster. The use of atmospheric, realistic locations, such as the faded gaiety of the Coney Island amusement park and the lighthouse, add believability and drama to the animation. Unlike many of its spin-offs, the movie avoids descending too much into camp melodrama and has some genuinely tense moments. *The Beast From 20,000 Fathoms* was the first movie to use the "dynamation" technique, where a a split screen is used to insert the model animation into the live action.

Lured by the sensationalist trailers proclaiming "Is mankind challenging powers behind the cosmic barriers?" and "It Could Happen!" the cold war paranoia-era public flocked to the film, which earned five million dollars from its $200,000 budget, spawned a monster-movie genre (which included a whole Godzilla subgenre), and established Harryhausen as the man to call for animated monster effects.

Biography

Ray Harryhausen

The king of stop-frame animation, Ray Harryhausen has the ability to breathe life into inanimate models. Born in 1920 in Los Angeles, as a child he was fascinated by dinosaurs and fantasy subjects and began making puppets and models at an early age. He was inspired by marionette shows and movies, particularly *The Lost World* and *King Kong* (1933). Harryhausen made his own wooden models of dinosaurs and of Kong, trying to recreate the stop-frame effects he had seen on screen using a 16mm camera.

In 1938 he met the man behind the movies that had inspired him as a child, Willis O'Brien. He nervously showed O'Brien his own models during a visit to the MGM studio. O'Brien advised him to take art and anatomy classes, and taught him the importance of drawing his plans before animating his models. Harryhausen followed this advice and also began studying filmmaking techniques.

In 1940 he joined George Pal's studio, where he worked on the *Puppetoons* series. These wooden puppets did not suit Harryhausen, however, as Pal's replacement system of puppet animation did not allow enough scope for creativity. After army service during World War II, he produced a series of nursery rhymes using armatured models, which were released as *Mother Goose Stories* (1946) and distributed to schools. He then worked alongside O'Brien on *Mighty Joe Young* (1949); O'Brien designed and planned the animation, while Harryhausen did most of the stop-frame work. After working on several projects with O'Brien that were never completed, Harryhausen pursued his own work.

For *The Beast From 20,000 Fathoms* (1953), he produced fantastic effects, despite the low budget he had to work with. This is a testament both to his skill and his enthusiasm for the project. Over the course of his long career, he contributed outstanding effects to many features, including *It Came From Beneath the Sea* (1955), *The 7th Voyage of Sinbad* (1958), *Jason and the Argonauts* (1963), *The Golden Voyage of Sinbad* (1973), and *Clash of the Titans* (1981). He officially retired in 1984, but has continued to work on select projects, including contributing to the BBC series *Walking with Dinosaurs* (1999). He also helped animators Mark Caballo and Seamus Walsh to complete *The Tortoise and the Hare* in 2002, a short which Harryhausen had started but abandoned 50 years earlier.

1954

UK

NAPOLEON

Halas & Batchelor: Animal Farm

Handling Ships may have been the first British feature-length animated film, but as a training film, it was only distributed to the Navy. *Animal Farm*, also made by Halas & Batchelor, was the first British animated feature film to get a general release.

When American producer Louis de Rochemont suggested that John Halas and Joy Batchelor make a film of George Orwell's political allegory, they wanted to be sure to make a movie with wide appeal. *Animal Farm* was made in much more of a traditional semirealist style than the modernist designs that Halas & Batchelor were known for, presumably to increase the chances of the film being accepted in the same markets as Disney features. The increased realism of the animal characters also helps the audience to concentrate on the story, rather than thinking about the design. Despite its near-Disney stylings, *Animal Farm* remains above all a grown-up, intelligent film that steers away from cuteness to deliver a clear political allegory. The dark colors used in the animation reflect its somber theme.

The story concerns a farm where the farmer cruelly drives the animals like slaves, ruling over them with the aid of his ferocious dogs. The animals revolt and take over the farm with the aim of every animal being equal, but the pigs become corrupted by power and run the new system as a dictatorship that is no better than the farmer's regime. Orwell's book ends with the pigs in ascendency, but the film has a happy ending as the other animals revolt against the pigs and take over the farm in order to instill a democracy.

Critics in the UK hailed it as the best film of the year and the *New York Times* called it a masterpiece. It does indeed have reason to be described as one of the great animated features, not least because it was the first one that dared to tell a grown-up story aimed at a predominantly adult audience.

The happy ending, which attracted much criticism, is more commercially acceptable than Orwell's bleaker version, and indeed John Halas explained the change was needed to reward the audience for their emotional involvement with the animals. Decades later it emerged that an early incarnation of the CIA

had secretly been funding the film after their representatives had purchased the rights from Orwell's daughter. These financiers, via De Rochemont, had pushed for the changed ending with the intention of discrediting communism, rather than Orwell's original which is an attack on all totalitarianism, whether from the left or the right. Halas and Batchelor, pacifists who believed in trying to use animation to bring world peace, were of course unaware of any of this. These events are detailed in full in the book *Halas and Batchelor Cartoons* by Paul Wells and Vivien Halas and in *Animated Propaganda During the Cold War* by Karl F. Cohen, and were confirmed in a conversation between the author and Vivien Halas, daughter of the film's directors. Despite the existence of such pressure, the compromised ending that resulted does in fact seem to be opposed to all dictatorships and not specifically communism.

TEETH

MODEL SHEET ②

Animal Farm, 1954

1955

USA

Lady and the Tramp, 1955

Disney: Lady and the Tramp

The launch of *Lady and the Tramp* was somewhat overshadowed by the opening of the Disneyland theme park in California just a month after the movie's release, but it now seems like a fine entry to the line of Disney animated features and an improvement on the studios' films from the early 1950s. The cast of dogs and cats were wonderfully animated, have real individual personalities and emotions, and the songs have great spirit.

It was the first Disney movie to be filmed in widescreen and the first to tell a twentieth-century, urban type of story. Along with the warmth and sentimentality of the Romeo-and-Juliet-like love story, the portrayal of the Tramp character and his dog pals from the wrong side of the tracks hinted at a harsher side to modern life not often seen in children's cartoons. Characters like the sad street lady dog in the pound and the spoiled and spiteful pair of Siamese cats, Si and Am, are particularly memorable, as are their songs, performed by Peggy Lee.

Despite being dismissed by the critics, Disney clearly not being in favor at this time as UPA took the role of critics' darlings, *Lady and the Tramp* was a financial success and took more money for the Walt Disney Studios than any of their films since *Snow White*. It is one of the best-loved features from the studio, has a true universal appeal that transcends all age groups, which has not dated over the subsequent decades.

1955
USA

James Whitney: Yantra

After studying painting and traveling in England during his youth, James Whitney returned to his hometown of Los Angeles, where in 1940 he began making abstract films. He invariably collaborated with his brother John on these films, which would often take up to five years to complete.

Their first completed work was *Twenty-Four Variations on an Original Theme* (1942), made on 8mm film and lasting around 20 minutes. This was followed by the breakthrough *Five Film Exercises* (1943–44), in which the brothers filmed subtly shifting patterns of light filtered through animated elements to create one of the most memorable and influential moments of abstract film. In 1946 John and James showed some of this work at the first Art in Cinema film sceening at the San Francisco Museum of Art. After this period, James' work took on a more spiritual aspect as he pursued his interests in meditation, psychology, and quantum physics, subjects he researched and immersed himself in at a remote retreat where he withdrew from the world.

In 1955 James Whitney completed what many consider to be his masterpiece, *Yantra*. It took five years of intensive work using a method of punching precise patterns of holes in card and then painting through these holes before rotating the card and producing further images of rich, kaleidoscopic and complex patterns, often treated with photographic effects like solarization to finesse the process further. Although originally intended to be contemplated in silence, the film was later combined with a soundtrack taken from electronic music composer Henik Bading's *Cain and Abel*. This version was shown at the Vortex Concerts held at the Morrison Planetarium in San Francisco in 1957.

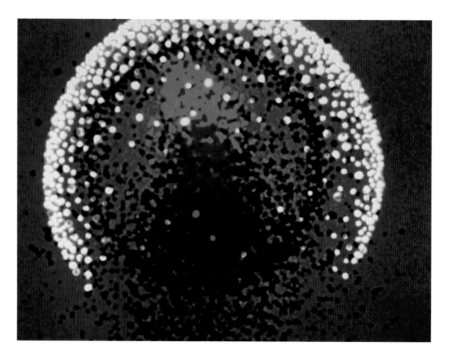

Yantra, 1955

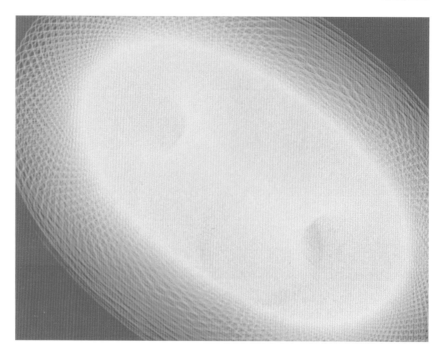

Lapis, 1966

USA

Partly helped by a primitive analog computer made by his brother John, James was later able to produce the follow-up film, *Lapis* (1966), which, although of even greater hypnotic complexity and intensity than *Yantra*, took under two years to complete. This pioneering use of computers aided the camera's movements, enabling it to film more precise and complex sequences of painted dots.

Taking long gaps between projects, which Whitney spent at his retreat planning and researching his work and contemplating the changing of the seasons, meant that James Whitney only made five films before his death in 1982. His last films were planned as a sequence of four, the first of which, *Dwija* (1973), represented fire. Later came *Wu Ming* (1977) representing water. *Li* (earth) and *Kang Jing Xiang* (air) were completed by others, including his nephew Mark Whitney, after James' death. These later films were praised as further masterworks and Whitney left the world of abstract animation a small, but powerful, mysterious, and original legacy.

Saul Bass: The Man with the Golden Arm movie titles

Following UPA's lead in illustration- and graphic-based animation, American designer Saul Bass started producing work for live-action feature films to give them an aspect of high style, as John Hubley had done for UPA in *The Four Poster* (1952). After working on the titles for director Otto Preminger's *Carmen Jones* (1954), Bass created the title sequence for Preminger's classic, hard-hitting story of drug addiction, *The Man with the Golden Arm*. In what is now seen as a milestone in graphic design, the titles are delivered within a mini narrative, almost transforming the title sequence into a super stylish short film in its own right.

The impact of his work on *The Man with the Golden Arm* ensured that Saul Bass went on to create many more famous title sequences, including *The Seven Year Itch* (1955) and *Around the World in Eighty Days* (1956). Perhaps his most famous works are his collaborations with Alfred Hitchcock, including the classic movies *Vertigo* (1958), *North by Northwest* (1959), and *Psycho* (1960).

1958–1985:
The Television Age

What has become known as the Golden Age of Animation came to a close in the early 1960s with the end of the commercial viability of movie theater shorts. This was partially due to the legally enforced ending of the American practice of "block booking," whereby movie producers could no longer insist on theaters buying shorts packaged along with the main features; instead, shorts had to be sold separately, resulting in owners of theater chains forcing the price down enough to make shorts unviable. The preference of theater owners was now for double bills of features to provide better value at the box office to compete with the new rival of television, cheap mass entertainment broadcast straight into consumers' homes.

The rise of television, while it cut the market for theater shorts, simultaneously provided new markets for animation in commercials and TV series. Broadcasters' demands for large quantities of cost-effective animation forced budgets down and instigated a culture of limited animation, using held drawings with moving areas, such as talking mouths, on separate levels, and much reuse of animation cycles. The simplified design approach of companies like UPA was seized upon by market leaders like Hanna-Barbera as a way of producing quick drawings, and this set the steadily declining quality of television animation for the next three decades. Feature animation budgets were also cut back in line with declining movie theater audiences. For makers of commercials, however, the budgets were increasing, as global brands wanted to be associated with the clever ideas and eye-catching designs that were possible with animation.

1958

USA

Hanna-Barbera: The Huckleberry Hound Show and other TV series

After MGM's animation unit closed down in 1957, successful *Tom and Jerry* directing team Joseph Barbera and William Hanna formed their own production company. They had already produced animated inserts for *Anchors Aweigh* (1945), directed by George Sidney, and it was Sidney who aided them to start a company with the intention of creating animation for the new medium of television. With an eye on the modest success of the first television cartoon series, *Crusader Rabbit*, they produced *The Ruff & Reddy Show* (1957), an idea they had developed at MGM but had been turned down. A year later they hit the jackpot with *The Huckleberry Hound Show*.

The canine character that carried the show's name was a hillbilly type with a characteristic slow-talking southern drawl, voiced by Daws Butler. Two other cartoons also formed the show, but Huckleberry was the undoubted star and gained a fervent following in the USA and worldwide. The shows involved Huckleberry taking on a variety of different jobs, with the hero frequently addressing the audience and commenting on his adventures.

Taking the UPA stripped-down, limited-animation model but dispensing with UPA's high style, Hanna-Barbera productions became an animation factory that dominated television animation for the next few decades. Hanna-Barbera's television budgets were a fraction of the average budgets for theatrical shorts that they'd had at MGM, and the minimal quality of their animations led Warner Bros. legend Chuck Jones to describe their work as "illustrated radio."

After *Huckleberry Hound*, Hanna-Barbera Productions produced many more hit shows, which will be, along with their catchy theme tunes, instantly familiar to anyone alive in that era. *Yogi Bear* was a support act from *The Huckleberry Hound Show*, but the wise-guy bear and his sidekick Boo Boo soon became stars in their own right, even spawning a feature film *Hey There, It's Yogi Bear* (1964).

Hanna-Barbera's *The Flintstones* (1960–1966) was the first animated sitcom and the only cartoon to successfully fill a prime-time slot rather than children's scheduling until *The Simpsons* landed 30 years later. The studio also had success with the space-age set sitcom, *The Jetsons*.

In the late 1960s, the company produced more notable hits such as *Scooby Doo*, *Wacky Races*, and the live-action/animation psychedelic experience *The Banana Splits and Friends Show*. These are just a few of the many Hanna-Barbera hit shows that, while based on cheap and limited animation, managed to maintain a funny and memorable watchability due to the writing, characters, and catchy tunes that created a bubblegum-pop-culture freshness with every new flavor that came off the production line.

1958
USA

Robert Breer: A Man With His Dog Out For Air

In the 1950s, an artistic movement called the "beat generation" started to emerge, with its philosophy of free-form expressionist "stream of consciousness" prose and poetry from writers such as Jack Kerouac and Allen Ginsberg. The work of certain animators at the time seemed to relate to this style and these artists were recognized by, and loosely linked with, the beats. The expression "underground" came into use in this era, as this kind of art would often be experienced by the counterculture in dark, smoky cellars, hidden underneath the street level of mainstream life.

Robert Breer was a visual artist rather than a filmmaker, often working in sculpture and paint, and was inspired by the likes of Man Ray's use of film as a medium. Much influenced by the avant-garde, beat poetry, jazz, and the new performance art, Breer incorporated these art forms into his films, creating devices for creating and showing his animation in galleries.

Breer started making his free-form animation in the mid-1950s by the means of fast, sketchy, unrelated drawings on filing cards, his early work attracting the attention of recognized beatnik writers such as Ginsberg. Breer's short *A Man With His Dog Out For Air* consists of quick, spontaneous, mainly figurative line drawings of simple things encountered on a walk: clouds, birds, houses, etc., until we see the subjects who are seeing all this: a man and his dog. The film rejects analysis and celebrates the simple momentary pleasures of being alive.

Breer had a career as a filmmaker spanning over 50 years, in which he moved through many new styles and influences and transcended the connection with the beat generation to become recognized as a great of avant-garde animation.

1958
USA/ Hungary

George Pal: tom thumb

George Pal, now working in Hollywood mainly as a live-action movie director, produced and directed this spectacular version of the Brothers Grimm fairy tale, using his flair for special effects with a mixture of giant sets, superimposition, and stop-frame animation of the many toys who tom thumb (the lower case letters are deliberate) befriends. The effects are immaculately crafted and the film stands up today as a great, although somewhat forgotten, childen's classic. The animation was by Wah Chang (the designer of the *Star Trek* props, including the communicator on which the modern flip-top cell-phone is supposedly based) and Gene Warren. The film won the 1959 Oscar for best special effects.

1958

Czech Republic

Karel Zeman: Vynález zkázy (The Fabulous World of Jules Verne)

Like a psychedelic, Eastern European version of Ray Harryhausen, Karel Zeman created unique films that combined stop-frame creatures and live-action actors in stylized sets and rich, vivid, and imaginative fantasy worlds.

Born in Bohemia (now the Czech Republic) in 1910, Zeman worked as a window dresser and poster designer and studied at business school. Following an early interest in Czech puppet theater, Zeman moved to Paris to study commercial art and work in advertising. Returning to his native land, he continued working on commercials until he was offered a job in the animation studio run by Hermina Tyrlova. Zeman and Tyrlova then collaborated on *Vánocní sen* (*Christmas Dream*, 1946), which won the award for best animated film at the Cannes Film Festival. In 1949 Zeman created the incredible *Inspirace* (*Inspiration*), which used miniature glass models and sets to create remarkably fluid figures in a unique stop-frame world.

After creating a series of short, comic stop-frame films featuring the character Mr Prokouk, Zeman made his first feature, *Král Lávra* (*King Lavra*), in 1950, followed by his first live-action/animation film, *Cesta do praveku* (*Journey into History*), a genre for which he would become world renowned. It was Zeman's next film, *Vynález zkázy* (*The Fabulous World of Jules Verne*) which brought him international acclaim and which many consider his masterpiece. Based on Jules Vernes' novel *Face au drapeau* (*Facing the Flag*), the movie was designed to look like the kind of illustrations that would have been in the original 1896 publication by artists such as Edward Riou. The sets and backgrounds in this Victorian illustrative style give the feel of a toy cardboard puppet show from that era, except in this case containing real actors. A favorite on television in the 1960s, *The Fabulous World of Jules Verne* is now rarely seen, and like the rest of Zeman's beautiful work, is criminally neglected.

He followed this with other Jules Vernes adaptations such as *Na komete* (*Journey by Comet*, 1970) and the whimsical fantasy *Baron Prasil* (*The Fabulous Baron Munchausen*, 1961), seemingly influential on Terry Gilliam's later version of the tale, as indeed is much of Zeman's work on Gilliam's style. His later work includes a version of Sinbad, *Pohádky tisíce a jedné noci* (*A Thousand and One Nights*, 1974) and the fantasy story of love conquering evil, *Carodejuv ucen* (*Krabat: The Sorcerer's Apprentice*, 1977).

Vynález zkázy (The Fabulous World of Jules Verne), 1958

1958

Croatia

Zagreb Film: Samac (Alone)

In 1956 the founders of Duga Film regrouped within the Zagreb Film studio to produce work influenced by UPA's stylized, limited animation approach. After their first release, *Nestasni Robot* (*The Playful Robot*, 1956) won a prize at the Pula Film Festival, they hit gold with 1958's *Samac* (*Alone*), which won a prize and attracted much attention at the prestigious Venice Film Festival. This dialog-free short tells the story of a lonely office worker who spends his days surrounded by female coworkers, and his nights in a tortured dream world.

Directed by writer, critic, and live-action director Vatroslav Mimica, *Alone* put the Zagreb studio on the map and initiated a wave of existential films, questioning and commenting on the human condition. Directors such as Mimica, Dusan Vukotic, and Vladimir Kristl, often swapped roles and became writers, directors, and designers on each other's subsequent films.

Samac (Alone), 1958

Biography

Zagreb Film

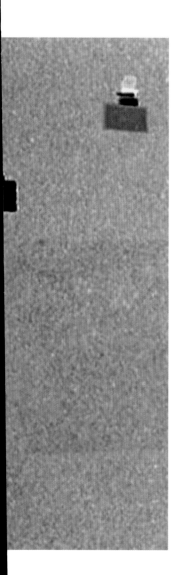

Along with America's UPA studio, Zagreb Film's animation division created pioneering work using modernist styles and limited animation. The Duga Film studio, founded by caricaturists from the satirical magazine *Kerempuh*, had produced Croatia's first animated film in 1951 *Veliki miting* (*The Big Meeting*). After only a year's existence, in 1952 Duga Film was dismantled by the Croatian government, who saw animation as an unnecessary luxury.

In 1956, Dusan Vukotic, Nikola Kostelac, and other former members of Duga Film formed Zagreb Film with the aim of producing creative and experimental animation. As well as the original Duga Film members, the studio attracted new talent, such as Vatroslav Mimica, Branko Ranitovic, Pavao Stalter, Dragutin Vunak, Nedeljko Dragic, Ante Zaninovic, Zdenko Gasparovic, Milan Blazekovic, Zvonimir Loncaric, Zlatko Pavlinic, and, later Josko Marusic and Kresimir Zimonic.

In 1948, Yugoslavia (now Croatia) had split from Stalinism; this meant that the animators at Zagreb Film had more freedom than their counterparts in other Eastern European countries. They did not have to follow the soviet realist style and there was less censorship. At the studio, each animator was allowed the freedom to develop their own unique style, and the resulting work won international acclaim.

1958

Japan

Hakuja den (Legend of
the White Snake), 1958

Taiji Yabushita: Hakuja Den (Legend of the White Snake, aka The Tale of the White Serpent)

Taiji Yabushita's *Hakuja den* (*Legend of the White Snake*) was the first Japanese full-length animated feature in color, and its success acted as a starting point for the modern Japanese animation industry. Its production company, Toei Doga, made a steady stream of features based on ancient legends and science fiction. Soon imitated by many other companies, these films were usually produced faster than Western features, and were more based on spectacle and special effects than character animation. This style of animation is regarded as the roots of what we now know as manga and anime, although *Legend of the White Snake* is more Western in tone, featuring musical numbers and cute animals.

Based on a Chinese fairy tale, *Legend of the White Snake* recounts the love affair between a boy and a magical snake goddess reincarnated as a pretty girl, until the boy is killed by an evil wizard and the goddess tries to resurrect him. The film achieved success in Japan and abroad, winning a prize at the Venice Children's Film Festival, and was released in the USA as *Panda and the Magic Serpent*. It also served as an influence on a young Hayao Miyazaki.

1959
USA

Disney: Sleeping Beauty

Sleeping Beauty was Walt Disney's return to his grand ambition for animated features. He not only invested a lot of money in the movie, but also his studio's reputation as the masters of animation. Disney hoped it would answer criticisms of his films being behind the times in terms of modern design.

Like *Lady and the Tramp* four years earlier, *Sleeping Beauty* was made in widescreen, which created certain difficulties, such as the need for different kinds of wider staging of small numbers of characters and the need for longer backgrounds and production cels. Almost a decade in development, the movie was Disney's longest-running animated feature and was intended to be his masterpiece. It featured some beautiful designs, which were more graphic, angular, and contemporary than those previously attempted by the company. The wider frames also allowed for a more detailed approach. Pulling back from the pursuit of realism, the studio intended the design of the film to look like "living illustrations," and took inspiration from the flat style and colors of medieval tapestries. Disney regular Ken Anderson was the production designer, while a lot of the design work and background painting was done by Eyvind Earle.

The film's music, presented in stereophonic sound, was adapted from Tchaikovsky's ballet *Sleeping Beauty* and Princess Aurora's name was also taken from this source, although her name while in-hiding, Briar Rose, was taken from the original Brothers Grimm fairy tale. Her suitor, Prince Phillip, was named for the Duke of Edinburgh, the husband of Britain's Queen Elizabeth II.

Despite now being admired as one of the most sophisticated and best of Disney's movies and one of history's greatest animated features, *Sleeping Beauty* was met with a cool reception from critics at the time, who compared it unfavorably with *Snow White* and *Cinderella*. It was considered slow-moving and cold compared with the emotional pull of Disney's earlier films (once again the rotoscoped main characters didn't help in this regard). The movie was Disney's most expensive animated feature at a cost of $6 million, and this, combined with the outlay on the theme parks, took The Walt Disney Company close to bankruptcy. Although the film turned a profit, this would be the company's last expansive and expensive animated feature made during Walt Disney's lifetime.

1959

USA

1959

USA

John Whitney: Vertigo movie titles

After his first experiments in film, such as filming a solar eclipse through a homemade telescope, John Whitney collaborated with his brother James on abstract films, developing techniques of punching holes in card to create complex, animated patterns. In 1959, in collaboration with designer Saul Bass, he used his "mechanical" animation techniques to produce the title sequence for Alfred Hitchcock's classic, *Vertigo*. The iconic spirals were created using an analog computer Whitney had constructed using surplus anti aircraft guidance hardware. Whitney had realized the potential this technology had for motion graphics while working with high-speed missile photography during WWII.

John and Faith Hubley: Moonbird

After leaving UPA, John Hubley set up a commercial studio in Los Angeles before moving to New York in 1955 with his wife and collaborator, Faith Hubley. They then set to work fulfilling their marriage vow of making one independent film a year.

Their short film *Moonbird* was funded by the Guggenheim Museum and was based on the improvised play of their young children, Mark and Ray. The film's soundtrack consisted of the children's unscripted, tape-recorded play talk, edited down to tell a loose, rambling story of an imaginary search for the "Moonbird."

Like their previous film *The Adventures of an* * (1957), *Moonbird* leaned toward abstract, expressionist stylings. The Hubleys used experimental animation methods, such as using double exposures to produce overlaid images and filming the layers half-exposed to make them semitransparent. Other techniques included coloring the image with wax crayon and black ink, which resulted in the ink resisting the wax to give a wild, loose feel in keeping with the imaginary child's world the film creates. *Moonbird* was acclaimed by critics worldwide and won the animated short film Oscar for that year. Despite their prolific and prize-winning output, *Moonbird* remains one of the Hubleys' most well-loved films and one of the greatest independent animated shorts.

John & Faith Hubley

John Hubley was born in New York in 1914, into a British family with an artistic heritage. In the 1930s, Hubley moved to Los Angeles to live with a well-to-do uncle who supported his studies, but with whom Hubley never saw eye to eye, and who was reportedly the model for Hubley's most famous creation, Mister Magoo. After college Hubley got a job at the Walt Disney Studio where he worked as a background and layout artist at the time when the studio was at its peak of excitement, learning, and expansion. Hubley later fondly remembered that time, despite his later involvement with the 1941 animators' strike. Although Hubley worked on such classics as *Snow White*, *Pinocchio*, *Dumbo*, *Bambi*, and

Fantasia, he had found some other kindred spirits at Disney who disliked the increased regimentation of style and the pursuit of greater commerciality. He left during the 1941 strike and enlisted in the army. He joined UPA to make the election film for Roosevelt, *Hell Bent for Election*, in 1944.

Faith Elliott grew up in the tough Hell's Kitchen area of New York; little is known of her childhood but it did not seem to be a happy one. In 1942 aged 18 she moved to Los Angeles where she worked at a variety of jobs at Columbia Pictures including as a messenger, as a sound editor, a script clerk, and a script supervisor. She met John Hubley while they were both working at UPA and they married in 1955.

John Hubley was released by UPA in 1952 following pressure on the studio from the House Un-American Activities Committee. Hubley had refused to cooperate with HUAC's investigations and was blacklisted. John and Faith set up Storyboard Studios in New York in 1956. With the aid of a Guggenheim fellowship, the two artists produced a string of original and influential independent films throughout the 1960s and 1970s, winning three Oscars and countless other awards together, with Faith Hubley continuing to make films after her husband's death in 1977.

Moonbird, 1959

1960

USA

Harry Smith: Film No 12: Heaven and Earth Magic

Probably Harry Smith's best-known work, *Film No. 12* (named *Heaven and Earth Magic* by Smith's fellow abstract filmmaker and friend Jonas Mekas) seems to have been made between 1950 and 1960. During this process Smith often used sleep deprivation as a gateway to spirituality and the subconscious, continuously falling asleep next to his camera, then awakening and resuming work. In Smith's words this was "to make the whole thing automatic…some kind of universal process was directing these so-called arbitrary processes."

Harry Smith gave a typically mysterious summary of the film's narrative as follows: "The first part depicts the heroine's toothache consequent to the loss of a very valuable watermelon, her dentistry and transportation to heaven. Next follows an elaborate exposition of the heavenly land, in terms of Israel and Montreal. The second part depicts the return to earth from being eaten by Max Müller on the day Edward VII dedicated the Great Sewer of London." A more simple description of the plot might say that a magician creates some elaborate spells that he injects into a woman in a dentist's chair. She rises to heaven and breaks into fragments. As the magician attempts to piece her back together, they are both eaten by a giant head and return to earth in an elevator, arriving at some kind of grand celebration. The end is an exact reversal of the start, giving the whole film a cyclical path.

According to Smith, the original was made on 35mm film with a running time of six hours, although if this version existed, it is now lost. What survives is an hour long 16mm edit containing this obscure seminarrative, in which for long periods small cutout figures, white against black, jerkily manipulate a variety of cutout or real symbolic objects. Watching the film now the monochrome minimalism disappoints compared with Smith's early works, which resembled beautiful moving abstract expressionist paintings. What has to be remembered is that the film was designed to be enhanced with color masks, lights, music, and sound effects manipulated by Smith, along with masking slides that transformed the screen itself to appropriate symbolic shapes. This would give the overall feel of an elaborate magic lantern theater embellishing an animated shadow play. Also integrated into many of its legendary screenings was a whole other theater of activity with Smith letting off fireworks, giving a running "stream of consciousness" commentary, while fending off hecklers and scorning members of the audience who weren't sufficiently appreciative.

Strong iconic images of death, birth, marriage, and violence clash with banal household objects, birds, insects, pets, and machines. Overlapping sound effects of clocks, wolves, voices, machines, screams, wind, babies, and dogs accompany the film, all meticulously recorded by sound collector Smith, creating a disorientating effect. This film really exists so much in its own universe that it's almost impossible to decipher, resembling at various times dark mystical witchcraft, or a giant visual puzzle of obscure references to be pieced together, or an obscure coded confessional therapy, or darkly funny, lo-fi surrealism about death. Or, more likely, it is all of these things and more.

4

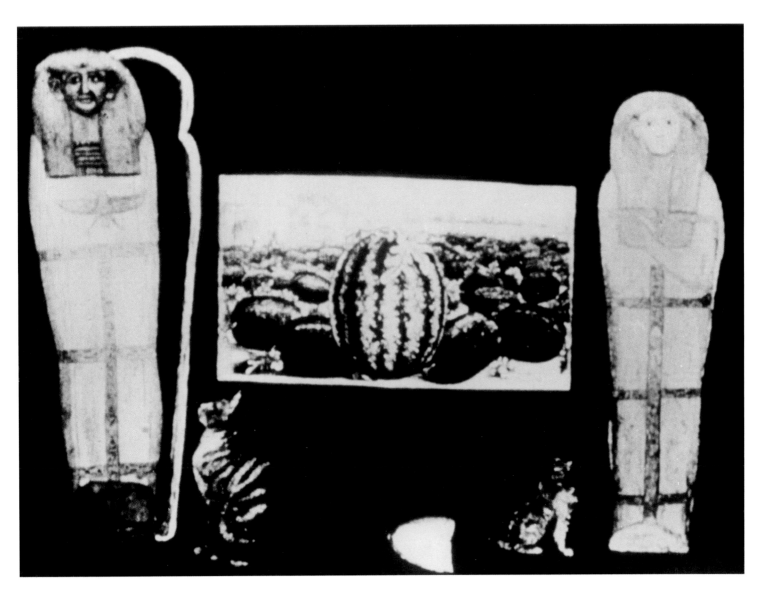

Heaven and Earth
Magic, 1960

1961
USA

One Hundred and One
Dalmations, 1961

Disney: One Hundred and One Dalmatians

Perhaps with an eye on the popularity of *Lady and the Tramp*, Disney's next feature film was another canine story in a modern setting. Adapted from the book *The Hundred and One Dalmatians* by Dodie Smith, *One Hundred and One Dalmatians* was the first Disney movie to use the Xerox process. Disney veteran Ub Iwerks, now in charge of "special processes," had adapted Xerox copying technology to copy the animators' drawings onto the cells on which they were painted and filmed in front of the backgrounds. This eliminated the process of handtracing the drawings onto the cells, but meant that the animators' slightly rougher pencil line, and not a line

traced by someone else, was seen in the film. This gave a looser, softer feel to the animation and slightly changed the feel of Disney movies for the next two decades.

This technical change may have played a part in the more stylized and caricatured feel of most of the central character designs in *One Hundred and One Dalmatians*, again a departure for Disney features where the central human characters had always tended to be in a realistic style, with the exception perhaps of *Pinocchio*. The Xerox and its rougher line, after initial doubts, was welcomed by the animators, as were the stylized designs. The animation could now be freer and not so constricted by the need for realism or as tied to the rotoscoping of live actors, which had been a bone of contention on *Sleeping Beauty*.

The arrival of Xerox technology was timely for this project with its many puppies, each with many spots. Without it, it is possible that the movie may not have even been made. The budget would have been much higher and the schedule much longer were it not for this labor-saving breakthrough which could, for instance, duplicate the same puppy animation many times across a frame.

Like *Lady and the Tramp*, *One Hundred and One Dalmatians* is one of Disney's sweetest and most loved features, and in Cruella De Vil it has one of cinema's greatest villainesses. Superbly animated by Marc Davis, Cruella steals the show from a gallery of charming, eccentric, and wonderfully designed characters. Like Disney's *Mary Poppins* released a few years later, the movie makes for a delightful and affectionate vision of London family life. It is said to have been the first Disney feature in a modern setting, which is technically true, although apart from a few background details, *Lady and the Tramp* had the feeling that it could be set in the modern day.

1961
USA

1961
UK

Jordan Belson: Allures

Like Harry Smith, Jordan Belson was a member of the West Coast Experimental Film Movement inspired by the Art in Cinema film screenings. These events were held annually from 1946 until 1954 at the San Francisco Museum of Art. The films of Oskar Fischinger, Viking Eggeling, Maya Deren, and others were screened at the early events, and Smith, Belson, and other artists from the California scene also showed their work at the later exhibitions.

During the 1950s Belson experimented with methods of animation such as stop frame and stream of consciousness-type scroll painting. He worked with electronic musician Henry Jacobs to create a series of events called the Vortex Concerts at the Morrison Planetarium in San Francisco. The concept of what would now be called a "VJ" can be traced back to these groundbreaking events, in which Jacobs played taped music while Belson coordinated up to 70 projectors to produce live abstract light images on the domed ceiling of the planetarium.

Recommended by Oskar Fischinger, Belson was awarded a grant from the Museum of Non-Objective Painting, which later became the Guggenheim Museum. He started making films from a specially-constructed optical bench, and in 1961 produced *Allures*. Like a lot of the work of his contemporaries, Belson's films were designed to invoke a spiritual or mystical type of experience, influenced by his interest in Eastern beliefs and possibly also by the psychedelic drugs that were gaining popularity at the time among certain audiences.

Jacobs and Belson provided an electronic soundtrack for *Allures*, which visually consists of galaxies of lights, dots, and sparks of different colors moving hypnotically around cosmic spirals. *Allures* was an acknowledged influence on special-effects legend Douglas Trumbull's "Stargate" sequence in *2001: A Space Oddessy* (1968) and was the blueprint for psychedelic computer-aided animation in years to come.

Bob Godfrey: Do It Yourself Cartoon Kit

After working with Peter Sachs at Larkins Studio in London, Bob Godfrey set up his first company, Biographic, where he made *Do It Yourself Cartoon Kit* in 1961.

The film is a fast-moving, crazed, cutout animation, based on a spoof sales pitch for the "do it yourself cartoon kit," during which the voiceover artist (comic actor Michael Bentine) digresses and wanders off on a number of random tangents.

The eccentric, surrealist humor is of the type that was popular in Britain at the time with radio series such as *The Goon Show* (of which Bentine was a cast member). In the 1970s the television comedy series *Monty Python's Flying Circus* continued this comedy style, and also featured surreal, cutout animations by Terry Gilliam. In fact, *Do It Yourself Cartoon Kit* has sometimes been wrongly credited to Gilliam as it is so similar in style to his future work. Indeed, Gilliam later published his own surreal and silly book on how to make cartoons, entitled *Animations of Mortality*.

The animation in Godfrey's film, which really could be done by anyone themselves at home, takes animation into minimalism beyond even the limited styles common in this era, and into what could be called lo-fi animation. It is this kind of playful subversion of animation tradition to produce work that utterly refuses to take itself, or anything else, at all seriously that made this film so influential.

1961

Croatia

Dusan Vukotic and Zagreb Film: Surogat (Ersatz)

The Oscar for animated short film went out of the USA for the first time in 1962 when it was awarded to Dusan Vukotic's *Surogat* (*Ersatz*). Made at the Zagreb Film studio, it is a highly modernist short, here taking a simplified design aesthetic to its further extremes. While the designs are more geometric, angular, and simplified than Fyodor Khitruk's *Istoriya odnogo prestupleniya* (*Story of One Crime*, 1962) and other modernist shorts that predominated in the Eastern Bloc around that time, the animation has a smoother and more finessed approach, giving the movement a level of sophistication and quality missing from many other films of its kind.

An acerbic and darkly comic tale about the absurdities of the modern age, the story concerns a man's increasingly surreal attempts to show off his autoinflatable gadgetry at the beach—including an encounter with the ultimate, unobtainable pneumatic woman—until, finally, his self-importance is deflated.

Surogat (Ersatz), 1961

USA

1001 Arabian Nights,
1959

Gay Purr-ee and UPA's later work

After the departure from UPA of John Hubley and Phil Eastman during the dark times of the Hollywood Un-American Activities blacklist, the company had lost much of its creative drive by the late 1950s. Producer and manager Steve Bosustow tried to keep the company alive by taking a series of business decisions driven by commercial pressures. UPA's earlier, beautiful one-off films had given the company its reputation and had literally changed the world of animation, with many other studios mimicking what had become known as the "UPA style." Now under pressure from financial backers Columbia, and following

the high-profit, low-finesse production-line methods of Hanna-Barbera, the one-off shorts were abandoned in favor of cheap television series of *Mister Magoo* and *Dick Tracy*. Of the later output, only a short series called *Ham and Hattie* (1957) received the acclaim of the earlier work, with the first episode nominated for an Oscar. Some longer-format TV specials of *Mister Magoo* were also more ambitious and well received, most memorably *Mister Magoo's Christmas Carol* (1962), directed by Abe Levitow.

Following the collapse of the market for theatrical shorts, the only other game in town apart from television was feature animation, a direction which Bosustow first explored with Mister

Magoo's vehicle *1001 Arabian Nights* (1959). The movie had a difficult production life, during which director Pete Burness resigned to be replaced by Disney veteran Jack Kinney. Visually the film is well made, although the script is slow moving and clumsy, with the Mister Magoo character tacked on to a traditional Aladdin story.

In the wake of the success of Disney's London-set dog story *One Hundred and One Dalmatians* (1961), UPA came up with a European-set story about cats. *Gay Purr-ee* concerns a rural cat who dreams of the excitement of Paris until she is kidnapped by a criminal cat gang. Abe Levitow again directed, Judy Garland provided the voice of the central character

Mewsette and sang eight songs by Yip Harburg, with Mel Blanc providing other voices. Chuck Jones supervised the animation and wrote the story with his wife Dorothy while moonlighting from the austerity of the later regime at Warner Bros.

Gay Purr-ee is an enjoyable, nice-looking, and fondly remembered feature, although the low budget is often apparent in comparison with Disney's movies. As with *1001 Arabian Nights*, the story is a bit slow moving and strung out, with the company's inexperience in feature films somewhat evident. Sadly, the film never generated enough box office interest to save UPA, which closed in 1964.

1962

Russia

Istoriya Odnogo
Prestuplenlya
(Story of One Crime),
1962

Fyodor Khitruk: Istoriya Odnogo Prestupleniya (Story of One Crime)

In 1938, two years after graduating from Moscow's OGIS College for Applied Arts, Fyodor Khitruk started work as an animator at the state-funded studio, Soyuzmultfilm. In 1962 he made his debut as a director with a film that is credited with changing the course of Russian animation.

Istoriya odnogo prestupleniya (*Story of One Crime*) was made in the modernist style, and although visually similar to UPA's work, this film is much darker in tone, as it starts with a furious man beating two old ladies to death with a frying pan. Its apartment block setting is of the kind that many people were being rehoused in during the 1960s, as part of an optimistic plan for urban renewal. Khitruk's film is a black-humored warning about the city planners' utopian dream, as the central character is driven to his wit's end by human noise pollution keeping him awake all night. The film caused concern among the Communist Party officials, who saw it as an attack on government housing policies. The film was, however, allowed to be released theatrically to appreciative soviet audiences.

The minimal, stylized animation, flat perspectives, fabric patterns, and concrete brick textures brought Russian cartoons right up to date after the Disney-influenced traditional tales of the soviet realism style; in fact, *Story of One Crime* feels like it is more soviet and more real than any Russian animation for decades. This little gem is a standout of soviet animation and, with its determined nontraditional style, it opened a door for a new generation of Russian animators to make modern, grown-up films containing irony, social satire, and original ideas.

Khitruk went on to direct many more satirical, award-winning shorts, such as *Chelovek v ramke* (*Man in the Frame*, 1966), *Ostrov* (*Island*, 1973), *Film, film, film!* (1968), *Ikar i mudretsy* (*Icarus and the Wise Men*, 1976), and *Lev i byk* (*Lion and Bull*, 1984).

In 1993 Khitruk, along with leading animators Yuriy Norshteyn, Eduard Nazarov, and Andrey Khrzhanovsky, founded the animation school and studio SHAR in Moscow.

1963

USA

Ivan Sutherland: Sketchpad software

In 1963 Ivan Sutherland developed Sketchpad (also known as the Robot Draftsman), a revolutionary piece of computer software, for his PhD thesis. Running on the Lincoln TX-2 computer at the Massachusetts Institute of Technology (MIT), it was a breakthrough in computer graphics and a forerunner of modern computer-aided drafting software (CAD). With Sketchpad, Sutherland showed not just how people might create art with computers, but also how they might interact in general using a graphical user interface (GUI), and inspired further development of similar systems worldwide.

1963

USA

Stan Brakhage: Mothlight

An abstract filmmaker with a long and varied career, Stan Brakhage made films from the 1940s right through until his death in 2003. Spending many years in an isolated log cabin with his family, his films engage with nature, emotions, relationships, and family life. Scratching, painting, and pressing natural objects directly onto the film stock, Brakhage's work also relates to ideas of altered states of consciousness between sleep and waking. *Mothlight* was created by a form of "direct cinema," in that no camera was used to create it; instead, found objects of insects' wings, beetles' legs, and leaves were glued between two strips of film. This ultra-short short (its running time is just four minutes) is certainly like no other film before it, and has a strange, hypnotic fascination and unique beauty.

Mothlight, 1963

1963

Japan

Osamu Tezuka: Tetsuwan Atomu (Astro Boy)

In 1952 Osamu Tezuka created the manga comic known as *Tetsuwan Atomu* (*Astro Boy*), which he later developed into the television series of the same name, first broadcast in Japan in 1963 and soon popular worldwide. Although it was not the first anime television series—*Instant History*, a Japanese documentary series using cartoons to illustrate history, was broadcast in 1961—it was *Astro Boy* that demonstrated to the world the particular style of cartoon that later became known as anime. The series was remade in color in the 1980s, again in 2003, and a CG feature followed in 2009.

With a deliberate nod to the story of Pinocchio, *Astro Boy* concerns a robot boy created by a scientist who has lost his own son in an accident. Upset because his robot substitute son can't grow up, he sells the baby-featured, rocket-booted Astro Boy, programmed to be forever good, to an evil robot circus master. Happily the robot boy is rescued by a kind professor who adopts him, encourages him to devote himself to fighting evil, and eventually builds him a robot girlfriend.

The designs of *Astro Boy* have a genuine appeal, originality, and impact missing from later, more derivative examples of anime, which use the sci-fi elements but dispense with the charm and classic design.

Biography

Osamu Tezuka

Born in 1928, Osamu Tezuka developed a childhood love for comic strips and began producing his own comics while still in school. He graduated as a doctor in the early 1950s, but he never practiced this profession. Instead, he pursued his artistic interests and became Japan's biggest art celebrity of the 1950s. He wrote hundreds of manga comics, many of which have never been translated from the original Japanese. Tezuka founded Mushi Productions in 1962, which became a major studio producing animated versions of several other comic artists' works as well as those of Tezuka.

Inpired by the work of early American animators, Tezuka is known as the Godfather of Anime, and is credited with inventing some of its distinctive features, such as characters with oversized eyes. Best known for *Tetsuwan Atomu* (*Astro Boy*), Tezuka worked to promote animation as an art form and used the funds from his commercial work to produce experimental animated films aimed at an adult audience. He continued to make animated films, both commercial and arthouse, until his untimely death from stomach cancer in 1989.

A hugely influential figure, the Osamu Tezuka Museum was inaugurated in 1994. Among many other honors, he was awarded the Winsor McCay award for lifetime achievement in 1990.

1964
USA

Depatie-Freleng: The Pink Panther movie titles

After Warner Bros. shut down its animation studio in 1963, Isadore "Friz" Freleng and business partner David DePatie founded DePatie-Freleng Enterprises.

The company was commissioned to create the opening titles for the live-action Peter Sellars comedy, *The Pink Panther*. Freleng and layout artist and director Hawley Pratt created a

long, languid cat character, which became so popular that a short cartoon, *The Pink Phink* (1964), was commissioned, winning the 1965 Oscar. Freleng and DePatie then produced a popular series of Pink Panther cartoons. The success of this ensured that other series followed, including *The Inspector* and *The Ant and the Aardvark*. DePatie-Freleng would keep making *The Pink Panther* and other series for television and theatrical release until 1980.

1964

USA

Disney: Mary Poppins

In 1964 Disney produced their first serious attempt at mixing animation with live action since *Song of the South* in 1946. In this classic children's film, the magical nanny of the title (played by Julie Andrews) takes the two children in her care and her friend Bert (Dick Van Dyke) into a fantasy animated world where they ride on a carousel and play with animated animals. Highlights include some wonderful penguin waiters, who dance along with the cast—and who would be seen again in 1988's *Who Framed Roger Rabbit*—and the fairground horses, who are liberated from their carousel in order to carry the characters across the archetypal fairy-tale landscape. This magical

sequence accompanied the song "Jolly Holiday," one of the great numbers written by the Sherman Brothers for the movie.

The charming and lush dream world, which includes some of Disney's best animation of the 1960s, was directed by Ward Kimball, who was also in charge of the animated sequences for Disney's similar, although not as memorable, *Bedknobs and Broomsticks* (1971).

Mary Poppins is a timeless and entertaining children's classic, carried by a fine, energetic, and funny perfomance by Van Dyke, some great dancing and songs, and Julie Andrews shining in a role for which she will always be remembered.

USA/
Czech Republic

Gene Deitch: Munro And Nudnik

Gene Deitch, an animator at UPA in the early 1950s, later joined Terrytoons in 1955 where he created characters such as John Doormat, Gaston Le Crayon, and Foofle. In early 1958, his theatrical cartoon *Sidney's Family Tree* (1958) was nominated for an Acadamy Award, but later that year he was fired from Terrytoons after some infighting at the studio. He opened his own studio, but closed it down quickly, and in 1960, moved to Prague, Czechoslovakia (now the Czech Republic). There he worked at Rembrandt Films with producer William L. Snyder, and directed approximately a dozen *Tom and Jerry* cartoons, outsourced from MGM, along with *Krazy Kat* and *Popeye* for King Features.

In 1960 Deitch made the Oscar-winning short *Munro* (1960), a loose naturalistic film written by cartoonist Jules Feiffer, featuring a droll commentary about a Charlie Brown-like boy who is drafted into the army.

Following this, Paramount bought Deitch's series *Nudnik* for the US market. *Nudnik* features a short, lumpy, scruffy character called Yaramaz Nudnik (based on Deitch's Foofle character) and the hapless scrapes he gets into. Watching *Nudnik*, its dual roots are apparent; it has a loose, Eastern European feel to the design and an American solidity to the animation, which ultimately creates something with an originality and quality rare in television cartoons, particularly at this time of threadbare production values. Between 1964 and 1966, 12 Nudnik cartoons were produced in Prague for Paramount, of which the first, mysteriously called *Nudnik No 2*, was nominated for the short film Oscar in 1965.

USA

Chuck Jones: The Dot and the Line: A Romance in Lower Mathematics

The Dot and the Line was a short made by Chuck Jones during his time at MGM. Adapted from the book by Norton Juster, the film is perhaps the ultimate in stripped-down, geometric modernism in animation, reducing the characters in a love story to literally a dot and a line, and in doing so somehow saying as much about human relationships as the entire works of Jane Austen.

Narrated by Robert Morley, the funny and clever story tells of a boring straight line who is in love with a graceful round circle, who, unfortunately for the line, would rather hang around with a crazy, jazz-dancing squiggle. Eventually the dot tires of the antics of the unruly and unreliable squiggle and the line learns how to bend, finally impressing the dot by making a variety of lovely, precise geometric shapes.

1965
USA

Bill Melendez: A Charlie Brown Christmas

After making a 1965 documentary about *Peanuts* creator Charles Schultz, producer Lee Mendelson put together this animated Christmas TV special. Schultz suggested hiring animator and director Bill Melendez, whom Schultz had worked with on a *Peanuts*-based commercial.

Melendez had an amazing resume, his list of employers reading like a who's who of the Golden Age of American Animation. Joining Disney in 1938, Melendez had worked on films such as *Bambi*, *Fantasia*, and *Dumbo*. A campaigner for unionization of the animators, he left as part of the 1941 Disney animators' strike, and moved to Leon Schlesinger Productions, which became Warner Bros. Cartoons. In 1948, Melendez, moved over to UPA where he animated on cartoons such as *Gerald McBoing-Boing*. Later, Melendez directed thousands of television commercials. In 1963 he founded his own studio, Bill Melendez Productions, in the basement of his Hollywood home.

Funded by the Coca-Cola Company and scored by jazz composer Vince Guaraldi, *A Charlie Brown Christmas* is a charming cartoon. Its simple expressionistic backgrounds, jazzy music, and simple but gracefully drawn characters give it the feel of a UPA short updated for the 1960s, and it captures the well-defined world of the *Peanuts* comic strip. It became a standard fixture for many Christmases to come and is fondly remembered by the 1950s-born generation.

1965
China

Wan Laiming: Da nao tian gong (Havoc in Heaven/Uproar in Heaven)

Da nao tian gong (*Havoc in Heaven*) is perhaps the most famous and successful movie by the masters of Chinese animation, the Wan brothers, and one of the most influential films in Asian cinema. Wan Guchan began planning the film after the completion of *Tie shan gong zhu* (*Princess Iron Fan*, 1941), of which he was one of the main creators and animators. The project was delayed by the Japanese capture of Shanghai and, later, by the Chinese Civil War. Returning to the Shanghai Animation Film Studio in 1954, Wan Guchan and the studio's director Wan Laiming started work on the project and the first part was completed and released in 1961, followed by the second part in 1964. The two parts were edited and screened together for the first time in 1965; various versions now exist with lengths between around 85 and 120 minutes. This was the last major Chinese animated film of its era, as a year later the whole movie industry was effectively stopped by the Cultural Revolution.

Like *Princess Iron Fan*, the story was taken from the traditional Buddist tale, *Journey to the West*. It concerns the monkey king, Sun Wukong, who while searching for a suitable weapon, causes trouble by taking a magic pillar from the palace of the dragon king. He is then summoned to heaven and given the task of looking after the stables, where he causes more havoc by setting the horses free. The monkey king represents the virtues of cunning and bravery triumphing over brute force.

This impressive movie is smoothly animated and richly detailed with beautiful painted backdrops in the Chinese style. The percussion-based music and certain visual stylizations of the movements and design are influenced by traditional Chinese operas. For modern Western tastes, the story can seem a little slow and complicated, but this merely reflects cultural differences between Western and traditional Chinese storytelling rather than any shortcomings of the movie itself.

1966

USA

彩色动画片

Da nao tian gong
(Havoc in Heaven),
1965

Chuck Jones: How The Grinch Stole Christmas!

Following the success of Bill Melendez's *A Charlie Brown Christmas*, Chuck Jones took Dr. Seuss' popular short story about the commercialization of Christmas, and produced what has now become a perennial Christmas classic on American television. The 26-minute short was broadcast annually on the CBS network from 1966 until 1987, after which it was bought by Turner Broadcasting. *How the Grinch Stole Christmas* is now shown several times every Christmas on the Turner networks, making it one of the most popular festive specials and one of the few from the 1960s that is still shown regularly.

Jones was a friend of Ted Geisel (Dr. Seuss), whom he had met during World War II when they both worked on the instructional *Private Snafu* shorts at Warner Bros. Well-animated and crafted, there were claims at the time that this was the most expensive TV animation to date, the budget reflecting Jones' wish to make the best possible adaptation of his friend's book. Jones based the animation as closely as possible on Seuss' distinctive designs, although the cartoon was made in color, in contrast to the original book, which was printed in red and black. The film follows the book's plot faithfully, the main points of departure being the addition of three songs and a larger role for the Grinch's dog, Max. The film features a wonderful narration from Boris Karloff, which gave him a resurgence of attention in the USA a few years before his death.

1966
Spain

Francisco Macián: El mago de los sueños (The Magician Of Dreams)

Barcelona-born Francisco Macián came to animation through his early interest in drawing and music. After working on Balet y Blay's *Los sueños de Tay-Pi* (*The Visions of Tay-Pi*, 1951) he opened his own animation studio in 1955. Here he mainly made commercials, although he also produced interesting projects such as a documentary on French illustrator Gustave Doré and an animated version of Laurel and Hardy.

In 1966 Macián completed his most ambitious project, *El mago de los sueños* (*The Magician of Dreams*). Using television characters licensed from Estudios Moro and based on a Hans Christian Andersen tale, the film weaves a story out of the dreams of six children. It is recognized as a milestone of Spanish animation and some critics have even described it as the best postwar European animated feature film. This charming film, almost forgotten outside of Spain, is indeed beautifully crafted and animated and not only compares well with other European features of its era, but also to most of the production-line animation coming out of the USA at this time, whether feature films or television.

Macián tragically died as he set to work on the follow-up to this great achievement, leaving a glittering promise unfulfilled.

1966
Russia

Andrei Khrjanovsky: Zhil-byl Kozyavin (There Lived Kozyavin)

Andrei Khrjanovsky's *Zhil-byl Kozyavin* (*There Lived Kozyavin*) is a dark comedy about the dangers of the machinations of a regimented state. In the film an emotionless bureaucrat sets about his duties in a rigidly determined manner, walking in one direction in a straight line, as he has been instructed, until he walks around the planet and back to where he started, trampling over whatever and whoever stands in his path. Using a basic straightforward drawing style, the short film uses the character's journey to experiment with perspective and landscape with increasingly surrealist backdrops and shades of Russian constructivism in many of its designs.

The film was clearly a comment on the absurdity of faceless communist bureaucracy, and yet paradoxically, despite the heavy KGB interference in all soviet film production, it was approved for production by the state-owned Soyuzmultfilm studio. Fyodor Khitruk's *Chelovek v ramke* (*Man in the Frame*) made in the same year, was also approved. *Man in the Frame* follows a similar theme, telling the story of an obedient bureaucrat who is afraid of breaking free from a picture frame that slowly grows bigger and eventually obliterates him.

Khrjanovsky's *Steklyannaya garmonika* (*The Glass Harmonica*, 1969) was not so lucky, however. This story of a city presided over by heartless bureaucrats to which a visiting musician demonstrates the liberating power of music and art, was the first animated film to be officially banned in Russia.

Khrjanovsky was an intellectual filmmaker who made animation with the determined seriousness of the live-action soviet arthouse filmmakers of his era. His films were multilayered studies of the human condition in a multitude of styles. He later adapted literary works, such as poems by Alexander Pushkin—*Ya k vam lechu vospominanem* (*I Fly To You in Memory*, 1977), *I s vami snova ya* (*I Am With You Again*, 1980), and *Osen* (*Autumn*, 1982)—and scripts by A. A. Milne, *Korolevskiy buterbrod* (*The King's Sandwich*, 1985).

Japan

Vietnam

Toei Doga: Saibogu 009 (Cyborg 009) and Kaitei Shonen Marin (Marine Boy)

Saibogu 009 (*Cyborg 009*) was a Japanese manga comic created by Shotaro Ishinomori concerning a champion athlete who, after being injured in an accident and kidnapped by evil forces, is rescued by a kind-hearted professor who transforms him into a half-human/half-machine cyborg with a mission of fighting evil. Treading the same pop sci-fi ground as *Astro Boy*, the comic was adapted into animation, although without quite the craft and quality of drawing and design of its predecessor. *Cyborg 009* was marketed into a successful franchise with a 1966 TV movie, followed by a sequel, *Saibogu 009: Kaiju senso* (*C009: Kaiju Wars*, 1967). A television series followed in 1968, with a color TV revival in 1979, and again in 2001 as *Cyborg 009: The Cyborg Soldier*, building a devoted following of teenage boys worldwide as Japanese TV animation began to challenge the American stranglehold of children's schedules.

Also launched the same year by the Toei Doga studio was *Kaitei Shonen Marin* (*Marine Boy*), inspired by Arthur C. Clarke's story *Deep Range*. The story of a boy who has been genetically modified by his father, Marine Boy can survive for long periods underwater with the aid of oxygen chewing gum, where he fights undersea monsters and bad guys with the help of a dolphin and a mermaid. The series was first created in 1967 by Suguru Sugiyama as *Dolphin Prince*; an early experiment in TV color anime, this was quickly cancelled and then restarted as *Marine Boy* a year later. Seventy-eight episodes of *Marine Boy* were made and the series helped spread the manga message as it became a hit in the USA. It was also the first successful anime in the UK.

Ngo Manh Lan: The Kitty

Founded in 1959, the Hanoi Cartoon Studio was established by the Vietnamese military to make propaganda shorts and morality tales using a variety of traditional animation techniques. Directed by ex-soldier Ngo Manh Lan, *The Kitty* was the first international success for the studio, a prize-winning short that tells of a kitten who organizes a fightback against an invading army of rats.

Born in 1934, Lan studied fine art before joining the army. He came to attention as an artist by producing war sketches during the Dien Bien Phu Campaign, and later went on to study animation in the Soviet Union. The cute animal films he produced form a stark contrast with his war drawings.

The Hanoi Cartoon Studio formed the basis of the early Vietnamese animation industry, although, since the late 1960s, the main form of animation produced in Vietnam has been production work "outsourced" from Western companies.

1967

USA

Disney: The Jungle Book

After the success of 1964's *Mary Poppins* came another Disney musical smash hit with excellent dance sequences and great songs. The new rough look to the Xeroxed lines of the drawings, first used in *One Hundred and One Dalmatians*, especially suited *The Jungle Book*, which has an overall loose and jazzy style. Despite being criticised for taking liberties with Rudyard Kipling's book, the film went on to become one of the best-loved Disney features. This looser, more spontaneous feel was also reflected in the voices; for the first time the characters' movements and acting were based on the personalities and filmed performances of the voice actors, who were encouraged to improvise as they recorded. This has since become standard practice in feature animation. Particularly memorable are the bandleader/comedian Phil Harris' excellent portrayal of the bear Baloo, George Saunders as the tiger Shere Kahn, and Louis Prima as King Louie the orangutan. The work of animator Milt

The Jungle Book, 1967

Kahl in the film, in particular on Shere Kahn, has become regarded as some of the greatest ever character animation and established his reputation as one of the great animators.

This was to be the last animated feature Walt Disney was involved in, as he died of lung cancer on December 15, 1966. *The Jungle Book* was released after his death and his company would never, artistically at least, fully recover from his loss. He was mourned around the world and in the years since his death there has never been anyone to replace him. Undoubtedly the most important figure in the history of animation, it is impossible to imagine twentieth-century popular culture without him.

1967
USA/Japan

Jules Bass: Mad Monster Party

Mad Monster Party is a wild, stop-frame comedy horror, made at stop-frame specialists MOM Productions in Japan for US producers Rankin/Bass. Seemingly influential on the later work of Tim Burton, particularly *The Nightmare Before Christmas*, this feature-length TV special is a follow-up to other stop-frame productions from the same team, such as the highly successful TV special *Rudolph the Red-Nosed Reindeer* (1964), and the TV series *The New Adventures of Pinnochio* (1960).

Witten by *Mad* magazine creator Harvey Kurtzman, *Mad* artist Jack Davis also designed the characters. The voice artists included, among others, Phyllis Diller and Boris Karloff, continuing his late career as an in-demand voiceover artist following his success in *The Grinch Who Stole Christmas*. The all-star cast of famous monsters included the original stop-frame beast, King Kong, although due to copyright, his character is referred to as "It." In one scene of this cult classic, a character's head is replaced by a pig's head, perhaps an influence on the legendary deleted scene in *Who Framed Roger Rabbit*, where Bob Hoskins has a cartoon pig's head "painted" onto his.

1967
Belgium

Belvision Studios: Astérix le Gaulois (Asterix the Gaul)

The first in the long and continuing franchise of Asterix feature films, of which 12 have been made to date, *Astérix le Gaulois* (*Asterix the Gaul*) was adapted from the first volume of the highly-successful series of comics and graphic novels created by French writer René Goscinny and illustrator Albert Uderzo.

Incredibly, the movie was made in Belgium without Goscinny or Uderzo's knowledge, and by the time they found out it was too late to stop the film's release. They forced production of the sequel to be stopped, however, and negotiated a role in the future productions of the series. They maintained, rightly many would say, that *Asterix the Gaul* was a cheaply made and substandard movie, which did the comics a disservice. The film stays close to its comic source though, and was a favorite with fans at the European box office.

1967
France/Poland

Walerian Borowcyzk: Théâtre de M. et Mme. Kabal (Mr and Mrs Kabal's Theater)

Walerian Borowcyzk was a Polish artist and filmmaker who, after studying painting and lithography at the Krakow Academy of Fine Arts and early work designing movie theater posters, started making short live-action films and then animation. He would continue to successfully move between various disciplines during his lifetime.

His early films were surrealist animated shorts made with fellow emerging Polish animator Jan Lenica, the most successful being *Byl Sobie raz* (*Once Upon a Time*, 1957), *Nagrodzone uczucia* (*Love Rewarded*, 1957), and *Dom* (*The House*, 1958). Borowczyk and Lenica fell out in around 1958 over artistic differences and both emigrated to the West, leaving behind an influential legacy among a new generation of Polish filmmakers and artists.

After moving to Paris, Borowcyzk continued his animation work. In 1959 he made *Les astronautes* (*The Astronauts*) with another art filmmaker, Chris Marker. Marker is famous for *La jetée* (*The Pier*, 1962), which, while being a sequence of images, was not animation. For the stop-motion film *Renaissance* (1963), Borowczyk filmed objects deteriorating and breaking, and then reversed the film so that the objects reformed before being blown up by a bomb. *Les jeux des anges* (*The Game of the Angels*, 1964) was listed by director and animator Terry Gilliam in an interview with the *Guardian* newspaper as one of his 10 favorite animated films of all time, and the influence of Borowczyk's absurd, anticonventional humor and minimalist approach can be seen in Gilliam's cartoons.

Using the characters from his 1962 short film *Le concert de M. et Mme. Kabal* (*The Concert of Mr And Mrs Kabal*) Borowcyzk made his final animated statement, *Théâtre de M. et Mme. Kabal* (*Mr and Mrs Kabal's Theater*) in 1967. An extreme surrealist and absurdist experience, it features minimal scratchy drawings, animated photographs, and deconstructed live action, in which Borowczyk himself makes an appearance. During the course of the film, the witch-like Madame Kabal presides over a series of insane acts, like a host to some kind of horrible cabaret, while talking in an indecipherable, rapid spiel of words and sounds, cut together seemingly at random, and often sounding like the stuttering rythmic repetition of hip-hop music. Throughout the film, Madame Kabal uses her deeply unpleasant voice and personality to bully anyone who comes into her domain, including the unfortunate Monsieur Kabal. The film is an early exercise in "lo-fi" animation, and its minimalism and obscure sillyness at times come over like something cooked up by British cartoonist/artist/animator David Shrigley 30 years later. The combination of minimal aesthetics and the jarring soundtrack challenges the viewer to keep watching, and in this way it is not that dissimilar an experience to Harry Smith's *Heaven and Earth Magic* (1960), except with the mysticism replaced by savage, Eastern European humor.

This proved to be Borowcyzk's last animated film (apart from a brief return in 1984 with *Scherzo infernal)* as he later concentrated on live action, again proving his diversity by ranging from critically-acclaimed art films—*Goto, l'Isle d'Amour* (*Goto, The Island of Love*, 1968) and *Blanche* (1971)—to erotic B-movies, such as *Interno di un convento* (*Behind Convent Walls*, 1978), *Docteur Jekyll et les femmes* (*The Blood of Dr Jekyll*, 1981), and *Emmanuelle 5* (1987).

1967

Croatia

Zlatko Grgic: Professor Balthazar

By the mid-1960s, the Zageb Film studio was building its reputation as one of the world's best animation studios. A second wave of animators and directors took control as the founding members from the 1950s dispersed. Like UPA a decade before, which in some ways served as a model for Zagreb, the studio produced work in the commercial world of advertising and television, as well as the one-off films for which it was famous.

Professor Balthazar was a Zagreb Film television series that achieved worldwide popularity. Created by Zlatko Grgic, after his success with the Cannes-prizewinning short *Muzikalno prase* (*The Musical Pig*, 1966), 52 episodes of the series featuring the eccentric old inventor were made over seven years, finishing production in 1974. It featured the requisite catchy theme tune that lodges in a child's brain for a lifetime and the simplified designs and limited animation that the Zagreb studio was known for.

Grgic went on to work on the Zagreb series *Maxi Cat* in 1971, and directed three shorts for the National Film Board of Canada: *Hot Stuff* (1971), *Who Are We?* (1974), and *Deep Throat* (1977). He also worked with Bob Godfrey on the Oscar-nominated *Dream Doll* in 1979.

Professor Balthazar

1967
Japan

Hiroshi Sasagawa: Mach Go Go Go (Speed Racer)

Based on a manga comic, the television series adaptation of *MACH GO GO GO* was sold in the West as *Speed Racer.* The Western version toned down the mayhem of the Japanese original by having characters "stunned" instead of killed, as the main character, Speed, races his car while fighting dastardly, cheating foes. After *Astro Boy* and *Marine Boy* the market had opened up in the West for this under-animated but effects-heavy style of Japanese anime, and *Speed Racer* was an international success.

1967
South Korea

Dong-Heon Shin: Hong Kil-dong

South Korea's first animated feature, *Hong Kil-dong*, was made six years after a military coup that had resulted in state restrictions of cinema. Taking advantage of the new rules on quotas of home-produced movies in the theaters and the successful Korean rerelease of Disney movies such as *Snow White and the Seven Dwarfs*, Seki Productions embarked on the adaptation of a popular comic starring folk hero Hong Kil-dong. The movie was a huge domestic success and kick-started a series of Korean domestic productions and the later successful Korean animation industry.

1968
Canada

Eva Szasz: Cosmic Zoom

Cosmic Zoom is a simple but fascinating science-based short, which travels to the farthest known point in the universe and back again to the smallest particle of matter. Starting with live-action film of a boy rowing a boat, the frame freezes and changes to drawn animation as the camera slowly zooms out until we see the whole of the lake, the continent of North America, planet earth, the moon, the solar system, the Milky Way, and the galaxy. From distant space, the camera then moves back down to the boy and keeps going closer until we see a mosquito on his hand, then the insect's head, and further down through the skin to the subatomic level, before coming back out to show the boy rowing across the lake.

The animated zoom is impressively smooth and could probably not be much improved by CGI. Based on the 1957 book *Cosmic View* by Kees Boeke (also revised in 1982 and 1994), the film was directed by Eva Szasz for the National Film Board of Canada. *Cosmic Zoom* is one of those shorts that captures the imagination and sticks in the mind of everyone that sees it, especially children and late night student crowds, providing a mindblowing mental map of the entire universe.

Coincidentally, the designers Ray and Charles Eames released their film *Powers of Ten*, also based on *Cosmic View*, in 1968. This film opens on a picnic scene 10 meters square and zooms out, in scales of 10 to the power of one, 10 to the power of two, and so on. Another similar film was made for IMAX cinemas in 1996 entitled *Cosmic Voyage*, which, although made with high-definition CGI, lacks the handcrafted charm of the 1968 films.

1968
UK

George Dunning: Yellow Submarine

Following on from Beatles wigs, fan books, scarves, and dolls, a television cartoon series about the band was almost inevitable. In 1965 London-based studio TV Cartoons (TVC) got the job of producing this rather lacklustre cartoon series for King Features, who owned the Beatles cartoon rights. So when funding for a Beatles animated feature was raised, TVC got the commission. TVC had a secret weapon to unleash on the movie, however: the maverick genius of director George Dunning. Dunning worked with designer Heinz Edelmann and writers including Lee Minoff, Erich Segal, and poet Roger McGough to create a psychedelic masterpiece to complement the Beatles' musical talents. Although King Features executive Al Brodax is credited as the producer of *Yellow Submarine* and

TVC's John Coates as production supervisor, in reality Coates was the hands-on producer while Brodax had a more distant executive role. This lack of proper credit illustrates the inexperience of Coates and Dunning's company at the time they signed the contract, with King Features walking away with all the profits and merchandise rights from the hit movie after completion, while TVC actually made a loss when the production went over budget.

The film begins in Liverpool, in a backdrop constructed by Dunning out of cutout photos. In the story, the Beatles agree to travel in a yellow submarine to rescue the inhabitants of a land where music and happiness are banned by the Blue Meanies. From that point on, Dunning and Edelmann's colorful and surreal fantasy backgrounds take over as the Fab Four's journey unfolds, built around a series of marvellous musical sequences.

Yellow Submarine,
1968

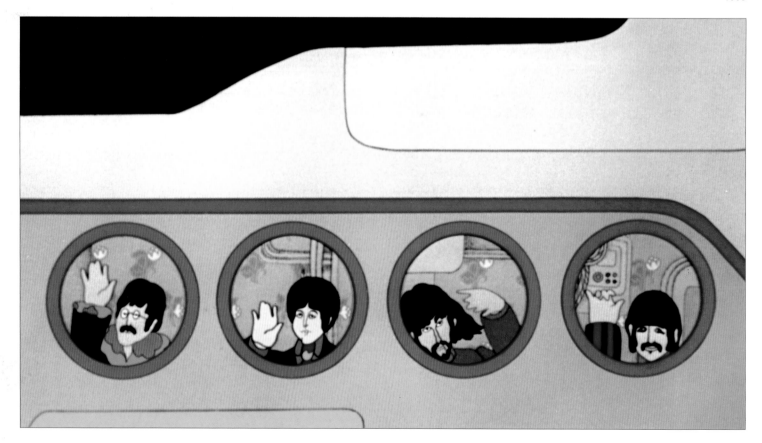

Each song was animated in a different visual style, making full use of the technology available at the time, as well as the talents of Dunning, Edelmann, Charles Jenkins, Robert Balser, Jack Stokes, and Alison de Vere. The kaleidoscopic shifting styles have influences ranging from the pop artists Peter Blake and Andy Warhol to the surrealists Salvador Dalí and René Magritte. Dunning was responsible for the "Lucy in the Sky with Diamonds" sequence, which featured paint overlaid on rotoscoped footage of live-action dancers. For "Eleanor Rigby," photos of certain crew members were integrated into the crowd, including Dunning and Edelmann (men with umbrellas), Alison de Vere (girl with camera), and Al Brodax (man smoking pipe), while the landlord of the production team's favorite pub also makes an appearance (man in phone box). Of the five new songs written especially for the movie, "Hey, Bulldog," and its sequence featuring a multiheaded dog, was edited out of the American release, perhaps considered too weird for kids. The sequence was reinstated for the thirtieth anniversary rerelease of the film.

Along with the Fab Four's wonderful live-action movies *Hard Day's Night* and *Help!*, *Yellow Submarine* captured the optimisim, charm, and humor of the band and the "swinging sixties" era that the Beatles presided over. Apart from the bright cartoon portraits of the Beatles, the film provided more iconic imagery evocative of the time, including the Submarine itself, the Blue Meanies, the Nowhere Man, and the nasty Flying Glove, and technically the film's wild mixing of techniques is still an inspirational reference today. An instant classic of British animation and one of the great "rock" movies, *Yellow Submarine*'s influence over graphic style, design, and advertising was huge, while it demonstrated to a generation of animators and directors that successful animated features were possible away from the standard Disney model.

Biography

George Dunning / TVC

A leading figure in both Canadian and British animation, George Dunning was born in Toronto in 1920. After studying at the Ontario School of Art and working as an illustrator, he joined the National Film Board of Canada in 1943, where he worked with Norman McLaren. At the NFB, Dunning began creating experimental work such as *Cadet Rousselle* (1946), a stop-motion short made using flat metal figures instead of puppets. In 1948 he spent a year in Paris, where he met and was influenced by the Czech animator Berthold Bartosch, and began experimenting with painting on glass. In the 1950s, Dunning worked for the UPA studio in New York on the *Gerald McBoing Boing* series, and in 1956 he moved to London to manage UPA's short-lived British office.

Dunning, along with his business partner John Coates, established TV Cartoons (TVC) in 1957, employing many of the former UPA London staff. Fellow Canadian Richard Williams was also employed as a freelance animation director. Although TVC mainly produced animated information films and commercials for the growing television market, Dunning continued to make experimental shorts such as *The Wardrobe* (1958) and *The Apple* (1962), as well as *The Flying Man* (1962) and *The Ladder* (1967), in which he developed the painted brushstroke technique that would later feature in the "Lucy in the Sky with Diamonds" sequence of *Yellow Submarine*. After completing work on the Beatles feature film, Dunning produced more noteworthy shorts, including *The Maggot* (1973) and *Damon the Mower* (1973), and began plans for an animated feature-length adaptation of Shakespeare's *The Tempest*. Sadly, ill health prevented him from completing this project and he died in 1979.

After Dunning's death, John Coates continued to manage TVC and decided to switch the studio's emphasis from commercials and information films to entertainment, particularly adaptations of children's literature. Coates mortgaged his house to help fund *The Snowman* (1982), TVC's most successful work. TVC adapted several other books by Raymond Briggs, including *When The Wind Blows* (1986) and *Father Christmas* (1991). Other notable works include *The World of Peter Rabbit and Friends* (1992) and a feature-length version of *The Wind in the Willows* (1995). Coates and his long-term associate Norman Kauffman are currently developing an adaptation of Raymond Briggs' *Ethel & Ernest*, a heartfelt story based on the relationship of Briggs' parents.

1968
UK/USA

Terry Gilliam: Storytime and Monty Python's Flying Circus

The American-born animator Terry Gilliam arrived in London in 1967. Here he looked up the only Englishman he knew, the actor John Cleese. Cleese gave him the name of a BBC producer and soon Gilliam was employed on a TV comedy show entitled *Do Not Adjust Your Set,* where he worked as a sketch writer alongside Michael Palin, Eric Idle, and Terry Jones. When the producer, Humphrey Barclay, found out about Gilliam's cartooning talent, he asked him to create some animation for the show. He later produced more cartoons to accompany various monologues and spin-offs, which were joined together to form the short film, *Storytime.*

Storytime was influenced by Stan van der Beek's *Death Breath* (1964), an absurdist art film Gilliam had seen in New York, featuring a cutout photo of Richard Nixon's head, sliced in half horizontally so that the mouth could open right up and swallow a big foot. Faced with creating animation with little money or time, Gilliam came up with his trademark anarchic animated mixture of cutout photos, Victorian imagery, surreal machines, and bizzarre illustrations.

The Christmas card sequence seen in *Storytime*, created for the *Do Not Adjust Your Set* Christmas special, is one of Gilliam's finest and funniest moments and encapsulates the good-natured anarchy and mischievous inventiveness of his work.

When Palin, Idle, and Jones started to put together a new show with John Cleese and Graham Chapman, Gilliam was brought in to contribute with his animation, writing, and, sometimes, acting. *Monty Python's Flying Circus* became an iconic television comedy of the 1960s and 1970s, and Gilliam's anarchic animations are an integral part of its identity. Gilliam also contributed animated elements to the Pythons' feature films, including *Monty Python and the Holy Grail* (1975) and *Life of Brian* (1979).

Monty Python's
Flying Circus

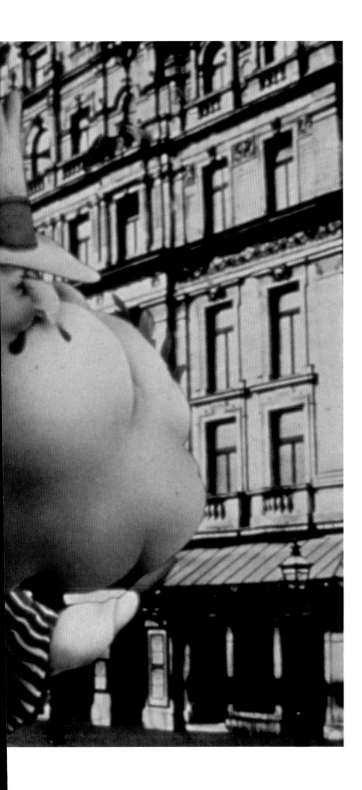

Biography

Terry Gilliam

After early years spent in Los Angeles (studying art and political science) and New York (as assistant editor, writer, and cartoonist on Harvey Kurtzman's magazine *Help!*), Terry Gilliam moved to the UK where, as part of the Monty Python comedy team, he established himself as a master of surreal, anarchic animation. His wild, inventive, and anticonventional style has proved influential on many future animators and directors, including lo-fi genius Michel Gondry and *South Park*'s Trey Parker and Matt Stone.

After the *Monty Python's Flying Circus* series finished its run, Gilliam took his particular aesthetic, attitude, and brand of gentle surrealism and widened its scope to become a visionary live-action movie director. He codirected *Monty Python and the Holy Grail* (1975) with Terry Jones, which he followed the next year with *Jabberwocky*, his first film as a solo director. His ambitious movies are typically surreal fantasies, with notable works including *Time Bandits* (1979), *Brazil* (1985), *The Adventures of Baron Munchausen* (1989), *12 Monkeys* (1995), *The Brothers Grimm* (2005), and *The Imaginarium of Doctor Parnassus* (2009).

1968
Japan

Isao Takahata: Taiyo No Oji: Horusu No Daiboken (Prince of the Sun: The Adventure of Horus)

In Isao Takahata's debut feature, *Taiyo no oji: Horusu no daiboken* (*Prince of the Sun: The Adventure of Horus*) can be seen a lot of the qualities and style that would become the hallmark of Studio Ghibli, the company he would later establish along with his younger collaborator and protégé, Hayao Miyazaki, who worked on this film with Takahata.

Produced by Toei Doga and Topcraft, the story concerns a young fisherman's son, Horus, who is rescued from a wolf attack by a giant, who has been awakened from centuries of sleep by the sounds of the fight. Horus returns the favor by removing a magic sword embedded in the giant, which Horus uses in further battles against the evil King Grunwald who has terrorized Horus' people for centuries. On his way to discover what happened to his ancestors, Horus rescues a fishing village from a giant fish and befriends Hilda, a lonely girl who is tied to his fate.

The movie, three years in the making, is distinguished by its precise, appealingly drawn and animated human characters, and beautifully realized natural scenery and animals. In fact, although some of the human designs have a more broad, cartoony feel, with its epic plot and a backdrop based on Scandinavia, in many ways it feels like the first Studio Ghibli production in everything but name.

1969
USA

Marv Newland: Bambi Meets Godzilla

As the credits roll on Marv Newland's 90-second debut (with everything credited to Marv Newland), we see a naïve animation of Bambi grazing among some flowers. The credits finish, a huge monster foot immediately flattens Bambi, to the accompaniment of a clanging chord. After a short pause, the closing credits roll. And that's it.

Apparently filmed on the side of Newland's fridge, *Bambi Meets Godzilla* is a lo-fi, anarchic classic, with a plot that could have come straight out of a Terry Gilliam *Monty Python* cartoon. The film's reputation spread as it started to be screened at midnight movie events and became a favorite of traveling animation shows like Spike and Mike's Fantastic Animation Festival and the Sick and Twisted Festival of Animation that toured college campuses in the 1970s and 1980s. It was even voted the 38th best cartoon of all time in a survey for animation historian Jerry Beck's book *The 50 Greatest Cartoons: As Selected by 1,000 Animation Professionals*. Highly unusual in its day, *Bambi Meets Godzilla* could be said to be an influence on the "shock humor" type of animation that emerged in decades to come, and if it now looks a bit predictable to modern audiences, that is because we have seen a million of the films and gags like it that followed.

1969

Canada

Ryan Larkin: Walking and Street Musique

A protégé of the National Film Board of Canada and Norman McLaren, Ryan Larkin produced a sequence of award-winning films in the 1960s in a freeflowing, psychedelic, figurative style, often involving a loose succession of scenarios and images morphing from one to another. His first film, *Syrinx* (1965), was based on Greek mythology and involved sequences of transforming drawings in a classical style, while *Cityscape* (1966) had the more contemporary theme of an evolving city.

Walking was another transformational film featuring impressionist-style walking figures who pass through many identities and forms while loping along a journey. Possessing a joyous, psychedelic energy and enthusiasm for the process of animation, *Walking* was nominated for the best animated short Oscar in 1970.

Larkin's next short, *Street Musique* (1972) concerned the effect on passersby of a street musician. It won many awards, but was Larkin's last completed film, although he created

animation for, and played a small part in, Mort Ransen's award-winning *Running Time* (1974).

Despite the quality of the animation and imagery, these films sometimes lack direction to the drifting narrative, perhaps reflecting the personality of the filmmaker. Over the next couple of decades, Larkin seemed to aimlessly slide out of animation and further into problems of depression, addiction, and homelessness, a tragedy considering the exuberance and potential shown in his early films.

In later years he was rescued from obscurity by animator and director Chris Landreth who tracked down the lost soul whose work he so admired and used Larkin's work as the basis for *Ryan* (2004). This attention inspired Larkin to conquer his demons and go back to work. He made some animated idents for MTV in 2005 and was planning a film called *Spare Change* with musician Laurie Gordon, drawing on his experiences as a homeless person, when he was tragically struck down by cancer. The film was finished after Larkin's death using his animation and storyboards.

Walking, 1969

1969

UK

Oliver Postgate and Peter Firmin: The Clangers

The Clangers, a race of animals living on a "small planet far far away," were the most surreal, and perhaps the most memorable, creations of the kings of lo-fi TV animation, Oliver Postgate and Peter Firmin. Together, Postgate and Firmin formed the company Smallfilms and produced many animated children's series, such as *Ivor the Engine*, *Bagpuss*, and *Noggin the Nog*. Working out of a converted cowshed, their animation was very basic, using handmade models usually designed and created by Firmin, or in the case of *The Clangers*, knitted by Firmin's wife. Yet despite this, all of their work had immense charm due to the sweet characters, whimsical storylines, and Postgate's delightful narration. Their work, beloved of British children, has been an inspiration to a generation of European animators.

The Clangers,
1969

Italy

Croatia

Osvaldo Cavandoli: La Linea (The Line)

In his early years as an animator, Osvaldo Cavadoli worked for Pagot Film on the first Italian animated feature *I fratelli Dinamite*, (*The Dynamite Brothers*, 1949). In the 1950s he worked on animated commercials, including work in stop frame, but his most successful work wasn't produced until 1969, when he created an advertising film for Italian television show *Carosello* called *La Linea* (*The Line*). *The Line* features a character drawn from, standing on, and traveling on one continuous line, and, in established animation tradition, calling on the hand of the artist to solve problems he encounters en route.

This clever and skilfully drawn piece broke out of its advertising origins and was turned into comics and a television series, with 90 episodes being produced between 1972 and 1991.

Pavao Stalter and Branko Ranitovic: Maska Crvene Smrti (The Masque of the Red Death)

A former restoration artist, Pavao Stalter was introduced to the Zagreb School of Animation in 1957 by art director Zlatko Bourek, himself a painter, set designer, and also a director, famous for shorts based on traditional tales such as *Becarac* (*Dancing Music*, 1966) and *Captain Arbanas Marko* (1968).

Like Bourek, Stalter began his animation career by working mainly as a background painter and designer, breaking through as a director with his adaptation of Edgar Allen Poe's classic horror tale *The Masque of the Red Death* in 1969. One of the great animated horror shorts, the film uses Stalter's scratchy style to great unsettling effect and was codirected by nomadic Yugoslavian animator/director Branko Ranitovic. Most of Stalter's other films were also made for Zagreb Film and were produced in a variety of different styles, including *Peti* (*The Fifth One*, 1965) and *Kuca Br.42* (*House No 42*, 1984).

Maska Crvene Smrti (The Masque of the Red Death), 1969

1969
Japan

Fuji Television: Sazae-san

Sazae-san, an animated television sitcom, began transmission in 1969 and is still in production today, making it the world's longest-running animation series. Based on Machiko Hasewaga's manga comic strip, which featured in a Japanese newspaper from 1946 until 1974, it tells simple stories of suburban domestic life. Over the years the series has changed style with the times, clothes have become more modern and Westernized for instance, but still the cartoon retains its nostalgic appeal. Managing to appeal to a wide demographic, Fuji Television's *Sazae-san* remains the most watched anime in Japan.

1970
USA

Lillian Schwartz: Pixillation

Painter Lillian Schwartz was an artist pioneer in computer animation. Her 1970 gallery video piece, *Pixillation*, was made with the help of Bell Labs engineer Kenneth Knowlton. Whereas other pioneers of computer animation created meditative, spiritual works, influenced by ancient mysticism, Schwartz's *Pixillation* was like a piece of bright, futuristic pop art. Ultra bright colors and strobing computer-created geometric images clash with more organic fleshy imagery, all meshed with a moog-synthesized soundtrack in more of an aggressive attack on the viewer than a calming aid to meditation.

Anime

Anime was invented by the pioneers of Japanese animation in the early twentieth century. Influenced by the art of manga comics, its visual style is commonly characterized by characters with large eyes, elongated limbs, and exaggerated facial expressions. Backgrounds are designed to appear three-dimensional and enhance the sense of atmosphere.

1970
USA

John and Faith Hubley: Eggs

The Hubleys' *Eggs* has a more serious and heavy-handed feel than the charming, light touch of films like *Moonbird* (1959), *Windy Day* (1967), and *Cockaboody* (1973). *Eggs* maintains the loose, spontaneous visual and narrative style of these works, but the drawing and design seem grittier, cruder, and scruffier than usual, perhaps reflecting the film's subject matter of overpopulation and social problems.

The short revolves around a fantasy discussion between Nature and Death on the subject of fecundity versus population control. Subplots explore future possibilities of needing a licence to have a baby or advances in medicine meaning people could live forever. To resolve the issue, a Hindu-based god appears and provides Nature and Death with a new planet to start again, telling the people of earth that they are now on their own and advising population control.

With a soundtrack by Quincy Jones, *Eggs* continued the Hubleys' trademark freeform style of drawing and painting on paper using multiple techniques and multiple exposure. The film uses a conversational character-based approach to tackle political issues, as in some of the Hubleys' other shorts, such as *The Hole* (1964), in which construction workers (Dizzy Gillespie and George Matthews) discuss nuclear war, and *The Hat* (1964), concerning war and the arms race. Faith Hubley continued to explore scientific and moral issues after her husband John's death, in films such as *Enter Life* (1982).

Eggs, 1970

1970

USA

Disney: The Aristocats

The Aristocats was the last film to be green lit by Walt Disney before he died in 1966. German-born Wolfgang Reitherman directed the film in his fourth decade working for Disney, having worked as an animator on the first Disney feature *Snow White and the Seven Dwarfs* in 1937, where he was credited as Woolie Reitherman.

In the story the aristocratic Duchess (voiced by Eva Gabor) and her three kittens, Berlioze, Toulouse, and Marie, have to find their way back home to their wealthy owner after they are kidnapped by a scheming butler. In peril, they are helped and befriended by an alley cat called O'Malley (played by Phil Harris, who also voiced Baloo in *The Jungle Book*). O'Malley is smitten by Duchess and proves himself an indulgent potential step-father to the three little ones on their journey back to the city. The movie has some great animation and music from the experienced Disney team and has a similar, light foot-tapping appeal to *The Jungle Book* and *One Hundred and One Dalmations*. However, like other Disney features of the 1970s, the bad guys don't seem to pose any real threat to the protagonists and therefore do not provide momentum to the story. The bumbling butler character Edgar doesn't really stand up to the heavyweight, nuanced menace of *One Hundred and One Dalmations*' Cruella de Vil or *The Jungle Book*'s Shere Khan.

The Aristocats, 1970

The score was composed by another Disney stalwart, George Bruns, using both French-style dance music and jazz to create, respectively, the ambience of the refined Parisian world of Duchess and the punchier, rawer street life of the alley cats. The soundtrack has become a classic as the Sherman Brothers—now famous for their songs in *The Jungle Book*, *Mary Poppins*, and *Chitty Chitty Bang Bang*—contributed such songs as "The Aristocats" (which French romantic singer Maurice Chevalier came out of retirement to sing), "She Never Felt Alone," and "Scales and Arpeggios." Other songs include "Everybody Wants to Be a Cat," by Floyd Huddleston and Al Rinker, and "Thomas O'Malley" by Terry Gilkyson.

The voice of the alley-dwelling Scat Cat was provided by Scatman Crothers, the musician, actor, and prolific voiceover artist, in what was his first voiceover animation work. He later provided the voice for Hanna-Barbera's Hong Kong Fuey and Jazz in the 1986 feature film, *The Transformers*.

1970
USA

Chuck Jones and Abe Levitow: The Phantom Tollbooth

Based on a book by New York architect Norton Juster, *The Phantom Tollbooth* tells of a bored young boy, Milo, who receives a strange delivery: a tollbooth that he drives his toy car through to enter the Kingdom of Wisdom. Milo then sets off on a journey that will help him find meaning in his life.

The Phantom Tollbooth was directed by Jones and another veteran animator/director Abe Levitow, who had animated with Jones at Warner Bros. in the 1940s and then worked at UPA in the 1950s. Warners veteran Dave Monahan directed the live action, and the legendary Mel Blanc provided the voices.

Despite the talent involved, *The Phantom Tollbooth* is rather an oddity; it has a lot in its favor, but somehow never really takes off. The animated world is imaginative, fascinating, and well animated, although it feels a bit threatening at times for small children. The transition between the live action and the simplified animation style is pretty jarring and is actually less sophisticated than Disney's *Song of the South,* made 25 years earlier. *The Phantom Tollbooth* was made in line with Hollywood's general preoccupation at the time with connecting with the younger "love generation," who were keen to find meaning in contemporary society and "find themselves." This gentle psychedelia is a charming reminder of the positivity and freedom of the times, and did make a good impression on many adults. However, this aspect, along with some of the wordplay-based jokes, must have gone over the heads of all but the most sophisticated child, and unfortunately at times the analogies and moralizing seem a bit heavy-handed, a potential "turn off" for adults and children alike.

Perhaps due to critical and public indifference for *The Phantom Tollbooth*, MGM's animation department was closed soon after this production. MGM did not fund another animated film until 1982's *The Secret of NIMH.*

1970
France

Pollux et le chat bleu (Dougal and the Blue Cat)

After working as a cleaner in a film studio and as an advertising executive, Serge Danot made a pilot for a television series called *Le manegè enchanté* (*The Magic Roundabout*). Over 500 episodes of this stop-frame children's classic were produced from 1963 to 1971, and in 1970 a feature film was released, *Pollux et le chat bleu* (*Dougal and the Blue Cat*).

Rather darker and more sinister than the light and whimsical television episodes, the movie features the garden where the Magic Roundabout characters live being threatened by an evil cat. The Blue Cat wishes to destroy the happy and colorful utopia and turn everything blue. Sugar-lump eating Dougal the dog saves the day and banishes the color blue from the garden.

As with the TV series, for the English-language version of the movie, Eric Thompson adapted the script and narrated the film. Rather than using a direct translation of the French script, Thompson made up what fitted best with what was happening on the screen. His charming and surreal interpretation resulted in this version gaining a cult following among adults, which extended the life and appeal of the English-language version beyond that of the original French. Some of this cult appeal was based on supposed references to alternative culture, such as the belief that the guitar-strumming character Dylan represented Bob Dylan. An underground theory that Thompson's interpretation was littered with references to sex and drugs was later denied by Thompson's wife, the actress Phyllida Law. Somewhat due to this cult appeal, and of course its enduring success with children, the television series was remade in the 1990s, and in 2006 a CGI *Magic Roundabout* feature film was produced by BolexBrothers/Pathé, with a similar evil blue theme. However, neither the 1970 nor the 2006 movies were big successes, failing to capture the small but perfectly formed, sugar-lump-sized, stop-frame whimsical charm of the original TV series.

Pollux et le chat bleu
(Dougal and the Blue
Cat), 1970

1971

USA

Ralph Bakshi: Fritz the Cat

Despite its title, which at first glance seems to place it in the genre of a mainstream cartoon, this film's content is a serious deviation from traditional, child-targeted material. Animation for adults was not a new idea; in fact, it goes right back to the early European pioneers of the late nineteenth and early twentieth centuries, and was also seen in the work of studios such as Halas & Batchelor and UPA. However, it was a somewhat forgotten idea in the American mainstream. Ralph Bakshi believed that, with all the changes in society and the new social power and economic freedom of young people, it was time to take adult animation seriously once more. Taking the comic strip character created by Robert Crumb, he made what became the first X-rated American cartoon, with the poster's tagline stating: "We're not rated X for nothin' baby."

Despite being quickly made for a relatively low budget, *Fritz the Cat* is a decent attempt at adapting Crumb's underground comic style, although without the beautiful, but time-consuming, cross-hatching that defines Crumb's work. The backgrounds have an impressively realist, grubby, and gritty feel to them, having been traced from photographs taken of New York at the

Fritz the Cat,
1971

time. The story concerns Fritz, a young cat in a contemporary cartoon version of New York full of anthropomorphicized animals. Fritz lives an alternative lifestyle among students, beatniks, and bohemians experimenting with free love, drugs, and rock and roll.

Bakshi, who cut his teeth in mainstream animation studios such as Terrytoons and Paramount, came across Crumb's underground comic work in an East Side New York bookstore. Although Crumb was initially impressed by Bakshi, he took a lot of convincing before he gave permission for the film, with Bakshi having to lay virtual siege to Crumb's California home. Eventually Bakshi got his agreement and the film was made. Later, Crumb decided he disliked the film and claimed that the Fritz in the film represented Bakshi's hang-ups more than anything else. Crumb then killed off his creation in a mocking comic book called *Fritz the Cat Superstar*, which contains a scene where Fritz discusses a sequel for the movie. Crumb also claimed that Bakshi had got the agreement with his ex-girlfriend more than with him, and that she had no ownership rights on Fritz, which Bakshi denied. The bitterness may stem from the fact that, while Crumb earned $50,000 from the rights to the film, it went on to gross $100 million around the world and became one of the most successful independent animation films of all time.

Biography

Ralph Bakshi

Ralph Bakshi was born in Israel in 1938, and his family moved to New York in 1939. He began his career at Terrytoons, where he worked as an animator and director on cartoons such as the *Mighty Mouse* series. Later he worked at Paramount and then at Steve Krantz Productions in Canada, where he produced and directed the animated *Spiderman* series. In 1968 Bakshi opened a studio in New York, where he worked on commercials. Aiming to reach the counterculture audience that had made movies like *Yellow Submarine* (1968) and *Easy Rider* (1969) so successful, in 1971 he made the first X-rated animated feature, *Fritz the Cat*. Notorious for its depiction of sex and drugs, it was a big hit and convinced some film critics to take animation a bit more seriously.

Bakshi followed this success with *Heavy Traffic* (1973), generally considered to be his best film, telling of the life of a struggling cartoonist in New York's ghettos and showing the underbelly of urban life. His next film was shelved and he followed this with *Coonskin* (1975), which was withdrawn after accusations of racism. Bakshi maintains he is a liberal and not a racist, and claims that the people making the accusations had not actually watched the film.

Bashki went on to make two fantasy films; *Wizards* (1977), a postapocalyptic sci-fi, and *The Lord of the Rings* (1978), which was a minor hit on the back of Tolkein's popularity, but suffered from a falling-off in quality due to budget problems towards the end of the production. Although criticized for its extensive use of unrefined rotoscoping—the 1970s-style costumes traced directly from the cast looking somewhat out of place in a fantasy setting—the movie is remembered fondly by many who saw it as children. Peter Jackson, director of the *Lord of the Rings* trilogy, has said that Bakshi's work was his first introduction to Tolkein's universe.

His next two films *American Pop* (1981) and *Fire and Ice* (1983), did not do well and Bakshi turned his back on feature films. He moved to television, where he seemed to find his form again, reviving the 1940s character, Mighty Mouse. He made another feature film, *Cool World* (1992), a TV live-action film *The Cool and the Crazy* (1994), and then an adult animated sci-fi TV series *Spicy City* (1997), before retiring from animation.

1971/1974

UK

Bob Godfrey: Karma Sutra Rides Again and Great

Made during the early-1970s craze for adult animation, in *Karma Sutra Rides Again* middle-aged Stanley (voiced by Godfrey) and Ethel demonstrate their behind-closed-doors hobby—sex and its many possibilities. For Bob Godfrey, who believed that animation should concern the surreal and the fantastic rather than striving to imitate realism, this was an exercise in finding the exotic inside mundane suburbia while poking fun at British attitudes to sex. Made in Godfrey's unpretentious wobbly lo-fi style, *Karma Sutra Rides Again*, was given an X certificate by the British Censor, was screened alongside Stanley Kubrick's *A Clockwork Orange* in the UK, and was nominated for the Oscar for best animated short.

Godfrey again found the extraordinary in uptight British subject matter in his 1974 Oscar-winning short, *Great*, a biography of the ninteenth-century British engineer Isambard Kingdom Brunel. Using different animation styles to show events in Brunel's life while mocking stuffy Victorian values, it excelled in its portrayal of mechanical engineering achievements, like the launch of the Great Western Railway. *Great* won the Academy Award for best animated film in 1976.

Great, 1974

1971
UK/USA

1972
Japan

Richard Williams: A Christmas Carol

Canadian-born Richard Williams began his career at UPA, where he worked with Chuck Jones, who was the executive producer on Williams' first major film, *A Christmas Carol*. Despite being a made-for-TV product, it was later released in movie theaters and won the 1972 Academy Award for best animated short film. The controversy this caused led to the Academy changing its rules, deeming that TV movies could not be considered for Oscars.

Michael Redgrave as the narrator, Michael Horden as Marley's ghost, and Alastair Sim as Scrooge, all reprised their roles from the 1951 live-action movie classic, while Williams' young son, and future animator, Alex provided the voice of Tiny Tim. Veteran animators Ken Harris and Abe Levitow helped guide the character work, while technically, the film makes great use of inventive traveling establishing shots and bridging sequences, perhaps evidence of Williams' award-winning early work on titles and linking scenes for live-action movies such as *What's New Pussycat* (1965) and *Charge of the Light Brigade* (1968).

Its dark mood and disturbing imagery moves away from the Victorian whimsy usually associated with Christmas, and places the movie in a more realistic nineteenth-century setting. Williams was inspired in this by the original illustrations to Dickens' tale by John Leech and the 1930s illustrations by Milo Winter. *A Christmas Carol* failed to become a perennial Christmas television favorite, however, being deemed too harsh and downbeat. However, Williams had never intended it as a children's film—he insisted to Chuck Jones that it would be, as the original novella is subtitled, "A Ghost Story of Christmas."

Renzo and Sayoko Kinoshita: Nippon Seizou (Made in Japan) and Pica-don

Renzo and Sayoko Kinoshita's *Nippon Seizou* (*Made in Japan*) is a playful critique of Japanese culture, which concerns the people of Japan putting the economy before anything else. *Made in Japan* combines simple cartoon characters with detailed backgrounds of Japanese urban life; it won awards worldwide, including the Grand Prix at the New York International Animation Festival in 1972.

The couple made commercials to fund more independent work, using social and economic themes to stimulate debate about Japanese culture and history. Finding little other independent animation being made in Japan, the Kinoshitas were central to developing the independent animation scene in the country and helped to establish the Hiroshima International Animation Festival.

Their 1978 short *Pica-don*, a depiction of the nuclear bombing of Hiroshima, is one of the most harrowing and disturbing animation shorts of all time. Based on survivors' accounts, the opening scenes of peaceful Japanese family life are unbearable to watch because you know what's coming next. The scenes of the bomb's aftermath, showing the burnt flesh of the dead and the few survivors melting as they stagger about in search of family, are stylized but nonetheless represent a gut-wrenchingly vivid vision of the hell on earth that man can inflict on his fellow man.

1973

France/Czech Republic

Réne Laloux: La planète sauvage (The Fantastic Planet)

Réne Laloux's *La planète sauvage* (*The Fantastic Planet*) was released in 1973 after a long production process. Laloux, a former painter, was previously best known for his startling debut short film *Les dents du singe* (*The Monkey's Teeth*, 1960), made with the help of inmates from a psychiatric clinic.

Work on *The Fantastic Planet* began in 1968 at the Jiří Trnka Studios in Prague. The movie's extended production was the result of various factors, perhaps most importantly the invasion of Czechoslovakia (now the Czech Republic) by the Russian army, which began in August, 1968. There were also internal problems at the studio. At one point, with nationalistic feelings running high (understandable at this time of political oppression from the Soviet Union) the Czech crew wanted to oust Laloux, the only non-Czech working on the film, and replace him with Josef Kábrt, the film's designer. This move was abandoned and Laloux survived as director, but the film, seen as an analogy of Soviet oppression, came under pressure from the new Czech political regime and Laloux was forced to move to France to finish production.

La planète sauvage
(The Fantastic Planet),
1973

Based on the novel *Oms en Série* by the French writer Stefan Wul, the film tells of a society where humans, Oms (from the French "l'homme") have been taken to the planet Ygam by the large blue Traags, to be their pets (blue being a recurring color motif during this period of animation for villians and oppressors). Laloux also turned Wul's story *L'Orphelin de Perdide* (*The Orphan of Perdide*, 1958) into the 1982 French/Hungarian movie *Les maîtres du temps*. Writer and designer Roland Topor had previously collaborated with Laloux in the mid-1960s on the shorts *Les temps morts* (*Dead Times*, 1964) and *L'escargot* (*The Snails*, 1965).

The movie is distinctly of its era, with fantasy visuals, exotic creatures, and dreamlike situations, alongside an avant-garde jazz and electronic soundtrack. Against this exotic backdrop, the movement of character and camera is quite limited, although as the whole film is different from any other, it creates its own rules. The surreal visuals mix with analogies aluding to the real social concerns of fascist repression and war, as well as alternative culture and Eastern mysticism.

The movie was a hit in France, won the critics' award at the 1973 Cannes Film Festival, and has become something of a cult favorite in subsequent years.

1974
USA

Robert Breer: Fuji

Inspired by the likes of Man Ray's use of film as a medium for fine art, visual artist Robert Breer has worked in film and animation, as well as sculpture and painting. His early work was influenced by the European abstract animators Fernand Léger, Hans Richter, Viking Eggeling, and Walter Ruttman.

In the early 1970s, Breer began using rotoscoping in order to focus more on individual images of film. His short *Fuji* was made while he was working on sculptures for the Pepsi Pavilion project in Osaka, Japan. The film was built around a recording of a woman's face, filmed in front of Japan's Mount Fuji from a speeding train. Breer interspersed this with increasingly abstract, flickering images of the mountain, in a reference to nineteenth-century printmaker Hokusai's series of works, *Thirty-six Views of Fuji*.

1974
USA

Michael Benveniste and Howard Ziehm: Flesh Gordon

Flesh Gordon was a wild, soft porn cult parody of the sci-fi serial *Flash Gordon,* featuring stop-frame animated creatures. Despite such monster names as Penisaurus and the Great God Porno, the film was an affectionate spoof on science fiction and monster movies. The effects crew featured many young artists who would go on to become successful in film effects, and one of the monsters was named Nesuahyrrah, in a backwards tribute to stop-frame master, Ray Harryhausen.

1974

France/ Poland

Piotr Kamler: Le Pas (The Step)

Polish-born Piotr Kamler made the experimental short film *Le pas* (*The Step*) through the ORTF research department in Paris—a place that nurtured many experimental animators during the 1960s and 1970s. In order to take the "step" of the title, a small cube sheds itself into sheets of paper, and, to an electronic soundtrack which couples as the sound effects of the peeling paper, the cube reassembles itself a little way away from its starting point. Typically of Kamler's work, the film is meticulously constructed and features simple but exact geometric shapes, animated by stop frame, into a narrative so subtle that it at times seems to be a nonnarrative abstract piece of work. *The Step* was Kamler's last film before his 1982 feature, *Chronopolis.*

Kamler's early shorts like *The Step* and *Coeur de secours* (1973), with their ambient feel, precise clean-edged 3D shapes, and mathematical motion, look more like our idea of computer animation than the real CGI of the time. *Chronopolis*, however, a science-fiction story about a city lost in space and time, was one of the first features to actually use CGI animation.

1974

Japan

Hayao Miyazaki and Isao Takahata: Arupusu no shôjo Haiji (Heidi)

This Japanese television series adaptation of Johanna Spryri's children's book *Heidi* was popular in many countries and was dubbed into 19 different languages. *Arupusu no shôjo Haiji* (*Heidi*) represents another stage on the collaborative history of director Isao Takahata with animator, layout artist, and future director Hayao Miyazaki. Its beautiful color design and the freshfaced appeal of its child characters, seen in early form here, would later become familiar the world over when the two men formed the legendary Studio Ghibli to produce their own feature films.

1975
USA

John Whitney and Larry Cuba: Arabesque

In 1960 John Whitney set up a company called Motion Graphics Incorporated using an analog computer of his own invention to produce title sequences and commercials. In 1961 he produced a film called *Catalog* that was a record of his visual effects to date. By the 1970s he had moved on to faster digital computers and produced his most famous film, *Arabesque*, in 1975.

In this milestone of Computer Generated Imagery (CGI), the mathematical concepts that underlie CGI and the artistic sensibilities of the filmmakers fuse in an hypnotic ballet of lines and music. The mathematical symmetries and the illusion of three-dimensionality made possible with CGI are explored, celebrated, and enhanced by the Eastern-style music with an almost mystical reverence. Strings of curving and looping lines take the form of Asian designs, medical graphical traces, and structures of great complexity, before returning to a circle as if to a starting point, mathematically and metaphorically.

Overlaying, transparency, and the blending in and out of the shifting colors all combine into a beautiful demonstration of what Richard Shoup, Harry Smith, and others made possible a few years earlier. The film also gives us a glimpse into the future and to the role computing was to go on to play in the history of animation.

1975
USA

Sally Cruikshank: Quasi at the Quackadero

American independent animator Sally Cruikshank is a true original. Her fourth film *Quasi at the Quackadero* was a popular and critical success and has become a cult favorite. Along with *Make Me Psychic* (1978) and *Quasi's Cabaret Trailer* (1980) it is part of her "Art Deco" trilogy, a style of design that enjoyed a fashion revival in the mid-1970s. This is, however, a pretty wild take on Art Deco, by way of naïve outsider art and colorful *Yellow Submarine*-style trippy surrealism.

Another 1970s film where creativity was allowed to flow unrestrained, the loose narrative of *Quasi at the Quackadero* features regular Cruikshank characters Quasi and Anita, two stylized ducks, who visit a very strange funfair with their robot. In 1994 it was voted into Jeff Beck's book *The 50 Greatest Cartoons*, and in 2009 it was selected for preservation as "culturally significant" in the US National Film Registry.

Renowned movie composer Danny Elfman provided music for Cruikshank's 1987 film *Face Like a Frog* and, like fellow independent animator Marv Newland (most famous for 1969's *Bambi Meets Godzilla*), she later spent time working on the animated sequences for cult children's TV show Sesame Street, and also contributed to Newland's film *Anjam* (1984).

1975

UK/USA

1975

Norway

Ronald Searle and Bill Melendez: Dick Deadeye, or Duty Done

Experienced animation director Bill Melendez, best-known for his Charlie Brown TV specials, joined forces with revered British cartoonist Ronald Searle to create this wild pastiche of Gilbert and Sullivan's comic operas. In a rather contrived plot, Dick Deadeye, the villian from HMS Pinafore, sets out on a mission from Queen Victoria, which brings him into contact with a series of Gilbert and Sullivan characters, interpreted into Searle's spindly creations. The film was made as an affectionate but irreverent celebration of the hundreth anniversary of the composers beginning to write their Savoy Operas. The soundtrack uses Gilbert and Sullivan's songs, although some of the lyrics were altered.

Ivo Caprino: Flaklypa Grand Prix (The Pinchcliffe Grand Prix)

Animator and director Ivo Caprino came to prominence in the 1950s in Norway with his puppet shorts *Tim og Toffe* (*Tin of Toffee*, 1949), made with a technique perfected by Caprino for manipulating the characters in real time, an early version of animatronics. His films were hugely popular in Norway, with high public interest in the secret "magical" method behind his films. Later Caprino switched to stop-frame animation, although still maintaining the impression with the public that he was using his "mysterious" technique. He produced many shorts and commercials, a series of animated folk tales, and a live-action feature containing stop-frame sequences, *Ugler i mosen* (1959). His animation work culminated in the stop-frame feature *Flaklypa Grand Prix* (*The Pinchcliffe Grand Prix*), based on the characters of cartoonist Kjell Aukrust.

The movie's central character is Theodore Rimspoke, who invents madcap contraptions with the aid of his two trusty animal sidekicks, Sunny Duckworth and Lambert. Rimspoke discovers that his invention of a racing car engine has been stolen by his former assistant, Rudoph Gore-Slimey, who has used it to become a racing champion. This spurs Rimspoke to create the ultimate racing car and challenge Gore-Slimey in a Grand Prix.

The film took three and a half years to make and was a huge hit in Norway, creating box office records that still stand; reportedly it was shown daily in certain theaters for 28 years. The movie's sets were meticulously detailed and the character animation has a smoothness and fluidity that seem magically lifelike at times. *The Pinchcliffe Grand Prix* is a forgotten gem that would fascinate children and adults anywhere and deserves a wider release.

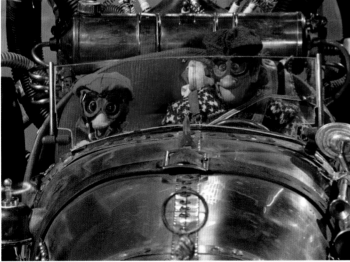

Flaklypa Grand Prix
(The Pinchcliffe Grand Prix), 1975

1975
Hungary

Hugó, a víziló (Hugo the Hippo), 1973

William Feigenbaum and József Gémes: Hugó, a víziló (Hugo the Hippo)

Hungary's state owned and funded Pannonia studio had created its reputation with animated television series and award-winning short films, before venturing into feature production. *Hugó, a víziló* (*Hugo the Hippo*) was (supposedly) a children's film that was so psychedelic, at times dark and strange, and in fact "phantasmagorical," as it quite rightly says on the poster, that it has become a cult favorite with adults.

The story tells of how, when the Sultan of Zanzibar has a problem with sharks, he employs 12 hippos to patrol the harbor. After doing their job the hippos are abandoned and go wild; 11 are killed with only Hugo surviving. He is found and cared for by some children, but is eventually blamed for the destruction of the town, only to be saved at the last minute by the Sultan.

Hugo the Hippo was the first international release of a Hungarian feature-length animation. It was a movie very much of its time in which the "turned-on" mindset of its creators was allowed to flow unrestricted onto the screen.

1976
USA/Canada

Caroline Leaf: The Street

While studying Visual Arts at Harvard University, Caroline Leaf developed her own personal style of animation. Using sand animation, she made *Sand, or Peter and the Wolf*. The technique for sand animation involves placing sand on a lightbox and moving it around to create each frame, exploiting the translucent qualities of sand. *Sand, or Peter and the Wolf* won her a scholarship to stay at the college and make her next film, *Orfeo* (1972), by the method of painting on glass.

After making *How Beaver Stole Fire* in 1971, which she later disowned as she did not approve of the soundtrack, she was invited to work with the National Film Board of Canada where she made an adaptation of a traditional Canadian Inuit tale, *The Owl Who Married a Goose* (1974), using a soundtrack of Inuit voices. In 1976 she made the film that made her international reputation, *The Street*.

Mixing watercolor washes with paint and glycerine animation, *The Street* has an impressionistic looseness, like a hazy childhood memory, which nicely expresses the feel of the story by Canadian writer Mordecai Richler. The short film follows life in a small apartment as a family politely, and not so politely, wait for their grandmother to die in the back bedroom. Like *The Owl Who Married a Goose*, this is another bittersweet family tale; the naturalistic voices further the organic nature of the film, giving it something of the feel of John and Faith Hubley's *Moonbird*.

Leaf's film was an instant success at screenings around the world, receieved much praise, and in a 1984 critics poll *The Street* was voted the second best animated film of all time. The next year she made *The Metamorphasis of Mr Samsa* based on Kafka's story, but then moved away from animation in favor of live-action documentary. Nearly a decade later she returned with *Entre Deux Soers* (*Two Sisters*, 1990), winning first prize at the Annecy Animation Festival in 1991.

1976
Belgium

La flûte à six schtroumpfs
(The Smurfs and the
Magic Flute), 1976

Eddie Lateste and Peyo: La flûte à six schtroumpfs (The Smurfs and the Magic Flute)

Les Schtroumpfs (or the Smurfs, as they are known in English) were created by the cartoonist Peyo in 1958. They first appeared in comic strips in the Belgian magazine, *Le Journal de Spirou*, which became hugely popular. Much Smurfs merchandise was produced, including musical releases. In the 1960s, 10 black-and-white animated Smurfs shorts were made for Belgian television, and in 1976 a feature-length color movie was released, *La flûte à six schtroumpfs* (*The Smurfs and the Magic Flute*). The movie was produced by the Belgian studio Belvision and was directed by Peyo and Eddie Lateste; it was based on one of the Smurfs' comic-strip adventures. In 1981 Hanna-Barbera began producing an animated Smurfs series for US television; the success of this led to a US release for *The Smurfs and the Magic Flute* in 1983.

1976

Italy

Bruno Bozzetto: Allegro Non Troppo

Based around famous classical music pieces, *Allegro Non Troppo* is divided into segments focusing on different aspects of life, often using mythology or science fiction themes. Comparisons to Disney's *Fantasia* are inevitable, although stylistically Bozzetto's film was more graphical, modernist, and had something of the *Yellow Submarine*-style gentle psychedelia of the age. Also typical of the times, while *Fantasia* was a positive reflection on Western ideas and potential, *Allegro Non Troppo*, meaning "slow down" or "not so fast," takes a more considered attitude. The overall tone of light-hearted cynicism is broken with the downbeat segment where a lonely ghost cat explores his old house and life. The film also contains live-action sequences, often parodies of the "glamor" of movie-making.

Allegro Non Troppo, 1976

Biography

Bruno Bozzetto

Born in Milan, Italy, in 1938, Bruno Bozzetto caught the attention of animation veterans Norman McLaren and John Halas when his first short, *Tapum! La storia delle armi* (*Tapum A History of Weapons*) was screened at the 1958 Cannes Fi Festival. In 1960 the Bruno Bozzetto Film Company was established in Milan to produce movies, television shows, and commercials, including vehicles for Bozzetto's creation Mr Rossi, who went on to star in three feature films and many shorts and comics.

In 1965 Bozzetto directed the stylish and stylized animate spoof western *West and Soda*, the first Italian animated featur to be released for two decades, standing up well visually with any animated features from this era. This was followed by *Vip, mio fratello superuomo* (*VIP: My Brother Superman*, 1968), a superhero spoof. In the 1970s Bozzetto created comic strips based on *VIP: My Brother Superman* and *West and Soda* and also made some live-action moves. *Allegro Non Troppo* (1976) continued Bozzetto's trademark of parodying Hollywood content such as superheroes and cowboys.

One of Italy's most prolific and influential animators, Bozzetto continues to explore these ideas in his award-winning films and television animation. Always interested in technological progress and how this affects animation, he has embraced computer-generated animation, and has also create many animation shorts for the internet using Flash software. His experiments with 3D have included the short *Looo* and the television series *I Cosi*.

977

SA

isney: The Rescuers

sney's first big success since 1967's *The Jungle Book*, e *Rescuers* stuck faithfully to the characters and stories in argery Sharp's books. Orphan Penny's message in a bottle found by the animal organization Rescue Aid Society, who ring into action sending two mouse agents to find Penny and scue her from the evil Madame Medusa.

The film, directed by Wolfgang Reitherman, John unsbery, and Art Stevens, broke the record for the largest pening weekend animation gross, a statistic it kept until 1986 hen the record was broken by *An American Tail*, directed by

Rescuers animator Don Bluth. Bluth was one of the young generation of animators working on the movie, many of whom would steer the Walt Disney Studios into its 1990s revival. They worked on the film alongside Walt's old guard; *The Rescuers* was the last Disney movie for veterans Milt Kahl, Ollie Johnston, and Frank Thomas, with young animators Glen Keane, Ron Clements, and Andy Gaskill stepping up to fill the void. *The Rescuers* is a great parting salvo from these old legends and a fine entry in the Disney catalog. Lively and well paced with some great animation, it is perhaps the last great film from the studios' (relatively) more modernist and stylized midperiod, stretching from *Sleeping Beauty* onward.

The Rescuers,
1977

Like all the best Disney features of these years, *The Rescuers* features some great voice performances, in this case from the low-key Bob Newhart (Bernard), Eva Gabor (reprising her performance in *The Aristocats*), and Geraldine Page, voicing Madame Medusa, enjoying a return to powerful and extravagant Disney villains of the past. Indeed, the memorable villain may be the missing ingredient of the preceding Disney films that failed to make a big impact, like *Robin Hood* (1973). Another key ingredient for a Disney success is a memorable supporting character or two, which *The Rescuers* delivers in the albatross "airline," Orville.

1977

UK

Jeff Keen: The Cartoon Theatre of Dr Gaz

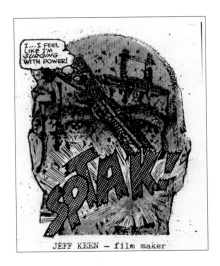

Jeff Keen

Since the early 1960s British filmmaker Jeff Keen's work has existed in its own universe; he is a true outsider filmmaker. Beyond the wildest fringes of avant-garde and for many years claiming to be unaware of even the existence of other experimental filmmakers, Keen is seemingly more inspired by the trashiest and most banal moments of pop culture, lurid pulp fiction, and the underground world of biker and beatnik lifestyles than by high art. Keen often mixes and superimposes stolen fragments of monster movies and sci-fi with home movies, action painting, and rough homemade animation. He then edits all these pieces together at such a breakneck blur that the whole film almost becomes animation in itself. Because his work has existed separate from other genres and movements, his personal vision seems somehow timeless, not categorizable, and somehow not out of place with many of the eras he has lived and made films through.

The Cartoon Theatre of Dr Gaz is a machine-gun paced edit of such things as crude stop-frame clips involving monster models and vandalized dolls, mixed with crazed live-action antics, and animation of Keen's painted work growing on the canvas. His many films include *Instant Cinema* (1962), *Flik Flak* (1963), and *Irresistable Attack* (1995). Since Keen retired from filmmaking, his films have been collected and released on DVD by the British Film Institute.

The Cartoon Theatre
of Dr Gaz, 1977

1977

Australia/Poland

Yoram Gross: Dot and the Kangaroo

In order to make something with a unique and Australian style, Polish émigré Yoram Gross used the technique of laying animated characters over photographic backgrounds for his 1977 feature film, *Dot and the Kangaroo*. This technique had earlier been used by "father of Australian Animation," Eric Porter in *Waste Not want Not* (c. 1939), but it became Gross' trademark. The movie concerns a young settler, Dot, who gets lost in the bush and is rescued by a kangeroo, who carries Dot in her pouch on a journey to find her parents. They encounter many native Australian creatures on the way and the use of indigenous art influences is seen in many moments, such as the frightening Bunyip scenes. *Dot and the Kangaroo* sold well abroad and Gross followed it up with seven sequels. Gross, who had set up a studio in Australia in 1968, also produced successful television cartoons featuring typically Australian characters, such as the koala, Blinky Bill.

Dot and the Kangaroo, 1977

1978
UK

1978
UK

Ubu, 1978

Geoff Dunbar: Ubu

This animated version of Alfred Jarry's 1896 play *Ubu Roi* (*Ubu the King*) was perhaps, in animation terms, another sign of the end of the hippie influence. It was a time of recession, the culture of the 1960s had gone stale, and punk was starting to sweep the old guard away, although to label this as a punk film might diminish the craftsmanship and design skill involved. The film does seem, like much punk culture, to be a raw attack on the corruption of power and wealth, depicting the foul-mouthed Pere Ubu usurping King Wenceslas' crown and celebrating his supremacy. The images are rendered with violent slashes of black paint with speech bubbles relaying the dialogue.

Dunbar made commercials for the likes of Guiness and Dulux through his company Grand Slamm to finance his personal projects and also obtained funding for *Ubu* through the UK Arts Council. The film won several festival prizes, including the 1979 Golden Berlin Bear for best short film.

Martin Rosen: Watership Down

Despite being marketed as a family-friendly, mainstream film, *Watership Down* was no cute children's story. Not completely devoid of cuteness—it is about rabbits after all—the movie was faithful to the dark and violent story of Richard Adams' best-selling book, which depicts man and nature's cruelty.

John Hubley was originally hired as the director, but left early in the production after completing the opening scene. An impressive cast of British film, television, and theater stars voiced the often frightening story of rabbits forced to leave their warren when one of them has a premonition of disaster. Embarking on a journey to create a new idealized society on Watership Down, they find that life there does not come without a struggle, and the final battle is the goriest scene in the film. *Watership Down* has a realistic, sensitive, and unsentimental style, and, apart from talking in human voices, the characters have very little in the way of human attributes. Seeing the countryside through the rabbits' eyes gives the viewer a nonidealized, nonsentimental vision of nature. Rosen's film was a brave and uncompromising attempt to tell a powerful, grown-up story.

Watership Down suffered at times from rather minimal animation, which, along with the limited range of expression in the naturalistic animal faces, often contrasts with the dramatic voice performances by the excellent cast. This is compensated by the strong design of the characters and environments, plus the powerful sense of danger throughout which gives the film its unique character.

Croatia

China

Zdenko Gasparovic: Satiemania

Zdenko Gasparovic worked for the renowned Zagreb Film studio in the 1960s as an animator and in 1966 directed the short *A Dog's Life*, before traveling to the USA to work for Hanna-Barbera, among others. Later, back in Croatia, his work included a stint on the television series *Professor Balthazar*, before he produced one of the most critically successful shorts to come out of Zagreb Film.

In *Satiemania* the piano music of Eric Satie links a stream of conciousness that seems to frankly expose male obsessions in a way only perhaps possible during the unrestrained 1970s. Starting off with innocent rythmic walk cycle studies, the animator seems to bore with this exercise as the walks become more caricatured and sexual, becoming dominated by short skirts and pimp stylings. As the music changes, the next phase of the film is devoted to women in many facets; sweet and innocent, wanton and provocative, eating, drinking, taking drugs, laughing, crying, sometimes handsome, sometimes grotesque, ecstatic, innocent, their faces, breasts, hair, mixed in with images of nature, food, rivers, supermarkets, rain, canyons, and meat. The tone changes again with the music, and in the next phase the intensity heightens into violence, both cartoonish and realistic, with male characters receiving blows and beatings until this subsides into images of nature once more. It's a psychiatrist's dream, or nightmare, come true.

The figures in these dreamlike snippets of animation and still images are skillfully drawn in loose, three-dimensional life sketches of pencil, charcoal, and watercolor, often giving a feel similar to the bohemian underworld of the French impressionist painters a century before or the later, grotesque caricatured realism of animators like Bill Plympton or Joanna Quinn. Poetic, honest, and psychological, the film was a huge critical success and won many awards in festivals worldwide.

Xu Jingda: A Night in an Art Gallery and Nezha nao hai (Nezha Conquers the Dragon King)

In 1965, during the Chinese Cultural Revolution, the government-run Shanghai Animation Film Studio was closed under orders from Mao Zedong. As animation was considered to be decadent, elitist, and counterrevolutionary, the animators were sent to serve on farms for "reeducation" by hard labor. After this virtually no animation was made or shown until 1978 when reforms allowed the studio to reopen.

The years of repression and the 1976 fall of the Gang of Four (those responsible for the long cultural purge) inspired the 1978 short film from Xu Jingda, *A Night in an Art Gallery*. Based on caricatures of the Four that the director had secretly drawn while in the labor farm, the film tells the story of the four owners of a gallery banning all art they don't understand.

1979 saw the release of the feature-length *Nezha nao hai* (*Nezha Conquers the Dragon King*). Based on a segment of the traditional tale *Fengshen Yanyi* (*Investiture of the Gods*), it tells of how Nezha, a tiny boy born from an egg, fights the dragon king, and frees the people from oppressive rulers (a common theme in animation from communist countries).

The film was screened at the 1980 Cannes Film Festival and was much admired. It features stylized animation and a colorful, 1970s interpretation of traditional Chinese styles.

Xu Jingda, also known as A Da, followed the film up with *Three Monks* (1980), a story of quarrelsome monks who learn to work together in order to rebuild their temple. The film won many awards and was again admired for blending traditional styles with contemporary animation techniques.

1979

USA

Ed Emshwiller: Sunstone

After creating experimental films in the New American Cinema movement of the 1960s, Ed Emshwiller first worked with video art and early computer graphics systems in the early 1970s. His best-known work, *Sunstone* (1979) was a milestone in 3D computer animation over a decade before the widespread use of 3D CGI.

Working mainly as a sci-fi illustrator, Emshwiller began making films after getting a Ford Foundation grant in 1964. Fifteen years later, *Sunstone* was made with financial support from the Guggenheim Foundation and was produced at the New York Institute of Technology. Helped by CGI pioneers like Alvy Ray Smith, the film utilizes all the emerging resources of computer animation, and, like other early computer-generated films produced by the 1960s generation, was influenced by Eastern mysticism and "enlightenment." Technically, *Sunstone* is one of the first CGI films to create a convincing, solid three-dimensional object that spins in space. Still retaining a strange power even when viewed today, its key image of a living sculpture of a human face set in a circular stone must have seemed magical and alien to audiences of the time.

1970s computer animation milestones

Ed Catmull developed a breakthrough computer graphics language while he was a PhD student at the University of Utah and presented it at the 1972 ACM (Association for Computing Machinery) annual conference. Inspired by his tutor Ivan Sutherland's program Sketchpad, he experimented with computer graphics and made breakthrough discoveries in the areas of Z Buffering, texture mapping, and anitialiasing. Catmull's work made it possible to generate an animation of a human hand lasting a little over a minute that was used in the 1976 sci-fi movie *Futureworld*. This was one of the first instances of CGI animation in a mainstream feature film. Catmull later became one of the central figures in Pixar Animation Studios and was subsequently president of Pixar and Walt Disney Studios.

Richard Shoup's SuperPaint was one of the first graphics programs to use a sophisticated graphical user interface, and was one of the earliest to use pixel-based drawing and painting in display as a video image and to feature antialiasing. The SuperPaint frame buffer system was designed in 1972 in the Computer Science Lab at the Xerox Palo Alto Research Center. The minicomputer that Shoup used for his experiments cost the Xerox company hundreds of thousands of dollars, and SuperPaint didn't have any foreseeable use in the office market, which left his supervisors unimpressed. Nevertheless Shoup was permitted to develop the program and make improvements.

Working with early video cameras, in 1973 Shoup and his team of Larry Clark, Alvy Ray Smith, Bob Flegal, and Patrick Baudelaire got the program to produce images, and created one of the earliest uses of computer technology for computer animation and video editing.

Alvy Ray Smith later joined the Computer Graphics Laboratory at the New York Institute of Technology, where he worked from 1975 to 1979 and developed paint programs. He invented the Alpha Channel, a system of transparency that allows elements to be overlaid, aided Ed Emshwiller with his landmark film *Sunstone* (1979), and cofounded Pixar.

The early images produced by SuperPaint may not look much today, but what was produced in these experiments and others like it would change the world of entertainment forever. Shoup's program was able to develop algorithms to clarify images, create sharp lines, produce a subtle range of colors, capture images from video, change the hue and saturation of digital images, choose from a preset color palette with virtual paintbrushes and pencils, and autofill images—all big steps forward and part of the computer graphics methodology we now take for granted. This contribution was acknowledged in 1983 when Shoup was awarded an Emmy for Outstanding Achievement in Engineering Development and then in 1998 Shoup, Alvy Ray Smith, and Thomas Porter were awarded an Academy Award for Scientific and Technical Achievement for their contributions.

1979
UK

Roger Mainwood: Autobahn

Halas & Batchelor was one of the first studios in the world to use CG, and as early as 1969, John Halas had experimented with computer graphics. The short *Autobahn* was directed for Halas by Roger Mainwood, a young animator fresh out of college; it was typical of Halas to encourage young talent. Also typical of Halas' spirit of experimentation was *Autobahn*'s use of early computer graphics images. Halas foresaw the eventual widespread adaptation of CGI in animation and, unlike many other animators at the time, welcomed its arrival. The use of the computer at London's Imperial College for *Autobahn* proved to be less practical than hoped, however, and the primitive images it produced were little used in the film, and, like other films at the time, the computer-style images were mostly produced by traditional animation techniques. Nevertheless, Halas saw the experiment as worthwhile and as good publicity. *Autobahn* is essentially a music video for the Kraftwerk song of the same name, perfectly capturing the cold robot glamor of the band and wonderfully evocative of its era.

Autobahn, 1979

1979

Russia

1979

Japan

Yuri Norstein: Skazka skazok (Tale of Tales)

After initially being quietly released to a few festivals by the Soviet authorities without much fanfare, as if not sure of what they had on their hands, in the next five years Yuri Norstein's *Skazka skazok* (*Tale of Tales*) would build an almost mythical reputation among critics and animators. Although still little seen, it is routinely described as the *Citizen Kane* of animation and was voted the greatest animated film of all time by a large international panel in 1984 and once again in 2002.

The film, Norstein's follow-up to the short *Yozhik v tumane* (*Little Hedgehog in the Fog*, 1975), is a bittersweet poem about childhood, about Russia, and about being human. The narrative consists of a series of fragmented, interlinked stories that play in order of random association rather than in logical order. The film is intended to work like the structure of human memory, with one thing leading to the memory of something else. It is all about memories: the personal memories of the animator and how these link to the collective memories shared by Russia and its people and to universal human memories, and how, even though these are often sad, they can still be beautiful.

Tale of Tales was made with the methods that Norstein had developed during 15 years of working for Soyuzmultfilm. He had worked on many different styles of film and with many different people, including one of the fathers of Russian animation, Ivan Ivanov-Vano. Because of this, the film contains a variety of techniques, the main one an intricate but basic cutout animation embedded in complex multiplane backgrounds and foregrounds. This means that, like the story, the characters often seem tangled in complex elements and obscured by fog. Audiences approaching the film expecting a linear story with an obvious meaning can find it impenetrable, but those who approach it with an open mind and a willingness to do a bit of thinking to meet it halfway, can find it a mesmeric and moving experience, with an ultimately uplifting conclusion.

Hayao Miyazaki: Rupan Sansei: Kariosutoro no shiro (Castle of Cagliostro)

One of a series of adventures starring Lupin, a lovable rogue and master thief, *Rupan Sansei: Kariosutoro no shiro* (*Castle of Cagliostro*) is notable for being Hayao Miyazaki's first movie as a writer/director after working as the art director on the television series *Arupusu no shôjo Haiji* (*Heidi*). In the movie, Lupin finds he has stolen counterfeit money and heads off to the European duchy of Cagliostro to find out who made the forgeries. He gets involved in a historical mystery and saves a princess from an evil count. The film is a great animated crime thriller and tense action movie, featuring many of the European historical-style settings to be found in Miyazaki's later work.

Hayao Miyazaki / Studio Ghibli

Taking over from Osamu Tezuka as the "Japanese Disney," Hayao Miyazaki and Studio Ghibli have enjoyed national and international success. Miyazaki was born in 1941, and began his animation career at Toei Animation in 1963. In 1971 he joined the A-Pro studio, where he began collaborating with fellow animator Isao Takahata. He directed his first feature, *Rupan Sansei: Kariosutoro no shiro* (*Castle of Cagliostro*), in 1979, and following the success of this and

1984's *Kaze no tani no Naushika* (*Nausicaä of the Valley of the Wind*. See page 257.), he and Takahata cofounded Studio Ghibli in 1985.

Most of Studio Ghibli's output has been made using traditional drawn animation techniques, although computer animation was used for the first time in 1997's *Mononoke-hime* (*Princess Mononoke*. See page 311.). This was also the first movie to really bring Miyazaki's work to attention in the West, thus spreading his

influence on the wider animation world. Many leading contemporary figures, such as Pixar's John Lasseter and Peter Docter, have acknowledged Miyazaki as an influence on their own work.

As well as animation, Miyazaki is also a successful manga comic book artist. He has won numerous awards, including the animated feature Oscar for *Sen to Chihiro no kamikakushi* (*Spirited Away*. See page 332.)

Rupan Sansei: Kariosutoro
no shiro (Castle of
Cagliostro), 1979

1980

France

Le roi et l'oiseau (The King and the Mocking Bird), 1980

Paul Grimault: Le roi et l'oiseau (The King and the Mocking Bird)

In 1936 French animator Paul Grimault and his business partner André Sarrut formed a small animation company called Les Gémeaux, and in 1941 Grimault made the short animated film *Les Passegers de la Grande Ourse* (*The Passengers of the Great Bear*). Following this, Grimault made a series of well-received shorts, such as *L'épouvantail* (*The Scarecrow*, 1943) and *La flute magique* (*The Magic Flute*, 1946), before embarking on a feature film. Supported by his friend and collaborator Jaques Prévert, Grimault began work on *La bergère et le ramoneur* (*The Shepherdess and the Chimneysweep*) in 1948. When Grimault's partner André Sarrut screened the film in an unfinished state in 1952, the two fell out and production was halted.

The movie was much anticipated as the French answer to successful American animated features, and there was an outcry when the project was abandoned. Infuriated by this experience, Grimault left the world of animation for a few years. In 1967 Grimault won the sole rights to *The Shepherdess and the Chimneysweep* and resurrected the project 15 years after abandoning it. During the next decade he continued work on his feature while also producing more award-winning shorts, such as *Le diamant* (*The Diamond*, 1970) and *Le chien mélomane* (*The Music Loving Dog*, 1973). Grimault's feature was eventually finished in 1980, retitled as *Le roi et l'oiseau* (*The King and the Mocking Bird*), 32 years after production had commenced.

The movie is beautifully animated and painstakingly put together, as any great animated film must be. By the time of its release, however, inevitably it looked dated and the character design has a vintage style, similar to something from the Fleischer brothers' work from the *Gulliver's Travels* era. These minor issues aside, it is now rightly regarded as a classic and is certainly one of the greatest European animated features. It was also one of the few foreign movies to be distributed in Japan by Studio Ghibli.

1980/1981
Hungary

Pannonia Studio: A Légy (The Fly) and Vuk (The Little Fox)

Released by Hungary's Pannonia Studio, Ferenc Rófusz's short *A Légy* (*The Fly*) won the Oscar in 1981 for best animated short. Told from the fly's point of view, the film is rotoscoped in a realistically-drawn style, from photographs or film taken through a fisheye lens. Through the insect's eyes, we experience flying around a garden, before going inside a house where the fly is pursued and then swatted by the owner. Rófusz followed the film with two others showing a death from the first person perspective; *Dead Point* (1982) concerns the victim of a firing squad and *Gravitation* (1984) is about an apple falling from a tree.

Vuk (*The Little Fox*), directed by Attila Dargay for Pannonia, tells the story of a fox cub–renamed Vik in the English-language version–whose family is wiped out by humans while he is away from home. Taken in and raised by his uncle, he later finds a vixen trapped in a cage and rescues her. When his uncle is killed, Vik gets revenge on the person who killed him. Based on Istvan Fekete's novel, the movie includes cute-looking characters set against striking, stylized watercolor backgrounds, and was Hungary's most successful animated film of the 1980s.

1981
Canada/ Germany

Frédéric Back: Crac!

Telling the story of the life of a rocking chair through the years from its construction in 1850, this poignant and charming short film uses humor, imaginary sequences, and traditional music to show life and change in Quebec, Canada. "Crac" refers to the sound of the wood being felled, and of chairs creaking and rocking and eventually breaking

Although a German by birth, many of Back's films are examinations of the culture of Canada, his adopted homeland. The Oscar-winning *Crac!* is an early example of the pastel-shaded look that became popular in animation in the 1980s in films such as *The Snowman* (1982).

Back won a second Academy Award in 1987 for his film *L'homme qui plantait des arbres* (*The Man Who Planted Trees*). Based on Jean Gino's story of the same name, this beautiful, soft pencil-shaded film tells of a man who lives in a barren area and tries to restore it to life by planting one tree at a time.

Vuk (The Little Fox), 1981

1981/1983
Canada

Gerald Potterton: Heavy Metal and Clive Smith: Rock & Rule

Heavy Metal was a 1981 feature-film adaptation of the cult adult comic of the same name (not a particular reference to heavy metal music), which itself is an American version of the French adult comic *Metal Hurlant*. The movie is composed of several psychedelic, sci-fi fantasy adventures from the magazine, featuring sex, violence, and rock 'n' roll. The stories were written and designed by various leading comic artists, including Moebius, Richard Corben, and Bernie Wrightson. The animation was divided among several studios and directors, each handling different stories, using a lot of rotoscoping of human characters mixed with fantasy backgrounds to create some generally well realized imaginary worlds. The film gained a mixed response from the critics and a limited success on its initial movie theater release, but went on to become a late night TV cult favorite.

Of similar appeal was *Rock & Rule* (1983), a rock 'n' roll animated feature about a postapocalyptic world where mutant animals have taken over. The film was a spin-off from producer Nelvana's earlier TV special, *The Devil and Daniel Mouse*, and featured the music and voices of rock stars Lou Reed, Iggy Pop, Debbie Harry, Chris Stein, and Earth Wind and Fire. *Rock & Rule* was the first animated feature film for Canadian studio Nelvana, which would go on to produce much animated television and film. The movie cost $8 million to make and nearly bankrupted the company. Its failure stemmed from the limited theatrical release it received due to distributor MGM changing management and the adult classification awarded to the film for its scenes of "drug use, implied devil worship, and mild sexuality." *Rock & Rule* later gained a cult following from screenings on the HBO television channel.

1981
UK/USA

John Halas: Dilemma

For the short *Dilemma*, Halas looked to CG experts in the USA, following the limitations of his previous experiment with CG in 1979's *Autobahn*. *Dilemma* has been claimed as the first fully-digitized CG film, although, like *Autobahn* and *Tron* (1982), which also made such claims, how much of it is actual CG and how much is cel animaton made to look like CG is open to question.

Dilemma uses the graphical style that was Halas' trademark, incorporated with computer morphing effects and electronic music, to take us through history and into the future to show how technology has been used for destruction and to make a plea for the ethical use of technology. Despite this pessimistic vision, Halas was generally positive about the role of computers in animation and art; influenced by the Bauhaus movement, he followed their belief in embracing technology and trying to use it for the benefit of humanity.

Dilemma, 1981

1981
Japan

1982
USA

Nintendo: Donkey Kong

Nintendo's arcade video game *Donkey Kong* was launched in 1981, and is credited as the first game to use animation to create real characters, albeit in a limited form. Created by games design genius Shigeru Miyamoto, this was the first appearance of Super Mario who would later become the most famous character in video games, and indeed, one of the most recognizable cartoon characters in the world.

Tim Burton: Vincent

While working in the concept department at Disney, a 24-year-old Tim Burton impressed executives enough for them to fund a short stop-frame film based on a poem he had written. *Vincent* is the story of a young boy (who looks rather like Burton), who is obsessed with the actor Vincent Price (Burton's hero), and imagines himself to be in the stories of Edgar Allen Poe, although he is actually living in suburban America (where Burton grew up).

The black-and-white film is shot in a German expressionist style and shows influences from the gothic music subculture that was emerging at this time. The Edward Gorey/Charles Addams-style horror/black comic subject matter and thin, curly designs would become familiar trademarks of Burton's future work, as he rose to stardom as a director and producer of both quirky, independent features and Hollywood blockbusters.

Vincent, 1982

1982

USA

Don Bluth: The Secret of NIMH

In 1979, after spending nearly a decade at the Walt Disney Studios learning from the living legends of animation, Don Bluth, Gary Goldman, and John Pomeroy set up Don Bluth Productions. Later joined by eight more artists, for the first few months the company operated out of Bluth's garage.

Disillusioned with Disney management's cost-cutting leading to what they saw as a betrayal of the company's heritage, they had been working on a special project during nights and weekends for several years. Using methods based on those used by Disney animators in the 1940s, techniques now often abandoned due to issues of time and expense, they produced first the feature *Banjo the Woodpile Cat* (1979), which was sold to television, and then *The Secret of NIMH*.

Taken from Robert C. O'Brien's children's book, *Mrs. Frisby and the Rats of NIMH*, it had been suggested as a Disney project but was rejected as being too dark for the studio's preferred light output at that time. Bluth was financed by Aurora Productions, a company established by former Disney executives, and, in another old-style Walt Disney-type move, Bluth, Goldman, Pomeroy, and the executive producers at Aurora mortgaged their homes to complete the movie.

As well as the highly traditional, full-quality character animation, more painstaking effort was taken with novel visual techniques, like color Xerography and split exposures and diffusion to create shadows, translucency, and reflections. There was also a return to classic, Disney-style use of the multiplane camera. Despite the care lavished on it, the film still only cost about half that of an average Disney feature.

In the story, a widow mouse called Mrs Brisby must move out of her field because the plow is on its way, but one of her children is ill. They escape with the help of super-intelligent rats who have escaped from NIMH—the National Institute of Mental Health. Mrs Brisby then repays the rats by saving them from extermination by NIMH with the aid of a magic amulet. The movie is beautifully crafted, but (as in many films directed by animators) the lush animation and effects seem to come at the expense of pacing problems and a meandering story. An advantage the old Disney company enjoyed was that Walt Disney was ruthless about letting a great piece of animation interfere with the telling of the story. Disney was also, in the early days that Bluth wished to emulate, looking to innovate and create new types of films. Critics of Bluth's films would argue that emulating an innovator is somehow missing the point of their innovation.

The Secret of NIMH got generally good reviews, receiving much praise for the quality of its animation, but only performed averagely at the box office, partly due to having to compete with Steven Spielberg's smash hit, *E.T.* This caused financial difficulties at Bluth's company, which they solved by creating animated sequences for the video game *Dragon's Lair*, which became a huge hit. Impressed by the company, Spielberg became executive producer of the next Bluth film, *An American Tail* (1986).

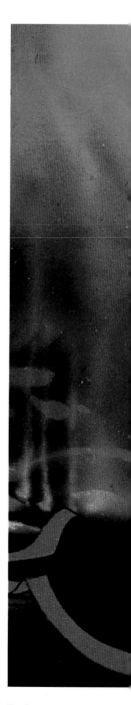

The Secret of NIMH, 1982

1982

USA

Steven Lisberger: Tron

For *Tron*, the first feature film to be based around computer animation, Disney worked with the Lisberger/Kushner animation studio set up by Steven Lisberger and Donald Kushner in 1977. Lisberger was a traditional animator who had an epiphany when he saw the video game *Pong* and animation produced by computer graphics company MAG, one of the companies that would later work on *Tron*. Lisberger was a visionary, with the belief that one day all movies would be made by computers. Disney's head of production, Thomas L. Wilhite, bought into this to the tune of $20 million invested in *Tron* and its new technology, believing it would give Disney a lead over its rivals and futureproof the company.

In the movie, Flynn (Jeff Bridges), a video game programmer, is usurped by a dishonest programmer who steals his work and gets Flynn fired from the corporation ENCOM. Flynn hacks into ENCOM's network where his digital self is caught and erased by the computer's Master Control Program (MCP). The MCP is out of control and has designs on taking over the Pentagon, but with the aid of another victim of corporate corruption—Bradley and his "security program" Tron—Flynn invades the computer again to do battle with the MCP.

Contrary to the hype however, because the technology was not as ready as Lisberger would have liked, a lot of the movie was made by Disney's animators using traditional methods. This caused a lot of tensions with the Disney animators, unionized since the 1940s, with many of them refusing to work on the film fearing that their jobs would be eventually replaced by computers. They had a point: 20 years later, Disney closed its traditional animation production in favor of CGI.

Tron has over 800 shots in which the actors are put in CGI environments, but while computer animation was used in some scenes, the technology did not yet exist for a shot to contain both live action and computer animation. So with techniques not too dissimilar from the ones developed by Ub Iwerks for *Song of the South* 40 years before, live-action shots were combined with traditional cel animation shots using "backlit animation" to make them look like they were computer generated and then edited in with the genuine CG shots. Strangely, this technique wasn't uncommon in this era as, in an effort to seem cutting edge, producers would fake computer animation using traditional animation methods, even though this actually required even more work than regular animation. Ironically, this faking of CGI by traditional methods actually helped to create a demand for and public acceptance of computer animation, which enabled CGI to eventually make many traditional methods largely obsolete.

Lisberger had set out to make an animated movie with live-action segments at the beginning and end, but ended up with a live-action movie with less than a quarter (approximately 20 minutes) of animation. He also wanted to make films using the new technologies of video games and computing, and to open this new aesthetic to mainstream audiences. However, the "computer generated" animation in *Tron* was dismissed at the time as soulless and only of appeal to video game and computer enthusiasts and the movie faired averagely well at the box office. Yet despite these failures, *Tron* is a fascinating film with a unique look, and Lisberger was ultimately proved right in his vision of a digital future for Hollywood. In hindsight, he was just 20 years ahead of the technology and attitudes. Incredibly, *Tron* was refused a nomination for the Academy Awards for special effects as its use of computers was considered to be cheating at the time.

Tron, 1982

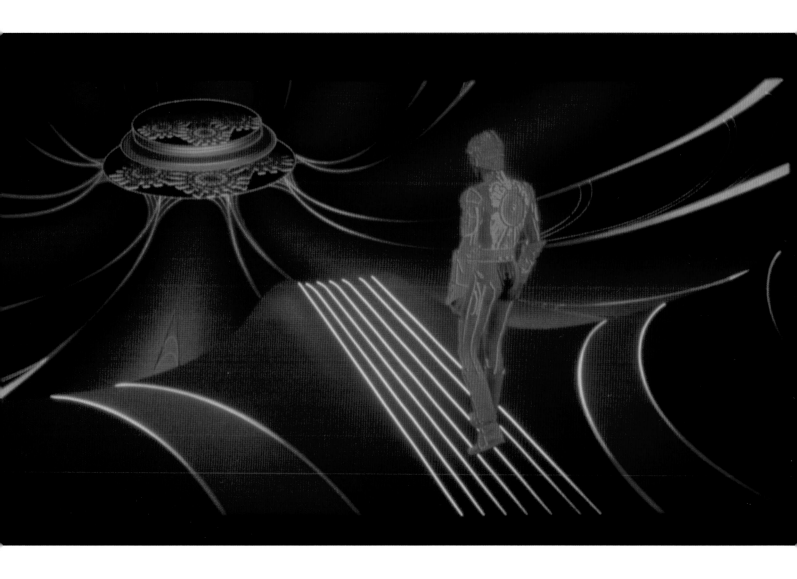

1982

UK

Dianne Jackson: The Snowman

In the 1980s the UK's newly-launched television network Channel 4 funded many animated films, the first of which was their most commercially successful. In 1982 *Yellow Submarine* creators TV Cartoons (TVC) produced the Channel 4-funded adaptation of Raymond Briggs' children's graphic novel *The Snowman*. Directed by Dianne Jackson, this sweet children's classic has become a Christmas TV tradition around the world, and began a fruitful relationship between Briggs and TVC.

In the film, a boy's snowman comes to life and takes him on adventures during the night, including a trip to meet Santa. The scarf that Santa gives the boy is the only proof that it was not all a dream, because the next day, the snowman has melted. The film, silent but for the famous score by Howard Blake, was handrendered in pastel colors for both the characters and the backgrounds, giving it a very organic, crafted feel. Despite the potentially schmaltzy nature of the story and the soaring orchestral score, the skill of the filmmaking is such that *The Snowman* never descends into oversentimentality and is genuinely sweet and moving for children and adults alike.

An introduction was recorded by Raymond Briggs for the first screenings of *The Snowman*, explaining his inspiration for the story, which were the only spoken words in the production. This was replaced in later broadcasts by, somewhat bizarrely, introductions by rock star David Bowie and comedian Mel Smith.

Nominated for the 1983 Academy Award for best animated short film, *The Snowman* was probably the most successful British example of family-oriented animation to date, a record later to be superseded by the work of Aardman Animation.

The Snowman, 1982

UK

Gerald Scarfe: Pink Floyd The Wall

The Wall is a partly-animated movie based on Pink Floyd's 1979 album of the same name. Written by Pink Floyd bassist and singer Roger Walters, *The Wall* tells the life story and mental breakdown of a rock star called Pink (played by Bob Geldoff and said to be based on Waters and former Pink Floyd member Syd Barrett, who suffered a drug-fuelled breakdown). This is combined with the story "The Wall" by philosopher and writer Jean Paul Sartre and experiences Walters had while reading Sartre's work. The movie uses symbolism and metaphors to explore the feelings of isolation and alienation.

The film's 15 minutes of animation are fantasy sequences portraying the tortured mind of Pink. The animation was designed and directed by the satirical cartoonist Gerald Scarfe, using his signature style of wild and aggressive ink-spattered designs. Scarfe had already collaborated with Pink Floyd, having produced animated clips and set designs for use during their concerts, as well as drawing the cover illustration for *The Wall* album. The animation in the movie includes nightmarish scenes of the German bombing of England during World War II, for which Scarfe drew on his own childhood experiences. The characters called The Frightened Ones are based on his memories of having to wear gas masks and hide in shelters during the bombing raids. Iconic images in *The Wall* include the Nazi-like marching hammers. As part of what Scarfe has described as the "magic" of animation, objects morph from one thing to another—doves become vultures and then war planes.

1982/1988
Czech Republic

Jan Svankmajer: Moznosti dialogu (Dimensions of Dialogue) and Neco z Alenky (Alice)

Surrealist genius Jan Svankmajer's masterpiece *Moznosti dialogu* (*Dimensions of Dialogue*) drew on his experience with puppetry and experimental theater to create an examination in three parts of how humans communicate and what, according to this, can often go horribly wrong.

In the first part, the most famous and influential section, Svankmajer recreates and animates the paintings of sixteenth-century artist Giuseppe Arcimboldo, who created images of human heads out of fruit and vegetables. In Svankmajer's film, a fruit-and-vegetable head meets another head made of metal tools and mechanical parts; they attack each other and the tool head swallows and vomits up the vegetable head, who now incorporates some metal tools. They attack each other again, and so it goes on with the heads slowly changing their construction. This sequence summarizes Svankmajer's aesthetic of familiar, banal household objects brought disturbingly and maliciously to life.

In the next sequence, two young clay lovers embrace, melt together, and then spit out a smaller clay ball. They reject the ball and are upset by it, and because of this, the lovers fight and destroy each other. In the third chapter, clay heads of two bald middle-aged men try to cooperate by spitting useful objects to each other out of their mouths, until in their eagerness to please, they start combining the objects with disastrous results.

Made with the aid of animator Vlasta Pospisilova, *Dimensions of Dialogue* is a classic of surrealist stop frame, won many awards worldwide, and cemented Svankmajer's reputation.

For the feature film *Neco z Alenky* (*Alice*, 1988), Svankmajer retold Lewis Carroll's *Alice in Wonderland* in his unique and unsettling style, with a mixture of live action and stop-frame animation. The White Rabbit is a stuffed rabbit that leaks sawdust, meaning he constantly has to eat more. The other inhabitants of Wonderland are mostly made of household objects, bones, or food. The film, funded by the UK's Channel 4, is for many people the best screen version of Carroll's story as, without being a literal interpretation, it celebrates the underlying creepiness of the source material.

Neco z Alenky
(Alice), 1988

Biography

Jan Svankmajer

Jan Svankmajer is a surrealist artist who has never confined himself to one medium; he has worked in puppetry, theater, painting, sculpture, engraving, and film. Born in Prague in 1934, he attended the Institute of Applied Arts and then studied puppetry at the Prague Academy of Performing Arts. His first involvement with film came about during his time at the Laterna Magika Puppet Theatre; he produced his first film, *Poslední trik pana Schwarcewalldea a pana Edgara* (*The Last Trick*) in 1964. His early works show the influence of his puppet theater background.

Svankmajer is married to fellow surrealist artist Eva Svankmajerova, and he joined the Czech surrealist group in 1970. His interest in surrealism was first shown in *Zahrada* (*The Garden*, 1968). *Zvahlav aneb Saticky Slameného Huberta* (*Jabberwocky*, 1971) and *Leonarduv denik* (*Leonardo's Diary*, 1972) show stronger elements of surrealism. In 1972, following the release of *Leonardo's Diary*, he was banned from making films by the communist government of Czechoslovakia. In 1982, after his ban was lifted, he completed his stop-motion masterpiece *Moznosti dialogu* (*Dimensions of Dialogue*). This film was also banned, but he went on to make dozens more films, including the feature *Neco z Alenky* (*Alice*, 1987), and became one of the world's most celebrated animators.

While his films sometimes occupy the fringes of the mainstream, they always retain strong elements of surrealism and gleefully defy convention. Frequently adapting myths and fairy tales, Svankmajer's unique-looking stop-frame films have influenced many animators, including Tim Burton and the Brothers Quay. With his later feature films, *Lekce Faust* (*Faust*, 1994), *Spiklenci slasti* (*Conspirators of Pleasure*, 1996), and *Otesánek* (*Little Otik*, 2000), Svankmajer has moved more into live action, but has retained his surrealist vision.

Otesánek (Little Otik), 2000

1983

USA

John Korty and Charles Swenson: Twice Upon a Time

Twice Upon a Time is an almost forgotten animation feature, although the few people who saw it often remember it so enthusiastically that it has achieved a kind of legendary cult status. The fact of its obscurity seems strange considering it was executive produced by George Lucas, after he'd produced two of the most famous movies of all time in the form of *Star Wars* and *The Empire Strikes Back*. *Twice Upon a Time* got virtually no promotion on its release as its producers, The Ladd Company, were going out of business. Consequently, the film was only shown for two weeks in one theater. It had a few screenings on HBO years later, where seemingly everybody who saw it has never forgotten it. Its short cable TV run was terminated when director John Korty objected to the channel showing a version that was unapproved by him.

Korty was an award-winning independent San Francisco-based filmmaker who had a studio in his barn and was an inspirational figure for Lucas and Francis Ford Coppola. He had made animation for *Sesame Street*, and would also direct a *Star Wars* spin-off for Lucas. Codirector and writer Charles Swenson was an animator who would work for many more years in films and animation, including directing *Rugrats* for

television and writing *An American Tale: Fievel Goes West* (1991).The crew also featured some future big names, like directors David Fincher and Henry Selick, yet despite its cult following and amazing history, *Twice Upon a Time* has never been released on DVD, although some battered copies taken from VHS can be watched online.

Aimed at a young adult audience, the movie featured dialogue improvised by young comedians and a rock soundtrack. Described as an action-adventure comedy, it had a crazy convoluted fantasy plot full of wild characters and hip, ironic dialogue including contemporary slang and swear words, quite a shocking novelty in animation at this time. Various different versions of the movie were created, with different amounts of swearing included.

The film was produced in a house converted into a studio and made with a unique system of cutout animation called Lumage, developed by Korty, that involved translucent cut fabric or plastic filmed on a light table. Korty had previously used this method on his 1964 award-winning short *Breaking the Habit*. *Twice Upon a Time* has a unique, rich glowing look to it, like intricate cutout animation that's been plugged into an electric grid, and one can imagine that if Lotte Reiniger was working in California in the 1980s, this is the kind of film she might have made.

1983
USA

John Lasseter: Test for Where the Wild Things Are

In 1983, while John Lasseter was working for Disney, he created a test for a proposed CGI version of Maurice Sendak's children's picture book, *Where the Wild Things Are*. The test, like *Tron*, was a cooperation with pioneering CG animation company MAGI. Lasseter had an idea for making movies that were computer-generated but retained Disney's traditional animation techniques in order to produce quality character animation with personality and warmth. Following the somewhat disappointing reaction to *Tron* the year before,

however, Disney apparently were not convinced that computer animation had much of a future. They passed on the project, and the disappointed Lasseter left soon after, convinced he was right about the potential of CG.

The test, a mix of CG and traditional animation, was shown at the 1984 Canadian International Animation Festival and demonstrated to many in the industry the possibilities of CG animation. Two decades later, Disney bought Lasseter's CG animation company Pixar Animation Studios, and made him Chief Creative Officer of the corporation. *Where the Wild Things Are* was successfully filmed in 2008 by Spike Jonze, using extensive CG facial animation.

1980s computer animation milestones

Computer programmer, artist, and animator Yoichiro Kawaguchi was a pioneer of computer software that grows images in an organic way. His program Growth Model uses growth algorithms to generate brightly-colored psychedelic worlds, populated with metallic-shaded, organic life-forms. Environments are created with variable parameters in which "life-forms" develop, flourish, or die away with infinite variety. Films produced in this way include *Tendril* (1982) and *Ocean* (1986).

Karl Sims and William Latham are other creators of computer films who use software to grow their images. They have made films and artworks from the digital virtual universes and creatures that are created from the Darwinian ecosystems they set up. Sims used early 3D CGI particle techniques to create work such as *Panspermia* (1990) and *Particle Dreams* (1998). Latham created the short film *Biogenesis* (1993), and later an interactive consumer version of his software Organic Art.

In 1983, the video game *Dragon's Lair* caused a sensation in the arcades with its full-quality animated sequences, made by Don Bluth. In the same year, the Commodore 64 computer was released. The C64 was one of the first affordable home computers and, like the launch of the Sinclair Spectrum the year before in Europe, opened the creation of computer graphics to everyone and inspired a generation of computer artists and programmers. Also in 1983, Jim Clark founded Silicon Graphics in California. This company developed a series of high-spec workstations, which for a while were essential for high-level CGI, and on which many animated and effects films such as *Jurassic Park* were created.

Wavefront Technologies was formed in 1984 by Bill Kovacs, who, along with Roy Hall and others, had developed some of the software used in *Tron*. After Kovacs left, Hall and others developed video manipulation and animation software. In 1995 Silicon Graphics bought

Wavefront Technologies and Canadian firm Alias Research, and merged them to produce advanced computer animation software Alias/Wavefront for its machines, which was later developed, with the collaboration of the Walt Disney Studios during the making of *Dinosaur*, into the Maya software, released in 1998.

In 1986 former National Film Board of Canada animator Daniel Langlois formed Softimage and in 1988 released the first version of the Softimage software, becoming an industry standard in CGI animation and the preferred choice for character animation. In 1990 the first version of 3D Studio (later renamed 3DS Max), another hugely popular 3D CGI package, was released by Autodesk. Autodesk later purchased the rights to both Maya and Softimage and became the market leaders in high-end 3D CGI animation products. Maya won the Oscar for technical achievements in 2003.

1983
UK

Mark Hall and Chris Taylor: The Wind in the Willows

Cosgrove Hall Productions, based in Manchester, England, produced this stop-frame version of *The Wind in the Willows* for British television. It is considered by many to be the finest filmed version of Kenneth Grahame's much adapted classic tale. In the story, Mole, Rat, and Badger try to control the reckless Toad, but he ends up in prison. He escapes, but in the meantime, Rat has to stop the weasels from taking over Toad Hall.

Mark Hall's beautifully produced film presents a rural world that is rich in detail and texture; the models are well crafted, managing to succeed with the challenge of depicting realistically-shaped animals with human characteristics. The film also makes use of some excellent voice talent, with dialogue taken straight from the original book. The worldwide success of the project led to a 52-episode television series and a second film, *A Tale of Two Toads*, produced in 1989.

The Wind in the Willows, 1983

1984
Japan

Hayao Miyazaki: Kaze no tani no Naushika (Nausicaä of the Valley of the Wind)

Taken from a segment of his own graphic novel of the same name, Hayao Miyazaki wrote and directed *Kaze no tani no Naushika* (*Nausicaä of the Valley of the Wind*), his second feature after *Rupan Sansei: Kariosutoro no shiro* (*Castle of Cagliostro*, 1979). *Nausicaä* was an instant classic, a massive box office hit in Japan, and its success led the novel's publisher to fund Miyazaki in setting up Studio Ghibli.

In the film, the young and noble Princess Nausicaä fights for peace as she tries to prevent two tribes from destroying each other and the planet. It features the beautiful natural backgrounds, clean precise character design, and fluid animation that fans of Miyazaki have come to recognize, with the design of Princess Nausicaä being the original version of the classic Miyazaki girl design.

A badly edited and dubbed English version was released in the USA and worldwide by New World in the 1980s as *Warriors of the Wind*, and was later shown on HBO cable TV. More than 30 minutes were cut from the film, losing a lot of the environmental theme, as it was felt to be "slow moving." Also for this version, most of the characters were renamed and the plot was not explained to the voice actors before they recorded their lines. Miyazaki was furious at this lack of respect and for a long time mistrusted Western distributors of his work.

1984
France

Jean-François Laguionie: Gwen, le livre de sable (Gwen, or the Book of Sand)

A virtually forgotten animated feature from the 1980s, *Gwen, le livre de sable* (*Gwen, or the Book of Sand*) is a fascinating and original film in terms of visuals as well as story. In order to avoid the black outlined flat cel look, the film is rendered with gouache, the fabrics and textures in every frame are shaded and animated almost three dimensionally, giving a very lifelike feel, while the characters are quite simplified.

The poetic and philosophical story, often told through voiceover, is set in a postapocalyptic sand-covered world, where the hero Gwen is adopted by a tribe of nomads. At night some terrible creature leaves objects from the modern world in the sand while the humans hide away. One night Gwen stays outside with her friend, a young boy who is kidnapped by the night creature. Gwen and the boy's mother, Roseline, set out to find the boy and discover the secret of their strange world and The City of the Dead.

Gwen is an intelligent and enigmatic film that does not talk down to its audience. Its surreal imagery of mysterious objects left in the desert creates a mystery that drives the thoughtful narrative forward, and its painstaking and skillfully rendered look makes it an interesting film to watch.

1985

USA

Will Vinton: The Adventures of Mark Twain

Inspired by Walt Disney and the architect Antoni Gaudí (who made design models from clay), Will Vinton and fellow architecture student Bob Gardiner began experimenting with stop-frame animation after creating architectural models at University of California, Berkeley. Their first film together, *Closed Monday* (1974), about a drunk in an art gallery, won them an Oscar. A couple of years later Vinton and Gardiner parted ways on their second film *Mountain Music* (1976).

The Adventures of Mark Twain was the first feature-length "claymation" film, as Vinton called his stop-frame process, and took three and a half years to shoot. The film is based on excerpts from the stories of Mark Twain, mixed with a statement the author made about having "come in" with Halley's Comet and wanting to "go out with it" (Twain died one day after the comet appeared in 1910). The film's highly original storyline, well told with the nicely constructed and animated models and sets, follows the adventures of Tom Sawyer, Huck Finn, and other characters as they ride on Mark Twain's interplanetary balloon, and relates the author's philosophy and real life events that inspired him.

Every single item that appeared in the movie was made of clay, even the skies. The film showcased all the skills that Vinton had been developing, but also required him to introduce new innovations, such as "moustache synch" where replacement moustaches were used to simulate speech. The lengthy production schedule meant that the design of the models had to be modified so that parts could be easily replaced as they wore out. The half-body models used for close-up shots tended to be rather top-heavy, so were made with heavy steel bases to stabilize them.

The film deals with many aspects of life, good and bad, happy and sad, and for that reason is perhaps unsuitable for children and has been edited down when shown on television. It is a beautifully made, original, and fascinating film, although

sometimes the semirealistic nature of the characters and their world seems to emphasise the slight stiffness inherent in the stop-frame technique.

Vinton achieved greater fame with the California Raisins, a funny and expressively animated group of raisins, created for the California Raisin Advisory Board, who became a media sensation, starred in television specials, and had several hit records.

The Adventures of
Mark Twain, 1985

Claymation

Clay animation is a form of stop-frame animation where all the models are made from a malleable substance, such as clay or Plasticine. The models are moved and shifted frame-by-frame, in a laborious and time-consuming process. Will Vinton coined and trademarked the term "claymation" in 1976 to describe the technique used in his work.

1985

Canada

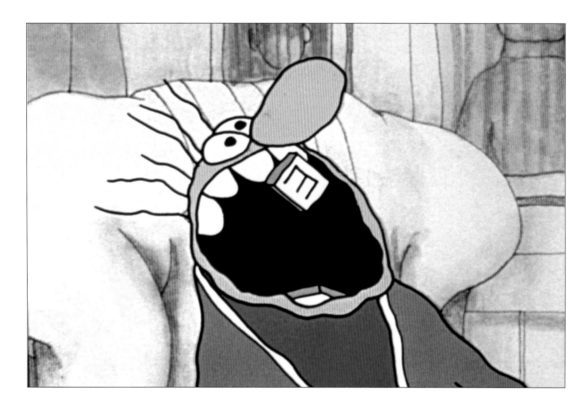

The Big Snit, 1985

Richard Condie: The Big Snit

The Big Snit is a classic of Canadian animation; a short cartoon that everyone loves, it is perfect in a way that is inexplicable—it just is. A middle-aged couple hang out, play Scrabble, he cheats, they argue, they annoy each other, he saws the chair, she shakes her eyeballs in her glasses, they argue, fight, cry, make up ... and meanwhile earth-shattering events are happening outside.

Richard Condie's style is similar to that of Bob Godfrey, with its simple drawings, wobbly lines, refusal to take anything seriously, and general silliness. He collaborates with a small group of people on his films, including musician Patrick Godfrey his sister Sharon Condie, who created backgrounds for

The Big Snit, and animator Cordell Barker. Barker is the creator of another classic of Canadian silliness, *The Cat Came Back* (1988), a slapstick-style story based on a comic song. *The Big Snit* was nominated for an Oscar for best animated short and was voted the 25th best cartoon of all time in the 1994 survey for Jerry Beck's book.

The basic message of *The Big Snit* seems to be: despite our petty conflicts, the world is a nice place and we should appreciate it more. Stop taking everything so seriously and enjoy your life. Stop taking this cartoon seriously, it's just a cartoon.

1985
UK/Canada

1986
USA

Steve Barron: Take on Me and Money for Nothing

In 1981 the words "Ladies and Gentleman, rock and roll" launched MTV, an American cable channel with the simple idea of showing nothing but music videos. It soon became a global phenomenon. The first channel ident was animated, and so were many of the videos.

In 1985 Norwegian band A-ha released the single "Take On Me," which became a worldwide hit. The success was largely due to the music video directed by London-based Dubliner Steve Barron. It was animated by American animator Michael Patterson and featured the singer of the band coming alive from a comic's pages in the form of a rotoscoped animated character.

Also directed by Steve Barron in 1985 was the video for "Money For Nothing" by Dire Straits, one of the first computer animated videos and a landmark in CGI. A satire on the whole MTV rock star culture, the video also features a rotoscoped performance of Dire Straits on the video's virtual "TV." Although produced in London, it was animated by the Canadian company Mainframe, pioneers of computer animation, who also made the first CGI television series *Reboot* in 1994.

Don Bluth: An American Tail

After *The Secret of NIMH* Steven Speilberg teamed up with Don Bluth with a mission to make Disney-style features better than the ones that Disney were currently producing. On its release, *An American Tail* seemed to have succeeded in this, beating Disney's *The Great Mouse Detective* at the box office and attracting generally more favorable reviews. Indeed it became the highest grossing non-Disney animated feature, until beaten by Bluth's next release, *The Land Before Time* (1988).

An American Tail concerns a family of mice who, suffering persecution from cats, stow away aboard a ship to the promised land of America. Like *The Secret of NIMH*, the movie featured the same rounded, bouncy Disney-type mice characters, plus lush backgrounds and effects, but also like *NIMH*, the story sometimes loses momentum. Its hero, Fievel, named after Spielberg's grandfather, became a popular enough character to star in more movies and a television series.

Bluth followed up *An American Tail* with the even more successful *The Land Before Time* (1988), the story of a group of cute dinosaurs on a quest across a harsh prehistoric landscape, a movie that eventually spawned more than 10 direct-to-video sequels. For *The Land Before Time* Bluth moved his studio to Dublin, and made several more films there, while for *American Tail 2: Fievel Goes West* (1991), Spielberg established his own studio, Amblimation, in London, which made three animated features and whose staff later became the foundation of DreamWorks Animation in Los Angeles.

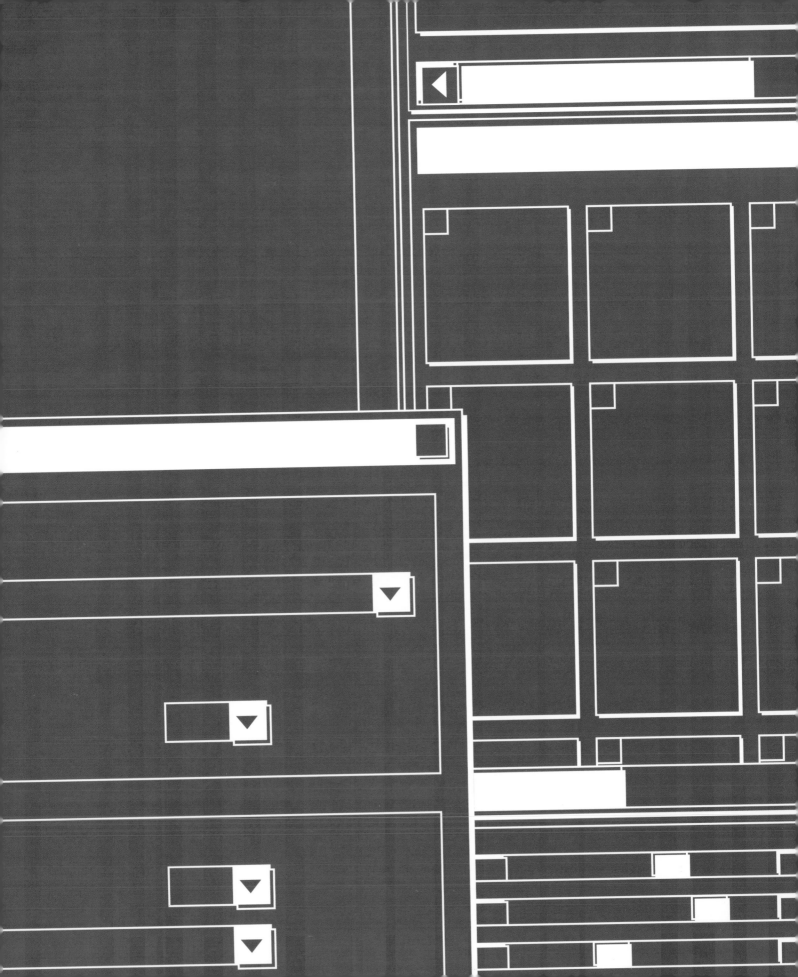

1986-2010:
The Digital Dawn

The late 1980s and early 1990s saw a number of positive developments for animation: movie theater attendances increased, the popularity of *Who Framed Roger Rabbit* and *The Simpsons* caused a boom in animated features and television series, Asian anime injected energy, the rise of the video games industry created a new market, and the internet provided new distribution possibilities. Animation was on the rise again, and this time round, anyone could have an animation studio in their desktop computer.

For the first few years of the CGI boom, the obsession was with making films and effects more and more photo realistic. Recreating reality has its place and can be exciting, but ultimately what is more exciting is creating different realities, and that's where the artist and animator become important again. So as with animation in the 1950s, outside Hollywood style FX, a lot of CG is either super-stylized and elaborately finessed or purposefully lo-fi, scratched, and scribbled. Any method is seized on to not look like computer graphics, often by taking computers out of the process. In video games, the super machines promising ultimate power and realism are now outsold by less powerful consoles with inferior graphics but superior imagination, creativity, and fun. The old techniques and values of drawing, design, imagination, and animation have been absorbed and applied to the digital age.

The production of television animation underwent a minor revolution in the digital age, as low-cost desktop computers and software programs such as Flash meant that production no longer had to be stripped down so much it became "visual radio," nor sent to lower wage economies, but could be kept in-house meaning tighter controls on quality. After the boom and bust years of the late 1990s, the internet reestablished itself as a viable entertainment platform when household high-speed broadband became commonplace, and websites like YouTube achieved massive popularity with their open access to homemade clips, short films, music videos, and TV excerpts. The phenomenon of "viral" distribution, where people email a link for a favorite video clip to their friends, became a powerful alternative and cost-effective method of distribution, and a whole new advertising industry tried to invisibly infiltrate this "new media" world. Things were changing fast and many filmmakers and animators broke through from outside the traditional industry channels to achieve success by this kind of viral distribution.

Editing, compositing, motion tracking, and digital animation systems that 20 years ago would have been prohibitively expensive for all but the biggest production houses, are now compressed into far superior software, usable on a decent laptop and affordable to most. This has, of course, meant a lot of terrible films being produced. There is a sense that the fact of something being difficult to produce, as animation was in the past, filters out a lot of those who lack the burning desire and the determination needed to work long and hard to achieve excellence. On the other hand, this liberating of the means of production, as Karl Marx might put it, has also led to a lot of work from talented people who would have found producing animation almost impossibly expensive and difficult in the past. Francis Ford Coppola once stated that the next Mozart might be a little fat girl in Ohio with a camcorder. Give her a computer, and she could be the next Disney too.

1986
USA

John Lasseter: Luxo Jr.

After leaving Disney, John Lasseter worked at Lucasfilm Computer Graphics Project, helping produce the early CG animated short *The Adventures of Andre and Wally B* in 1984. This two-minute film about a duel between a cartoon man, who sounds a little like Donald Duck, and a wasp, was an early example of how CG could produce character animation and funny cartoons, even if the characters are made up of little more than colored spheres and tubes. Lasseter is credited with the character design and animation for the short.

In 1986 this division of Lucasfilm was bought by Apple founder Steve Jobs, after being sold by George Lucas when he needed money after the disastrous flop of *Howard the Duck* (1983). Lasseter produced short films such as *Luxo Jr.* for the new company, Pixar Animation Studios, to demonstrate the capabilities of the company and its main product, the Pixar Image Computer, which they sold to Disney and others, mainly for coloring animated films. With the two-and-a-half minute long *Luxo Jr.*, Pixar started hitting their stride; the film is a charming story of a baby lamp who hops playfully around its mother with a ball. The characters, comprising of simple shapes, communicate a variety of emotions, and it is the quality of the animation alone that changes the household objects into entertaining characters. The lamp would later become Pixar's logo.

Biography

John Lasseter / Pixar

When John Lasseter first worked for The Walt Disney Company as a Jungle Cruise skipper at Disneyland Park, he began a career that would eventually take him to the very top of the company. Perhaps the true heir to Walt Disney, Lasseter has pioneered new techniques, but has always remembered that a successful animation must be founded on appealing characters and a great story. Born in 1957, Lasseter grew up in Los Angeles. While at high school, he was inspired by reading Bob Thomas' *The Art of Animation*, and realized that his passion for cartoons could become his career. He studied at the California Institute of the Arts, and while there, he took part in Disney's character animation training program (fellow trainees included the future directors, Tim Burton and Brad Bird).

He was hired by Disney in 1982, but, wanting to pursue his interest in the exciting possibilities of computer animation, he joined LucasFilm in 1984. At this studio, he worked on his first 3D short, *Andre and Wally B*, and he also designed and animated a sequence for the live-action movie *Young Sherlock Holmes* (1985).

In 1986 Steve Jobs bought the computer division of LucasFilm and, along with Ed Catmull, cofounded the Pixar studio with Lasseter on board as a director. The new studio's aim was to develop computer technology and use it to tell wonderful stories. Pixar quickly became a world leader in the field of computer animation, and their groundbreaking work has changed the face of the industry. Initially making shorts and commercials, in 1991 Pixar signed a deal with Disney for three feature films. The first of these, *Toy Story* (1995), directed by Lasseter, was a huge success and showed the potential of computer animation. (For more on *Toy Story*, see page 298.) In 2006 Disney purchased Pixar, and Lasseter became the chief creative officer of both studios, confirming his status as one of the key figures in world animation today.

Luxo Jr., 1986

1986
UK

Jimmy Murakami: When the Wind Blows

Channel 4 funded *The Snowman* follow-up, *When the Wind Blows*, another adaptation of a Raymond Briggs graphic novel by TVC, this time directed by Jimmy Murakami. Although a nuclear holocaust is a more somber subject than a flying snowman, like Briggs' book, the film managed to tackle the subject through gentle black humor. The story concerns an old couple called Jim and Hilda who, when war breaks out, naively and comically follow the government's survival instructions for the event of a nuclear attack, with terrible results. The couple's touching yet pathetic faith in the "powers that be," based on their nostalgic memories of World War II, is sad and affecting and brings the nuclear disarmament debate down to a clear cut human level. The film had more of a traditional cel-painted look than *The Snowman*, but used photographed model sets for the backgrounds. Never likely to be as commercially successful as *The Snowman*, *When the Wind Blows* was a brave and grown-up animated feature, much praised by the critics, and presenting a powerful argument against the nuclear arms race.

When the Wind
Blows, 1986

1986

UK/USA

Brothers Quay: Street of Crocodiles

Made during Channel 4's golden years of animation funding, *Street of Crocodiles* is the Brothers Quay's best-known work and is typical of their enigmatic and claustrophobic style. Influenced by Eastern European animation, writing, and surrealism, in particular Jan Svankmajer's work, the brothers create nightmarish and mysterious stop-frame worlds, like peering at bizzare and obscure fragments of stories from the subconscious mind, "seen through a dirty pane of glass" as they have described it.

Street of Crocodiles is loosely based on a story by Polish writer Bruno Schulz; the plot involves a puppet exploring a museum as the exhibits and objects come to life. The strange happenings include some screws that unscrew themselves and dance, a broken watch that opens up to reveal that it's full of meat, and some nasty broken Victorian zombie dolls that perform vivisection on the puppet. The camera swings and tracks as if by clockwork, as Leszek Jankowski's haunting, scratchy score heightens the sense of desolation and threat. The film ends with a quote from Shulz's book about the barren life in The Street of Crocodiles, where nothing can ever succeed or reach a conclusion.

There are several references to Poland in the film, and the end credits are similar in style to old communist films. The obscurity of it all means it is difficult to tell how much of this is an exercise in style and homage, like a music video, and how much is attempting to communicate ideas and black humor, like Svankmajer's work. Either way, it's an atmospheric and memorable film.

Street of
Crocodiles, 1986

1986
UK

Stephen R. Johnson: Sledgehammer

In 1986 the video for "Sledgehammer" rejuvenated singer Peter Gabriel's career. The video, an amazing pixillation/stop-frame animation epic directed by Stephen R. Johnson, was made by Aardman Animations and The Brothers Quay. Somewhat influenced by Jan Svankmajer's films with its animated fruit and objects, it featured Gabriel singing while immersed in a variety of crazily imaginative surreal situations, including being made of vegetables, pixillated dancing, and animation being painted onto him. It became one of the most played videos on MTV and is considered to be one of the best music videos ever made.

1986
Russia

Nina Shorina: Dver (Door)

This beautifully-made stop-frame short seems to be an analogy of contemporary Russia, shortly before Mikhail Gorbachev introduced political and economic reforms. The door of a large apartment block is kept permanently boarded shut, but in these difficult circumstances the residents manage to carry on with their lives. When the door is eventually left open, they continue with their old habits and avoid using it. A child sees the absurdity of the situation, but when he points it out, he is ignored by the adults, who are unable or unwilling to change their ways. The superb design of the crumbling old building and the characters makes *Dver* (*Door*) a satisfying experience for the eyes as well as the mind.

1987
UK

Joanna Quinn: Girls Night Out and Alison de Vere: Black Dog

In Joanna Quinn's debut film, a character called Beryl leaves her husband slumped in front of the TV as she is taken on a wild night out by her factory worker friends. The women get drunk, watch a male strip show, and Beryl lets go of her inhibitions. Quinn began work on the film in 1985 when she was still at college. After moving from England to Wales, she completed the film and added the riotous soundtrack with the aid of funding from Channel 4 and the Welsh television channel, S4C. *Girls Night Out* showed Quinn's potential as a filmmaker and animator and perhaps remains her best remembered film. Drawn in Quinn's signature loose and organic style and with a bawdy physical humor, the film captures the abandon of a wild night out. This six-minute short won several awards at the 1987 Annecy Animation Festival.

Quinn followed the film up with more award-winning shorts, including *Body Beautiful* (1990), *Elles* (1992), the Oscar-nominated *Famous Fred* (1998), and what is often considered her masterpiece, *Britannia* (1993). These shorts were often subsidised by her work on worldwide advertising campaigns for products such as Charmin toilet paper and Whiskas catfood.

Channel 4 screened *Girls Night Out* alongside Alison de Vere's *The Black Dog*. Another Annecy award winner told from a woman's perspective in a sketchy style, de Vere's film was a much darker and psychological "soul journey," dealing with a woman haunted by the appearance of a black dog. She tries to shake the beast off by shopping, makeovers, and nightclubs, but is preyed on by all manner of parasitical beasts, who come after her for payment in the morning. Rescued by the black dog, she finds herself in a city where the story, mixed with ancient mythology, becomes even more symbolic and allegorical.

A veteran of British studios such as Halas & Batchelor and TVC, de Vere produced several more award-winning works as a director before her death in 2001.

1987
USA

Girls Night Out,
1987

Brad Bird: Family Dog

The original *Family Dog*, developed as part of Steven Spielberg's anthology television series *Amazing Stories*, was a highly-rated animated comedy that became a cult show among animators. Many of the illustrious *Family Dog* crew would go on to become big names in animation, such as Ralph Eggleston, future Pixar production designer and director of the short *For The Birds* (2000); Rob Minkoff, future director of Disney's *The Lion King* (1994) and the live-action/CG animation feature *Stuart Little* (1999); and Chris Buck, director of Disney's *Tarzan* (1999); and for many, this was their first real exposure to the talents of star director Brad Bird.

The film told three separate stories about a long-suffering family dog; as well as being superbly written and directed and very funny, the film featured an angular retro design, a future hallmark of Bird's work. It had a very high production quality by the standards of mid-1980s TV animation, which, at the time, was dominated by low-budget, mass-produced, Saturday-morning children's fare.

Family Dog was an influential landmark production that is credited with having a role in the 1990s revival of quality animation that came through movies such as Spielberg's *An American Tail* (1986), Disney's *Who Framed Roger Rabbit* (1988) and *The Little Mermaid* (1989), and, in TV terms, Ralph Bakshi's *The New Adventures of Mighty Mouse* (1987), Matt Groening's *The Simpsons* (1990), and John Kricfalusi's *Ren and Stimpy* (1991).

1987
Estonia

Priit Pärn: Eine murul (Breakfast on the Grass)

In the 1980s, animation from the Soviet bloc was enjoying new freedoms; Gorbachev's reforms were loosening state control, yet animators still received funding from the state, something they would lose under the new capitalist free markets. Emerging under the wing of Rein Raamat, who had established Estonian animation as an important force in the previous five years, Pritt Pärn became a hugely influential figure in Eastern Europe, and indeed worldwide, with his roughly drawn but expressive, powerful, and darkly ironic personal films. His early works *Kas maakera on ümmargune?* (*Is the Earth Round?*, 1977) and *Kolmnurk* (*Triangle*, 1982), caused ripples in the Eastern Bloc with their simplistic drawings and downbeat and critical perspective, avoiding both the often childish efforts of the government-dictated Soyuzmultfilm studio and the overly moralizing tone of the "serious" animators such as Rammat.

In Pärn's multi-award-winning 23-minute masterpiece *Eine murul* (*Breakfast On The Grass*) four interlocking stories explore everyday life in Russia. In the first part, a young woman struggles against poverty and shortages of goods and services leaving her vulnerable to corruption and lechery. Part two concerns a man's idealized fantasy of the materialistic high life and his pursuit of this, which leads him to be thrown between one corrupt figure and another, finding his money to be of little value. In part three a woman sees or imagines herself as losing her own face/beauty/identity, and her preoccupation with this causes her to neglect her young daughter. In the fourth story a bureaucrat receives some news which makes him literally shrink in stature, and then go on a surreal journey ending in murder to restore his status. The final part, based on Èdouard Manet's painting *Le déjeuner sur l'herbe* (*Luncheon on the Grass*), the four main characters are admitted into a symbolic, private gated garden of decadence and pleasure.

Pärn released *Hotell E* in 1992, the year after Estonia gained independence. This short uses the stereotype of the gray East miserably regarding the colorful, happy West to attack hypocrisy. On the one hand Pärn shows how the East prevents freedom by repressing art and language, while on the other hand the Western free market is driven to appeal to the lowest denominator, ignoring art and language, and therefore, in a different way, repressing individual freedom.

Many Ukranian animators were heavily influenced by Pärn's style and often brought this influence to foreign industries during their subsequent careers abroad. An example of this is Igor Kovalyov, who brought Pärn's style to the US industry where it can be clearly seen in animation such as his children's television series, *Rugrats*.

1987

Japan

Japan

Yoshiaki Kawajiri: Yoju Toshi (Wicked City)

An undercover human agent working in the Dark Realm teams up with a sexy agent from this dark dimension, and they embark on a passionate, forbidden relationship as the two worlds prepare to sign a treaty. A dark violent, erotic, and disturbing fantasy, the tone is set by an early encounter with a creature which is a cross between a spider and a predatory woman, with a vagina lined with sharp teeth. Unlike lots of anime of this kind, *Yoju Toshi* (*Wicked City*) had a fairly high budget and was aimed at theatrical release in Japan and Asia by its producers, Madhouse. This influential dark gothic sci-fi thriller was later released in the West on video, where it gained a cult following.

Yoshiaki Kawajiri, Katsuhiro Otomo, Rintaro: Neo Tokyo

Maintaining a dark moody look to its 2D drawn anime worlds and stylized direction techniques, *Neo Tokyo* was an experimental and influential milestone. An anthology movie containing three interwoven shorts by directors who are among the leading figures in anime, *Neo Tokyo* is interesting for its use of Western classical music. Rintaro directed the framing film *Labyrinth*, the story of a small girl who ventures through a mirror into an eerie and surreal carnival world. Katsuhiro Otomo's *Order to Stop Construction*, is a more wordy and philosophical piece about a robot construction project in the jungle going out of control. Some see this short as a rehearsal for *Akira* (1988), and while it does have the technology out of control aspect, a common theme in anime, it is perhaps closer to, and inspired by, Francis Ford Coppola's *Apocalypse Now* (1979). The third film in the anthology is *Running Man* by Yoshiaki Kawajiri, a more traditional techno anime about a champion racing driver who can't stop winning.

Eine murul (Breakfast on the Grass), 1987

1988
USA/UK

Disney: Who Framed Roger Rabbit

By 1986 The Walt Disney Company was in the doldrums as cartoons were deemed to be out of public favor. The studio's decision to invest $70 million, at that date one of the biggest budgets of all time, on a revolutionary animated movie based on a little known book seems incredible in retrospect and possibly shows how much they wanted to work with Steven Spielberg. It also shows just how good the short test sequence was that Richard Williams and his special-effects man Chris Knott had created at Williams' studio in London.

This test sequence showed a cartoon rabbit falling down some live-action stairs, but unlike previous attempts to merge animation and live action, the camera moved about, the character looked very three-dimensional, and as he went in and out of different lighting effects, he cast shadows that exactly matched the live-action shadows. In short, the cartoon felt totally immersed in the film. The finished movie was a continuation of this, its 1940s film noir look and private eye story providing a shadowy world in which the live action and animated characters could merge. A few of the set pieces, and particularly the finale, featured a roll call of animated characters from history.

Richard Williams, the animation director chosen for the project, insisted on working in London. A handful of top Disney animators were mixed in with a mainly British crew of about 200, including the best animators from Williams' studio. The movie was composited at ILM in Los Angeles and used no computers in its sophisticated animation process.

Two years later, the film was released in a blaze of publicity and was a huge critical success, becoming 1988's biggest box office smash and launching a revival in the art of animation. Many young British animators benefited from the somewhat intense working experience and from being trained by Disney. When the production was over, Disney took a handful of the best young animators back to Los Angeles, and some of them would go on to lead the company's big revival of the 1990s, starting with *The Little Mermaid* (1989).

When Walt Disney first set up his company, he made films that combined animation with live action, and now, as with *Mary Poppins* in the 1960s, *Roger Rabbit* rescued the company's animated features from lean times.

Who Framed Roger
Rabbit, 1988

1988

USA

Bruce Bickford: Prometheus Garden

Bruce Bickford is an outsider, underground artist who has been producing his own extraordinary brand of stop-frame animation since his work in the early 1970s with rock maverick Frank Zappa and the films *Baby Snakes*, *Dub Room Special*, and *The Amazing Mr Bickford*. Working alone in Seattle, he produces stream-of-consciousness worlds that veer between enchanted forests and bad trips from hell, filled with mutated human forms morphing into monsters, into hamburgers, into fairies, into anything this deranged imagination can drag forth.

The warped visuals distract from the lack of any real plot in *Prometheus Garden*, which, at a running time of 28 minutes, is Bickford's longest film to date and the only one he claims he had complete power over after Zappa took editorial control of his work. *Prometheus Garden* is loosely inspired by the Greek myth of Prometheus, who created mortals from clay; the extraordinary vivid visual grotesqueries disguise the lack of story or real variety to the work. Like a series of increasingly nightmarish hallucinations, in a garden filled with waving mutant plants, heads grow out of the ground like fungi and are molded into armies of naked humans, who fight for survival, disembowel each other, merge into bizarre creatures, and act out Greek myths involving cowboys, cops, and pizzas.

UK

Mark Baker: The Hill Farm

The Hill Farm is a beautiful, 18-minute, dialogue-free short; it covers the events of three days and shows how different people use the same hilly countryside in different ways. The farmer cares for the animals, a group of holiday-makers camp nearby and take photos, and hunters hunt everything they see. A storm and a big bear cause problems, but everything is resolved as the different groups shelter in the farmhouse.

The Hill Farm was made over a three-year period at the UK's National Film & Television School, and was completed in 1988. It had a budget of around £18,000 and used mainly traditional animation techniques. Mark Baker worked on the film alone, with some input from visiting lecturers. Baker also had some help from the paint department at Richard Purdum Productions, where he had worked previously. *The Hill Farm* won the Annecy Grand Prix, and Baker's other shorts *The Village* and *Jolly Roger* were both Oscar nominated and have won major awards around the world. The backgrounds and characters in *The Hill Farm* are simple, but beautifully designed and animated, and with the trademark hilly terrain that would later feature in Mark Baker and Neville Astley's worldwide hit television series *Peppa Pig* in 2005.

Prometheus
Garden, 1988

1988
Japan

Katsuhiro Otomo: Akira

Japanese manga artist Katsuhiro Otomo released the animated version of his epic sci-fi masterpiece *Akira* in 1988. This apocalyptic and mind-blowing techno thriller was a massive success, bringing anime to a whole new worldwide audience. With its stunning design, effects, and groundbreaking digital and cel animation, *Akira* ran way over budget, but it was a worldwide smash and broke open the market in the West for Japanese anime. Although it increased awareness and acceptance of anime, no Japanese adult-aimed animation has since achieved a similar success in the West.

Akira is the story of young members of a motorcycle gang in postapocalyptic Neo Tokyo, a new city built on an island in Tokyo bay after the destruction of the original city in World War 3. When captured by the army, one of the boys, Tetsuo, is discovered to have psychic superpowers similar to the awesome destructive energy possessed by Akira, a small boy who was responsible for destroying Tokyo 30 years earlier.

This leads to a spectacular confrontation at the Olympic Stadium, underneath which the remains of Akira are stored.

Akira was reported to be the first Japanese film to use the standard Western technique of recording the sound before the pictures; the usual practice in Japan was to dub the sound over the picture.

After this project, Otomo worked with fellow manga creator Satoshi Kon, who provided layouts and animation for the animated feature *Rojin Z* (*Old Man Z*, 1991) written by Otomo, while Kon wrote the script for Otomo's live-action *Warudo apâtomento horâ* (*World Apartment Horror*, 1991). Otomo then part directed *Memories* (1995), and in 1988 he was credited as supervisor on *Spriggan*, although many believe he directed it due to the closeness to his style. In 2001 he wrote and produced *Metropolis*, and in 2004, moving from cyber-punk to steam-punk, he directed the stunning *Steamboy*, perhaps the true follow-up to *Akira*.

Akira,
1988

1988

Japan

Isao Takahata: Hotaru no haka (Grave of the Fireflies); Hayao Miyazaki: Tonari no Totoro (My Neighbor Totoro)

The success of 1984's *Kaze no tani no Naushika* (*Nausicaä of the Valley of the Wind*) led Hayao Miyazaki and his friend and fellow director Isao Takahata to set up Studio Ghibli and begin to produce a string of anime features of unequalled originality, quality, and critical and commercial success.

The studio's first few releases set a benchmark for the visual beauty and diversity of Ghibli's output. The charming and unique *Tenkû no shiro Rapyuta* (*Castle in the Sky*), was released in 1986. Written and directed by Miyazaki, it tells a moving story of robots guarding ancient flying cities.

Miyazaki's next movie, *Tonari no Totoro* (*My Neighbor Totoro*), is a charming and warm-hearted children's fantasy. It captures, from a child's point of view, a world where simple things are full of excitement and imagination, although the film is not afraid to give a more realistic world view by also touching on downbeat subjects. Two young sisters move to the countryside and find that their house and the woods that surround it contain magical creatures who help nature. The design of the natural world is as gorgeous as it is in all Miyazaki's movies, while the delightful Totoro creatures have become iconic Japanese

characters and the symbol of the Ghilbli company. The scene where the two girls quietly wait for a bus in the rain and gradually realise a Totoro is waiting with them, is one of the most magical moments in animation.

In contrast, Takahata's *Hotaru no haka* (*Grave of the Fireflies*) is an intense film set in the last days of World War II, which examines the consequences of the US airforce dropping fire bombs on Japanese cities. These events are portrayed on a human scale, in fact a child's scale, but the raw emotions and combination of innocence and instinct the characters portray make this a very adult film. Despite the beautiful scenes and poetic pace, it is harrowing and hard to watch.

My Neighbor Totoro and *Grave of the Fireflies* were, somewhat strangely, released together in a double bill to theaters in Japan. This strategy proved unsuccessful, as although *Totoro* was a commercial family movie, the harrowing nature of *Fireflies* was a tough sell to a family audience. Both films however gained critical praise and reputations over the following years.

Hotaru no haka
(Grave of the
Fireflies), 1988

1989
USA

Disney: The Little Mermaid

The Little Mermaid was a classic princess story, Disney's first princess tale and first feature based on a fairy tale since 1959's *Sleeping Beauty*. Adapted from the Hans Christian Andersen fairy tale, it tells the story of the mermaid princess who rescues and falls in love with a human prince and dreams of joining the human world.

    Disney had first considered making a movie of *The Little Mermaid* in the 1930s, and illustrator Kay Nielsen had prepared pastel and watercolor sketches for it. These preliminary designs were used as a starting point by the the animators when they began work on the modern feature. With a sassier take on this familiar subject matter, the movie features a new, modern style of character design, a colorful undersea world, and the best songs in a Disney film since the 1960s. The underwater setting meant that approximately 80 percent of *The Little Mermaid* required special-effects work, as the animators brought to life schools of fish and tried to recreate storms, explosions, reflections, and waves. After its great success at the box office, *The Little Mermaid* was credited, along with *Roger Rabbit*, with starting the animated feature revival of the 1990s.

The Little
Mermaid, 1989

1990
USA

Matt Groening: The Simpsons

According to legend, Matt Groening came up with the idea for *The Simpsons* outside the office of producer James L. Brooks while waiting for a meeting. He had been asked to pitch some ideas based on his cult *Life in Hell* comic strips, but not wanting to give up the rights to these, he came up with a dysfunctional family with characters named after his parents and sisters (the name Bart was chosen as an anagram of brat). The cartoon was first given short slots in *The Tracy Ullman Show*, and when this started to attract a cult following, it was given its own series, the first prime-time cartoon on American television for 20 years.

The early shorts were animated in rather a crude style due to a misunderstanding between Groening and the animators. Groening had produced rough sketches that he thought would be redrawn, but instead the animators just traced over his drawings. The animation was later refined as the show became successful. The main characters were designed so that they would be easily recognizable even when seen in silhouette—the mark of a classic cartoon character. One of the most distinctive features of the show, the characters' yellow skin, came about as a way of disguising the fact that several characters have no hair line.

The fact that it was a cartoon gave the talented writing team free reign to create a sitcom that was free of any moralizing tone and full of irreverent humor; they filled every frame of the show with background gags, in-jokes, satire, spoofs, and cultural references. The show constantly satirized celebrities, who were only too happy to lend their voices to the show and make "guest appearances." Managing to get away with a more liberal and subversive attitude than many American live-action sitcoms, and appealing to children and adults alike, *The Simpsons* grew to become a massive worldwide phenomenon.

Controversial from the start, many in the USA hated it, saying it provided terrible role models. Famously, President George Bush Sr. remarked in a speech that his Republicans would make American families "more like The Waltons and less like The Simpsons." The show's mischievous response was to write an episode called "Two Bad Neighbors," where Bush moved to Springfield and began a feud with Homer.

When it began, *The Simpsons* focused on Bart as the primary character, but it soon became clear that dopey dad Homer was the star of the show, and he became the central character in most stories. *The Simpsons* is one of the longest running animated series of all time, the longest running sitcom of all time, and has at various times been voted the greatest sitcom and the greatest ever TV show.

The Simpsons

MAH GROENING

1991

USA

Disney: Beauty and the Beast

Directed by Kirk Wise and Gary Trousdale, Disney's *Beauty and the Beast* concerns Belle, a modern girl dissatisfied with life in a provincial French town. When her father is taken prisoner by Prince Adam, Belle goes to the dark castle and takes his place. The arrogant prince has been turned into a beast by an enchantress until he learns to love, and he has until the last petal falls off the enchanted rose to do it. In the beginning, Belle views him as nothing more than a monster, and he sees her as difficult and stubborn, but slowly they develop feelings for each other.

Before work began on the movie, Disney's production designers traveled to the Loire valley in France and studied the great French romantic painters, Fragonard and Boucher. The result was a richly detailed design, with the outdoor scenes having an authentic, European look. For other scenes, notably the ballroom dance sequence, computer-generated three-dimensional backgrounds were used, provided by up-and-coming company Pixar, who were establishing ties with Disney. Some traditional animators who had worked on *Roger Rabbit* used this experience of animating in perspective over moving background frames for these scenes. The Beast animation was supervised by Disney star animator Glen Keane, while James Baxter, recruited from the London-based *Roger Rabbit* team, was put in charge of the heroine Belle.

The memorable songs were carefully written to move the plot along, and the movie was later adapted as a stage musical. *Beauty and the Beast* is considered by many to be Disney's best feature of this period, and indeed one of their greatest of all time, and became the first animated movie to be nominated for an Oscar for best feature.

Disney's other release in 1991, *Aladdin*, was Ron Clements and John Musker's follow-up to *The Little Mermaid*. The genie character, animated by Eric Goldburg and voiced by Robin Williams (who was allowed to improvise freely), stole the show, and *Aladdin* was a massive box office success.

Beauty and the Beast,
1991

1991
USA

1992
USA

John Kricfalusi: Ren and Stimpy

Ralph Bakshi's 1987 critically successful revival of the 1940s character Mighty Mouse laid the groundwork for many animators who would go on to have great success with other shows, and who played their part in the resurgence of television animation. After working as a supervising director on *The New Adventures of Mighty Mouse*, John Kricfalusi directed *Ren and Stimpy* for the Nickelodeon network. The cartoon quickly attracted a following among children and adults with its crazy designs, which managed to be both highly original and retro, radically different but old-school inspired. The show starred Ren, a psychotic chiuhuahua, inspired by a picture of a chihuahua on an old postcard, and Stimpy, a fat Manx cat, supposedly inspired by Bob Clampett's *Looney Tunes* short, *A Gruesome Twosome* (1945). Both were extremely ugly to the point of grotesquerie, but were also very expressive and funny. The humor was engagingly violent, with plenty of juvenile slapstick and also some fruity adult jokes smuggled aboard.

Kricfalusi was a fan of the old Warner Bros. shorts and took the idea of the extreme and dynamic poses from those cartoons into the limited TV animation format, as well as the method of a team developing, storyboarding, and animating the whole episode themselves rather than the industrialized method of dividing the different stages up to different people. Suffering a similar fate to Bakshi's *Mighty Mouse*, which was cancelled for supposed drug references, Kricfalusi was sacked after just a couple of series of *Ren and Stimpy* for wanting to make the show too violent, gross, and adult for children. Nickelodeon also claimed that Kricfalusi was bad at hitting deadlines.

The show carried on without Kricfalusi, but finished soon afterwards. Despite its relatively short life, *Ren and Stimpy* was hugely influential and is credited with inspiring the return of "creator driven" shows, as well as helping to kick-start the general revival of television animation in the 1990s.

Bruce Timm: Batman: The Animated Series

Like Kricfalusi, Bruce Timm was another talented animator and designer who had worked on the 1987 *Mighty Mouse* revival. His relaunch of the Batman character into a dark, noir-inspired 1940s style was a milestone in television animation, and was also part of the retrieval of the Batman concept, originally quite a dark figure, from the tongue-in-cheek 1960s TV series. Timm was inspired by Frank Miller's 1986 comic *Batman: The Dark Knight Returns*, in which the concept and hi-tech but retro-styled design of the Batman world was taken seriously again.

Timm's series was acclaimed by the animation world and was inspirational to other superhero revivals, such as Timm's own 1996 *Superman: The Animated Series*. Timm also went on to produce other DC Comic-owned superhero adaptations, known as the DC Animated Universe (or DCAU), such as *Batman Beyond* (1999) and *Justice League* (2003).

1992
UK

1992
Japan/India

Barry Purves: Screenplay

Former Cosgrove Hall animator Barry Purves produced this minor classic of stop-frame animation in his bedroom, apparently making it in just one take. In the style of Japanese Kabuki theater, the story of doomed love is told by a visible narrator while characters act out the fable on a revolving stage, fading in and out of shadow until the tale reaches its genuinely shocking finale. The beautifully poised animation is immaculately controlled and staged as if performed by dancers and the stylized special effects are achieved by unfolding fans and tapestries in real-world theatrical style.

Funded by Channel 4, *Screenplay* won many prizes worldwide and has achieved cult status among animators. Among Purves' other films is *Next* (1989), also made for Channel 4, in which William Shakespeare pitches his plays to an unimpressed director.

Ram Mohan and Yugo Sako: Ramayana: The Legend of Prince Rama

Based on a section of the Hindu verse epic the *Ramayana*, this Indian and Japanese coproduction was directed by Indian animation legend Ram Mohan and Japanese filmmaker Yugo Sako. The animation reflected this multicultural alliance, as it combined the look of traditional Indian art with the style of Japanese anime. Sako's background was in documentary making rather than animation, however, when he became interested in the *Ramayana*, he decided that animation would be the ideal medium for telling the story.

The movie had a protracted production life; work began in the mid-1980s in India, but the government objected to a sacred subject being depicted as a cartoon. After four years of attempting to convince the Indian government to support the project, production was switched to Japan where it took a further two years to complete. Mohan made regular trips to Tokyo to supervise the designs and to advise the Japanese animators on the subtleties of Indian culture and traditions.

Ramayana: The Legend of Prince Rama won several festival awards, including the best animated film award at the Santa Clarita International Film Festival. It was released in the West in 2000 with a narration by James Earl Jones.

Screenplay,
1992

1993

USA

Tim Burton and Henry Selick: The Nightmare Before Christmas

Like the 1982 short *Vincent*, the idea for *The Nightmare Before Christmas* was taken from a poem written by Tim Burton, inspired by seeing a Halloween display in a store window being taken down and replaced with Christmas merchandise. The movie was influenced by the rather creepy stop-frame work of Ladislaw Starewicz, particularly *The Night Before Christmas* (1913), as well as the animated TV special *How The Grinch Stole Christmas* (1966), and also seemingly by the crazy, bubblegum gothic *Mad Monster Party* (1967).

The Nightmare Before Christmas* was funded by Disney and was the first feature to be directed by stop-frame master Henry Selick, like Burton a former Disney employee and also a trained 2D animator. With Burton away making the live-action *Batman Returns*, Selick made the film in San Francisco; he later commented that on this movie, he learned to appreciate the importance of working a distance away from the producers. Selick would go on to direct *James and the Giant Peach* (1996) and *Coraline* (2009).

In the story, Jack Skellington, the pumpkin king of Halloween Town, is bored with doing the same thing every year. By accident, he comes across Christmas Town, and is so taken with the idea of Christmas that, with a lot of difficulty, he gets the resident bats, ghouls, and goblins of Halloween Town to help him put on Christmas instead of Halloween.

The movie featured intricate, computer-controlled camera moves programmed on state-of-the-art motion-control rigs, while using the same replacement animation techniques as George Pal's 1940s Puppetoons for the facial expressions and lip-synch, with Jack for instance apparently having around 400 heads.

The Nightmare Before Christmas features gorgeous design and animation and it defined Burton's style for many of his fans. The movie features fantastic songs and musical numbers by Danny Elfman, but perhaps the story feels a bit overstretched for a feature-length film and suffers a loss of momentum and emotional involvement. Despite these minor flaws, it was a success at the box office and has been rereleased several times, including in 2006 in 3D, and sold a huge amount of merchandise. An inspiration to many future animators, it also went some way to restoring The Walt Disney Company's reputation for pioneering and experimental animation.

Burton made a follow-up of sorts, *The Corpse Bride* (2005), the story of a man in Victorian England who inadvertently marries a corpse and is swept away to the Land of the Dead. It was visualized in the characteristic Burton stop-frame style, as first seen in *Vincent*, and, as with *The Nightmare Before Christmas*, the sets, animation, and model design were of exceptional quality.

The Nightmare
Before Christmas,
1993

1993
USA

1993
USA

Steven Spielberg: Jurassic Park

Steven Spielberg's *Jurassic Park* was the movie that showed the world that, with CGI, anything was possible. The film's photorealistic dinosaurs were created by mixing animatronic creature effects, created by Stan Winston and Phil Tippet, with CG animation created by Industrial Light and Magic. The CGI was animated by Mark Dippe and Steve Williams, alongside Phil Tippet's team, using "Dinosaur Input Devices" to feed stop-frame animation poses into the computer models.

Elements seen in *Jaws* and other Spielberg hits are present, such as scared kids, unknown terrors, white knuckle chases, and gory visual jokes. The story concerns a theme park featuring living dinosaurs drawn from prehistoric DNA. Three scientists and two children are invited to test the computer-controlled park, but the system goes down due to human failings and the monsters go on the rampage.

Jurassic Park became the biggest box office hit to date, and along with James Cameron's *The Abyss* (1989) and *Terminator 2: Judgement Day* (1991), caused Hollywood to stampede toward CGI special effects.

Cartoon Network: 2 Stupid Dogs, Dexter's Laboratory, and Johnny Bravo

In 1991 Ted Turner's Cartoon Network purchased Hanna-Barbera and in 1993 started producing its own "creator driven" animated series, to add to the stream of Warners, MGM, and Fleischers shorts they were broadcasting. This policy of giving the creation of cartoons back to the animators, instigated by John Kricfalusi's *Ren and Stimpy* a couple of years earlier, injected a whole new energy and excitement into TV animation, a genre that had been stale for so long, and revived the Hanna-Barbera studio. Notable among these new shows were Donovan Cook's *2 Stupid Dogs* (1993), Craig McCracken's *The Powerpuff Girls* (1995), Genndy Tartakovsky's *Dexter's Laboratory* (1995), and Van Partible's *Johnny Bravo* (1995).

2 Stupid Dogs was a revival of the traditional Hanna-Barbera brand of animation, drawn in a retro, simple flat style and, in the old Hanna-Barbera tradition, featuring another cartoon, the vintage favorite *Secret Squirrel*, in between two episodes of the main show. *Dexter's Laboratory* was coproduced by Cartoon Network and Hanna-Barbera and concerned a boy genius with a hidden lab behind his bedroom wall. In this angular, zingy 1950s-fest, Dexter is a squat, square little geek battling his annoying tall skinny sister and an evil genius kid neighbor. *Johnny Bravo* featured the rock 'n' roll stylings of a posturing Elvis-alike and his hapless adventures, and involved many Hanna-Barbera veterans, including Joseph Hanna himself, in its creation.

Jurassic Park,
1993

USA/UK

Richard Williams: The Thief and the Cobbler

After Richard Williams directed the animation for 1988's *Who Framed Roger Rabbit* he was able to return to the work that had been his life's obsession.

In 1964 Williams had started work on a film which he worked on for around 25 years and never completed. It was eventually taken away from his control, hurriedly finished by the financiers, and completed in 1993, making it the movie with the longest ever production period. It had gone through several title changes over the years, but was released as *The Thief and the Cobbler*.

Williams had been making the film bit by bit over time, using the money he had earned through making commercials and animated sections for live-action movies such as *The Charge of the Light Brigade* (1968) and *The Pink Panther Strikes Again* (1976), as well as directing animated features like *A Christmas Carol* (1971). He wanted the *Thief* film to be his masterpiece and an animation classic, but his obsessive attention to detail proved to be both his greatest strength and also his undoing.

In 1990, after the success of *Roger Rabbit*, Williams signed a deal with Warner Bros. to pay for the movie to be finished. It all ended badly when Williams, apparently never satisfied and remaking scenes repeatedly, failed to deliver the finished film by 1991 as agreed. Warner Bros. pulled out and the film was taken away from him. One factor in the loss of confidence by Warners in Williams' masterwork may have been that Disney, rejuvenated after *Roger Rabbit* and *The Little Mermaid*, had started work on *Aladdin*. This new Disney feature was similar to *The Thief* in many ways, such as the environments, the characters, and even parts of the story. As *The Thief* had been in production for so long, many people in the industry had moved between Williams' and Disney's studios, particularly during the production of *Roger Rabbit*, so they would have been aware of these similarities.

The movie that was finished without Williams on board was very different to the one he had been making. Released in the USA as *Arabian Night* in 1995, it had been massively changed from Williams' version, with characters cut out, new and cheaper song sequences inserted, voices of young American actors dubbed over much of the film that was supposed to have been silent, the voices of legendary British actors removed, and most of the stunning climactic battle sequence taken out.

The film only made back a tiny fraction of its $24 million budget and at one point was actually given away with cereal packets on a free DVD. Richard Williams retired from animation and for several years disappeared from public view. Even now on his highly successful lecture tours, promoting his wonderful best-selling instructional animation books, he refuses to speak about this film.

In circulation among animators, however, are bootleg copies of Williams' cut of the movie, a lot of which is still uncolored pencil animation, and there is a website outlining plans to create a restored director's cut for DVD. Whether the lost film is the classic of legend or perhaps the overlong and dated indulgence the financiers deemed it to be, it is certainly a unique labor of love touched with obsessive genius. From what is left to be viewed of the key sequences can be seen some of the most stunning and intricate animation ever filmed.

1994
USA

Disney: The Lion King

Disney's biggest hit of all and the peak of their 1990s success, came with *The Lion King*, a version of Hamlet set among a pride of lions. It features some super-slick African-inspired design and animation and some great spectacles, including the stampede scene, which, like sections of *Beauty and the Beast*, was a superbly successful blending of computer-aided and traditional animation.

Lion cub Prince Simba is the heir to his father King Mafusa's lion kingdom. Simba's evil Uncle Scar instigates Mafusa's death in a stampede with the aid of his hyena lackeys, then blames Simba. He tells the cub to flee the kingdom and orders his hyenas to kill him. Simba escapes and grows up in a rain forest with some wacky friends, until as an adult he returns to claim his rightful throne. As with *Bambi*, the scenes of Mafusa's death and the threat to Simba are genuinely powerful, gripping, and moving, and give the story its momentum.

The outstanding character design, stylized to various degrees from character to character, was aided by study of live animals brought to the studio—a similar practice was used in the development of *Bambi*—while artists visited Africa to get a feel for the backdrops. The music, by Tim Rice and Elton John, is particularly memorable, although sometimes overbearing, and led to a highly successful stage production that toured the world over the next decades.

Disney executives and animators believed that *Pocahontas*, their other animated production being made concurrently, would be the bigger critical and commercial success of the two. Proving screenwriter William Goldman's assertion concerning the film business, "nobody knows anything," *The Lion King* was the biggest grossing animated film of all time, a record it kept until the release of *Finding Nemo* in 2003.

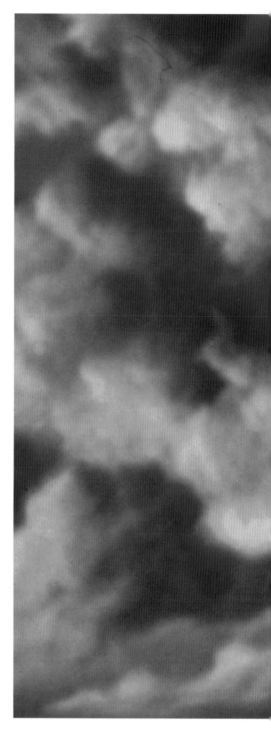

The Lion King,
1994

1994
USA

Ben Edlund: The Tick; Al Jean and Mike Reiss: The Critic; Everett Peck: Duckman

The massive success of *The Simpsons* opened the door for perhaps the greatest era of experimentation in television animation. In the mid-1990s, many wild and wonderful works were created, too many to name them all here, but suffice it to say no style was too extreme or character too offcenter for the networks, and an amazing parade of weirdness emanated from the minds of American animators at this time.

Based on Ben Edlund's absurdist superhero spoof comic, which he first created as a student, *The Tick* was adapted into an animated series for Fox in 1994. Intelligent, funny, and surreal, its look was a parody of 1970s superhero cartoons, except with ultra-bizarrely-themed superheroes.

The Critic was created by *Simpsons* writers Al Jean and Mike Reiss and produced by *Simpsons* producer James L. Brooks. It concerned the life of a self-important, overweight critic who hates pretty much all contemporary films, with each episode a parody of a famous movie. Using static, limited animation for its sophisticated dialogue-heavy approach, it was first broadcast on ABC and then on Fox. Although not achieving the popularity of *The Simpsons*, an impossible act to beat, its smart, low-key humor attracted a cult following through reruns on Comedy Central and a DVD release.

Based on characters from his surreal comic, *Duckman* was the creation of Everett Peck and was produced by Klasky Csupo for Paramount. Aimed squarely at an adult audience, the unsavory, angry, skirt-chasing Duckman, supposedly a private eye when he could be bothered, was voiced by Jason Alexander, best known for playing one of the all-time great sitcom antiheros in *Seinfeld*'s George Costanza. The unwholesome characters were like oddball and imperfect humans living on the margins of society, but in the form of animals. The first series featured Frank Zappa's music and his son Dweezil worked on the show as a voice artist.

The Critic

UK

Tim Watts and David Stoten: The Big Story

Former caricaturists and designers on the influential satirical puppet show *Spitting Image*, Tim Watts and David Stoten produced the stunning stop-frame short *The Big Story*. A simple idea brilliantly realized, the film features an argument between caricatures of a young Kirk Douglas and an old Kirk Douglas, both voiced by Frank Gorshin. The younger is a reporter and the older an editor in an old Hollywood style black-and-white newspaper office, and the mannerisms and angular features of both characters are captured brilliantly. The whole film was first animated as a pencil test, and this 2D companion piece was almost as good as the final version.

Quentin Tarantino liked *The Big Story* so much he requested it was screened before *Pulp Fiction* for its theatrical release. It was nominated for an Oscar and won the 1995 BAFTA for best animated short. A follow-up feature film was under discussion for some time featuring many other Hollywood caricatures, but securing permissions was found to be problematic. Watts and Stoten went on to work on many other movies including preparing storyboards and animation for Tim Burton's *The Corpse Bride*.

1995

USA

John Lasseter: Toy Story

Toy Story is a monumental landmark in animation history; it is the seismic moment when John Lasseter and Pixar proved to the world that it was possible to make fully-developed, sympathetic characters with human personalities through computer animation. Before *Toy Story*, most of the animation community was deeply unconvinced about CGI character animation and, partly through feeling threatened, resistant to the idea. Lasseter and his animators followed the principles of character animation, as developed by Disney and others in the first half of the twentieth century, and applied them to characters modeled in a computer. After the first few minutes, audiences forgot about computers, accepted the characters, and just enjoyed the story.

The first animated feature to be completely generated on computer, the real appeal of *Toy Story* lies in its characters and plot. Woody the cowboy, Andy's favorite toy, is the leader of the toy cupboard. But on Andy's birthday, a new toy called Buzz Lightyear arrives and becomes Andy's new favorite. Woody's resentment grows until, when Buzz falls out of the window, fingers point to Woody and he must go and rescue his rival.

An odd-couple bonding journey ensues, as Woody and Buzz escape from the nightmare world of the nasty kid next door and rejoin Andy before his family move house.

The choice of the toy subjects was inspired, fitting in with the limitations of computers at the time. Computer-animated humans and furry animals were still unconvincing, but toys made of plastic were perfect for the plasticky-looking animation and lack of suppleness that was typical of computer animation. This is perhaps best highlighted by the superb animation and characterization of the army of little green plastic soldiers, marching along on their stands.

Produced as a partnership between Disney and Lasseter's Pixar, *Toy Story* was the highest grossing domestic film in 1995, and, at the time, the third highest grossing animated film ever. It was nominated for three Academy Awards, with Lasseter receiving a special award for "the development and inspired application of techniques that have made possible the first feature-length computer-animated film." Suddenly, the rush was on for computer-animated features.

Toy Story, 1995

1995

Canada/the Netherlands

Paul Driessen: The End of the World in Four Seasons

After working for George Dunning in London on *Yellow Submarine*, Dutch animator Paul Driessen moved to Canada to work for the National Film Board. Driessen, interested in the idea of visually-told, nonlinear, multiple narratives, often experiments with split screens and parallel stories. His 1998 film *3 Misses* was nominated for an Academy Award and he has also taught animation in Germany, where two of his students' films have won Academy Awards, *Balance* (1989)

by Christoph and Wolfgang Lauenstein and *Quest* (1996) by Tyron Montgomery and Thomas Stellmach.

To the accompaniment of Vivaldi's *Four Seasons*, *The End of the World in Four Seasons* features eight interlocking stories in eight split screens, told in four seasonal sections. As is often the case with Driessen's work, a few viewings are required to piece together the narrative. The trademark wobbly lines and hapless characters act out seasonal scenarios relating to the cycles of nature, the activities beginning to intrude into other stories resulting in collapse and disaster at the end of every section.

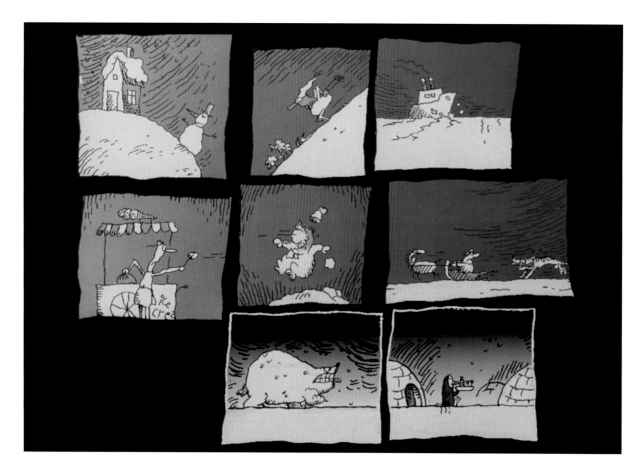

The End of the World in Four Seasons, 1995

1995

UK

Dave Borthwick: The Secret Adventures of Tom Thumb

This unique pixillation feature is a follow-up of sorts to the success of Borthwick and Aardman Animations' work on the Peter Gabriel music video *Sledgehammer*. Adapting the Tom Thumb story to a twisted future world where state programmed artificial insemination is the norm, Tom is the miniaturized result of man messing with nature. Kidnapped from his loving parents, he embarks on a series of adventures in this unsettling vision of the future, which satirizes animal experimentation, pollution, and the class system

Skillfully crafted using a pixillation technique whereby the human actors are posed and stop-frame animated, and substituting mumbling for real speech, the film, part funded by the BBC, is a unique arthouse experiment. However, this methodology is perhaps not a great aid to character development and drawing constant attention to the technique, makes it hard for the viewer to lose himself in the story.

The Secret Adventures
of Tom Thumb, 1995

Pixillation

Pixillation is a technique where live actors are used in the same way as models in stop-frame animation. Actors adopt poses and are photographed frame-by-frame. The technique was pioneered by experimental Scottish animator Norman McLaren in his 1952 film *Neighbours*.

1995
UK

Aardman Animations: Wallace and Gromit in A Close Shave

While Pixar was opening people's eyes to computer animation in the US, over in the UK another successful company was emerging with a new take on an old type of animation. Unlike Pixar, the people behind Aardman Animations weren't technical innovators, but, like Pixar, they produced funny stories with good animation and great characters. And like Pixar, they made something that was very difficult look simple.

The third film featuring scatterbrained cheese-loving inventor Wallace and his faithful, long-suffering dog Gromit, *A Close Shave* was a beautifully-crafted, stop-frame gem. Creator Nick Park realized that certain things are intrinsically funny the world over, and despite its very British nature, this and the other Wallace and Gromit films were successful around the world. The typically silly story of *A Close Shave* involves a lost sheep, Gromit being framed for sheep rustling, and Wallace falling in love with a mysterious wool-shop owning "femme fatale." Like its predecessor *The Wrong Trousers* (1993), *A Close Shave* won the Oscar for best short film. It also inspired two TV spin-off series, *Shaun the Sheep* (2007) and *Timmy Time* (2009).

Wallace and Gromit in
A Close Shave, 1995

Biography

Aardman Animations

Aardman Animations has been Britain's most prominent animation studio in recent years, and has a worldwide reputation as the leading producer of stop-frame model animation. Aardman's work is characterized by its quirky and very British sense of humor, along with its eccentric and loveable characters.

Founded by schoolmates Peter Lord and David Sproxton in 1972, Aardman's first project was the character Morph, who was created in 1976. Morph was a brightly-colored plasticine figure who appeared in the children's television series, *Take Hart*.

Lord and Sproxton were keen to create animation that also appealed to adults and for the Channel 4-commissioned *Conversation Pieces*, they developed their innovative technique of recording real-life conversations and adding humorous puppet animation to fit. This technique was also used in the popular *Creature Comforts* shorts.

In 1985, Nick Park joined the studio after Lord and Sproxton had seen his student work at the National Film and Television School (NFTS). Park created Aardman's most famous characters, Wallace and Gromit, while at the NFTS. The pair first appeared in Park's student film, *A Grand Day Out*. To date, Wallace and Gromit have starred in five shorts and one movie, as well as appearing in commercials, presenting a TV series about inventions, and featuring in a range of merchandise. (For more on Wallace and Gromit, see page 354.)

The studio has produced work in a variety of genres, including commercials, music videos, shorts, television series, and feature films. Their work has received awards from around the world, including four Academy Awards from seven nominations. Aardman has also been the subject of exhibitions at the Ghibli Museum in Japan (Hayao Miyazaki is a fan) and the UK's Science Museum. Sadly a fire at the company's warehouse in 2005 destroyed Aardman's 30-year archive of sets, figures, and props.

1995

Portugal

Estória do Gato e da Lua
(Story of the Cat and the
Moon), 1995

Pedro Serrazina: Estória do Gato e da Lua (Story of the Cat and the Moon)

This little gem is an atmospheric visualization of a feline love poem. Rendered in stark black and white, the visuals move between line drawings of a cat prowling over the wonderfully uneven rooftops of an old Portuguese town, to shifting flat monochrome of a black cat against a white sky and a white cat against a black sea. The cat, the town, the sea, and the music by Manuel Tentugal create the languid and liquid ambience of a cat who's got the cream.

1995
Japan

1995
Japan

Hideaki Anno: Shin seki evangerion (Neon Genesis Evangelion)

Shin seki evangerion (*Neon Genesis Evangelion*) from the production company Gainax, is a sprawling and ambitious anime, made as a TV serial, with spectacular sci-fi warfare and dark psychological subplots. After a meteorite strike wipes out half the earth's population, an experimental defence project called Nerv is called into action to fight the aliens, The Angels, who are behind the calamity. Nerv's strategy involves giant part-robot organisms called Evangelions that can only be controlled by children born after the disaster.

Hideaki Anno reportedly used the making of *Neon Genesis Evangelion* as therapy in his own personal fight against depression, as he weaved in heavy psychological themes, including aspects of Japan's fight in the Pacific War and Biblical ideology. The series ended on an anticlimactic note, and several extra episodes were added to the reedited version of the series, *Shin seiki Evangelion Gekijô-ban: Shito shinsei* (*Death and Rebirth*, 1997), which attempted to clarify the ending. A feature film, *Shin seiki Evangelion Gekijô-ban: Air/Magokoro wo, kimi ni* (*The End of Evangelion*) was also made in 1997.

Katsuhiro Otomo, Tensai Okamura, Koji Morimoto: Memories

Memories is an anthology film constructed of three shorts based on Katsuhiro Otomo's manga comics. The first story, *Magnetic Rose*, directed by Koji Morimoto, tells of a crew of space salvage hunters who discover a vast floating mausoleum in memory of a famous opera singer. The music of composers Puccini and Yoko Kanno adds to the rich atmosphere as the men explore the space station where holograms, robots, and virtual projections illustrate stories from the singer's life and fantasy begins to blend with reality and incorporate ghosts from the explorers' own lives, a thematic trademark of future director Satoshi Kon, who wrote the script from Otomo's story. Directed by Tensai Okamura, *Stink Bomb* is a comic tale of a worker in a research lab who inadvertently consumes a chemical that makes his body odor deadly to a distance of several miles, necessitating an ineptly handled military emergency. The final short, Otomo's *Cannon Fodder* is a serious antiwar statement about a city where everyone's life is devoted to manning thousands of cannons pointed at an unknown enemy. As his contribution to 1987's *Neo Tokyo* was considered by some to be a prototype *Akira*, so *Cannon Fodder* can be seen as a rehersal for Otomo's *Steamboy* (2004).

Drawn in a high detail 2D style, *Memories* avoids the usual "big eyes, small mouth" anime character design clichés, while its claustrophobic and lived-in environments are unlike the usual gleaming high tech. Although its three stories seem to have little but these high standards of creativity to link them, altogether *Memories* remains an intelligent and memorable anime entry.

1995

Japan

1995

South Africa

Mamoru Oshii: Kôkaku kidôtai (Ghost in the Shell)

Mamoru Oshii scored a huge critical success with the seminal anime TV series *Kidô keisatsu patorebâ* (*Patlabor*) in 1989, a sci-fi futuristic drama in which humans with real lives, problems, and emotions play out various dramas and deal with government red tape, budget cuts, and domestic problems while maintaining employment as pilots of giant robots.

Oshii's *Kôkaku kidôtai* (*Ghost in the Shell*) was the next big budget cyberpunk anime feature to cause ripples in the West after Katsuhiro Otomo's *Akira* (1988); in fact it was part funded by Manga Entertainment, the chief Western distributors of anime, who were looking to keep *Akira*'s mass-market momentum going. The look of *Ghost in the Shell* is a sophisticated rendition of the traditional 2D effects-laden anime style, notable in this case for its experiments with mixing in CG with the 2D drawings.

The story concerns a government experimental super computer, The Puppet Master, that goes horribly wrong and starts to slowly take over military functions for its own ends by hacking into other networks. A half-android girl is the key to stopping it, the title referring to her soul in the shell of her robot body, but she gets drawn into a kind of love affair with the machine. The complex and multistranded story, featuring Oshii's trademark realistic and flawed characters, is taken from Masamune Shirow's manga comic and proved a cult hit with Western anime fans, but didn't manage *Akira*'s crossover to mainstream audiences. It generated several television series, several straight-to-video spin-offs, and another big budget sequel, *Ghost in the Shell 2: Innocence* (2004). Also made by Oshii, and this time largely based on his own original story, the sequel marked a further progression in combining 3D CGI realism with traditional 2D drawn anime.

William Kentridge: Felix in Exile

Gallery artist William Kentridge uses animation as part of his overall multimedia installations, and to this end has made a series of short films. *Felix in Exile* is one of the best known of these, part of his *Drawings for Projection* series that was created from 1989 to 1999, and characteristic of the work he produced about South African history and society and the nature of memory and time.

Kentridge uses around 30 to 40 detailed charcoal drawings in these films and a technique of continuously altering and redrawing and then rubbing out and redrawing parts of it, and rephotographing the results. Leaving traces of the previous drawings, these then become overlaid by other traces, suggesting the natural or deliberate overwriting of memories or history. Kentridge's drawings are figurative and realistic, unlike the abstract art that dominated the twentieth century. The images have a gritty and realistic feel to them, but often contain elements of surrealism and symbolism.

Felix in Exile concerns a recurring character in Kentridge's work from this period: Felix Teitlebaum, a black South African. In this film, Felix is in exile in Paris during apartheid, longing for home. As well as the action involving Felix, the nonlinear, seminarrative shows the ongoing violent atmosphere of state repression in South Africa through events such as the shooting of a female land surveyor.

1996
USA

Henry Selick: James and the Giant Peach

One year after the release of Pixar's groundbreaking *Toy Story*, Henry Selick flew the flag for traditional stop-frame model animation with this delightful movie, another stop-frame diversion for Disney. Like Sellick's *The Nightmare Before Christmas*, this was also produced by Tim Burton, and was based on a classic children's book by Roald Dahl.

Like many successful animated features before and after, the movie begins with an emotional blow; the death of James' parents. The film starts and ends in live action, but when he enters the giant peach in an English garden to escape from his wicked aunts, he becomes a stop-frame model and meets model versions of the bugs who were his only friends in his cell-like bedroom. As the peach sails away across the Atlantic to the safety of New York, the gang of oddball characters are involved in many brilliantly realized adventures, including a Ray Harryhausen-influenced fight with skeletons on a shipwreck, an attack from a huge iron shark, and a flight with some lassoed seagulls.

With no restraints on the creativity of Burton, Sellick, and their team, each new sequence is a surprise and delight, one section of the film even goes into a cutout style. *James and the Giant Peach* won the best animation feature at the Annecy International Animation Festival and has become a cult movie among animators.

1996/1997
USA

Mike Judge: Beavis and Butt-Head Do America; King of the Hill

Mike Judge's cult MTV series *Beavis and Butt-Head*, which began in 1992, was influential in the rise of creator-driven animated television shows. *Beavis and Butt-Head* mainly consisted of the two crudely-drawn adolescent boys making juvenile comments from their couch as they watch music videos on TV. The idea of a feature film spin-off of this wouldn't seem to hold much promise, but with *Beavis and Butt-Head Do America*, Judge demonstrated that there was more depth to his talents. In this funny and engaging oddity, the story is widened out as the snickering, idiotic couple meet all manner of exotic characters as they set off across the USA in pursuit of their stolen TV. As with other feature film adaptations of animated TV shows, the sophistication of the animation and backgrounds were bumped up a few levels, although not enough to lose the loose, rough charm of the original series.

Judge later produced the equally funny, award-winning animated TV sitcom *King of the Hill*. Slower burning, quirkier, and more character driven than *The Simpsons* or *Family Guy*, *King of the Hill* was a more adult and subtle portrait of "ordinary" Americans than *Beavis and Butt-Head*, although Judge is the type of director who indentifies and celebrates the extraordinary in everyday suburban life. Judge, who also provided the voices for his animated characters, would later establish a career as a director of hilarious, left-field live-action comedy features, which further satirized the dumbing down of popular and consumer culture. However, along with the savage lampooning, Judge always maintains an affection toward his protagonists and the more absurd aspects of modern American life.

1996
Germany

1996
Japan

Trickompany: Werner–Das muss kesseln!!! (Werner, Eat my Dust)

In 1990 *Werner Beinhart*, an animated adult comedy feature adapted from the popular German comic books by Rötger Feldmann, was produced by Gerhard Hahn Filmproduktion and Hamburg's Trickompany. Popular in Germany, it was followed by two sequels starring its beer-drinking biker antihero, including 1996's *Werner–Das muss kesseln!!!* (*Werner, Eat My Dust*). In the movie, Werner and his friend Andi wager their beloved pet pig in a race against the rich and snobbish Nobelschröder.

Trickompany was founded by Michael Schaack and has produced commercials, feature films, and television series. In a similar broad comedy vein to the *Werner* movies was Trickompany's *Kleines Arschloch* (*Little Asshole*, 1997), an award-winning short featuring another popular German comic hero.

Shigeru Miyamoto: Super Mario 64

Shigeru Miyamoto and Nintendo's *Super Mario 64* is not only one of the greatest computer games of all time, but also one of the greatest works of art/entertainment of the twentieth century. From the moment the player takes control of Mario and finds that through some simple controls he can run, jump, swim, slide, or even fly in any direction of the beautifully-realized world, he or she is held in a similar state of wonder and exhilaration that the first audiences must have felt when watching Winsor McCay's *Gertie the Dinosaur* or Walt Disney's *Snow White and the Seven Dwarfs*.

The animation is also a milestone in video game history. Mario has been lovingly redesigned in three dimensions and all his movements perfectly convey his plucky, upbeat, never-say-die character, always willing to race toward any dangerous enemy or impossible looking puzzle in his hopelessly optimistic manner in order to rescue his beloved Princess Peach from the bullying tyrant Bowser.

Werner–Das muss
kesseln!!! (Werner, Eat my
Dust), 1996

USA

South Park

Matt Stone and Trey Parker: South Park

South Park was one of the wave of irreverent animation shows that followed in the wake of *The Simpsons*, and became quite a phenomenon in its own right. The main characters are four school-age boys, Stan, Kyle, Eric, and Kenny, from the small fictional town of South Park, Colorado, based on the kind of place Matt Stone and Trey Parker grew up. The scripts are cruder, darker, more surreal, and more gritty than *The Simpsons,* and the style of the animation is perhaps the most limited TV animation of all. The characters are little more than crudely animated flat circles, but this is an integral part of the show's humor and appeal, and is perhaps representational of a child's simplified view of the world. The cutout look and a lot of the surreal and anarchic humor come from Trey and Stone's love of British 1960s TV classic *Monty Python's Flying Circus*, with its Terry Gilliam animations, which they first saw on public television as teenagers. It was unlike anything they had ever seen on mainstream US television and seems to have been an epiphany for the pair.

The plots in *South Park* usually center around an extraordinary and often surreal event, often satirizing a real current event or media obsession. There are also running gags, such as Kenny being killed in every episode. The adults, as seen through the eyes of the main characters, often react more stupidly and childishly than the children themselves. To accommodate this topicality, the shows are made very quickly and often broadcast within about a week or two of being written, being put together digitally to speed up the process although still replicating the look of the simple cardboard cutouts of the pilot episode.

The first episodes were among the first internet virals and their word of mouth cult status led to the show being commissioned by the Comedy Central channel. Trey and Stone, who voice the main characters, are allowed a fee reign by the channel, who often directly screen the episodes only hours after receiving delivery of them. A feature film was released in 1999, *South Park: Bigger, Longer, and Uncut*, which earned the record for the most ever swear words in an animated film.

1997
USA

Bill Plympton: I Married a Strange Person

When illustrator Bill Plympton started making animated films it didn't take long for his visually and mentally warped universe to start attracting attention. His early short, *Your Face* (1988), was nominated for an Oscar, and his distinctive style soon attracted a cult following. Plympton began to make his own feature films, and is credited as being the only animator to draw every frame of an animated feature.

I Married a Strange Person is the highly prolific Plympton's third feature film and tells the story of a couple's wedding night and the husband's uncomfortable discovery that everything he imagines comes true, which leads to what has been described as "the most bizarre and hilarious sex scene ever put to film."

I Married a Strange
Person, 1997

Flash and the online animation boom

The last years of the 1990s saw a gold rush online, with every financier seemingly desperate to throw money at internet start-ups. Needless to say, the bubble burst and millions were lost. Among the things that money was thrown at was animation, an ideal medium for getting information across on a small, fuzzy screen. Unfortunately the technology available at the time meant that download times made any serious viewing of video online, or even simple interactivity, painfully slow, and the public were not prepared to pay for it. Ten years later, when broadband was ubiquitous, some of these ideas started to make sense.

The key to online animation was the development of Flash, a software that enabled animation to be made simply and in small files that could be viewed online without much download time. Many companies were set up to capitalize on this; websites like Icebox and Atom Films featured creator-driven, edgy, and controversial animation, such as Bill Plympton's short films, Pam Brady and Kyle McCulloch's *Mr Wong*, Mike Reiss' *Queer Duck*, and Peter Bagge's hilarious *Rock'n'Roll Dad*, based on the Beach Boys' dysfunctional family. Flash later became a key production tool for low-budget television animation, motion graphics, and other more traditional animation uses.

In 1997 *Ren and Stimpy* creator John Kricfalusi realized that on the internet he could bypass all the executives that kept censoring his work, and he started an online series called *The Goddam George Liquor Program*. Also in 1997, artist and animator Christine Panushka, best known previously for her 1984 art film *The Sum of Them*, was appointed curator of an online collection called Absolut Panushka, which supported and promoted experimental animation with essays and a film festival, and highlighted the work of 24 animators including Priit Pärn and Jules Engel.

Other online animation companies survived the big bust and went on to thrive by making "viral" films that were distributed by individuals emailing them to each other. These successes include Evan and Greg Spiridelli's jibjab.com, Joel Veitch's Rathergood.com, the surrealist genius of Cyriak, and, perhaps most successful of all, Matt Stone and Trey Parker's *South Park*, whose original episodes were internet viral hits.

1997

Japan

Hayao Miyazaki: Mononoke-hime (Princess Mononoke)

In ancient Japan, the boy prince Ashitaka is wounded when he defeats a supernatural boar creature that has been menacing his people. The wound is slowly sapping his strength and when he travels on his elk to find a cure, he meets Princess Mononoke, who lives with wolves. Ashitaka gets caught up in a war between the emperor of the humans and the woodland god and uses the powers that his wound has given him. The magical, semifantasy natural world and the neat clean designs and slick animation of the young protagonists are beautifully designed and drawn in the Miyazaki tradition, although the rambling storyline and themes are perhaps more accessible to audiences familiar with Japanese folklore.

After the rip-roaring adventure of *Kurenai no buta* (*Porco Rosso*, 1992), a superbly colorful and unique story about a biplane fighter pilot and bounty hunter who has turned into a pig, Miyazaki moved to a more thoughtful adult-aimed feature in *Mononoke-hime* (*Princess Mononoke*). The movie is seen as one of Miyazaki's more serious and epic ecologically-themed works, with influences from the British fantasy writer Rosemary Sutcliffe, and a kind of prequel to 1984's *Kaze no tani no Naushika* (*Nausicaä of the Valley of the Wind*). *Princess Mononoke* took over 15 years to develop and became the biggest box office hit in Japanese cinema history at that time.

For the American release of *Princess Mononoke*, a cast of well-known actors was expensively assembled and the film remained uncut on the insistence of Studio Ghibli. An animated film with a grown-up and serious story and scenes of violence and dismemberment, it left Western audiences confused and its Japanese box office success was not repeated. The DVD sales were very strong worldwide, however, and, like other Miyazaki films, its reputation grew by word of mouth.

1998
USA

Simon Wells, Brenda Chapman, Steve Hickner: Prince of Egypt

Hyped more than either *Antz* or *A Bug's Life*, Steven Spielberg, Jeffrey Katzenberg, and David Geffen had a lot riding on *Prince of Egypt*. They had poured millions into setting up DreamWorks Animation and its state-of-the-art animation facility in a bid to rival Disney's success in the animated feature revival of the 1990s. Directing duties were put in the experienced hands of Simon Wells, Steve Hickner, and Brenda Chapman. Chapman had been head of story on *The Lion King* and with *Prince of Egypt* she became the first female director of an American animated feature.

Telling the Biblical story of Moses and the Exodus, the movie was an animated epic; its mixture of computer backgrounds, drawn animation, and lavish special effects were impressive to look at, and it attempted to tell the story in a serious, grown-up way. A conscious attempt to get away from the Disney model of talking animals and zany sidekicks, it did well critically and at the box office, although not as well as the big Disney hits of preceding years. Perhaps like other 2D features of this period, it was overshadowed by the growing appetite for 3D CGI animation.

The massive hype pushed people into the multiplexes and the spectacle kept them entertained, but years later the film seems to have been somewhat forgotten. The lesson in Jewish history may have been too portentous for children while also containing few memorable moments of adult appeal, in contrast to the modern fairy tales with smart scripts that Disney had been producing.

Prince of Egypt, 1998

Biography

DreamWorks Animation

The Hollywood media production corporation DreamWorks SKG was formed in 1994 by three of the entertainment industry's biggest names, Steven Spielberg, David Geffen, and Jeffrey Katzenberg. From the beginning, animation was a big part of their plans with both Spielberg and Katzenberg having previous experience in hit animated features. The company's aim has been to release two features a year, no mean feat considering the amount of work in an animated feature film.

Although many of DreamWorks Animation's early features were traditional 2D animations and most of their in-house staff were from that background, they soon made a deal with Pacific Data Images (PDI) to produce CGI movies, and with the success of *Antz* (1998) and the even greater success of *Shrek* (2001), the company's films have been CGI since 2003. While the early 2D movies often aimed to be more grown-up and serious than Disney's, the studio eventually established its identity with fast-paced irreverent CG comedy films packed with hip, fast-talking characters, rock music, and pop culture references, aiming to appeal to adults as well as children. DreamWorks Animation has been a separate entity from the rest of DreamWorks since 2004.

This combination of comedy, superb animation, and entertaining stories and characters has made DreamWorks Animation one of the world's most successful animation studios. Notable DreamWorks Animation movies include the *Shrek* franchise, *Madagascar* (2005), *Bee Movie* (2007), *Kung Fu Panda* (2008), *Monsters vs Aliens* (2009), and *How To Train Your Dragon* (2010).

Tony Bancroft and Barry Cook: Mulan and Disney's Florida studio

The high Chinese style of *Mulan* makes it stand out as one of the more beautifully designed and entertaining of Disney's later 2D animated features. The story is based on a traditional Chinese tale which tells of a girl pretending to be a boy to sign up for the army in an effort to save her elderly father from conscription, eventually becoming a hero. *Mulan* could be said to be the last critical and commercial hit of Disney's 1990s animated feature revival period, but this relative success could not compare with the extraordinary profitability of *Aladdin* (1992) and *The Lion King* (1994).

Mulan was made in Disney's Orlando, Florida-based studio, established in 1989, which as well as the three classic *Roger Rabbit* shorts, also produced the other more critically and commercially successful Disney films from this period, *Lilo & Stitch* (2002) and *Brother Bear* (2003). Some speculated that, as with the production of *The Nightmare Before Christmas* in 1993, the East Coast studio's physical distance from the interference of Burbank executives was what gave its products the edge over the likes of *The Emperor's New Groove* (2000), *Atlantis* (2001), and *Treasure Planet* (2002), all made in Los Angeles. However the Florida-produced films were judged to be not sufficiently profitable to keep the Orlando studio open and it was closed down in 2004.

A few months before this closure, Walt's nephew Roy O. Disney had resigned in protest from the company at what he saw as chairman Michael Eisner's focus on maximizing short term profits at the expense of the core Disney values of innovation and quality. These strategies included trying to release an animated movie every few months instead of Walt Disney's ideal of one a year, and flooding the market with countless straight-to-video sequels, policies criticized for devaluing the brand. The closure of the seemingly valuable Florida studio came for Roy and other Disney traditionalists as a betrayal of values, although to the more hard-nosed observers it was simply more evidence of the big picture, which was the rise of CG animation resulting in the decline of 2D.

1998
USA

John Lasseter and Andrew Stanton: A Bug's Life; Eric Darnell and Tim Johnson: Antz

DreamWorks Animation/Pacific Data Image's *Antz* was the second computer-animated feature to be released, closely followed by Pixar/Disney's *A Bug's Life*. With both stories concerning ant colonies and individual ants who rebel against the system, the two movies brought into focus the rivalries between the two new animation giants, DreamWorks Animation and Pixar. Accusations of idea borrowing and spoiling tactics came from the Disney/Pixar side, as DreamWorks Animation boss Jeffrey Katzenberg had left Disney to form DreamWorks

Animation while they were planning *A Bug's Life*. Katzenberg stated that the idea for *Antz* had come from director Tim Johnson, independent of Pixar/Disney. The reason for two simultaneous insect films should also be seen, however, in the context of the computer animation technology available at the time. Like toys, insects were suitable subjects, as it was too difficult to achieve good results on computer with flexible, soft, and furry animals.

Although both movies carry a liberal message advocating personal freedom and the power of democracy and collective action to overcome tyranny, *Antz* was the more grown-up, political, and dark comedy of the two. The story concerns a neurotic and thoughtful ant, Z, voiced by Woody Allen, who

Antz, 1998

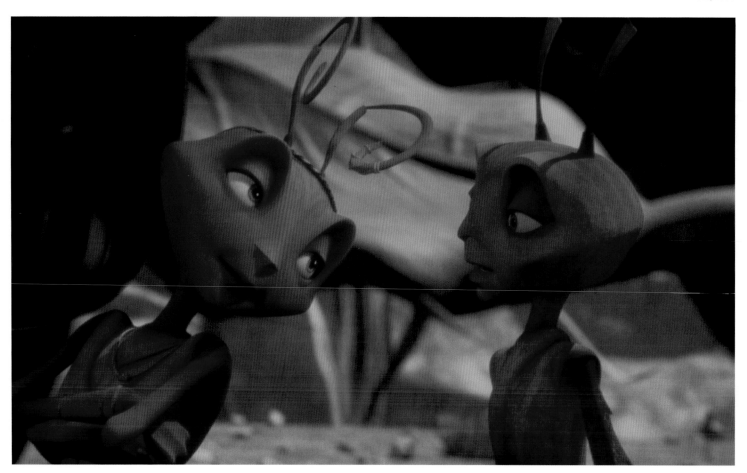

A Bug's Life,
1998

questions the lack of individual freedom in the underground, soviet-style society he inhabits. Destined to be a worker ant, Z unintentionally participates in a bloody war where all the other ants are killed and his dying friend urges him to think for himself. He survives by not fighting and running away, but to his dismay is hailed as a war hero by the colony's propaganda machine. Z falls in love with the Princess Bala and has to rescue the colony from destruction by the evil General Mandible.

   A Bug's Life is generally lighter in tone, although not without its dark moments. Set in a more anthropomorphized model of an ant colony, it concerns an eccentric inventor ant called Flik (voiced by Dave Foley). Flik's well-intentioned attempts to invent time-saving methods of performing the soul-destroying gathering of food lead to disaster and the loss of the food that the ants are forced to gather to feed the vicious gang of locusts who rule over them. Like Z, Flik is forced to leave the colony and survive on his own.

The different looks of the two movies illustrated their different tones; while the action in *A Bug's Life* mainly took place outdoors and demonstrated Pixar's work in developing CG representation of bright, lifelike natural environments, *Antz* was mainly set in a repressive underground colony. *Antz* had the edge with its more sophisticated facial expressions and technical advances in animating water, while Pixar had the better character animation, in particular the funny character design and animation of the flamboyant and theatrical circus insects who are brought in to fight the locusts.

   In the box office battle the lighter tone of *A Bug's Life* proved the more popular, but both movies won critical praise and proved that, far from being a temporary fad, the market for CG animation was big enough to sustain many features.

1998

France

Michel Ocelot: Kirikou et la Sorcière (Kirikou and the Sorceress)

French director Michel Ocelot drew on his childhood in Africa to produce the beautiful and unique style shown in *Kirikou et la sorcière* (*Kirikou and the Sorceress*) and its follow-ups. The story is loosely based on traditional African tales and tells of a special tiny baby born in a tribal village who can walk and talk from birth and helps to defeat an evil sorceress who is threatening his people. The lush and intricate designs are based on African art and the style of the French painter Henri Rousseau. The animation is in an elaborate cutout style, with the characters mostly shown in profile, which enhances the feeling of primitive art. The animation's simplistic flatness is at odds with the overiding preoocupation with three dimensions in most other features of this era. Comparisons with the work of

Lotte Reiniger are clear, but Ocelot cites his influences as Victorian illustrators, such as Aubrey Beardsley and Heath Robinson, and the art of ancient Egypt and Greece.

Kirikou and the Sorceress was a success in many territories, particularly continental Europe and Japan, where Miyazaki released it through Studio Ghibli and supervised the dubbing into Japanese. In the USA and UK, however, distributors were outraged at the nudity and tried to insist on some kind of undergarments to cover the characters' modesty. Ocelot, of course, refused, and the movie was restricted to a limited release. The film's success in other territories generated a sequel, *Kirikou et les bêtes sauvages* (*Kirikou and the Wild Beasts*, 2005), which told further stories from Kirikou's childhood. It also inspired a stage musical.

Kirikou et la sorcière (Kirikou and the Sorceress), 1998

1998
UK

Jamie Hewlett and Damon Albarn: Gorillaz

Created by Damon Albarn of rock band Blur and Jamie Hewlett, the comic artist and creator of Tank Girl, Gorillaz are a cartoon rock band, who are mainly known to the public via a series of animated music videos. Albarn and Hewlett were inspired to create the band by watching endless, vacuous music videos on MTV. Unlike the bubblegum cartoon pop bands of the past, such as the Hanna-Barbera created Josie and the Pussycats and The Banana Splitz, Gorillaz have an antiestablishment, punk/hip hop sensibility, and their music is a gritty mix of urban styles with guest appearances by cult figures.

The early videos used Hewlett's distinctive designs with limited animation, but when the band became successful, the videos became mini-masterpieces of the genre, brought to life with full animation in both 2D and 3D provided by London's Passion Pictures and often directed by animation director Pete Candeland.

1998
Japan

Satoshi Kon: Perfect Blue

The barriers between fiction and paranoid fantasy are completely blurred in this psychological story of a pop star whose decision to reinvent herself as an actress is challenged by possessive fans, press, and a murderous stalker. Told from different perspectives, the deliberately confusing story mirrors the disturbed state of mind of the central character, who has herself lost track of reality after her first acting role involves a traumatic rape scene. Director Satoshi Kon does away with the usual fades and transitions to signify what is real and what is imagined and makes atmospheric use of limited anime-style animation in this sophisticated psychological thriller that attempts to torment the viewer's mind. The superior script was written by Sadauki Murai from a novel by Yoshikazu Takeuchi for production company Madhouse, while director Kon was a protégé of *Akira* director Katshuhiro Otomo.

Kon's follow-up to *Perfect Blue* was *Sennen joyû* (*Millenium Actress*, 2001), which had similar themes of blurred fantasy and reality as an aging and reclusive actress is interviewed about her life. The story she tells mixes historical incidents with events from her life and the plots of her movies, leaving the viewer unsure what is the truth and how much of a reliable narrator she is. The epic 2004 television series *Môsô dairinin* (*Paranoia Agents*), directed by Kon, also has an ambiguity inherent in the story of two detectives hunting a killer who may exist or may be some kind of manifestation of modern paranoia and urban legend.

1999/2003
USA

1999
USA

The Wachowskis: The Matrix and The Animatrix

Influenced by anime's kinetic special effects and its blurring between reality and fantasy, as well as by martial arts action films and cyberpunk fiction, *The Matrix* and its sequels *The Matrix Reloaded* and *The Matrix Revolutions* (both 2003), were the ultimate in comic-book-style cinema.

Using many CGI animated characters as well as editing seamlessly between the actors and CG versions of themselves, the movies were most famous for their extreme camera moves, such as the much-imitated "bullet time" in which the camera orbits rapidly around a slow-motion event. This was a development of the time slice effect as pioneered by Michel Gondry for the 1995 music videos Bjork's *Army of Me* and The Rolling Stones' *Like a Rolling Stone*. Gondry's technique, with its circle of still cameras triggered in rapid succession, can also be traced directly back to Eadweard Muybridge's nineteenth-century photographs of animals in motion.

The Wachowskis refined the technique by using computer-programmed camera paths, laser-targeted cameras, and digital morphing to create further interpolation of the images. This rapid mixing and blurring of different visual effects characterizes the Wachowskis' work and their intention of staying ahead of FX savvy audiences and creating an atmosphere where the viewer doesn't know quite what he is looking at. The Wachowskis repeated this super-vivid disorientating style in an intensely colored live-action/CG adaptation of the TV anime classic *Speed Racer* in 2008.

The Animatrix were nine animated shorts set in *The Matrix* universe, mostly produced at Madhouse and Studio 4C. They were commissioned, overseen, and partly written by the Wachowskis in collaboration with some of the anime creators who had inspired them in their work, such as Koji Morimoto, Shinichiro Watanabe, Peter Chung, Yoshiaki Kawajiri, and Mahiro Maeda.

Brad Bird: The Iron Giant

A favorite of many animators, Brad Bird's *The Iron Giant* was a brilliant take on Ted Hughes' book about a boy who befriends a giant alien war robot who wants to learn how to not be "a gun." It was executive produced by Pete Townshend of rock band The Who, who owns the rights to the original poem and created a stage play based on it.

The story is brought to life with clean, contemporary-looking drawn animation, which was blended perfectly with a 3D, CGI-animated robot and background elements, all wrapped up in a retro 1950s aesthetic to fit the anti-Cold War, beatnik-age tale. Funny, sad, charming, and beautifully made, *The Iron Giant* was loved by critics and animators and won several awards, but perhaps due to poor marketing, it was never a hit at the box office.

1999
USA

1999
USA

Matt Groening: Futurama; Seth McFarlane: Family Guy

Futurama was Matt Groening's follow up to *The Simpsons*. Set in the future, it featured a high level of flat rendered 3D CG backgrounds and effects. Another witty and well-written TV cartoon, two of the more memorable characters are Leela, a sexy one-eyed spaceship captain, and Bender an alcohol-loving, bad-tempered robot. The series ran until 2003 on the Fox network and in 2007 four straight-to-DVD films were released. In 2010 the Comedy Central channel revived the show and began airing new episodes.

Seth McFarlane's *Family Guy* is an animated sitcom concerning an overweight father, Peter Griffin, and his brood who are at varying levels of eccentricity ranging from mopey teenage daughter Meg, to smoking and drinking dog Brian, to baby Stewie, who speaks like an English supervillain. Many of the characters are voiced by McFarlane himself. Cancelled by the broadcaster Fox after its third series, it was resurrected after popular reruns on Adult Swim and high DVD sales, and now has a huge cult following.

Stephen Hillenburg: Spongebob Squarepants

While working as a marine biology teacher, Stephen Hillenburg created a set of characters based on different kinds of crustacean and undersea life and incorporated them into a comic called *The Intertidal Zone*. Bob the Sponge was originally an actual sea sponge rather than the bathroom sponge that he evolved into. Hillenburg later retrained as an animator and on the strength of his short film *Wormholes*, got a job as a director on television series *Rocko's Modern Life*. Hillenburg presented a pilot of his ideas based on characters from *The Intertidal Zone* to Nickelodeon executives, and the result was *Spongebob Squarepants*.

The idea of a television series based on an anthropomorphic sponge who lives in the sea is so intensely strange that it is brilliant. Spongebob is a very funny character, cheerily voiced by Tom Kenny, with an equally odd supporting cast of underwater misfits, and the show's low-fi, pop-surrealist look is unique and engaging. It is one of the most successful series of all time, particularly for the massive popularity of its merchandise. *The Spongebob Squarepants Movie* was released in 2004.

1999
Canada/Russia

1999
UK

Alexandr and Dmitri Petrov: The Old Man and the Sea

Aleksandr Petrov and his son Dmitri used their unique style of finger painting with slow-drying oil paints on multiple planes of glass, often working for days and nights without rest, to create this incredible Oscar-winning film. *The Old Man and the Sea* is an adaptation of Ernest Hemingway's story of a fisherman's noble battle with a giant marlin, the film combining beautiful, figurative oil paintings with the astonishing fluidity of the camera. The point of view flows smoothly from high in the air with the seagulls, to swooping down into the sea under the fishing boat, all realized in a perfect moving perspective that could not be bettered by CGI. Petrov later said that he identified with, and was inspired by, the old man in the story as he represented the "struggle, the patience, and the determination needed as an animator."

The Old Man and the Sea,
1999

Richard Kenworthy and Shynola: The Littlest Robo and music videos

Directed by Richard Kenworthy while he was a student at the Royal College of Art, *The Littlest Robo* is a flat rendered CG short set in a desolate mid-west American landscape. It tells the story of a boy and his relationships with his silent father and their domestic help, a small, cheerful robot. The robot is appliance-like in appearance and has a personality similar to that of R2D2.

The Littlest Robo's gravelly-voiced narrator is Kurt Wagner of rock band Lambchop, one of the bands, along with Radiohead, Junior Senior, Blur, and Unkle, for whom Kenworthy's animation collective Shynola produced their seminal music videos. These videos are perhaps Shynola's most famous and best works and are some of the more outstanding animated works of the early 2000s. The Shynola collective consists of Richard Kenworthy, Gideon Baws, Chris Harding, and Jason Groves; they met at the Kent Institute of Art and Design and ended up sharing a house together in London, from where they made all their early work.

Shynola's video for Lambchop's "Like a Woman" (2002) is a beautifully simple depiction of a floating leaf's journey along a river, made in the style of traditional Chinese illustration and the Wan brothers' animation. The video for Junior Senior's "Move Your Feet" (2003) is a joyous and surreal celebration of bright, blocky pixel art, apparently made with the legendary early pixel animation software, DPaint. The collaboration with absurdist cartoonist David Shrigley for Blur's "Good Song" (2003) is a peculiarly moving lo-fi love story between a giant squirrel and a little man with wings, which ends in disaster when the squirrel gets carried away with his sharp teeth.

UK

Tim Hope: The Wolfman

Tim Hope's *The Wolfman*, as well as being a work of genius, is a great example of a lo-fi approach to computer animation, going completely against the grain of most CG at this time, which was determinedly clawing its way toward total realism. Hope had to make the best use of his limited resources; he had to borrow a friend's computer to make the film, and was working out of a shared house. He developed his earlier tinkering with CG, which he had previously used to produce stage projections and animated pieces for his comedy act with the actor Julian Barratt. For *The Wolfman* Hope scanned and mapped simple cartoon drawings into 3D Studio to create a mini universe, somewhere along the lines of Oliver Postgate's homemade approach or a 3D version of Terry Gilliam's work. Hope's film tells the story of a man reciting a love poem to the moon, turning into a wolfman, and then attempting to eat the universe, the tone of the piece moving from Victorian serenity to total insanity in the space of just three minutes.

Hope also produced notable music videos using his lo-fi approach to CG, including Coldplay's "Don't Panic" (2001) and King Biscuit Time's "No Style". He later designed animated sequences for former collaborator Julian Barratt's surreal TV comedy show *The Mighty Boosh*, and created commercials through London's Passion Pictures.

The Wolfman, 1999

1999
Germany/UK

1999
Japan

Steffen Schäffler: The Periwig Maker

Set during a seventeenth-century plague epidemic, the dark and highly atmospheric stop-frame short *The Periwig Maker* concerns a wig maker who is at first solely concerned with self-preservation as he observes the ghastly effects of the plague on the London street outside his window, before his interest is drawn to the worsening condition of a small girl across the road. Written by Steffen Schäffler's sister Annette and adapted from Daniel Defoe's book *A Journal of the Plague Year*, the film was narrated by Kenneth Branagh. *The Periwig Maker* was five years in the making, has beautifully crafted and highly detailed sets, and was nominated for an Academy Award.

Satoshi Tomioka: Sink

Former hydrodynamics student Satoshi Tomioka started producing his own films while at college, before combining work for commercial animation studios with making his unique personal CG visions at home. *Sink* is based on one of Tomioka's typically brightly-colored, yet worn and grubby surreal worlds. Among other things, we see commuter trains packed with colliding deep sea divers, reading pornography while sealed off behind their protective shells from any real human contact–a vision clearly inspired by Tomioka's experiences on the Tokyo underground. His other films *Coin Laundry XYZ*, *Gastank Mania*, and *Justice Runners* follow a similarly colorful and deranged aesthetic and have the same ambiguous atmosphere as Tomioka seems to simultaneously attack and delight in the impersonal aspects of modern technological society. Tomioka has also created commercials for Honda and Japanese Rail.

The Periwig Maker, 1999

2000
USA

2000
UK

Ralph Eggleston: For the Birds

Right from their early shorts such as *The Adventures of Andre and Wally B* and *Luxo Jr*, Pixar's policy was to produce regular short films that served not only as accompaniments to the main features, but also as tests for new technologies, techniques, and approaches before applying them to the bigger projects. In this way, they were following the same approach that Walt Disney took with his short films. These are the kind of things that may be difficult for an executive to quantify on a balance sheet, as a short film will never make a profit, but it is one of the ways that Pixar stays ahead of the game. It also helps to maintain Pixar's image as the kind of company that gives new directors a chance to prove themselves and some freedom to run with whatever funny, spontaneous, and inspired ideas that may crop up. And *For the Birds* is very, very funny. The short is a simple, yet inspired scenario about a tight social group of little round birds on a telegraph wire, who unkindly resent the arrival of a solitary big gawky bird, and how their unkindness toward the outsider backfires.

Jonathan Hodgson: The Man with the Beautiful Eyes

Jonathan Hodgson's work is informed by his interest in naive outsider art and the random unsophisticated scribblings of children. He has a lo-fi approach to drawing and animation, which is combined with a skilful use of color, texture, perspective, and graphics to create the visual poetry that he calls his "bad animation."

Hodgson's elegantly designed short *The Man with the Beautiful Eyes*, based on a poem by Charles Bukowski and made for Channel 4, tells the story of a group of children who encounter the dropout owner of the overgrown garden where they play, to the horror of their suburban parents. Designed by Johnny Hannah, the film is informed by Hannah and Hodgson's admiration of Bukowski's writings and also by the American/ Lithuanian artist Ben Shahn, the early twentieth-century English artist Edward Bawden, and 1950s record covers. The film was made nondigitally, shot on film using paint, ink, and collage.

The Man with the
Beautiful Eyes, 2000

2000

UK/the Netherlands

Michael Dudok de Wit: Father and Daughter

After success with his early shorts *Tom Sweep* (1992) and *Le moine et le poisson* (*The Monk and the Fish*, 1994), Dutch director Michael Dudok de Witt—who states his influences as Eastern European animation, Tintin, and the art of Tibetan monks—made the beautiful and emotive *Father and Daughter*.

In this elegant short film about how love can transcend time and death, a young Dutch girl witnesses her father inexplicably rowing out to sea, never to return. Over the years, she cycles to the same spot in the flat countryside and waits for him. Eventually, in her own old age, she makes a journey out to join him.

A simple and poignant dialogue-free story, it is complemented with elegant and graceful design and animation, and the use of sillhouettes and shadows. Made in the Netherlands and England using mainly traditional methods, the film deservedly won three British Animation Awards and the Oscar for best short film, and stands out as one of the great animation shorts of its era.

Father and Daughter,
2000

2000
Poland

Piotr Dumala: Zbrodnia i kara (Crime and Punishment); Jerzy Kucia: Strojenie instrumentów (Tuning the Instruments)

At the start of the twenty-first century, Poland's animation industry, like that of other Eastern European countries, had to reinvent itself from a centralized situation of state funding and control into smaller entities that endeavor to survive in the capitalist free market. In most cases, this means that the exploratory and personal short films that proudly characterized much Eastern European animation have generally taken second place to commercial interests. This usually means producing advertising or functioning as service industries, mainly for Western media corporations taking advantage of lower labor costs to outsource production of cartoon franchises for global television consumption. Reacting against this trend, Piotr Dumala and Jerzy Kucia have produced a series of animated shorts that are determinedly fine art.

Piotr Dumala's *Zbrodnia i kara* (*Crime and Punishment*), a loose adaptation of Dostoyevsky's novel, paints a psychological portrait of a man driven to murder. An oppressive shadowy atmosphere dominates the stationary scenes that form the film, while animated details draw out the tension. Dumala used a unique technique of scratching and painting images into plaster that was covered in glue, a method he first used for another Dostoyevsky adaptation, *Lagodna* (*Gentle*, 1985).

In Jerzy Kucia's *Strojenie instrumentów* (*Tuning the Instruments*), shadowy visuals combine filmed, animated, and abstract material with a jarring soundtrack of instruments being tuned, to which figures perform a mechanical kind of dance in place of any narrative. Like Dumala's films, Kucia's work has a dark and unsettling nature to it that is characteristic of many Eastern European art films.

Zbrodnia i kara
(Crime and Punishment), 2000

2000

Denmark/ Germany/Ireland

Stefan Fjeldmark and Michael Hegner: Hjælp! Jeg er en fisk (Help! I'm a Fish/ A Fish Tale)

After running into trouble during a fishing trip, kids Stella, Fly, and Chuck take shelter in the laboratory of an eccentric scientist, Professor MacKrill. Concerned about the effects of global warming, the professor has developed a potion that turns humans into fish enabling them to survive if the earth is flooded. Stella mistakenly takes some of the potion and is turned into a starfish. When she is released into the ocean the other children also take the potion and set off to rescue her, but must take the antidote within 48 hours to avoid being permanently stuck as fish, while also attempting to thwart the plans of the movie's villain, a power-crazed pilot fish called Joe.

Written and directed by Stefan Fjeldmark and Michael Hegner, *Hjælp! Jeg er en fisk (Help! I'm a Fish/A Fish Tale)* was produced by A. Film, Scandinavia's largest animation studio, and coproduced by German and Irish companies. The film was made using traditional 2D animation techniques with some digital 3D enhancement. Well animated and designed, with its contemporary character design and slick special effects it has the feel of a mainstream movie from across the Atlantic.

© 2000 HELP! I'M A FISH™

Hjælp! Jeg er en fisk
(Help! I'm a Fish),
2000

2000
India

Narayan Shi: Freedom Song

An animated version of Hans Christan Andersen's *The Emperor's Nightingale*, this short combines 2D and 3D effects to produce colorful scenes of meadows and jungles. Narayan Shi produced the film for Mumbai's Famous House of Animation, a studio that produces animation in 2D, 3D, and stop-motion. *Freedom Song* won several national and international awards.

Freedom Song,
2000

2001
USA

Shrek, 2001

Pete Docter and David Silverman: Monsters, Inc.; Andrew Adamson and Vicky Jenson: Shrek

3D CGI animation took a big step forward in 2001. Pixar's *Monsters, Inc.* had super fluffy fur, realistic cloth textures, and a fully-realized cartoon city. DreamWorks Animation's *Shrek* had squashy, stretchy animation of facial muscles, hair, and cloth, and a fully-realized fairytale countryside full of grassy fields and leafy forests. But most importantly, both movies had human characters that did not look too weird. Sure, there had been humans in *Toy Story*, but they somehow looked almost as much like plastic toys as the toys themselves, which didn't particularly matter as they were as peripheral to the story as the humans in the *Tom and Jerry* shorts.

In Pete Docter and David Silverman's *Monsters, Inc.*, a human character had a big supporting role, as a believably bouncy, overemotional, and expressive little girl follows a monster through the portal of her bedroom closet and into the city where all the monsters come from. Needless to say all the monsters are actually as scared of children as the kids are of them. In another nice twist, the barriers between monsters and children are revealed to be a big conspiracy perpetuated in order to divide and rule and enable corporate profits. The warm-hearted movie with its original and clever concept was Pixar's best since *Toy Story*, and consolidated the company's postion as the market leaders in CG-animation family features.

Monsters, Inc.,
2001

In *Shrek* most of the supporting cast are human, with big, flexible, caricatured faces and rather stiff little bodies, giving them the feel of Victorian satirical cartoons. Demonstrating, and perhaps deliberately establishing, the difference between DreamWorks Animation and Pixar, Andrew Adamson and Vicky Jenson's *Shrek* went for a more modern, hip appeal by creating an anti-fairytale populated by slang-talking, streetwise characters. The film's title character is a peace-loving ogre, voiced by Canadian Mike Myers in a Scottish accent. Many of the other characters, such as Shrek's sidekick Donkey (Eddie Murphy) shared similarities to Warner Bros.' "screwball" characters of the 1940s and 1950s, in that they seem to

be aware that they are in a cartoon with an audience watching, have a wisecrack put-down for every archetype they encounter, and little respect for the older generation of cartoon characters and their cute cartoon rules.

Shrek was a phenomenally successful movie, it was the highest grossing animated feature at that time, and created a multiplex franchise. *Monsters, Inc.* was also a big commercial hit, proving once again that animation is a "big tent" with plenty of room for many different approaches.

2001
USA

2001
USA

Bob Sabiston and Richard Linklater: Waking Life and Snack and Drink

Bob Sabiston first began to develop animation software at the Massachusetts Institute of Technology in the late 1980s, using it to create several short films of which one, *Grinning Evil Death* (1990) was seen on the first episode of MTV's adult animation strand *Liquid Television*. Later in the 1990s, Sabiston developed Rotoshop, the program that would make his name and define his style. Essentially a new kind of rotoscoping program that enabled artists to paint over the frames of live-action film and then interpolate between the images, Rotoshop created a continuous flowing painting in time, something that would have been a dream come true for the European "visual music" experimentalists of the early twentieth century.

Later working in Austin, Texas, Sabiston created further films, including the award-winning *Snack and Drink* (1999). Sabiston worked with local artists using his software to create what is one of the outstanding computer-aided short films of its era, a documentary subject following an autistic boy to his local supermarket as he talks about many subjects, including his favorite animated character, Fievel from *An American Tail*.

In 2001, Sabiston teamed up with film director Richard Linklater, who divides his work between independent films made in and around Austin, and mainstream Hollywood films. Using the same Rotoshop technique and employing 30 artists, Linklater and Sabiston produced the unique feature film, *Waking Life*. Like Linklater's 1991 feature S*lacker*, *Waking Life* follows the interlinking conversations and philosophizing of various Austin citizens, although in this case following one central character. The movie's title refers to a quote from Spanish-American philosopher George Santayana: "Sanity is a madness put to good uses, waking life is a dream controlled."

Cartoon Network: Adult Swim

Adult Swim, or [adult swim] as it likes to be styled, started as a channel within a channel on Cartoon Network, broadcasting adult-targeted animation late at night. In 2005 it was split off into a separate channel in the USA as well as an online portal. The name comes from the sessions in swimming pools where only adults are allowed, known as "adult swim" times in the US.

The bold and exotic line-up of shows included Dave Willis and Mat Maiellaro's surreal series about fast food characters, *Aqua Teen Hunger Force* (2000); Seth Green and Matthew Senreiche's crazy, stop-motion sketch show, *Robot Chicken* (2005); Jackson Publick, James Urbaniak, and Patrick Warburton's *The Venture Brothers*, a sci-fi spoof about the dysfunctional family of an unstable superscientist; Shinichiro Watanabe's Japanese futuristic drama *Cowboy Bebop* (1998); and Michael Ouweleen and Erik Richter's *Harvey Birdman, Attorney at Law* (2001), in which various Hanna-Barbera superhero characters now work behind desks in a law office.

Adult Swim is programmed and largely commissioned by Williams St Studios which is, like Cartoon Network itself, a company owned by Turner Broadcast Network. Mixed in with the Williams St Studios's creative and surreal animated comedy series on Adult Swim are various other adult-targeted short films and Japanese anime series, films, and OVAs (material made for video and DVD release). The bold, original, sophisticated, and funny animated shows created for Adult Swim have cult followings worldwide and have made the channel a success among its target demographic of young adults.

2001
USA

Genndy Tartakovsky: Samurai Jack

Samurai Jack was a Cartoon Network series that won great critical acclaim and a cult following, especially among animators. The series was devised and designed by Russian-born Genndy Tartakovsky, who had previously worked on *Batman: The Animated Series*, *The Critic*, *The Powerpuff Girls*, and *2 Stupid Dogs*. Set in a highly stylized future world influenced by Japanese samurai culture, kung-fu movies, UPA films, and Frank Miller's *Ronin* comics, the characters are angular and geometric, drawn without the traditional black surrounding line. Individual episodes often veer off in different style directions and the highly visual storytelling is almost dialogue free. Tartakovsky was later hired by George Lucas to direct *Star Wars: Clone Wars* (2004), an interesting and successful stylized CG interpretation of the *Star Wars* universe.

2001/2002
USA/ France

Michel Gondry: Fell in Love with a Girl and Hardest Button to Button

Michel Gondry is a French director notable for his innovative and highly creative use of nondigital animation effects, including single-frame methods and pixillation. He provides an example of a different path that certain animators and directors took in response to the slick perfection of CG. These kinds of techniques are particularly apparent in the music videos that Gondry made at the beginning of his career. Gondry's early music videos for his own band Oui Oui attracted the attention of the singer Bjork, for whom Gondry made a series of music promos, starting with *Human Behavior* (1993), which was influenced by legendary Russian animator Yuri Norstein's *Yozhik v tumane* (*Hedgehog in the Fog*, 1975). For the Bjork video *Army of Me* and The Rolling Stones' *Like A Rolling Stone* Gondry created early versions of the much-used "bullet time" effect, produced by a line of still cameras taking a sequence of images at differing angles of the same moment.

Gondry's *Fell in Love with a Girl* video for the White Stripes used the brilliant but simple technique of creating frame-by-frame images of the band's performance using Lego bricks in the band's signature colors of red, black, and white. For *Hardest Button to Button*, Gondry pixillated multiple drum kits and guitar amps appearing rhythmically across urban landscapes. Gondry went on to specialize in his own brand of lo-fi surreal movies, often using nondigital primitive effects and animation and explorations of naïve homemade design and staging.

2001

Japan

Hayao Miyazaki: Sen to Chihiro no kamikakushi (Spirited Away)

By the start of the twenty-first century, Studio Ghibli had produced a string of beautiful, unique, and critically-acclaimed films by Hayao Miyazaki and Isao Takahata, including Miyazaki's *Mononoke-hime* (*Princess Mononoke*, 1997), which broke box office records in Japan. In 2001 Ghibli released Miyazaki's masterpiece of imagination and childhood fantasy *Sen to Chihiro no kamikakushi* (*Spirited Away*). The movie set a new box office record, not only in Japan but also worldwide (for a non-US film), and won the Academy Award for best animated feature.

The incredibly imaginative story tells of a young girl, Chihiro, who strays into a secret magic palace after her parents become lost in their car, help themselves to the food in a mysterious deserted village, and are turned into pigs. The stunningly realized characters and creatures she encounters in this parable of greed and selfishness in modern society, make the film one of the all-time greats of creative animation.

Inside the palace, Chihiro's name is taken away from her, which represents the end of her childhood. Her struggle for survival forces her on a journey which represents her move from childhood to adulthood, and her transformation from being a rather negative, complaining, selfish young modern child into someone hard working, positive, and caring. In this sense, the cutoff fantasy world of the castle represents a view of teenage years as spent in an unreal world that rejects the rules of adult society and creates a kind of anarchy where the biggest monsters will rule.

The movie also contains critical allegories of other aspects of modern society such as pollution (the filthy slime-and-trash-encrusted creature in the bath house) and modern greed and consumerism (Chihiro's parents gorging themselves on huge amounts of food that isn't rightfully theirs). The consequences of this greed—the parents are turned into pigs—has similarities with the selfish hedonistic boys who turn themselves into "asses" in Disney's *Pinocchio*, a movie that is also about growing up, human decency, selflessness, and self respect.

Spirited Away contains many unforgettable characters and sequences with many more obscure and complex interpretations, such as the grotesque witch with the massive head, the six-armed old man, and the faceless ghost-like spirit who follows Chihiro and starts to react to the greed of other characters by eating and then regurgitating everything and everyone in sight.

2001
USA/Japan

Hironobu Sakaguchi: Final Fantasy: The Spirits Within

Final Fantasy: The Spirits Within was a spin-off of the cult *Final Fantasy* series of role-play video games, which became well known for their photo-real motion-captured introductory sequences. Although being more of a straight sci-fi adventure and having little in common with the sword-and-sorcery type games and their universe apart from the title, the movie was also a serious attempt at creating hyper-realistic characters and environments. Made at Square Studios in Hawaii, *Final Fantasy: The Spirits Within* was a coproduction between Japanese and American investors. Although noted for its impressively high levels of realism, the proximity to realism simply makes the viewer constantly notice the differences, pulling them out of the story experience. The movie failed to excite the general public outside of game players, was a box office failure, and was credited with causing the closure of the Hawaiian studio.

Final Fantasy:
The Spirits Within, 2001

A brief history of motion/performance capture

A big trend in animation in the early twenty-first century was motion capture, or performance capture as it is also known. This is essentially the digital age version of rotoscoping, whereby actors' movements are recorded and the motion applied to animated characters to create more realistic movements. Like rotoscoping, when used sensitively the technique of motion capture can be very effective, but it is often best when some stylization of the movements or character design is applied.

In the Fleischers' debut feature *Gulliver's Travels* (1939), rotoscoping is used very literally for the main character; this looks quite impressive at first but soon becomes somewhat tedious to watch. In Disney's debut feature *Snow White and the Seven Dwarfs* (1937) the rotoscope was also used, but the animators finessed the effect by stylizing the movements and making them more interesting. The results, and the movie, were much more successful. Similarly with motion capture, when the movements are too literal, too real and human, and the characters are too stylized, it can seem like a cartoon character has been possessed by the spirit of a thespian. But if the characters are too real, it can often seem like a slightly creepy, dead-eyed waxwork model has come to life.

Science has an interesting perspective on this, with a theory known as "uncanny valley." This was put forward by roboticist Masahiro Mori, and observes that when robots of human appearance get to the point where they look and act almost like actual humans, it causes revulsion among human observers, the "valley" referring to a dip in the positivity of human reaction relative to a robot's closeness to human appearance. The theory supposes that beyond that point, when the robot might become identical to a human, then the response would become positive again. The problem is that creating something identical to a human is almost impossible, so adept is the human brain at recognizing any tiny detail of abnormality, particularly in the human face. Still more fascinating is that further research into the theory, by David Hanson, has found that stylization or adding slight cartoony elements of design to the artificial face, can make the response more positive.

The history of motion capture can be traced back to the late 1800s when Etienne-Jules Marey and Eadweard Muybridge photographed and analyzed the motion of animals and humans. In the digital age, new possibilities opened up, and after early work in 1983 at the Massachusetts Institute of Technology, many more experiments in motion capture took place in the 1980s. Pioneer CG workstation developer Silicon Graphics created a virtual talking head controllable in real time by a puppeteer. Jim Henson's Creature Shop in conjunction with Pacific Data Images produced a digital version of *The Muppets* character Waldo, which was also controllable in real time by manipulating a puppet. In 1985 Robert Abel and Associates created a motion capture sequence entitled *Sexy Robot*, and in 1990 Jeff Kleiser and Diana Walczak created a music video, *Don't Touch Me*, featuring a motion-captured performance of singer Perla Batalla. The live-action sci-fi movies *Total Recall* (1990) and *Lawnmower Man* (1991) contained short motion-capture shots, as did Peter Gabriel's music video, *Steam* (1993). The 1997 sci-fi movie *Lost in Space* used further developments in Jim Henson's Creature Shop's motion capture for puppeteers.

Video games were the first industry to extensively use motion capture, starting with Atari's *Highlander; The Last of the McLeods* (1995). Within a few years, the technique was ubiquitous in games. The phenomenally successful Rockstars video game *Grand Theft Auto 3* (2001), was a milestone in graphics and gameplay, as it used motion capture for the characters in its fully-immersive gangster universe, where the player was free to roam, explore, and make his way in the criminal underworld.

The first feature film to be entirely animated with motion capture was *Sinbad: Beyond the Valley of the Mists* (2000), while *Final Fantasy: The Spirits Within* (2001) was the first attempt to create a photoreal world using motion-captured characters in a movie, with mixed results. *The Lord of the Rings: The Two Towers* (2002) was a more successful use of this method, with Andy Serkis' reptilian performance mapped into the CGI goblin character Gollum, the fantasy comic-book style setting and stylized characterization making for an ideal use of the technique. 2004's *The Polar Express*, from *Who Framed Roger Rabbit* director Robert Zemeckis, provided some beautiful CG effects animation, although the realistic, motion-captured characters had rather dead-looking eyes and faces. Much more successful was the digital conversion of Andy Serkis' physical performance into the empathetic giant gorilla in Peter Jackson's *King Kong* (2005), which was the central figure of a beautifully and terrifyingly realized fantasy prehistoric island world, before rampaging through a period recreation of New York. The French production *Renaissance* (2006) was set in a striking black-and-white cyberpunk universe, and by rendering in monochrome and using the trick of staging everything in half shadow, the animators managed to disguise any imperfections and make more dramatic the rather uninteresting motion-

Renaissance, 2006

captured, realistic characters. The haunted house story *Monster House* (2006) was produced by Zemeckis and Steven Spielberg and featured simpler, more cartoonlike characters, the motion capture here working well with this more stylized and crafted feel.

2007's *Happy Feet* featured hand-keyed animation mixed with motion capture for its cute penguin tale. The dancing of the motion-captured, realistic penguins works with an uncanny accuracy, but lacks some of the charm of Disney's hand-animated dancing penguins in *Mary Poppins*, which actually captured the feel of real penguins' movements more effectively. Robert Zemeckis' *Beowulf* (2007), like *Monster House*

and *The Polar Express*, was produced through Zemeckis' Imagemovers Digital Studio, which he set up in order to produce performance capture films. *Beowulf* is one of the more successful of the motion/performance capture movies, partly due to improvements in the process and the greater experience of the team, and also due to the fantasy subject matter. The faces and physiques of the actors are a few degrees closer to real, the "dead" eyes have improved, and the murky, torchlit, and snowbound fantasy world helps the viewer to suspend disbelief. Ultimately though, the use of synthetic actors creates a barrier between performer and audience, like a digital prosthetic mask. The success of *The Lord*

of the Rings, *Harry Potter*, and *Avatar* fantasy worlds suggest that *Beowulf* could have been more successful if it had been made with real actors instead of the synthesized humans pitted against the CGI creatures.

2001
Japan

Rintaro: Metropolis

Japanese director Rintaro's version of *Metropolis* is not a direct remake of Fritz Lang's 1927 film, with which Western audiences might be more familiar. It is rather an adaptation of "father of anime" Osamu Tezuka's epic 1949 manga comic, which he published when he was still a teenager and which formed the second part of a trilogy of books including *Lost World* (1948) and *Next World* (1951). Tezuka had not seen Lang's film when he created the comic, but was inspired by its poster and the famous image of the female robot to create a story about a future city where humanoid robots have been created as slaves, which has in turn created mass unemployment and an angry class of people ripe for exploitation by extreme politicians. The plot concerns Kenichi and his detective uncle, Shunsaku Ban, who must visit Metropolis in search of the criminal, Dr. Laughton.

Rintaro's *Metropolis* is a high budget, top class Japanese animation without the kind of cost-cutting, limited animation commonly seen in anime. Instead we have a no-expense-spared, lovingly crafted adaptation of the manga comic, which blends traditional handdrawn animation with CGI in a combination of technology and human endeavor that is much more successful than the disastrous situation depicted in the story. The backgrounds are alive with animation and FX detail making each sequence a rich experience and, perhaps in homage to Lang's 80-year old classic, the score is based on 1920s jazz music. A spectacular and epic tale, it was perhaps a little too ambitious, as the film tries to encompass the many facets of life in the city and condense the epic manga story into around 100 minutes.

The film's credits are a roll call of anime superstars, with seemingly everybody wanting to be involved, including *Akira* creator Katsuhiro Otomo as scriptwriter. Rintaro is one of the leading anime directors; a founder of the production company Madhouse, he worked for Tezuka directing *Astro Boy* in the 1960s.

Metropolis, 2001

Hong Kong

⑤

Toe Yuen: Mak dau goo si
(My Life as McDull)

McDull is a cartoon pig and has been highly popular in Hong Kong and China for over a decade in the comics of Alice Mak and Brian Tse. This feature adaptation, a big hit in Hong Kong and winner of the Grand Prix at the Annecy Animation Festival, combines realistic aspects and references to life in Hong Kong with the adventures of the cheerful, but dim little pig and his mother. The simply drawn 2D characters are immersed in a rich, colorful 3D urban world that combines 3D CGI animation and effects with primitive cutout styles.

2002

USA

Chris Wedge: Ice Age

Blue Sky Studios has a long history in the world of computer graphics. Many of the senior staff, such as director Chris Wedge, were involved in the early CG company MAGI, which worked on Disney's *Tron* and John Lasseter's Disney test short for *Where the Wild Things Are*. Wedge was a CG animator on both of these projects and later, through the new company Blue Sky, created many early CG commercials, the short *Bunny* (1998), and CG animation for Don Bluth and Gary Goldman's 2D/CGI sci-fi feature *Titan A.E.*

In 1997 Blue Sky were bought by *Titan A.E.* producers Fox, who were looking for a CG studio following the commercial failure of Bluth and Goldman's film. Their first release was based on a script that Bluth and Goldman had turned down, *Ice Age*. The story was simple but funny, involving a disparate bunch of prehistoric creatures migrating during the ice age and joining forces to rescue a human baby. Characters include a sloth named Sid, a woolly mammoth named Manny, a saber-toothed tiger named Diego, and an acorn-loving saber-toothed squirrel named Scrat, and some pretty advanced early (both in CGI and historical terms) humans.

The movie was visually strong with some great stylized character design plus naturalistic backgrounds and lighting enhanced by Blue Sky's rendering software, CGI Studio, the most advanced rendering software of all the main studios. The characters had loose, improvisational voice tracks, and the animation was solid for most characters and extreme and funny for others, in parts perhaps the closest to the crazy Warner Bros. style of animation that had been achieved in CG. Indeed, the movie had some of the loose feel of the classic Warner Bros. shorts, as though it had been lovingly put together by a talented team that were allowed the freedom to be inventive and spontaneous, and have fun with the characters. This was in contrast to the glut of me-too 3D features that were starting to appear, many of which felt like they had been dictated by marketing men and formula-driven executives. *Ice Age* attracted great reviews and did very well at the box office, spawning two sequels.

Ice Age, 2002

2002
USA

Lilo & Stitch, 2002

Dean DeBlois and Chris Sanders: Lilo & Stitch

In the 1940s, after a few big budget disappointments, Walt Disney decided to make a lower budget, simpler film called *Dumbo*, which went on to become one of the studio's best-loved works. Similarly, 60 years later, after a few expensive movies had failed to take off, Disney CEO Michael Eisner decided to make a smaller, sweeter, and less ambitious story: *Lilo & Stitch*.

In this underrated gem from the Walt Disney Studios, lonely Elvis-obsessed orphan Lilo is cared for by her struggling sister. She inadvertently adopts escaped space convict Stitch, who is trying to escape from alien detectives sent to recapture him. Stitch is slowly socialized by the love of the little orphan girl who, with the help of her new friend, regains her confidence.

CG was used for the spaceship, and digital coloring was used for the drawings, but aside from that, the fancy technology was kept to a minimum. Rather than going for multiplane sense of depth, a flat picture book feel was used and, as with *Dumbo*, bright watercolors were used for the sunny Hawaiian backdrops. (Not that it was all sun and no rain; the movie's nonconventional family unit showed the tension and stress as well as the love and warmth that are part of everybody's domestic life.) The character designs were fresh and original and they felt free from the design-by-committee syndrome, something that could also be said about the film as a whole. The story of outsider characters suffering prejudice for being different and then learning to use it as an advantage is also similar to *Dumbo*'s theme.

Nominated for the Academy Award for best animated feature, *Lilo & Stitch* was one of Disney's bigger successes of the early years of the century. Like *Dumbo*, it is looked back on with affection, and it generated several straight-to-video sequels as well as successful merchandise sales.

2002
UK/Denmark

Siri Melchior: The Dog Who Was a Cat Inside

The Dog Who Was a Cat Inside is a beautifully designed and animated short, where handdrawn styles are applied to a digital environment. Using expressive line drawings and simplified geometric styles, it looks like a 1950s modernist UPA short made in 3D CGI. The sweet story tells of a dog learning to get in touch with his internal other side, which we can see inside his body struggling against his actions. Siri Melchior studied in her native Copenhagen and the UK's Royal College of Art, and works through the London-based studio, Passion Pictures.

The Dog Who Was
a Cat Inside, 2002

2002
UK

2002
South Korea

Chris Shepherd: Dad's Dead

Chris Shepherd's short film *Dad's Dead* is a dark and uncomfortable childhood story of hanging around with the wrong crowd, or in this case, a child sociopath who draws the narrator (Ian Hart) into his at first funny and then increasingly nasty world. An amalgam of real stories and characters from Shepherd's working-class childhood in Liverpool, the film blends and overlays live action and drawn animation styles to create a both gritty and painterly surreal texture.

This multi-award-winning film was made for the UK's Animate! experimental animation scheme. Shepherd would later collaborate with surrealist cartoon artist David Shrigley on the short *Who I Am and What I Want* (2005), also for the Animate! scheme. Shepherd's next short, *Silence is Golden* (2006), explored similar themes of childhood fantasy and also mixed live action with animation.

Seong-kang Lee: Mari iyagi (My Beautiful Girl, Mari)

Like Hong Kong's *My Life as McDull* from 2001, *Mari iyagi (My Beautiful Girl, Mari)* is an Asian feature with a strong regional identity in its story and visual design. The plot tells of a boy on summer vacation escaping from his problems through his surreal daydreams and fantasizing about an imaginary girlfriend. The beautiful visuals combine flat rendered pastel backgrounds with simply drawn outline-free characters. It won the Grand Prix at the Annecy Animated Film Festival.

Dad's Dead,
2002

2003
USA/France

Disney and Salvador Dalí: Destino

The project *Destino* was first planned in 1945 as a collaboration between Salvador Dalí and the Disney studios, but was cancelled due to the financial constraints brought on by the war years. In 1999, Roy Disney rediscovered *Destino* and its storyboards by John Hench, and green lighted it for inclusion in the cancelled project, *Fantasia 2006*. The short was completed at Disney's Paris studios by Dominique Monfrey and was given a limited theatrical and festival release. Nominated for an Academy Award, the film is pure Dalí surrealism given a more contemporary feel involving elements of CGI, with figures dancing through an open landscape populated with melting statues, misshapen clocks, and other psychological symbols.

2003
USA

Andrew Stanton and Lee Unkrich: Finding Nemo

Andrew Stanton's story of a father clown fish and his journey to find his son, gained the highest ever box office takings for an animated feature at the time, plus the highest ever DVD sales of any movie. It also won the Oscar for best animated feature.

Stanton conceived of the story based on his observations of the protective feelings of parenthood. Like Stanton's *WALL-E* and Pete Docter's *Up*, the story starts with scenes of emotional impact which keep the viewer locked in. While Marlin the clown fish is looking forward to starting a family, a barracuda appears out of nowhere and eats his wife and eggs. The one egg that's left hatches into a baby fish, Nemo, of whom Marlin is understandably overprotective. When Nemo is captured by a diver and taken to a dentist's surgery in Sydney, the distraught Marlin sets out in pursuit, meeting many exotic undersea species on his epic quest.

The beautiful look of the ocean world—apparently partially inspired by the stunning underwater nature photography of the BBC series *Blue Planet*—captures perfectly the play of light filtering through water and the exotic colors of the barrier reef.

Pixar's supporting human characters in *Finding Nemo* had reached the same high levels of design and animation as the main animal characters, now involving a higher level of stylization that anchors them in the 3D cartoon world. The fact that, even using the limited potential of fish, as opposed to, say, a furry animal with expressive limbs, Pixar managed to create a genuinely emotional journey and characters with real depth and humor, showed the huge confidence and storytelling skill of the company at this time.

Finding Nemo,
2003

2003

UK/France/Belgium/Canada

Sylvain Chomet: Les triplettes de Belleville (The Triplets of Belleville/ Belleville rendez-vous)

Running with the Western world's 2D animation baton while all around others were dropping like flies, Sylvain Chomet's wonderful *Les triplettes de Belleville* (*The Triplets of Belleville/ Belleville rendez-vous*) became an instant European classic. Influenced by silent comedy and the great French comedy actor Jacques Tati, Chomet's film is almost entirely dialogue free, but the proof of its success is that you don't even notice this. In the same way that Tati collected characters he wanted to see onscreen and then constructed a film around them, *The Triplets of Belleville* takes a small group of misfits and lets them follow their own path through the open and spontaneous storyline.

The separate but converging plotlines take in an elderly trio of triplet dance stars in Belleville (a city based on New York), and Champion, a young cyclist competing in the Tour de France. Champion's grandmother, Madame Souza, acts as his guardian and trainer, and sets out to rescue him when he is kidnapped by a square-shaped Mafioso on a tall, triangular ocean liner.

The backgrounds have the beautifully classic yet stylized look of a 1960s Disney feature, but what differentiates Chomet's work is the more eccentric character designs, whose geometric physical aspects are often pushed to quite extreme levels. Chomet rejects much contemporary Hollywood animation as overacting, and draws from the more subtle Disney animation of the 1960s, the low-key acting and open poetic storytelling of Hayao Miyazaki features, and the powerfully understated work of certain British animators, such as Mark Baker.

Although the film has classic style and technique, CG was used for some background elements, such as cars and machinery, which Chomet is happy for computers to draw in order to save an animator from this boring work. A lot of the CG was created with deliberately deteriorated lines to match the imperfections of the drawings, and the CG-created cycles were drawn over by hand to match the characters' lines.

The Triplets of Belleville was not only cofinanced by companies from different countries, but also had teams of animators scattered across the world, meaning Chomet often had to direct via internet and email, an increasingly common way of working. The movie was nominated for the best animated feature Oscar, but lost out to *Finding Nemo*.

Les triplettes de Belleville (The Triplets of Belleville/ Belleville rendez-vous), 2003

2003
Australia

Adam Elliot: Harvie Krumpet

The winner of the 2003 Academy Award for best animated short was a darkly comic Australian stop-motion film. Adam Elliot wrote, directed, and animated *Harvie Krumpet*, the story of a man who suffers a lifetime of bad luck. Harvie Krumpet is born in a Polish village; he has Tourette's syndrome, which causes him to be abused by his fellow villagers. His parents freeze to death and, when the Nazis invade Poland, he escapes to Australia. He is then struck by lightning and has to have a testicle removed, but here his luck changes as he falls in love with his nurse at the hospital. Many years later, his wife dies, he develops, Alzheimers and is hospitalized.

Elliot had already established his reputation as one of Australia's leading animators with the trilogy of shorts *Uncle* (1996), *Cousin* (1998), and *Brother* (1999). Like *Harvie Krumpet*, each of these claymation films are biographies of "underdog" characters and employ a mixture of humor and pathos.

Harvie Krumpet uses primitive, gnomish characters, low-key character animation, and tableau-like held shots. The cartoon-strip simplicity of the visuals contrasts with, and provides the comedy for, the beautifully written and performed melancholic narration by Oscar-winning actor Geoffrey Rush, which, if heard in isolation, would perhaps be too downbeat. Rush recorded two versions of the voiceover, the first rough recording was made at the beginning of the filmmaking process as a guide track for the animatic and the second version after Rush had seen the finished film.

Harvie Krumpet,
2003

2003
Australia

Peter Cornwell: Ward 13

This dark horror/action/comedy stop-motion short from
Australian animator Peter Cornwell tells the story of Ben, who
wakes up after a car accident to find himself in hospital. As he
explores his surroundings, he discovers that, rather than caring
for their patients, the doctors of Ward 13 perform horrific
experiments on them. Ben's attempts to escape this terrifying
situation grow increasingly frantic, ending with a supercharged
wheelchair chase sequence.

Cornwell wrote, directed, and animated *Ward 13* in his
spare time while working at the Australian Broadcasting
Commission (ABC). ABC had previously supported Cornwell's
claymation short, *Little Piggy*, which was broadcast on
Australian television. Following this, he made several animated
shorts and commercials before beginning work on *Ward 13*.
Cornwell had very limited resources for making his film, and
chose to tell the story using stop motion in order to achieve high
production values on a low budget. He created the models
himself, using clay, silicone, and polyurethane. The wooden sets
had built-in lights to give an atmospheric lighting effect, and the
effect of motion was achieved by keeping the camera steady
and sliding these sets along a track.

The short falls somewhere between scary horror and
cartoonish stop-frame piece; the finale, although tense,
has somewhat the feel of the manic final chase sequence
in Aardman Animations' *The Wrong Trousers* (1993).
Overall, *Ward 13*'s subject matter, relatively realistic sets,
and naturalistic character animation, combined with its
sophisticated fast cutting, camera moves, and kinetic direction,
give it the feel of a rehearsal for a live-action horror/action
movie. This would seem to be borne out by Cornwell's later
career as a horror director in Hollywood. *Ward 13* won
numerous awards worldwide, including the Audience Award
at the 2004 Zagreb World Festival of Animated Films.

Ward 13, 2003

2004
USA

Brad Bird: The Incredibles

After the fabulously good *The Iron Giant*, a lot was expected of Brad Bird's Pixar debut and he didn't disappoint, delivering another instant classic in *The Incredibles*. Bird was an animation child prodigy, who had impressed the Disney animators at the age of 14 and had been taken under the wing of Milt Kahl, one of the greatest of Walt Disney's reliable team of "nine old men." Bird had worked as an animator on Disney's *The Fox and the Hound* (1981) and on Martin Rosen's *The Plague Dogs* (1982), and as a director and story consultant on *The Simpsons*. He had known Pixar head John Lasseter since they studied together at California Insitute of the Arts, and Lasseter had been trying to persuade Bird to come and work on Pixar's films for some time.

After the excellence of the animated human characters in *Finding Nemo*, Pixar were ready to make a movie where humans, rather than toys or animals, took center stage. The characters' angular and top-heavy style was perfect for *The Incredibles*' 1950s-futuristic-style designs, a reprise from the Cold War setting of *The Iron Giant*. The premise of a family of superheroes living incognito after health and safety has ruled them obsolete, is one full of potential. The story concerns Bob (aka Mr Incredible) being torn between what he really wants to do (be a superhero) and what's supposedly best for his family (being Bob). This theme was inspired by Bird's feelings of frustration at the failure of his film projects to get off the ground at the same time as starting a new family. *The Incredibles* was a huge critical and commercial success and won the Academy Award for the best animated feature.

After *The Incredibles*, Bird picked up another Pixar project in development, *Ratatouille* (2007). The story of a gourmet Parisian rat, it again featured some brilliant human characterization and won Bird his second Oscar.

The Incredibles, 2004

2004

Canada

Ryan, 2004

Chris Landreth: Ryan

In Canadian Chris Landreth's 2004 Oscar-winning short film *Ryan* he makes a kind of animated documentary about his hero, Ryan Larkin, a Canadian animator from the 1960s. Larkin achieved fame with beautiful films such as *Street Musique* (1972) and the Oscar-nominated *Walking* (1969). Landreth recorded interviews with Larkin, now homeless, alcoholic, and begging for change on a street corner, about his fall from the peak of his profession into drug and alcohol addiction. Landreth then recreated the two of them in a semisurreal 3D animated style, which attempts to portray Larkin's fragile state of mind.

Inspired by the renewed interest in his work that *Ryan* inspired, Larkin underwent rehabilitation and started work on a new animated film, *Spare Change*. In Febuary, 2007, however, Larkin died of lung cancer before completing his film.

2004

UK

2004

Switzerland/
Canada

Marc Craste and Studio AKA:
JoJo in the Stars

JoJo in the Stars is a dark little tale about a freakshow circus in a parallel nightmare universe. JoJo, a trapeze artist under the power of a tyrannical circus owner, is loved from afar by a mysterious figure, who eventually makes his move with disastrous results. Mark Craste's prizewinning CG short stemmed from three one-minute violent and disturbing shorts, made as a kind of reaction to years of working on commercials. *JoJo in the Stars* was inspired by the 1986 Nick Cave and the Bad Seeds song, "The Carny," and was also influenced by live-action movies like David Lynch's *Eraserhead* and Wim Wenders' *Wings of Desire*. It also has the scratchy, uneasy atmosphere of early silent black-and-white horror movies, such as *Nosferatu* and *The Cabinet of Dr Caligari*.

Georges Schwizgebel: L'homme sans
ombre (The Man Without a Shadow)

After studying at the École des Beaux Arts et des Arts Décoratifs in Geneva, Switzerland, Georges Schwizgebel established Studio GDS where he produced graphic design and animated commercials and films such as *78 Tours* (*78 R.P.M.*, 1998) and *La jeune fille et les noages* (*The Young Girl and the Clouds*, 2000). His paint-on-glass short film *L'homme sans ombre* (*The Man Without a Shadow*), a coproduction with the National Film Board of Canada and based on a story by German writer Adelbert von Chamisso, features Schwizgebel's strongest narrative while using his acute sense of color and design to tell a psychological fable. A man sells his shadow, representing his soul, to the devil in exchange for wealth and women, but finds that, without his shadow, he is only a shadow of a man. With people disliking and avoiding him, he tries to get his shadow back. The direction of the film is highly stylized, with many creative transitions and dissolves using color and perspective as devices to move from scene to scene, making for an often disorientating but always engrossing visual journey. *The Man Without a Shadow* won awards at the Cannes Film Festival and the Zagreb World Festival of Animated Films.

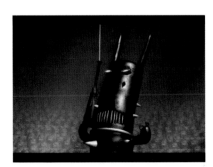

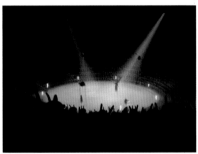

JoJo in the Stars,
2004

L'homme sans ombre
(The Man Without a Shadow), 2004

2004
Japan

Masaaki Yuasa: Mind Game

Mind Game won a string of awards and became an instant cult classic, living up to its title with a wildly unpredictable plotline and brain-popping psychedelic visuals in an extraordinary variety of styles. The story, based on Robin Nishi's comic book, tells of an irresponsible young man who is killed while trying to protect a girl from violent gangsters. In the crazily-realized afterlife he meets God and is allowed back to earth, where he ends up in another reality inside a whale and, as in *Pinocchio*, finds time for reflection and some kind of salvation.

Largely animated by the avant-garde Studio 4°C, Yuasa's film accelerates through a bewildering kaleidoscope of techniques including photomontage and video-game-type graphics; the main story on earth is told through a loose, freeflowing style of animation with squared-off character designs against gritty urban graphics, similar to the studio's later groundbreaking anime, *Tekkon Kinkreet* (2006). The psychedelia in *Mind Game* has an innocence free of tedious associations with drug use, as it lets rip with the kind of pure, unconstrained imagination that animation allows.

2004
Japan

Katsuhiro Otomo: Steamboy

Otomo's long awaited follow-up to *Akira* (1988), *Steamboy* took 10 years to make and again features military conspiracy plots and a child hero with connections to sources of massive psychic power, this time transported to a "steampunk" universe. Steampunk is a science-fiction genre, which blends sci-fi with nineteenth-century technology. *Steamboy* is set in 1866 in Manchester, England; Ray is a boy whose inventor father and grandfather have fallen out over their plans for a huge steam tower for the Great Exhibition in London. The boy receives a mysterious object in the post, a new awesome power source called the Steam Ball. The welded iron machines and effects build in complexity until the apocalyptically spectacular finale. Not for the first time in anime, the characters pale into insignificance next to the amazing visual bombardment of the technical detail.

Steamboy,
2004

2005
USA

Eric Darnell and Tom McGrath: Madagascar

DreamWorks Animation's *Madagascar* is the story of spoiled New York zoo animals who are shipwrecked on the island of Madagascar, where they are forced to survive in a jungle populated by crazy characters, including the memorable lemur leader, King Julien XII. The characters and design were more stylized than the majority of CG features; the animation was simplified and angled away from realism, similar to the approach of Chris Wedge's *Ice Age*. *Madagascar* has DreamWorks Animation's typical fast-paced, wisecracking style of direction, and is packed with pop hits and star names, including Ben Stiller, Chris Rock, and David Schwimmer. It was a big commercial success, generating sequels and much merchandise sales.

Madagascar,
2005

2005
UK/USA

Aardman Animations: Wallace and Gromit: Curse of the Were Rabbit

Wallace and Gromit's first feature film was funded by DreamWorks Animation, but managed to retain the quintessentially British charm of the hugely popular shorts that preceded it. An affectionate stop-frame homage to Hammer Horror films, the story tells of an unfortunate accident caused by one of Wallace's eccentric inventions, The Mind Manipulation O Matic, after which he becomes the Were Rabbit and menaces the town's prize vegetables. The supporting characters are hilarious, the animation is superb, and the sets of the town and Tottington Hall are lovely. The film won rave reviews and numerous awards, including the 2005 Academy Award for Best Animated Feature.

In 2007, both DreamWorks Animation and Aardman Animations announced their decision to end their partnership in creating animated films.

Wallace and Gromit:
Curse of the Were Rabbit,
2005

UK/USA

Sam Fell and David Bowers: Flushed Away

The third coproduction between the USA's DreamWorks Animation and the UK's Aardman Animations, *Flushed Away* was the first wholly CG feature produced by Aardman, best-known for their stop-frame work. The movie tells the story of Roddy, a spoiled but likeable upper class pet rat, who is flushed down the toilet. He embarks on a series of adventures with a gallery of crazy, sewer-dwelling animals, including a rodent-hating gangster toad, a notorious mercenary frog, some singing slugs, and a love interest rat called Rita, voiced by Kate Winslet. The script by British television comedy veterans Dick Clement and Ian La Frenais featured several Anglo obsessions, such as social class and soccer rivalries, which may have not connected fully with American audiences.

Codirectors Sam Fell and David Bowers also provided several voices for minor characters, as they would also do for *The Tale of Despereaux* and *Astro Boy*. Care was taken that the CG, used due to difficulties in creating the necessary sewer waters in traditional stop frame, managed to retain the simplicity and charm of an Aardman production. Indeed, the character design and animation, particularly in the simple but expressive facial expressions and lip sync, are immediately identifiable as products of the studio. In the glut of CG animation features from the era, *Flushed Away* stands out with its strong identity and sparky, quirky charm.

2005
UK

Peppa Pig

Astley Baker Davies: Peppa Pig; Tiger Aspect: Charlie and Lola

Desktop animation software rejuvenated the television animation industry in the early 2000s, making it cost effective to produce series locally rather than sending the labor-intensive parts of production out to low-cost economic areas. *Peppa Pig* and *Charlie and Lola* are preschool TV series made entirely in the UK, using their strengths of strong design identity and idiosyncratic sweet characters to achieve international success.

Peppa Pig is the work of Neville Astley, creator of the award-winning short *Trainspotter* (1996) and Mark Baker, famed for the award-winning *Hill Farm* (1988). The characters and designs in *Peppa Pig* are bright and simple, but clearly lovingly crafted, and its hilly landscape is similar in design to the setting of Baker's *Hill Farm*.

Charlie and Lola is created in an identical collage style to its source, Lauren Child's successful children's books, and features many delightful fantasy sequences which illustrate the imaginings of Lola and her brother.

2005
UK

2005
Japan

Run Wrake: Rabbit

Run Wrake has made a series of short films influenced by Len Lye, Oskar Fischinger, and Jan Svankmajer, among others. His early films *Jukebox* (1994) and *What is That* (2000) are figurative, but use narrative in nontraditional ways. His 2005 film *Rabbit* is a classic of digital surrealism, placing imagery from old children's sticker books into a darkly funny Svankmajer-esque parable about consumerism and the corruption of innocence. Wrake found the 1950s educational stickers in a junkstore, and combined them with hand-drawn animation and backgrounds. Despite being deeply strange, *Rabbit* is as entertaining as any Chuck Jones classic, in its own unique and disturbing way.

Yamatoworks: Kakurenbo: Hide and Seek

For a short film made by a four-man team working on ordinary computers and with little funding, *Kakurenbo: Hide and Seek* is outstanding. It achieves remarkably high standards in its shadowy production design and detail of the CG animation, and creates some genuine suspense.

Concerning a group of children who gather one night in a demon-haunted area of Tokyo, the story and characters could perhaps be better realized in a longer film, but there are plenty of fully-funded feature films that have lesser-formed characters and plots. While this 25-minute supernatural thriller retains the traditional handdrawn look of most anime, it was actually made in 3D CGI and then rendered in a flat 2D style using cel shading. The fact that the characters wear masks helps to disguise the difficulties of creating expressive CGI human faces. Kakurenbo attracted attention due to the small-scale personal nature of its production, won several awards, was distributed on DVD, and broadcast on cable television in the USA.

Rabbit, 2005

2006
USA

2006
UK

A Gentleman's Duel,
2006

Modern Toss

Sean McNally and Francisco Ruiz Velasco: A Gentleman's Duel

This short film made by Sean McNally and Francisco Ruiz Velasco at Blur Studio was a follow-up to their earlier Academy Award-nominated short *Gopher Broke* (2004). *A Gentleman's Duel* follows a polite argument about a lady between two Victorian gentlemen, which rapidly escalates into an all-out steampunk robot war, trashing the elegant surroundings and almost killing the lady too.

Funny and beautifully made, the film features great character and effects animation and one of the most lovingly animated voluptuous cartoon women since Jessica Rabbit. Mainly known for their spectacular mini epics for video game story scenes, work like this confirms Blur Studio's status as one of the most interesting and capable smaller studios in the crowded world of CG animation.

Mick Bunnage and Jon Link: Modern Toss

The television series of *Modern Toss* is a hilariously demented lo-fi adaptation of Mick Bunnage and Jon Link's scribbly and surreal cult cartoons. After working in the unstable world of magazine publishing, Link and Bunnage used a redundancy payoff to fund their cartoon project. The *Modern Toss* characters first appeared on a website, then in comic books and on T-shirts and greetings cards before the first TV series aired in 2006. Regular characters included two squabbling astronauts; Mr Tourette, the inappropriate sign painter; Alan, a pointlessly antisocial middle-aged scribble; and the Drive-By Abuser, who shouts his views on the population from the back of a scooter. Packed with profanities and in some ways recalling the traditions of UPA's simplified animation, *Modern Toss* combined animation with surreal live-action sketches, and featured voice overs from British comedy stars.

Two series of *Modern Toss* were shown on Channel 4 in the UK and on Adult Swim in the US, while the characters continue to propagate online, in books, exhibitions, and on a variety of merchandise.

2006
UK/Poland/Norway

Suzie Templeton: Peter and the Wolf

Suzie Templeton's stop-motion interpretation of *Peter and the Wolf*, winner of the Academy Award for best animated short, is a modern take on the dark fable and the symphony by Sergei Prokofiev. Countless recordings and film versions have been made of this popular piece, with the best-known film versions being animated. Filmed versions include the Disney cartoon of 1946, a 1958 Russian film directed by Anatoly Karanovich, and two American TV specials from 1958 and 1996, the latter featuring animation designed by Chuck Jones.

Templeton's version is one of the best, jettisoning the traditional narration and telling the story visually, an approach that is so often successful in animation with the medium's strengths for clearly and quickly conveying visual information.

Unlike the other adaptations which were usually made for child audiences in the West, Templeton retains the dark aspects of the story, for instance the duck character is eaten alive by the wolf and can be heard plaintively quacking from inside the animal. But Templeton also gives the film a more sensitive and noble ending as Peter frees the wolf to return to the forest, instead of leaving him chained in a zoo, as in the original. Largely based in a rural setting, the animation and visual style of the characters and the town have a contemporary Eastern European feel, an influence derived from the Russian story and the film's production base in Poland's Se-mar-for Studios.

Peter and the Wolf, 2006

2006

Norway

Christopher Nielsen: Slipp Jimmy fri (Free Jimmy)

Christopher Nielsen is a comic book artist whose works depict a Norwegian subculture of drug users and criminals. Two of his comic book characters starred in a computer-animated television series, *To trøtte typer* (2001), and more of his characters appear in the movie *Slipp Jimmy fri (Free Jimmy)*. Produced by Storm Studio, Free Jimmy was Norway's first computer-animated feature film.

The Jimmy of the title is a drug-addicted elephant, the star of a touring Russian circus. The film's four low-life heroes attempt to steal Jimmy in order to start up their own circus, but their attempt is bungled and Jimmy escapes. They set off to catch him and give him his drugs fix before he goes cold turkey. Jimmy is also being pursued by a group of animal activists, a hunting party, and the Lappish Mafia. Jimmy's only friend is a kindly moose who tries to helps him overcome his drug addiction.

A boldly unconventional and politically incorrect black comedy, *Free Jimmy* is crude, raucous, and grimy, using CGI software to bring the aesthetic of underground comic books to life. The gritty, semirealistic backgrounds, displayed to good effect in the film's opening sequence, are however perhaps more effective than the characters.

Free Jimmy was a critical and box office hit in Norway, where it has cult status. The British comedy writer and actor Simon Pegg wrote the screenplay for the English-language version, and also provided the voice of one of the characters. Other parts were played by Woody Harrelson and a host of British and American stars. Despite this, the English-language version failed to attract the same critical praise or cult audience, although Norwegian fans claim that a lot of the film's ironic humor and themes were lost in translation.

Slipp Jimmy fri,
(Free Jimmy),
2006

2006
Denmark

Anders Morgenthaler: Princess

Princess is an adult-aimed feature from Denmark that is 80 percent animation and 20 percent live action. It falls into the genre of an intelligent revenge movie, the avenger being a lapsed priest who takes his sister's young daughter into his care, after her mother, a porn star, has died of a drugs overdose. He discovers to his horror that the little girl has been corrupted and abused by the porn industry she has been brought up around, which sets him on a mission to destroy all the pornographic images of his famous sister, killing anyone who tries to stop him.

The well drawn and designed anime-style visuals make the harrowing story moderately more bearable, although the extreme cartoon violence is shocking, but this desensitization is one of the issues the film explores. The protagonist starts to take the little girl along to participate in his violent missions, destroying her innocence further and making him as bad as the people he is hunting. *Princess* is in the Danish tradition of Lars Von Trier's style of confrontational cinema, and is an interesting and challenging example of extreme animation.

2006
Japan

Michael Arias: Tekkon kinkuîto (Tekkon Kinkreet); Satoshi Kon: Paprika

Micheal Arias' *Tekkon kinkuîto* (*Tekkon Kinkreet*) was a critically-hailed adaptation of the 1993 manga comic published in English as *Tekkonkinkret: Black and White*. The stunning design of the movie features stylized, simply-drawn characters in a beautifully illustrated depiction of a rundown Tokyo suburb, realized in 3D and filmed with a live-action-type fluid camera style. The protagonists are two street urchins, a tough streetwise kid called Black, and a sensitive innocent with a special intelligence called White. Black and White get into a battle with a yakuza criminal gang who are trying to take over the neighborhood. The characters use a form of "freerunning" to effortlessly scale buildings and observe the neighborhood from the rooftops. Tokyo-based American Arias, producer of *The Animatrix* films, became the first non-Japanese director of a major anime movie in this work for Studio 4°C, known for their indie approach to anime and their connections with the superflat art movement of Takashi Murakami.

Paprika is an adaptation of Yasutaka Tsutsui's novel concerning a psychologist who, as part of the therapy, enters her patients' dreams. As is typical of Satoshi Kon's work, the boundaries between reality and fantasy are blurred, with a succession of spectacular sequences featuring surreal imagery.

Kon was a leading figure in the world of anime, writing and directing his own complex and cerebral movies. His best-known works *Perfect Blue* (1998), *Millennium Actress* (2001), *Tokyo Godfathers* (2003), and the TV series *Paranoia Agent* (2004), often used his trademark technique of segueing seamlessly between the reality of characters' lives and their memories, fantasies, dreams, and illusory worlds. Tragically, he died aged 46 in August 2010 of pancreatic cancer.

2006

South Korea

Jo Beom-jin: Aachi and Ssipak

Jo Beom-jin's *Aachi and Ssipak* is an incredible and unique animated feature from South Korea, set in a bizarre future world where human excrement is in high demand as the only form of fuel and the government pays people for its provision with an ice-cream-like drug. The protagonists Aachi and Ssipak are petty criminals who trade in the drug, "Juicybars," on the black market. The movie is an extreme combination of simplistically drawn 2D with hyper real 3D CGI backgrounds, and is packed with violence, uncompromising imagery, and the machine-gun-paced action that is typical of Korean action movies. *Aachi and Ssipak* is one of the more intense movie experiences in contemporary animation.

Aachi and Ssipak,
2006

South Africa

The Blackheart Gang: The Tale of How

The Tale of How is a beautifully intricate short that mines a similar area of Victorian eccentricity as the work of Karel Zeman, Terry Gilliam, and Tim Burton. The Blackheart Gang are a design and animation collective based in Cape Town, South Africa. Their work has a distinctive style, featuring dozens of digitally composited levels of (mainly 2D drawn) animated backgrounds, small characters, animals, and details. *The Tale of How* is the second in a series of shorts called *The Dodo Trilogy*. Constructed around an Edward Lear-style musical rhyme about fantastical creatures in a whimsical ocean world, the film picked up many prizes, including The Special Distinction award at the Annecy Animation Festival.

The Tale of How,
2006

2007
USA

2007
USA

David Silverman: The Simpsons Movie

Perhaps demonstrating that reports of its death were greatly exaggerated, in 2007 one of the biggest animated successes at the box office involved mainly drawn 2D animation. Aside from a few works of quality, the animated features market was now suffering from an excess of formulaic and forgettable 3D efforts. Many 3D features had become even more uninspired than many of the 1990s 2D flops had been, making traditionally animated 2D movies seem kind of fresh and interesting again. In this climate, *The Simpsons Movie* stood out from the crowd.

The movie was a faithful transition of the genius television series onto the big screen. The animation was given a little extra polish as it included some CG backgrounds, but there were no standout departures from the TV series' 2D look. The story was somewhat more ambitious than the average *Simpsons* episode, however, as Homer causes the entire town of Springfield to be quarantined under a giant glass dome. The family move to Alaska for a fresh start, but have to return to save the town from destruction.

The idea for a *Simpsons* movie had been around for as long as the show itself; in its first season, Groening had been asked to make a feature-length version. However, the production team chose to wait until they had the right story and enough resources to make the movie that *The Simpsons* deserved. In the opening credits of a later episode of the show, Bart wrote on the blackboard "I will not wait another 20 years to make a movie."

Disney: Enchanted

Another sign of the continuing health of 2D animation was the success of Disney's *Enchanted*. Directed by Kevin Lima, *Enchanted* poked affectionate fun at the studio's classic releases, notably *Snow White and the Seven Dwarfs*. In the opening animated sequence, Giselle, a typical Disney princess, is magicked out of the cartoon world by a wicked witch and is sent into modern day New York. The traditional cel animation is packed with visual references to classic Disney features, although Lima also drew on Art Nouveau influences to give the movie its own distinct style.

Enchanted marked a return to traditional animation after the company had taken the decision in 2004 to only create computer animation. Like Disney's previous live-action/ animation features *Song of the South*, *Mary Poppins*, and *Who Framed Roger Rabbit*, *Enchanted* was a welcome success that came to the studio's aid during a slump in its animated features.

Enchanted, 2007

2007
UK

2007
France/Iran

Magnetic Movie,
2007

Semiconductor: Magnetic Movie

Semiconductor are a directing duo who use digital animation, often controlled by software that links to sound or other events, to produce films and gallery works exploring the "physical world in flux, cities in motion, and systems in chaos."

The award-winning *Magnetic Movie* is a striking and atmospheric film, funded by Channel 4 and the Animate! scheme. To the recorded narration of scientists describing their experiments, the film visualizes the invisible magnetic fields emitted by equipment at Nato's Space Science Laboratories in Berkeley, California, as elaborate multicolored 3D patterns and sci-fi neon balls of light, tracked and composited into footage of the sterile labs.

Vincent Parronaud and Marjane Satrapi: Persepolis

Persepolis is a wonderfully idiosyncratic and personal animated movie, adapted from Marjane Satrapi's autobiographical graphic novel. Set in 1970s Iran, the film tells the story of the Islamic Revolution through the eyes of young Marji, powerfully evoking the fear of daily life at that time. As she becomes a teenager, Marji discovers punk and her love of Western pop culture and her stubborn nature set her in opposition to the new regime of the Islamic Fundamentalists. Fearing for her safety, her parents send her to a boarding school in Austria, where she finds Western values to be shallow and impersonal. She returns to Iran, but feels unable to live there, and so makes the decision to move to France.

Spain/
France

Persepolis, 2007

Nocturna, 2007

Drawn in the same style as Satrapi's novel, the monochrome animation is simple and stylish. Satrapi believes that this abstract graphic style helps make the story universal. *Persepolis* is a fascinating and funny story, and provides probably as good a lesson in understanding Iranian society as any outsider could have.

Adria García and Victor Maldonado:
Nocturna

This superior traditional 2D animated feature is a story about how an orphan's struggle with his fear of the dark leads to him being drawn into a fantasy nighttime world. The style owes something to filmmakers Tim Burton and Guillermo del Toro, but ultimately *Nocturna* creates its own unique, crooked world and Latin identity due to the talents of its directors and team.

This impressive movie, criminally underexposed and undistributed outside its area of origin, stands up well to other animated features of the 2000s through its fresh and original character design and art direction, quirky backgrounds, atmospheric lighting, and lovely animation.

2008

France

Julien Bocabeille, François-Xavier Chanioux, Olivier Delabarre, Thierry Marchand, Quentin Marmier, and Emud Mokhberi: Oktapodi

This memorable 3D CG short was the graduation film of six students at GOBELINS l'ecole de l'image, a college in Paris specializing in visuals arts and with a global reputation for producing fine animators. The students were tasked with making a high-quality short, with a running time limited to just two minutes. They came up with a frenetic story concerning two lovestruck octopuses employing ingenious and energetic means to escape from a determined chef in a small Greek coastal town. The fast-paced action allowed them to tell the story within the given time and ocopuses were chosen as subjects for their comedic potential and for the challenges they posed in terms of animation technique and character animation. Among its numerous awards and film festival screenings, *Oktapodi* was nominated for best animated short at the Academy Awards.

Although familiar from many other such cartoons throughout animation history, the manic chase unfolds in an absorbing manner thanks to the snappy character animation, simplified design, and crisp lighting, which gives *Oktapodi* the feel of a European version of a Blue Sky Studios production. The beautifully conceived models and environments demonstrate the importance of sculptural ability and an eye for lighting in 3D computer animation. When making family-aimed CG animation, you are entering a crowded ocean ruled by big fish like Pixar, DreamWorks Animation, and Blue Sky, but such is the quality on show here that these Octapodi can happily swim in the same water as their competitors from across the Atlantic.

Oktapodi, 2008

2008
USA

Pixar: WALL-E; DreamWorks Animation: Kung Fu Panda; Disney: Bolt

Of the many 3D CGI features released in 2008, the best and most sophisticated were *WALL-E*, *Kung Fu Panda*, and *Bolt*. Of these, Pixar's *WALL-E* was perhaps the most ambitious, setting a cute comedy within a somber warning about ecological irresponsibility and runaway consumerism. *WALL-E* is set largely in a burnt-out future where the earth is piled high with garbage. Humans have abandoned the planet and have reached extreme levels of laziness, and through decades of inactivity have been rendered incapable of any kind of intelligent thought or physical action. Disgusting blobs, they have become entirely dependent on robots. At the start of the movie, the small loveable robot of the title is performing his futile task of trying to tidy up the planet. After he encounters EVE, a more advanced robot who has been sent to find plants, he falls in love, and together WALL-E and EVE save humanity. In a bold move, the first third of the movie is virtually dialogue-free as we watch WALL-E's activities on the abandoned earth. The strength of the animation, however, is captivating and enables the viewer to fall in love with the little robot.

Taking a more traditional comedy approach to an animated feature, John Stevenson and Mark Osborne's *Kung Fu Panda* is a stylish martial arts story about a fat panda, Po, exuberantly voiced by Jack Black. Po is inadvertently selected to be the legendary Dragon Warrior, who must be trained by the Furious Five to fight the evil snow leopard, Tai Lung. The beautifully art directed and animated movie draws on Hong Kong martial arts movies, traditional Chinese design, and highly-stylized cartoons, such as Genndy Tartakovsky's *Samurai Jack*.

Disney's *Bolt* was the studio's first 3D CGI release under new creative director John Lasseter's regime. It showed a

WALL-E, 2008

marked improvement over previous efforts like *Chicken Little* (2005) and *Meet the Robinsons* (2007), both, like *Bolt*, released in stereoscopic 3D. The movie told the story of a small dog who has spent his life acting in a television series, and believes himself to be a real superhero. It is a return to the kind of warm, confident, and funny storytelling that is Disney's trademark. The characters and the backgrounds are designed with various levels of stylization, and the new technology of nonphotorealistic rendering was employed to give a handcrafted feel.

2008
USA

Don Hertzfeldt: I Am So Proud of You

A kind of spiritual descendant of Emile Cohl, Don Hertzfeldt is an animator who creates simple, anarchic works of playful surrealism that delight audiences while seeming to subvert the mainstream commercialized art world and create their own rules.

Hertzfeldt is either a fairly unique phenomenon or perhaps an example of a new way forward for individual animators surviving independently on their own terms. His following initially built momentum on the internet, and he now divides his time between the intensive work of making his personal films, and appearances at touring festivals and special screenings, where he attracts the kind of fanatical support from the student and alternative crowds usually associated with indie rock bands.

Part of Hertzfeldt's appeal comes from his standing as a kind of anticorporate and determinedly nontechnological figurehead, although this is not necessarily something he has aspired to, but comes from the techniques he chooses to work with, which include simplistic drawings on paper and antique rostrum cameras. He refuses to work in commercials or advertising, and even bypasses the mainstream animation industry and its methods. Hertzfeldt doesn't consider any need for a perception of conflict or delineation between traditional and digital methods and other approaches, dismissing the idea that one development should cancel another, and instead believes that all the technologies and approaches developed over the last century simply mean there is an exciting palette of tools for filmmakers, leading to healthy and stimulating choices for audiences.

Rejected, 2000

Stating his influences as more pointed toward live-action greats like Stanley Kubrick and David Lynch, as well as the comedy team Monty Python and silent film slapstick, Hertzfeldt began making cartoons as a teenager. He was pushed toward animation after seeing independent animated shorts in the Spike and Mike touring collections, as well as early works by Aardman Animations and Pixar, the films of Bill Plympton, and works from the National Film Board of Canada. Previous to this, like most people, Hertzfeldt's only experience of animation had been mainsteam work like Disney and Warner Bros., which he found funny but increasingly boring due to the adhesion to formulas. The independent work inspired him to start making animation and later, when attending film school to become a live-action director, Hertzfeldt continued making cartoons as a way to make films cheaply with complete freedom and without a big team. His films *Everything Will Be OK* and *Rejected* were nominated for Academy Awards.

I Am So Proud of You shows how his work has become increasingly philosophical, following early comedies such as *Billy's Balloon*, which had a disturbing and violent edge. Made and sold through his company Bitter Films, and using his recognizable style of stick figures combined with often-beautiful in-camera effects and stop-frame elements, *I Am So Proud of You* is the second chapter of a planned trilogy of films about Bill, a character developed from Hertzfeldt's web comics. The film, like its predecessor *Everything Will Be OK*, talks about the human condition by describing with oblique humor the obscure details and mundane existence of Bill, his thoughts, and memories, and the brief moments of joy and the dark moments of tragedy and sadness that define his life.

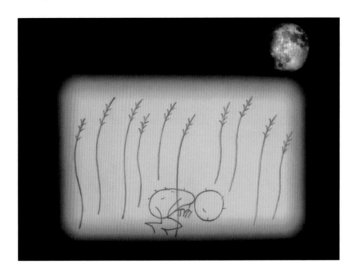

I Am So Proud of
You, 2008

2008
USA/UK

Robert Stevenhagen and Sam Fell:
The Tale of Despereaux

The Tale of Despereaux is an interesting and beautifully made movie, which stands out from the pile of other 3D CGI features made at this time. It suffers from story problems, which were probably not helped by various changes of director and the rather complex source material. Produced by Universal Pictures and made at London's Framestore animation studio, *The Tale of Despereaux* has a rich production design based on paintings by the Dutch masters, as well as some nicely designed and animated characters.

Sylvain Chomet was originally hired as director but fell out with the producers over creative and financial differences. Chomet was replaced by *Corpse Bride* codirector Mike Johnson, before Robert Stevenhagen and *Flushed Away* codirector Sam Fell were eventually installed. *The Tale of Despereaux* is based on the 2003 fantasy book of the same name by Kate DiCamillo, which told a story three times from the perspectives of different characters, and then used a fourth story to reveal the ending.

The movie's reception was perhaps hindered by a passing similarity to Pixar's smash hit *Ratatouille*, in that it featured a rodent hero. Also noticeable is the absence of the by now customary barrage of popular culture references, goofy wisecracking sidekicks, and ubiquitous pop music, which while refreshing to some, admittedly may not have helped with the laugh count (although there are many humorous moments). The in-jokes and influences here are often of a more cultured vein, featuring for instance a character made of fruit and vegetables in the style of sixteenth-century painter Arcimboldo.

The Tale of Despereaux,
2008

2008
UK

Smith & Foulkes: This Way Up

Directing team Alan Smith and Adam Foulkes created this kinetic and slapstick Oscar-nominated short about two determined undertakers overcoming enormous problems in transporting a body to its final destination. It is rendered in somber colors to suit its stony-faced heroes, who retain a dignified front through all manner of funny and extreme circumstances. Smith & Foulkes were influenced by classic silent slapstick comedians, such as Harold Lloyd and Laurel and Hardy, as well as later British comedy like Monty Python, Morecambe and Wise, and the 1967 silent short *The Plank*, in which two men encounter all kinds of trouble transporting the said piece of wood.

This Way Up,
2008

2008
UK

Stephen Irwin: The Black Dog's Progress

The Black Dog's Progress is an award-winning short, funded by experimental animation scheme Animate!. The film is made up of a series of flickbooks, the technique most often found in schoolboys' textbooks whereby frames of animation are drawn into a book which can then be viewed by rolling them rapidly. The film uses a growing number of looping flickbooks, drawn on paper in stark black and white and then assembled digitally, looping constantly so that we experience the past and the present side by side.

Telling the dark story of the unwanted orphan Black Dog, cast out by his uncaring owners only to experience the cruel and violent world outside, the concept has obvious echoes of William Hogarth's eighteenth-century morality tale engravings, *The Rake's Progress*. The multi-screen approach also bears similarity with some of the films of animator Paul Driessen. The accompaniment is a stripped down and haunting score by Danish musician Sorenious Bonk, which ends with a chilling scream.

The Black Dog's
Progress, 2008

2008

France

Various directors: Peur(s) du Noir (Fear(s) of the Dark)

This excellent anthology of stories, written and directed by renowned illustrators and comic artists, bears similarities with the portmanteau horror films that were popular in the 1960s and 1970s. Linked by an abstract psychological narrative written and directed by Pierre di Sciullo, the film contains chilling tales rendered in black and white by Blutch, Charles Burns, Marie Caillou, Lorenzo Mattotti, and Richard McGuire in their own distinctive styles.

Peur(s) du noir (Fear(s) of the Dark) plays on common fears and phobias and follows a monochrome trend in French animated movies, which also included *Renaissance* and *Persepolis*. The inventive and intertwined stories range from a Japanese girl haunted by a samurai ghost, a Spanish aristocrat and his deadly hunting dogs, and a town whose inhabitants disappear in the marshes. Perhaps the most stylish section is cult comic creator Charles Burns' bizarre story of doomed love involving a geeky teenage boy and his fascination with insects.

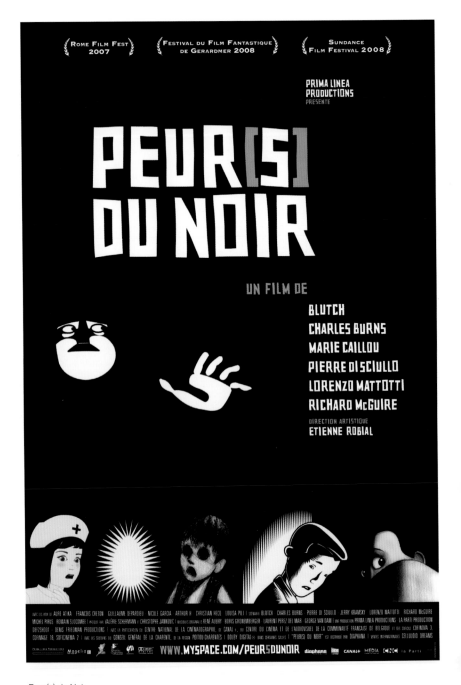

Peur(s) du Noir,
2008

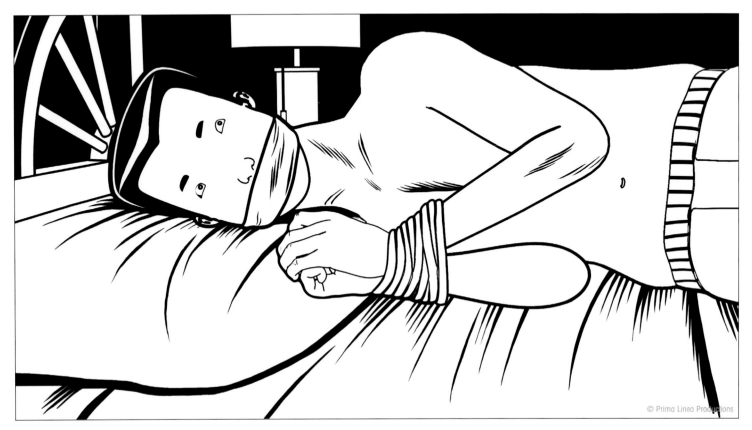

2008
Italy/ Argentina

Blu: Muto: An Ambiguous Animation Painted on Public Walls

This animation by Italian graffiti artist Blu features surreal black-and-white figures going through extraordinary and imaginative cycles of transformation and mutation, birth and death. The film would be impressive enough in any conventional format, but what makes it, and Blu's other work, so impressive is that it is all painted frame-by-frame on public walls, then photographed and overpainted. This particular piece of animated graffiti was painted in Buenos Aires, Argentina. The figures in Blu's works often use their unusual locations as part of the action, eating posters or kicking over objects that lean on the walls. Blu works all over the world creating massive public wall paintings, taking street art to a whole new level.

2008
Japan

Q-Games: Pixeljunk Eden

Kyoto-based artist Baiyon was commissioned by Q-Games to design this terrific-looking video game for the Playstation 3 platform. The experience of *Pixeljunk Eden* is like playing a game inside an abstract experimental animation film, as the gamer moves around various bright, highly stylized and flat colored garden environments. It features the ability to record the visuals as you influence them and put your own clips online.

2008
Japan

Hayao Miyazaki: Gake no ue no Ponyo (Ponyo)

Although based on an original concept, like much of Miyazaki's work *Gake no ue no Ponyo* (*Ponyo*) takes influences from various sources, including Hans Christian Andersen's *The Little Mermaid* and the Japanese children's story *Kaeru no Eruta* (*Elta the Frog*) by Yuriko Ohmura.

Ponyo tells the story of a young goldfish and her quest to become a human. The fish is rescued from a glass jar by a boy called Sosuke. Sosuke and the fish, who he names Ponyo, fall in love. Ponyo's father is a wizard and, against his will, she uses his magic to turn herself into a human. This disrupts the natural harmony of the world, and to restore order, Sosuke must pass a test to prove his love for Ponyo.

Studio Ghibli had experimented with computer animation in previous movies, but by the time *Ponyo* was made, they had returned to making entirely handdrawn animation. Hayao Miyazaki wrote and directed the movie, and was personally responsible for all the wave animation. The movie apparently features a record 170,000 separate drawings.

Although *Ponyo* is aimed at younger children, there is plenty for older viewers to appreciate. The beautiful 2D sequences of the magical undersea world and the spectacular results of the magic powers becoming unbalanced are as visually lush and stunning as anything previously produced by Miyazaki. As with much Asian cinema, the story moves in many unpredictable directions, naturally and imaginatively, free of the structural rules and formulas of much Western product.

Disney distributed *Ponyo* in the West and produced a high-quality English-language version featuring star actors. Miyazaki also traveled to the USA to promote the English-language release, where he made several public appearances alongside Pixar's John Lasseter. Although the two directors can perhaps be seen to represent the opposite ends of the technological scale, they share a mutual appreciation of each other's work.

2008
Japan

Kunio Kato: Le Maison en Petits Cubes (The House of Small Cubes)

This poignant 12-minute film with an ecological message by Kunio Kato won the Academy Award for best animated short in 2009. An old man lives in a city that has been almost completely submerged in water, and has to build further "cube" extensions onto the roof of his home to stay above the rising tide. When he drops his pipe into a hole in the floor, he swims down through the sections of the underwater tower he has constructed, each layer reminding him of a different phase of his life.

The story is told without any dialogue or narration, there is just a simple musical soundtrack. With its inked and handpainted illustration-style backgrounds and a loose, chunky character design, *Le Maison en Petits Cubes* (*The House of Small Cubes*) feels more European than Japanese in style.

Le Maison en Petits Cubes (The House of Small Cubes), 2008

2008

Israel/France/Germany/USA

Vals Im Bashir (Waltz with
Bashir), 2008

Ari Folman: Vals Im Bashir (Waltz with Bashir)

Vals Im Bashir (*Waltz with Bashir*) is an animated semidocumentary feature; made by the Israeli director Ari Folman, the movie was coproduced by companies in Israel, France, Germany, and the USA. *Waltz with Bashir* describes a man dealing with his traumatic experiences serving in the Israeli army during the 1982 Lebanon War and his mental block created by witnessing the massacres that took place there. Ultimately, the movie suggests that Israel as a nation suffers from collective amnesia about these events.

Influenced by graphic novels and the seminal philosophical war novels *Slaughterhouse Five* and *Catch 22*, *Waltz with Bashir* uses an elaborate combination of rotoscope-style techniques, Flash-style cutouts, and traditional frame-by-frame drawings to create its gritty atmosphere of the horrors of combat and the disorientating fog of war, as well as showing modern urban life. An extraordinary, personal, and powerful feature, it was the first animated production to be nominated for the Academy Award for best foreign film and, along with 2008's Israeli-Australian coproduction *$9.99*, was the first animated feature to come out of Israel since Yoram and Alina Gross' *Ba'al Hahalomot* (1962).

2009

USA

Pete Docter: Up

Up, another highly original story from Pixar, concerns an old man, Mr Fredricksen, and his decision to fly to South America by means of tying hundreds of balloons onto his house in order to pursue his deceased wife's unfulfilled dream. The first 15 minutes of the movie are extraordinarily touching as they tell, with very little dialogue, the story of the meeting, love, and marriage of Carl Fredricksen and his wife Ellie. As with *Finding Nemo* and, to a lesser extent, *WALL-E*, the emotional impact of this strongly drives the narrative of the rest of the movie, which allows the story to contain meandering and silly moments without losing too much momentum.

Released in stereoscopic 3D, which worked well with the flying sequences, the design of the characters, particularly of Fredricksen, were Pixar's most stylized to date. Like the Disney characters of the 1960s, the designs of *Up*'s characters are quite geometrically based. Fredricksen, loosely based on Spencer Tracy, has a very, square solid design, reflecting his stoical grumpy character, while Russell, the lonely boy scout he befriends, is very round and sweet. Pete Docter wanted these visual cues to give the audience an instant sense of the

Up, 2009

characters' personalities. The *Up* team invented the term "simplexity" to describe this process of simplifying the character design right down to its key elements, but then adding layers of texture and detail so that the characters are still believable.

The strengths of the movie—the opening sequence and the characterizations—more than make up for any weaker moments. *Up* quickly became one of Pixar's best-loved movies, winning the Academy Award for best animated feature.

2009
USA

John Musker and Ron Clements: The Princess and the Frog

When Disney bought Pixar in 2006, John Lasseter and Ed Catmull were put in charge of rejuvenating the Disney Animation Studios at Burbank, California. One of their first decisions was to allow directors to use whatever kind of animation they wanted, including traditional 2D animation, a reversal of the Disney executives' decision in 2004 to abandon 2D drawn animation in favor of the currently more profitable 3D CGI.

The Princess and the Frog was the first product of this revival and was a big commercial and critical success, creating another classic Disney princess story, and proving the argument that audiences simply want a good story well told and don't care about the technique. John Musker and Ron Clements were Disney 2D veterans, having previously directed the hits *Aladdin* and *The Little Mermaid*. In previous Disney movies the animators had tried to incorporate more CG-influenced contemporary trends in drawing, but for *The Princess and the Frog* Musker and Clements abandoned this approach. Instead, they looked back to the Disney styles of the past for inspiration, particularly the graphical and angular look of the 1960s films. They also based the look of their new movie on 1955's *Lady and the Tramp*, which the directors and Lasseter saw as the culmination of the classic Disney style.

The Princess and the Frog was also notable for being the first Disney movie with an African-American heroine. Despite the movie's retro animation, its lead character is a very modern girl. The feisty and hard-working Tiana is a more complex character than the typical cartoon princess. Set in 1920s New Orleans, as part of their research, the animators visited an old Louisiana plantation to find out about women's lives.

The Princess and the
Frog, 2009

2009
USA

Coraline, 2009

Wes Anderson: Fantastic Mr Fox; Shane Acker: 9; Henry Selick: Coraline

2009 was a strong year for stop-motion movies, which, like 2D drawn animation, had been written off many times before as uncommercial. The three movies that proved the technique was still relevant were *Fantastic Mr Fox*, *9*, and *Coraline*.

Fantastic Mr Fox is an excellent example of how successful a lo-fi approach can be. The cult live-action director Wes Anderson is know for his obsession with detail in the styling of his movies, and he insisted that *Fantastic Mr Fox* had a loose feel that recalled the early stop-frame movies. To help achieve this, "mistakes" such as the animators' finger impressions being visible in the characters' fur were left in.

An entertaining and engagingly eccentric adaptation of Roald Dahl's children's book, the movie has perhaps the best dialogue track of any animated feature, created by holding improvisational recording sessions with talented actors in a remote location away from a sound studio atmosphere.

Fantastic Mr Fox has an all-star cast, like much contemporary Hollywood animation, but in this case the film feels like a genuine George Clooney vehicle only with his physical image replaced by that of an animated fox. Clooney's charismatic soft-hearted rogue character is always at center stage, getting out of all kinds of impossible scrapes while delivering his trademark, freeflowing, but sharp as nails dialogue.

Rumors circulated concerning Anderson's over-fussiness while directing the movie from his Paris hotel suite and his refusal to spend much time on set in London. However, the process of directing remotely via internet is becoming far from uncommon, as many animated features are international coproductions and involve outsourcing.

Shane Acker's *9*, an extension of his Oscar-winning short of the same name, is set in a dystopian world where 9, a "stitchpunk" character with a cloth-textured design, fights against the evil overlord and various of his manifestations. Part produced by Tim Burton, the film had an impressive and original design and animation, along with some great creatures and battle sequences.

After the brilliant *James and the Giant Peach*, Henry Selick directed *Monkeybone* (2001), a badly received and unsuccessful adaptation of Kaja Blackley's graphic novel. He later created some great stop-motion exotic fish for Wes Anderson's *The Life Aquatic with Steve Zissou* (2004). After this Selick joined the Laika studio, formerly Will Vinton Studios. Here he wrote and directed the award-winning CG short *Moongirl* and the stop-frame feature *Coraline*. Also made in stereoscopic 3D, *Coraline* was an adaptation of Neil Gaiman's spooky "alternative universe in the closet" book. A story about the consequences of modern parents too wrapped up in their work to pay attention to their children, the stop-frame characters and sets were impressively imagined and realized, and the slowly unfolding story featured some genuinely creepy and tense moments.

9, 2009

2009
USA/New Zealand

James Cameron: Avatar

Epic sci-fi blockbuster *Avatar* broke box office records and became the movie "event" of 2009. Its lush and detailed creation of the alien world Pandora and its blue humanoid inhabitants, the Na'vi, was a milestone in CGI, stereoscopic 3D, and performance capture techniques, although whether or not it qualifies as an animated film is open for debate. Director James Cameron has claimed that, for the first time, no animators were used in the making of the synthetic characters and that it was purely performance capture seen on screen, although this is a claim met with a certain amount of scepticism in the industry.

Avatar's anti-imperialist, ecologically-themed story tells of a corporate mining expansion on Pandora leading to the employment on the planet of genetically-created replicants of the Na'vi, remotely operated by humans. The story relates how a paraplegic former marine is used in this capacity and finds his mission to infiltrate the rebellious inhabitants of the planet and obtain intelligence to be used against them conflicting with his feelings for the female Na'vi, named Neyteri, who rescues him. The movie's implicit condemnation of military practices such as remote-controlled technological warfare on distant lands, contains analogies with the Iraq war and other contemporary war zones.

Avatar cost over $200 million to make and then $150 million to promote. Even if it is perhaps rather needlessly overextended in terms of telling a simple story, it is a brave and mesmerizing work and a landmark in CGI. The effects were produced mainly through Peter Jackson's Weta studios in New Zealand, responsible for previous CG and performance capture milestones in *The Lord of the Rings* trilogy and *King Kong*.

After the success of *Avatar*, director James Cameron proposed that a new category of Academy Award should be created for the motion-capture performances of synthetic characters. While a valid proposal, this also relates back to and reopens the same debate about the performances of animated characters. If it can be argued that collaborative and technologically created characters such as those brought to life by performance capture are deserving of this kind of accolade, then there should certainly be inclusion for a character performance such as that of Carl Fredricksen in Pixar's *Up*, arguably a more nuanced, subtle, wider ranging, and more emotionally involving performance than the digitally-created ones in *Avatar*. Since the first animated feature films of the 1930s, animators have devoted literally years of their lives to the creation of these virtual personalities and have been responsible for some of the most memorable characters in cinema history. Considering that the animator's status is often way below that of voice actors, who are often awarded star billing and huge publicity during the promotion of animated films for what has been for them a few hours lucrative and undemanding work, the talent and genius of the actual creators of these animated stars is long overdue the recognition that it deserves.

2009

USA/UK/ Hong Kong

David Bowers: Astro Boy

Astro Boy is a remake (or reimagining) of Osamu Tezuka's seminal 1960s manga comic and TV series. In a futuristic, high-tech flying Metro City, a scientist driven mad with grief creates the superpowered Astro Boy using his dead son's DNA. When the robot boy behaves erratically, he is rejected by his father and falls to the polluted earth below. This superior kids' sci-fi adventure retains the original's *Pinocchio*-like concept, but adds to the source material some updated technology and sharp ecological, social, and political themes. The top-drawer CG animation and effects were produced by Hong Kong's Imagi Studios, while director David Bowers injected some irreverent British humor to the exotic mix of influences on show.

2009

France

H5 (François Alaux, Hervé de Crécy, and Ludovic Houplain): Logorama

Logorama is a clever and engrossing 3D CGI short that tells a low-life crime story with an imaginative and apocalyptic ending. The visually-striking setting is a version of Los Angeles made up of thousands of corporate logos and brand characters. The film, rendered in a flat cartoon style and influenced by the live-action movies of Quentin Tarantino, Paul Thomas Anderson, and Robert Altman, was created by directing collective H5 and was produced by Autour de Minuit. Among many awards, *Logorama* won the Oscar for best animated short.

Logorama, 2009

2010
USA

2010
USA

Lee Unkrich: Toy Story 3; Teddy Newton: Day & Night

Problems mount as beloved owner Andy grows up and goes to college while the toy gang end up at a day care center for destructive toddlers ruled by a sinister toy cartel. While the plot may not be as elegant as in previous installments, *Toy Story 3* more than makes up for this by hitting new highs in other areas. Pixar's usual wide emotional palette is demonstrated by scenes such as the characters' harrowing slide toward what seems like certain destruction in a hellish inferno of burning trash, an extraordinarily bleak moment for a children's film and, like 2008's *WALL-E*, a powerful warning about humanity's slide toward ecological disaster. At the other end of the spectrum, the hilarious discovery of a "Spanish mode" for Buzz Lightyear, already one of the funniest characters in cartoon history, is a flamenco tour de force of keyframe animation that throws down a mighty challenge for the producers of motion capture. Among many other notable moments in this Oscar-winning movie are the toys' backstory vignettes, such as the origins of the gangster teddy bear Lotso-Huggin, plus a love story between metrosexual Ken with "tougher than she looks" Barbie, and a cameo by Studio Ghibli's mascot, the Totoro.

The accompanying short, *Day & Night*, wonderfully combines traditional 2D animation with 3D CGI to create something like a charming, 1960s festival gem, with a styling similar to Osvaldo Cavandoli's *La Linea*. This respect for the lessons of animation history is what sets Pixar apart from the rest and, along with their masterly blending of cutting-edge technology with pure artistry, has enabled the studio, along with Studio Ghibli, to create a new Golden Age of feature cartoons. And, like the Walt Disney Studio in their Golden Age of cel animation of the 1930s to 1960s, they make it look effortless.

Chris Sanders and Dean DeBlois: How To Train Your Dragon

This beautifully made stereoscopic 3D feature was loosely based on the children's books by Cressida Cowell about the puny but clever Viking, Hiccup Horrendous Haddock the Third, and his friendship with a dragon, the Vikings' traditional enemy.

When Chris Sanders and Dean DeBlois, directors of the Disney 2D animated feature *Lilo & Stitch*, took over some way into the extended six-year development of this 3D CGI DreamWorks Animation production, they moved the script further from the source books, jettisoning some of the quirkiness and bringing in more grown-up and emotional aspects to the story, including for a children's animated feature a suprisingly downbeat aspect to the ending. The sequences of the hero riding his flying dragon make spectacular and effective use of the stereoscopic 3D, and the movie overall is a sophisticated piece of work, which perhaps manages to outshine some of Pixar's lesser product.

2010
USA

Kirsten Lepore: Bottle

Bottle is a charming and unique stop-frame short, which proves that it is ideas and not big budgets that really count. The story is about a long distance love affair between a character made of sand on a warm beach and a character made of snow on an icy coastline. After exchanging messages in a bottle across the sea, they arrange to meet, with disastrous consequences. Like most great short films, this is a simple and entertaining story built on deeper themes, as by entering this relationship and moving into the other's world, the characters identities are eroded away.

This love story between elements was made single-handedly by Kirsten Lepore while she was studying experimental animation at CalArts. Lepore painstakingly animated snow and sand frame-by-frame on location, recording the results on a Canon 7D digital camera. The relatively rapid movement of the sun and shadows, often a problem in outdoor stop-frame animation, here adds a believable dimension as the elemental characters seem to move at a slower pace to human time.

Bottle, 2010

2010
France/UK

Sylvain Chomet: L'illusionniste (The Illusionist)

Sylvain Chomet's acclaimed follow-up to *Les triplettes de Belleville* (*Triplets of Belleville/Belleville rendez-vous*, 2003), *L'illusionniste* (*The Illusionist*) is a movie that communicates with its audience with great subtlety and understatement, qualities that are traditions in French cinema but are rare in most animated features and in contemporary film in general. After Belleville's wild, meandering story of old ladies, old dogs, and young cyclists, *The Illusionist* features a quieter, but more linear narrative in its story of an aging magician coming to the end of his career in the late 1950s, the era that saw the birth of rock 'n' roll and the death of music hall. The story has its origins in a hithero unproduced 50-year old script by the legendary French director and comic actor Jacques Tati. The original script was for a live-action movie set in Czechoslovakia and starring Tati and his daughter Sophie. Chomet relocated the story to France, England, and Scotland—including a beautifully-realized Edinburgh backdrop—nicely expressing the French and British identity of the film. The central character of the French magician Tatischeff has a lot in common with Tati's gentle, gangly persona, his name being the real family name of Tati and his daughter Sophie. It was Sophie who suggested that Chomet use her father's script after he had asked about using a clip of one of Tati's films in *Belleville*.

The magician's paternal friendship with a naïve, small-town girl coming of age in the big city is the emotional heart of the slow-burning story, its bittersweet melancholy coming to life in the last quarter. Like other great animated movies, *The Illusionist* realizes the value of moments of genuine sadness to counterbalance comedy and confirms the undervalued potential animation has for communicating downbeat emotions.

As in *Belleville*, Tati's speciality of largely silent (or dialogue-free) comedy is revisited. The lack of conversation is rationalized here by the different nationalities of the characters and is carried off by the strongly visual nature of the animation, creating a treat of visual storytelling and a film that leaves space for its audience to use their minds and discover the detail for themselves. Also like *Belleville*, Chomet's talent for caricature creates a large and lovingly realized supporting cast of larger-than-life characters who populate every frame. This memorable and often grotesque cast, combined with the charming backdrops, demonstrate the simple and timeless appeal of great drawing. This, along with his courage to tell untraditional stories, is what makes Chomet one of the most interesting contemporary directors of animation, and one with the potential to be a kind of Western answer to Hayao Miyazaki.

It is tempting in a book like this to draw an analogy between the fortunes of 2D drawn animation and Tatischeff's old-world magic tricks, fading away in the face of new, more popular forms of entertainment. In fact, the film confirms the validity of drawn animation and what it has to offer to modern audiences. If *Belleville* showed that for traditional 2D animation there's life in the old dog yet, The Illusionist's rave reviews and enthusiastic audiences demonstrates an acceptance that the form is more than a nostalgic novelty and still has a prestigious place in the twenty-first century outside its accepted generic destinations of cute preteen fodder and Eastern anime. Not only does *The Illusionist* show drawn animation's potential for critically-praised independent cinema and the way forward for animators to create art-house hits, it also confirms the possibilities of telling all varieties of stories using the unique beauty of moving drawings.

L'illusionniste
(The Illusionist),
2010

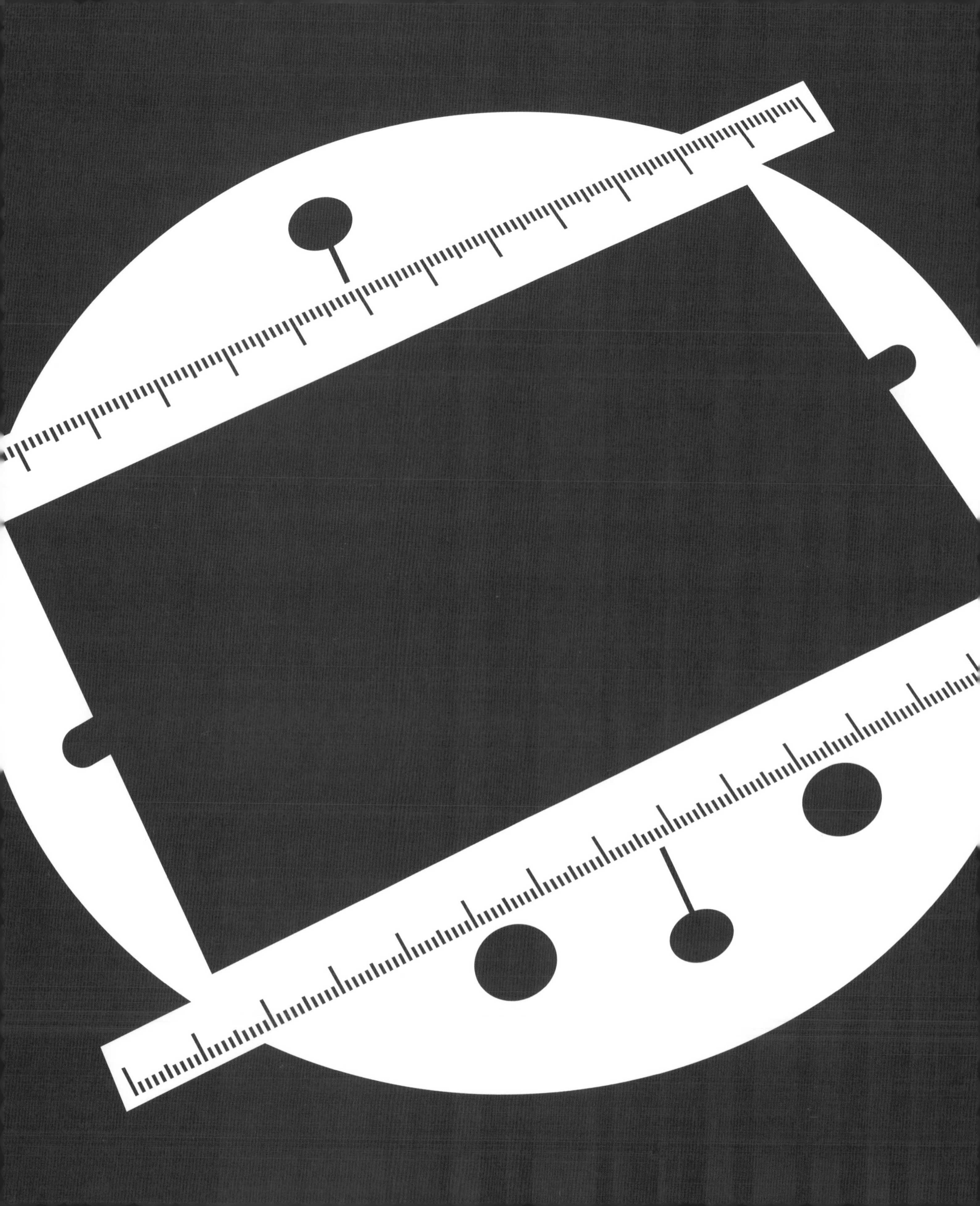

Resources

In this final section of the book, you'll find all the resources you need to become an animation expert. There's an extensive glossary of key animation terms and techniques, plus a list of Academy Award–winning animated shorts and feature films, some suggested books and websites, and links to the world's leading animation colleges.

Glossary

2D animation

See Cel animation.

3D CGI

In the late twentieth century, this took over from cel animation as the dominant form of animation. Precise and detailed graphical worlds and animated characters are generated in a three-dimensional (i.e., not flat) environment in a computer memory and viewed with a virtual camera that can be moved around in any direction. Can be used to create imaginative or cartoony worlds, but is also used to create ultrarealistic creatures and special effects for many live-action movies. Referred to as "3D CGI" to distinguish it from 2D CGI.

Abstract animation

Animation that is abstract rather than figurative in appearance, usually dispensing with a conventional narrative.

Animatic

A storyboard that is photographed and then edited in sequence with a (usually rough) soundtrack. This gives an early impression of the flow of the story and serves as a precise guide for the length of the animated scenes. As animation is completed, it is dropped into the animatic over the storyboard. In the digital era for 3D CGI films, a further stage of a 3D animatic is usually made, in which the drawn storyboard is visualized in an early version of the 3D environment with the 3D characters' movements roughly "blocked out." This 3D visualization is also increasingly used in live-action movies (where the process is known as previsualization or previz) to plan the film before shooting. It is especially used for effects-heavy movies, which invariably contain animated effects.

Animation

Animation is notoriously hard to define but is essentially sequential images designed to be viewed in quick succession by means of some kind of device. Thus prehistoric sequential cave paintings or images on pottery probably cannot really be considered animation as they were not able to be viewed in rapid enough succession, whereas something like sequential images on a lantern that spun rapidly over a fire or images in a flick book, could be considered as animation. However the term animation is mainly used to describe the areas of the film, television, and video world that use many

differing single-frame techniques, as opposed to "live action" in which subjects are filmed with a camera.

Animation desk

A peg bar is generally mounted on a semitransparent perspex disc that enables the animator to turn the drawings to any angle at which it is comfortable to draw the lines with precision. This is all usually fixed onto a desktop, the angle of which can also be adjusted to suit the animator. This type of apparatus has been in use since the development of industrialized animation in the decades preceding World War II.

Anime

A style of animation associated with the Japanese and Asian industries, which grew out of early Japanese cartoons and the postwar popularity of comics and Western animation and pop culture. Influenced by manga comics, anime's visual style commonly features characters with large eyes and exaggerated facial expressions. The animation is often of a limited quality, compensated for by extensive special effects set pieces, particularly in the straight to video/DVD productions. In the more prestigious productions however, such as those of Studio Ghibli, the animation is fully developed and the backgrounds are lush and detailed.

Cel animation

Also known as "2D," "paper," "drawn," or "traditional" animation. The process whereby an animator or team of animators produces a sequence of drawings which are usually then colored, traditionally by reproducing them onto transparent sheets known as cels, which are then photographed sequentially over a background by a movie camera. Moving into the digital age, the drawings are more commonly colored and recorded digitally inside a computer environment. Until the late 1990s cel animation was by far the most commonly used animation technique, but was then superseded commercially by 3D CGI, hence cel animation is often now known as 2D.

Cel shading

A technique whereby three-dimensional computer imagery is output using flat colors and black outlines to resemble traditional cel animation. When skillfully used the technique can be hard to differentiate from actual 2D cel animation. The perfect rotation of objects and characters in perspective, difficult and therefore sparingly used in 2D, is an advantage of this kind of CGI, although more sensitive processes such as conveying emotions through appealing and expressive human faces can be problematic in CG, and this is where 2D drawn animation may still have the edge.

CGI

Computer-generated imagery. The application of computer effects to animation.

Character animation

The art of animating characters using acquired knowledge of, and/or reference to, the movement of real life figures, combined with levels of stylization, exaggeration, and artistic license, with the ultimate intention of delivering a "performance" much like that of an actor and bringing the characters to life. The character's dialogue is usually prerecorded and used as a guide for the animation.

Claymation

Term coined by Will Vinton to describe the use of malleable models to create stop-frame animation. *See also Stop motion.*

Compositing

The process of overlaying different elements of animation and/or film with a high degree of accuracy and precision to create visual effects. In predigital times this was achieved by multiple passes of film, which were then combined with each other optically. In the digital era, the elements are combined within the computer's digital environment.

Cutout

The technique of cutting out drawings on card, often into various sections that are put on a background and then moved and photographed frame by frame. The same effect can also be achieved inside a computer environment.

Direct animation

See Drawn-on-film animation.

Direct film

Any kind of filmmaking that dispenses with the camera and involves the artist making images directly onto the frames of the film stock, a category that falls somewhere between art and film. Generally this means drawing, painting, or scratching straight onto the film, as in drawn-on film animation, which was famously practiced by Len Lye, Norman McLaren, and Caroline Leaf. Direct film can also include using found footage (using bits of film discarded by others) or such exotic techniques as Stan Brakhage's use of insect wings pressed onto the film.

Doubles

Filming animated images over two frames instead of one, therefore effectively reducing the frame rate from, for example 24 frames per second (fps) to 12 fps, in order to halve the number of drawings needed.

Drawn animation

See Cel animation.

Drawn-on-film animation

Also known as "direct animation." One of the few techniques of animation that does not require a camera, images are scratched or painted directly onto the film strip.

Function curves (F curves)

Adjustable curves (or straight lines) in an animation package that are graphical representations of the many different transformations possible in the digital animation environment. The shape of the curves are defined by points (keys), representing a value (position, rotation, scale, or other quantifiable transformations against a timeline (frames) on the other.

In-between

A drawing between a keyframe that helps to create the illusion of motion, usually created by a junior animator. In-betweening is an efficient process that allows a studio's senior animators to concentrate on the main drawings.

Keyframes

In traditional 2D commercial animation studios, the animator will often draw the main poses or keyframes, assistant animators will draw the halfway poses between these, then in-betweeners (trainee animators) draw the in-between frames. In digital animation, the animator defines the keyframes which contain the main poses of the character or other variable criteria, and the computer then calculates the in-between frames.

Limited animation

The labor-saving techniques of having fewer drawings per second—as few as eight or six per second in some cases—and of having parts of the drawings held still on different layers while other parts are kept moving, for instance a talking mouth moving on a still face. Limited animation was used in the 1950s by companies such as UPA, who compensated for having fewer drawings with high style and design. From the 1960s onward the techniques were pushed to the limits by studios such as Hanna-Barbera and producers of Asian anime in order to create cheap animation to fill television schedules.

Live action

Films that are not animated, including anything made on movie or video cameras using filmed subjects, rather than from individually-created frames, as in animation.

Lo-fi animation

A term used to describe often deliberately primitive animation that seems to consciously move against the shiny perfection and glossy realism of high-tech production methods. This approach became commonplace in the digital age as many creators and audiences tired of the sterile and impersonal work often produced by computers. Early examples of lo-fi works include Bob Godfrey and Terry Gilliam's animations, with later examples being the TV series *South Park* and *Modern Toss*, the feature film *Fantastic Mr Fox*, and the work of Don Hertzfeldt.

Machinima

A technique developed from the culture of video game "mods" (modifications), whereby the same tools used for customizing games are used to create animated films. After modifying the look of everything somewhat, the characters and cameras are manipulated using the game's controllers, and this is recorded as video footage. Voices are added, usually with offbeat and irreverent dialogue, often with entertaining results. The creators are accepted as "fan laborers" and circulate their work free of charge, and are thus able to use the copyright-protected games' assets. User-friendly software using this technology has now been made commercially available, designed to allow people without any expertise to produce animated films.

Model sheet

An animator's guide to the characters in a film, usually showing views from all angles, a variety of poses, and relative scale.

Modernist animation

Animation made using modernist, expressionist, or other more abstract design styles associated with modern art, usually based on geometric shapes and straight lines, rather than the soft, rounded, more "realistic" designs in the traditional Disney style. Popularized in the two decades following World War II by studios such as UPA in the USA, Halas & Batchelor in the UK, and Zagreb Film in Croatia.

Motion capture

Also known as "performance capture." A digital form of rotoscoping, actors' movements are recorded by a computer, processed, and then applied to CGI characters. For best results the raw data is invariably interpreted and stylized by an animator.

Multiplane camera

A variety of rostrum camera in which the camera points at multiple layers of glass surfaces on which different layers of background areas can be placed in front of and behind the animation frames, so that when the camera is panned sideways or tracked in or out, the layers move in perspective giving an illusion of depth. This can now be done within a digital environment, which has made the multiplane camera something of a museum piece.

Otaku

The original Japanese meaning of otaku is someone with unhealthily obsessive interests and limited social skills, similar to the Western meanings of nerd or geek. Otaku later came to be used specifically for fans of anime and manga, and is often used by the fans themselves in the East and West to describe the whole culture that has developed around these forms.

OVA

Original Video Animation. Animated films, almost exclusively Asian anime, that were made exclusively for release and distribution on video or DVD formats, thus bypassing the traditional means of movie theater and TV distribution (and their greater degree of censorship) and connecting directly with a fan base or cult audience.

Paint and trace

The department that traced and then color painted the animator's drawings onto cel, a practice now almost made extinct by digital coloring.

Paint-on-glass animation

Slow-drying oil paint is painted on glass, photographed, and moved about to create new frames.

Panning

A camera moving sideways along a background. Usually achieved in animation by moving the background along in small, even distances as it is photographed frame by frame.

Paper animation

See Cel animation.

Particle systems, simulations, and dynamics

Tools in a CG environment by which the computer will calculate the movement of particles (as in an explosion or petals blowing in the wind) or simulate the movement of secondary animation (such as cloth or hair on a character), or environmental effects (such as the flow of water or smoke), according to adjustable criteria inputted by the animator.

Peg bar

A small bar, generally fastened to a desk or light box, on which are two or three small round pegs that correspond with holes punched in the paper on which frames of animation drawings are created. The peg bar keeps the different drawings in register and allows the animator to easily flick and roll the paper and constantly check the flow of the animation. A light box is used to backlight the papers so that multiple drawings can be seen at once.

Pencil test

The animator's rough drawings filmed to test the movements before the drawings are cleaned up and then either transferred onto cel for coloring and filming, or, in the digital era, scanned for digital coloring.

Performance capture

See Motion capture.

Pinscreen

This method of animation uses a screen from which thousands of pins extrude. These pins can be pushed in to various lengths and, when lit from the side, this creates images of light and shadow. These images are then photographed sequentially, generally from the direction in which the pins point. The technique was invented and used to great acclaim in the 1930s by Alexandre Alexeieff and has rarely been used since.

Pixels

Tiny colored squares that are the building blocks of flat, 2D digital image types such as bitmaps or JPEGs. In early computers the pixels were larger due to processing power, giving a blocky, jagged look to the images.

Pixillation

Stop-frame animation technique using human actors instead of models or puppets.

Polygons

Small, usually triangular shapes from which simple 3D models are built in a 3D digital environment.

Puppet animation

An older term which refers to stop-motion animation in which human figures or animal character models are used, referred to in this case as puppets.

Rendering

In traditional animation, rendering is generally used to refer to techniques of pencil or crayon coloring of the drawings to produce a texture, rather than the more common flat color, painted-cel look. A good example of rendering technique is Dianne Jackson and TVC's 1982 short, *The Snowman*. In digital terms, rendering is the final process whereby the computer performs all the calculations and outputs the frames of animation.

Rostrum camera

A camera fixed on a lit desk or frame that is used for filming the still frames of traditional animation. Now rarely used due to the introduction of digital production methods.

Rotoscoping

The process of filming a subject and then drawing over the sequential stills of the frames for realistic movement. Usually, and most successfully, interpretation and stylization of the original images is employed during their transformation into drawings. Interesting results can be achieved digitally by using a combination of computer processing and human manipulation to transform the frames.

Sand animation

Similar to the paint-on-glass technique, sand is used to create images, which are photographed and then changed by moving the sand.

Singles

Creating one image per frame. This takes longer than using doubles, but creates a smoother movement and can be useful for animating fast action and precise lip synching.

Soviet realism/Socialist realism

A communist-government-imposed period of soviet art, resulting from a rejection of modern art movements, such as Impressionism and Cubism, and any other "decadent bourgeois" art, including abstract or experimental animation. After a decree by Joseph Stalin in 1932, this became official government policy for all artists in the Soviet Union and defiance of this was punishable by law. After a screening of Disney's Mickey Mouse shorts in Moscow in 1934, which hugely impressed many soviet animators and officials alike, animation became centralized and state funded through the Soyuzmultfilm Studio. It had to conform to Disney-style children's cel animation, usually telling traditional folk stories or fairy tales and promoting party policies and ideas. Using a rotoscoping technique known as Éclair, animators had to derive all movements of characters from filmed live-action sequences. Interestingly, at the other end of the political spectrum, Nazi Germany also had laws banning "decadent" abstract art, including animation.

Stereoscopic 3D

In which a subject is photographed or filmed from two slightly differing angles designed to replicate the differing perspectives of the human eyes. This process is particularly well suited to animation produced in 3D CGI, which is easily rendered from the two different virtual camera angles.

Stop frame

See Stop motion.

Stop motion

Also known as stop frame or claymation. The oldest form of animation, stop motion is the technique of moving and photographing objects or specially articulated models frame by frame. This method is used less often in modern animation, but it has a timeless appeal.

Storyboard

A sequence of illustrations used to plan and visualize an animated film.

Strata cut

The technique by which a slice is cut across an object and then the revealed cross-section photographed before another slice is taken off, and so on. The subject is usually a specially created loaf of multicolored clay, plasticene, or wax. The technique was invented and developed by Oskar Fischinger in the 1920s and 1930s.

Texture maps

Flat 2D images that are wrapped around, attached to, or projected onto 3D models in order to give them color and detail, in a 3D digital environment. Usually these images will consist of textures (such as cloth, brick, or skin) or of drawings or photographs of faces or other details. Texture maps can also be 3D-type textures which contain bumps, cracks, scales, rivets, etc., for added detail and realism.

Visual music

A term used to describe certain abstract animation (or film) that is intended to be a visual interpretation of music or perhaps intended to create a similar effect on the eyes of the audience as music has on the ears, i.e. stirring subconscious emotions and feelings, in this case through color, shape, and design. Abstract animators associated with this tradition include Oskar Fischinger, Len Lye, Norman McLaren, Mary Ellen Bute, Harry Smith, John and James Whitney, Jordan Belson, Jules Engel, and Ed Emshwiller.

Xerography

The practice of quickly and cheaply reproducing images by Xerox machine, used in animation from the 1960s to copy the drawings onto cels. In many cases, this replaced the older method of hand tracing. It was also used to reproduce multiple copies of the animation frames, as in Disney's 1961 feature, *One Hundred and One Dalmations*.

Zoetrope

An early device for watching sequential images in rapid succession by means of a spinning disc.

Academy Award Winners

Animated feature film

2001: *Shrek*. Aron Warner.

2002: *Spirited Away*. Hayao Miyazaki.

2003: *Finding Nemo*. Andrew Stanton.

2004: *The Incredibles*. Brad Bird.

2005: *Wallace & Gromit: The Curse of the Were-Rabbit*. Nick Park & Steve Box.

2006: *Happy Feet*. George Miller.

2007: *Ratatouille*. Brad Bird.

2008: *WALL-E*. Andrew Stanton.

2009: *Up*. Pete Docter.

2010: *Toy Story 3*. Lee Unkrich.

Animated short film

1931/32: *Flowers and Trees*. Walt Disney.

1932/33: *The Three Little Pigs*. Walt Disney.

1934: *The Tortoise and the Hare*. Walt Disney.

1935: *Three Orphan Kittens*. Walt Disney.

1936: *The Country Cousin*. Walt Disney.

1937: *The Old Mill*. Walt Disney.

1938: *Ferdinand the Bull*. Walt Disney.

1939: *The Ugly Duckling*. Walt Disney.

1940: *The Milky Way*. Metro-Goldwyn-Mayer.

1941: *Lend a Paw*. Walt Disney.

1942: *Der Fuehrer's Face*. Walt Disney.

1943: *Yankee Doodle Mouse*. Frederick Quimby.

1944: *Mouse Trouble*. Frederick Quimby.

1945: *Quiet Please!* Frederick Quimby.

1946: *The Cat Concerto*. Frederick Quimby.

1947: *Tweetie Pie*. Edward Selzer.

1948: *The Little Orphan*. Frederick Quimby.

1949: *For Scent-Imental Reasons*. Edward Selzer.

1950: *Gerald McBoing-Boing*. Stephen Bosustow.

1951: *The Two Mouseketeers*. Frederick Quimby.

1952: *Johann Mouse*. Frederick Quimby.

1953: *Toot, Whistle, Plunk and Boom*. Walt Disney.

1954: *When Magoo Flew*. Stephen Bosustow.

1955: *Speedy Gonzales*. Edward Selzer.

1956: *Mister Magoo's Puddle Jumper*. Stephen Bosustow.

1957: *Birds Anonymous*. Edward Selzer.

1958: *Knighty Knight Bugs*. John W. Burton.

1959: *Moonbird*. John Hubley.

1960: *Munro*. William L. Snyder.

1961: *Ersatz*. Zagreb Film.

1962: *The Hole*. John Hubley & Faith Hubley.

1963: *The Critic*. Ernest Pintoff.

1964: *The Pink Phink*. David H. DePatie & Friz Freleng.

1965: *The Dot and the Line*. Chuck Jones & Les Goldman

1966: *Herb Alpert and the Tijuana Brass Double Feature*. John Hubley & Faith Hubley.

1967: *The Box*. Fred Wolf.

1968: *Winnie the Pooh and the Blustery Day*. Walt Disney.

1969: *It's Tough to Be a Bird*. Ward Kimball.

1970: *Is It Always Right to Be Right?* Nick Bosustow.

1971: *The Crunch Bird*. Ted Petok.

1972: *A Christmas Carol*. Richard Williams.

1973: *Frank Film*. Frank Mouris.

1974: *Closed Mondays*. Will Vinton & Bob Gardiner.

1975: *Great*. Bob Godfrey.

1976: *Leisure*. Suzanne Baker.

1977: *The Sand Castle*. Co Hoedeman.

1978: *Special Delivery*. Eunice Macaulay & John Weldon.

1979: *Every Child*. Derek Lamb.

1980: *The Fly*. Ferenc Rofusz.

1981: *Crac!* Frédéric Back.

1982: *Tango*. Zbigniew Rybczynski.

1983: *Sundae in New York*. Jimmy Picker.

1984: *Charade*. Jon Minnis.

1985: *Anna & Bella*. Cilia Van Dijk.

1986: *A Greek Tragedy*. Linda Van Tulden & Willem Thijssen.

1987: *The Man Who Planted Trees*. Frédéric Back.

1988: *Tin Toy*. John Lasseter & William Reeves.

1989: *Balance*. Christoph Lauenstein & Wolfgang Lauenstein.

1990: *Creature Comforts*. Nick Park.

1991: *Manipulation*. Daniel Greaves.

1992: *Mona Lisa Descending a Staircase*. Joan C. Gratz.

1993: *The Wrong Trousers*. Nick Park.

1994: *Bob's Birthday*. Alison Snowden & David Fine.

1995: *A Close Shave*. Nick Park.

1996: *Quest*. Tyron Montgomery & Thomas Stellmach.

1997: *Geri's Game*. Jan Pinkava.

1998: *Bunny*. Chris Wedge.

1999: *The Old Man and the Sea*. Alexander Petrov.

2000: *Father and Daughter*. Michael Dudok de Wit.

2001: *For the Birds*. Ralph Eggleston.

2002: *The ChubbChubbs!* Eric Armstrong.

2003: *Harvie Krumpet*. Adam Elliot.

2004: *Ryan*. Chris Landreth.

2005: *The Moon and the Son: An Imagined Conversation*. John Canemaker & Peggy Stern.

2006: *The Danish Poet*. Torill Kove.

2007: *Peter & the Wolf*. Suzie Templeton & Hugh Welchman.

2008: *La Maison en Petits Cubes*. Kunio Kato.

2009: *Logorama*. Nicolas Schmerkin.

2010: *The Lost Thing*. Shaun Tan & Andrew Ruhemann.

Animation books and websites

Books

The 50 Greatest Cartoons: As Selected by 1,000 Animation Professionals. Edited by Jerry Beck. Turner Publishing, 1994.

Amidi, Amid. *Cartoon Modern: Style and Design in Fifties Animation.* Chronicle Books, 2006.

The Animate! Book: Rethinking Animation. Edited by Benjamin Cook and Gary Thomas. LUX, 2006.

Animation Art: From Pencil to Pixel, the World of Cartoon, Anime, and CGI. Edited by Jerry Beck. Flame Tree Publishing, 2004.

Animation Now! Edited by Julius Wiedemann. Taschen, 2004.

Bacher, Hans. *Dream Worlds: Production Design for Animation.* Focal Press, 2007.

Barrier, Michael. *Hollywood Cartoons: American Animation in its Golden Age.* Oxford University Press, 1999.

Bendazzi, Giannalberto. "African Cinema Animation." Translated by Emilia Ippolito with Paula Burnett.

Bendazzi, Giannalberto. *Cartoons: One Hundred Years of Cinema Animation.* John Libbey Cinema and Animation, 1994.

Blair, Preston. *Cartoon Animation.* Walter Foster, 1994.

Brophy, Philip. *100 Anime.* BFI, 2005.

Clements, Jonathan and McCarthy, Helen. *The Anime Encyclopedia: A Guide to Japanese Animation Since 1917.* Stone Bridge Press, 2006.

Faber, Liz and Walters, Helen. *Animation Unlimited: Innovative Short Films Since 1940.* Laurence King Publishing, 2004.

Furniss, Maureen. *The Animation Bible: A Guide to Everything—From Flipbooks to Flash.* Laurence King, 2008.

Gabler, Neal. *Walt Disney: The Triumph of the American Imagination.* Random House, 2007.

Gifford, Denis. *British Animated Films, 1895–1985: A Filmography.* McFarland & Co., 1988

Glebas, Francis. *Directing the Story: Professional Storytelling and Storyboarding Techniques for Live Action and Animation.* Focal Press, 2008.

Halas, Vivien and Wells, Paul. *Halas & Batchelor Cartoons: An Animated History.* Southbank Publishing, 2006.

Harry Smith: The Avant-garde in the American Vernacular. Edited by Andrew Perchuk and Rani Singh. Getty Research Institute, 2010.

Holliss, Richard and Sibley, Brian. *The Disney Studio Story.* Octopus Books, 1988.

Jensen, Paul. *The Men Who Made The Monsters.* Twayne Publishers, 1996.

Leslie, Esther. *Hollywood Flatlands: Animation, Critical Theory and the Avant-garde.* Verso Books, 2002.

Maltin, Leonard. *Of Mice and Magic: History of American Animated Cartoons.* Penguin Books, 1987.

McCarthy, Helen. *Hayao Miyazaki: Master of Japanese Animation.* Stone Bridge Press, 2001.

Muybridge, Eadweard. *Animals in Motion.* Dover Publications, 2000.

Muybridge, Eadweard. *The Human Figure in Motion.* Dover Publications, 2000.

Napier, Susan. *Anime from Akira to Howl's Moving Castle: Experiencing Contemporary Japanese Animation.* Palgrave McMillan, 2006.

Osmond, Andrew. *100 Animated Feature Films.* BFI, 2010.

Postgate, Oliver. *Seeing Things: A Memoir.* Cannongate Books, 2010.

Purves, Barry. *Basics Animation: Stop-motion.* AVA, 2010.

Purves, Barry. *Stop Motion: Passion, Process and Performance.* Focal Press, 2007.

A Reader in Animation Studies. Edited by Jayne Pilling. John Libbey Cinema and Animation, 1997.

Robinson, Chris. *Canadian Animation: Looking for a Place to Happen*. John Libbey Cinema and Animation, 2008.

Solomon, Charles. *The History of Animation: Enchanted Drawings*. Knopf, 1989.

Thomas, Frank and Johnston, Ollie. *Disney Animation: The Illusion of Life*. Abbeville Press, 1981.

Whitaker, Harold and Halas, John. *Timing for Animation*. Focal Press, 1981.

Williams, Richard. *The Animator's Survival Kit*. Faber and Faber, 2009.

Useful websites

100 Greatest Animated Shorts
www.100animatedshorts.com

Animate Projects (Animate!)
www.animateprojects.org

Annecy International Animated Film Festival
www.annecy.org

ASIFA Hollywood Animation Archive
www.animationarchive.org

British Film Institute
www.bfi.org.uk

Cartoon Brew
www.cartoonbrew.com

French Cinematheque
www.cinematheque.fr

German Cinematheque
www.deutsche-kinemathek.de

The Lost Continent
ukanimation.blogspot.com

National Film Board of Canada
www.nfb.ca

Quebec Cinematheque
www.cinematheque.qc.ca

Zagreb Animation Festival
www.animafest.hr

Animation colleges

Animation Mentor (online)
www.animationmentor.com

Ballyfermot College (Ireland)
www.isa-bcfe.ie

Beijing Film Academy (China)
www.bfa.edu.cn

California Institute of the Arts (CalArts) (USA)
calarts.edu

Centre for Animation (Denmark)
www.animwork.dk

GOBELINS l'ecole de l'image (France)
www.gobelins.fr

Royal College of Art (RCA) (UK)
www.rca.ac.uk

Sheridan College (Canada)
www.sheridanc.on.ca

Supinfocom (France)
www.supinfocom.org

Tokyo Design Academy (Japan)
www.tda.ac.jp

Index

Picture credits

The publishers would like to thank the following sources for their kind permission to reproduce their images in this book.

Every effort has been made to acknowledge correctly and contact the source and/or copyright holder of each picture. The publisher apologizes for any unintentional errors or omissions, which will be corrected in future editions of this book.

6–7: © Pathé
Ronald Grant Archive

8: © Disney
British Film Institute

9: Left: Courtesy Gaumont Pathé Archives
The Kobal Collection
Right: © Passion Pictures

11: © Aardman/Wallace & Gromit Ltd. 1993

15: © Disney
British Film Institute

16: Photo used with permission of the National Film Board of Canada. Ryan, 2004, National Film Board of Canada

19. © Jonathan Hodgson

21: THE TRIPLETS OF BELLEVILLE
A film by Sylvain Chomet
© 2002 Les Armateurs/Production Champion/Vivi Film/France 3 Cinéma/RGP France/Sylvain Chomet

23: © Zagreb Film

25: British Film Institute

27: © 1988 MASHROOM/AKIRA COMMITTEE All Rights Reserved.

29: Shanghai Animation Film Studio
British Film Institute

30: © Jo Beom-jin

31: The Freedom Song
Director: Narayan Shi
Executive Producer: Shashanka Ghosh
Head of Production: Suresh Eriyat
Produced at: Famous House of Animation
Animation Supervisor: Vaibhav Kumaresh
Styling and Background design: Nilima Eriyat
Music: V.J. Traven

37: The Kobal Collection

39: The Kobal Collection

40: The Kobal Collection

43: British Film Institute

47: British Film Institute

48: The Kobal Collection

49: British Film Institute

50: Courtesy Gaumont Pathé Archives
The Kobal Collection

51–52: British Film Institute

55: British Film Institute
Photo used with permission of the National Film Board of Canada

56: © Semiconductor

59: British Film Institute

63: British Film Institute

67: Inkwell Studios
The Kobal Collection

69: British Film Institute

71: The Kobal Collection

73: Jewel
The Kobal Collection

75: © FTCP, Inc.
British Film Institute

76: The Ronald Grant Archive

79: © Disney
British Film Institute

80: British Film Institute

82–83: British Film Institute

84: British Film Institute

86: British Film Institute

88: British Film Institute

91: British Film Institute

92: British Film Institute

97: © Disney
British Film Institute

98: © Disney
The Ronald Grant Archive

101: Reproduced with the kind permission of King Features, a division of Hearst Holdings, Inc.
British Film Institute

102: Wladyslaw Starewicz Production
British Film Institute

104: The Kobal Collection

107: Reproduced with the kind permission of King Features, a division of Hearst Holdings, Inc.
British Film Institute

110: British Film Institute

112: The Ronald Grant Archive

115: GUFK/Mosfilm
The Kobal Collection

116: © Royal Mail Group Ltd. 2010, courtesy of The British Postal Museum & Archive
British Film Institute

117: Courtesy Len Lye Foundation
British Film Institute

119: © Disney
British Film Institute

120: © Disney
British Film Institute

125: © Royal Mail Group Ltd. 2010, courtesy of The British Postal Museum & Archive
British Film Institute

129: © Disney
British Film Institute

130–133: © Disney
The Ronald Grant Archive

134–135: © Disney
The Ronald Grant Archive

138–139: © Disney
British Film Institute

145: © UPA/Bosustow Media Group

147: © The Halas & Batchelor Collection

148: © Disney
British Film Institute

150: © Soyuzmultfilm/FSUE

151: Ceskoslovensky Statni Film
The Kobal Collection

153: IMA Film
The Kobal Collection

154: © Disney
British Film Institute

156: © UPA/Bosustow Media Group

157: © UPA/Bosustow Media Group
The Kobal Collection

159: Photo used with permission of the National Film Board of Canada. Neighbours, 1952, National Film Board of Canada

160: © The Ray & Diana Harryhausen Foundation

162: © The Halas & Batchelor Collection

163: © The Halas & Batchelor Collection
British Film Institute

164–165: © Disney
British Film Institute

166: Top: James Whitney (American, b. Altadena, Cailfornia 1922–1982)
YANTRA, 1955, Still Frame
16mm film, color, sound, 8 minutes
© Estate of John and James Whitney
Bottom: James Whitney (American, b. Altadena, Cailfornia 1922–1982)
LAPIS, 1965, Still Frame
16mm film, color, sound, 10 minutes
© Estate of John and James Whitney

173: CSF/Filmove
British Film Institute

Acknowledgments

Thanks to:

Sylvain Chomet
ASIFA California
Margaret Adamic
Lela Budde
Rob Stevenhagen
Amid Amidi
Giannalberto Bendazzi
David Bowers
Andrew Ruhemann
Gary Thomas
Chris O'Reilly
Smith and Foulkes
Siri Melchior
Ruth Fielding
Fraser Maclean
Vivien Halas
Don Hertzfeldt
Helen Grundy
Tim Hope
Tee Bosustow
Graeme Struthers
Ciaran Brennan
Jonathan Hodgson
Luke Vernon
Liz Farrelly
David Curry
Jon Link
Patrick Beirne
Richard Shoup
Ruth Ducker
Sevil Bajarama
Marc Craste
Kim Craste
Suzie Templeton
John Hardwick
Caprino Studios

Jo Beom-Jin
Kerry Baldry
Chris Shepherd
Tony Ealey
Nick Harrop
Colin Alexander
Caroline Miller

Many thanks to my parents, Alan and Diana, for their encouragement, and to my family, Helen, Louis, and Elsie, for their patience.

Researchers:

Marian Cleary
Andrew Thomas
Erik Kuska
Ceu D'Ellia
Anne Lise Andreasen
John Walker
Izzy Archer
Martin Richardson

To contact the author or to make suggestions for further editions of the book email:
WHOA.Stephen.Cavalier@gmail.com